ECOLOGICAL
PSYCHOACOUSTICS

ECOLOGICAL
PSYCHOACOUSTICS

EDITED BY JOHN G. NEUHOFF

The College of Wooster
Department of Psychology
Wooster, Ohio

AMSTERDAM • BOSTON • HEIDELBERG • LONDON
NEW YORK • OXFORD • PARIS • SAN DIEGO
SAN FRANCISCO • SINGAPORE • SYDNEY • TOKYO

ELSEVIER
ACADEMIC
PRESS
Academic Press is an imprint of Elsevier

Elsevier Academic Press
525 B Street, Suite 1900, San Diego, California 92101-4495, USA
84 Theobald's Road, London WC1X 8RR, UK

This book is printed on acid-free paper. ∞

Library of Congress Cataloging-in-Publication Data

Neuhoff, John G.
    Ecological psychoacoustics / John G. Neuhoff.
        p.   cm.
    Includes bibliographical references and index.
    ISBN 0-12-515851-3 (hardcover : alk. paper)—ISBN 0-12-515851-3   1. Auditory perception.
2. Environmental psychology.   I. Title.
    BF251.N48 2004
    152.1'5—dc21

                                                                                                2003028202

British Library Cataloguing in Publication Data
A catalogue record for this book is available from the British Library

ISBN: 0-12-515851-3

For all information on all Academic Press publications
visit our Web site at www.academicpress.com

Printed in the United States of America
03   04   05   06   07   08   9   8   7   6   5   4   3   2   1

CONTENTS

1

ECOLOGICAL PSYCHOACOUSTICS: INTRODUCTION AND HISTORY

JOHN G. NEUHOFF

2

AUDITORY PERCEPTUAL ORGANIZATION INSIDE AND OUTSIDE THE LABORATORY

RHODRI CUSACK AND ROBERT P. CARLYON

3

ATTENTION AND TIMING

MARI RIESS JONES

4

Auditory Motion and Localization

John G. Neuhoff

5

From Gibson's Fire to Gestalts:
A Bridge-Building Theory of
Perceptual Objecthood

David Van Valkenburg and Michael Kubovy

6

ECOLOGICAL PSYCHOACOUSTICS AND
AUDITORY DISPLAYS: HEARING, GROUPING,
AND MEANING MAKING

BRUCE N. WALKER AND GREGORY KRAMER

7

ENVIRONMENTAL ACOUSTICS PSYCHOLOGICAL
ASSESSMENT OF NOISE

SEIICHIRO NAMBA AND SONOKO KUWANO

8

ECOLOGICAL DEVELOPMENTAL PSYCHOACOUSTICS

LYNNE A. WERNER AND LORI J. LEIBOLD

9

PERCEIVING ARTICULATORY EVENTS: LESSONS FOR AN ECOLOGICAL PSYCHOACOUSTICS

LAWRENCE D. ROSENBLUM

10

INTERACTING PERCEPTUAL DIMENSIONS

JOHN G. NEUHOFF

11

PITCH AND PITCH STRUCTURES

MARK A. SCHMUCKLER

12

LOUDNESS

ROBERT S. SCHLAUCH

Foreword

Sometimes a collision is a good thing. A hammer striking a nail can lead to magnificent creations. A clapper striking a bell can signal important events. In many ways, this book represents a collision between two perspectives on the study of hearing that historically have remained far apart. On the one hand, we have the perspective of traditional psychoacoustics, rich in tradition and grounded in rigorous experimental methods. On the other, we have more ecological and cognitive approaches to the study of hearing, with a focus on listening situations that are more similar to those encountered *outside* the laboratory. Each approach has its own particular strengths and weaknesses. However, combined, they have the potential to be much more fruitful than any additive effects that they might have separately, perhaps even the potential to create a new and more comprehensive perspective on the study of auditory processing. As with any new endeavor, there are often difficulties encountered in the face of discovery. Some of these difficulties result from a reluctance to relinquish years of dogmatic tradition in one discipline or another. Others stem from stepping into new ground that has yet to establish its own agreed upon vocabulary. For instance, in the following chapters there is considerable disagreement over relatively "simple" terms, such as exactly what a *sound* should be called. Some authors have developed theoretical positions around "*auditory objects*" while others prefer to call sounds "*auditory events.*" Still others use these terms interchangeably. Sometimes, even different authors using the same terms disagree over exactly what these terms denote. Such disagreement over basic terminology illustrates the youth of this collision between ecological and psychoacoustic approaches to the study of hearing. Initially, such difficulties might be somewhat disconcerting. Yet, this type of discussion and others like it will no doubt move the study of auditory perception, cognition, and action in a direction that will reap tremendous benefits. In Chapter 9 of this volume, Larry Rosenblum writes, "The time is ripe for a science of auditory *perception*. A majority of the research on human audition has concentrated on how the ear works rather than on what the ear hears." The idea is that in addition to studies of sensory physiology and psychoacoustics, more realistic studies of auditory perception, cognition, and action are necessary if we are to gain a comprehensive understanding of audition. A new science of auditory *perception* might well result from the collision between psychoacoustic, ecological, and cognitive perspectives. This volume is intended to provide a stepping stone into that science.

CONTRIBUTORS

Numbers in parentheses indicate the pages on which the authors' contributions begin.

Robert P. Carlyon (15) Medical Research Council Cognition and Brain Sciences Unit, Cambridge CB2 2EF United Kingdom

Rhodri Cusack (15) Medical Research Council Cognition and Brain Sciences Unit, Cambridge CB2 2EF United Kingdom

Mari Reiss Jones (49) Department of Psychology, The Ohio State University, Columbus, Ohio 43210

Gregory Kramer (149) Metta Foundation/Clarity, Portland, Oregon 97229

Michael Kubovy (113) Department of Psychology, University of Virginia, Charlottesville, Virginia 22903

Sonoko Kuwano (175) Department of Environmental Psychology, Graduate School of Human Sciences, Osaka University, Osaka 565-0871 Japan

Lori J. Leibold (191) Department of Speech and Hearing Sciences, University of Washington, Seattle, Washington 98105

Seiichiro Namba (175) 7-5-604, Obana-2Chome, Kawanishi 666-0015 Japan

John G. Neuhoff (1, 87, 249) Department of Psychology, The College of Wooster, Wooster, Ohio 44691

Lawrence D. Rosenblum (219) Department of Psychology, University of California, Riverside, Riverside, California 92521

Robert A. Schlauch (317) Department of Communication Disorders, University of Minnesota, Minneapolis, Minnesota 55455

Mark A. Schmuckler (271) Division of Life Sciences, University of Toronto, Scarborough, Ontario M1C 1A4 Canada

David Van Valkenburg (113) Department of Psychology, University of Virginia, Charlottesville, Virginia 22903

Bruce N. Walker (149) School of Psychology, Georgia Institute of Technology, Atlanta, Georgia 30332

Lynne A. Werner (191) Department of Speech and Hearing Sciences, University of Washington, Seattle, Washington 98105

1

ECOLOGICAL

PSYCHOACOUSTICS:

INTRODUCTION AND HISTORY

JOHN G. NEUHOFF

Some might argue that the title of this book, *Ecological Psychoacoustics*, is itself an oxymoron. Many psychoacoustic investigations lack any semblance of ecological validity, and most ecological investigations of audition bear little likeness to traditional psychoacoustics. However, detecting and recognizing a sound are the result of a complex interaction of physics, physiology, sensation, perception, and cognition. The process involves an interaction of the listener with the environment. Identifying a familiar voice, for example, involves complex vibrations of the sound source, compression and rarefaction of a medium; reflecting and filtering of the signal by objects in the environment, the head, torso, and pinnae; transduction of the mechanical energy into an electrochemical signal in the nervous system; and the activation of an entire network of correlated physiological mechanisms from cochlea to cortex. This entire process finally results in some conscious recognition and identification of the familiar speaker. The range of approaches that have been used to study these processes varies as widely as the processes themselves. However, over the years a methodological dichotomy between approaches to studying hearing has emerged.

On the one hand, much of the research on how we hear the world has focused on the physics, physiology, and sensation that occur in this chain of events. Many psychoacousticians have focused their efforts on understanding the specific manner in which acoustical energy is transduced into an electrochemical signal in the nervous system. Central issues have included the manner in which frequency and intensity are coded, how sound sources are localized, and the thresholds of detection and discrimination. Often, the goal of this research was to better understand how the peripheral auditory system functions in order to develop better techniques to assist the hearing impaired. With the focus on lower level sensory processes and the functioning of the peripheral auditory system, both cognitive processes and perception–action cycles were thought to be somewhat out of the scope of investigation and were often treated as confounds. Thus, perhaps because such things could not be duplicated in a hearing aid, traditional psychoacousticians were faced with the unlikely prospect of dealing with cognition and perception–action cycles as somewhat of a nuisance. Few doubted that higher level cognition could influence responses in psychoacoustic experiments. The approach, therefore, was to develop experimental controls for cognitive effects. Researchers took great steps to ensure that listeners in their experiments were not "thinking" about their responses to sounds and used statistical methods, such as signal detection theory, to factor out decision criteria and other consequences of cognition.

The obvious advantage to studying the pieces of the auditory puzzle in this way is that one can gain a better understanding of how the hardware of the peripheral auditory system functions and perhaps develop more effective solutions for auditory pathology. Furthermore, the approach provides a more fine-grained analysis of the topic of interest while controlling for the effects of the other phenomena that are not of immediate concern. The disadvantage of this approach, perhaps, is that the stimuli (often pure tones and noise bursts) and listening conditions employed (headphones, sound-attenuating booths, and anechoic chambers) are often unrealistic, leaving the larger question of environmentally and ecologically important cognition, listening behaviors, and the linkage between perception and action relatively unexplored.

On the other hand, a more recent approach to studying audition has emerged. Influenced by Gibson's "ecological" approach to studying perception and bolstered by a greater acceptance of cognitive psychology, those who study auditory event perception and auditory cognition, as well as many music and speech researchers, have treated cognitive psychology and ecological psychology as tools rather than confounds. The goal of this line of research has typically been to understand the complex higher order processes that occur when a listener hears a sound or intricate acoustic pattern. Clearly, lower level sensory processing is a prerequisite for both auditory cognition and perception–action relationships. However, the focus of many of these investigations is often on what might be called "listening behavior." Identification, recognition, similarity scaling, and categorization are frequently employed methodologies. The results of these types of investigations often have implications that reach beyond simply perceiving music, speech, and auditory events. They may shed light on perception and action in other highly complex situations that involve overlearned stimuli. Those who study music performance, for example, may provide insight into other areas in which perception and the planning and execution of complex motor behaviors are intricately linked. The advantage of this approach is that it often comes closer to the listening experiences and behaviors that are encountered in everyday life. The disadvantage is that, because of either the conceptual complexity of the issues being investigated or the acoustic complexity of the stimuli, the level of precision and experimental control found in the work of traditional psychoacoustics is sometimes missing from the work of those who study auditory cognition. It should be noted that the fields of ecological and cognitive psychology are by no means synonymous. Vigorous debate, particularly over the issue of mental representation, still exists between the two fields. Yet, their common focus on listening behavior, coupled with approaches by moderate researchers in both groups who are comfortable with the coexistence of perception–action linkage and mental representations, has yielded a common line of research that stands in stark contrast to the approach of traditional psychoacoustics.

The relationships and commonalities between these two broad subdivisions of hearing science (traditional psychoacoustics versus the cognitive–ecological approach) have been studied very little. Psychoacoustic journals typically published papers on sensory processes and auditory physiology. Auditory cognition and ecological acoustics papers were published in either perception and cognition journals or music and speech journals. When psychoacoustics began to emerge as its own discipline, the instrumentation of the day and dominant behaviorist paradigms in psychology were such that an integrated approach to studying auditory perception was not a realistic undertaking. Even within organizations dedicated to the study of acoustics (such as the Acoustical Society of America), music, speech, and psychoacoustic researchers had clear and formal divisions that continue to exist today. However, as the cognitive revolution began to take hold in psychology and technology began to develop at faster and faster rates, more comprehensive investigations of auditory function became possible. Advances in computer science, virtual environments, neurophysiology, and neuroimaging, coupled with emerging perspectives in evolutionary and ecological psychology, have now made it more plausible to begin to tie together lower level psychoacoustic work with perception–action relationships and higher level auditory cognition. Open-field ecological studies of auditory localization, for example, can now begin to draw on evidence from single-cell recording work to develop hypotheses further, and neuroimaging researchers can employ traditional psychophysical studies to identify structures responsible for processing classic psychoacoustic effects.

One of the goals of this book is to review some emerging work in psychoacoustics as well as work in auditory cognition and ecological psychology, highlighting the areas in which the lines of research intersect. The plan is to examine some of the complex interactions between these divergent areas of hearing science, tying together the occurrence of acoustic events, physiological responses of the auditory system, the perceptual and cognitive experience of the listener, and how this experience influences behavior, action, and subsequent perception. Where this is not possible, the goal is to address the potential reasons for the disparity or lack of convergence between the lines of research. Illuminating some of the converging evidence that is emerging from these traditionally divergent paths may yield a broader and perhaps more informative perspective on auditory function. Areas of inquiry that are useful in developing this perspective range from physics to physiology and from evolution to behavioral science.

Of course, the corresponding disadvantage of addressing the study of audition with such a global perspective is that at this time there is much that we do not know about each individual piece in the auditory puzzle. Thus, tying them all together is often an incomplete task. Perhaps more important when examining the big picture is the fine-grained analysis of each subarea becomes much coarser. Nevertheless, there are numerous exemplary sources that delve more thoroughly into fine detail of these areas and a few that attempt to tie them together. Thus, the approach of the book is to examine relationships that exist and provide a review of studies that incorporate environment, and cognition, as well as traditional psychoacoustics.

To gain some perspective on what we do and do not know about hearing, it is useful to begin by examining some of the historical forces that have driven psychoacoustic research. In the remainder of this introductory chapter, we first examine some of the influences that have shaped the questions that auditory researchers have traditionally asked. These forces include (but are certainly not limited to) the available technology and instrumentation of the time and the dominant theoretical perspectives that are in place when the research is conducted. Next, we examine briefly the role of evolution in shaping the form and function of the auditory system. Few would argue with the concept that the ability to hear has evolved. However, the evolution of the physiological structures that enable hearing is generally more widely accepted than the evolution of the behaviors that those structures support. We then discuss the distinctions between internal, external, and ecological validity, while examining the strengths and weaknesses of approaches that emphasize each. Finally, we further explore the distinction between research in psychoacoustics and research in auditory cognition.

HISTORICAL PERSPECTIVE

THE AVAILABLE TECHNOLOGY

In some ways, the traditional psychoacoustic research has mirrored the old joke about the bar patron who has had too much to drink and is on his hands and knees beneath a streetlight looking for his car keys. A police officer happens by and asks, "Well, where did you lose them?"

"Across the street" is the reply.

"Then why not look over there?"

"Because the light is better here."

Early on in the history of modern psychoacoustics, the difficulty in generating complex, controlled, dynamic stimuli limited many investigations of auditory function to studies of static sine wave tones or bursts of noise. In the 1930s and 1940s the scientific study of psychacoustics began to expand rapidly with the use of such stimuli. The widespread commercialization of the electronic vacuum tube made it possible not only to present these kinds of sounds with great control but also to amplify and measure the physiological responses in the auditory system (Wever & Bray, 1936a, 1936b, 1937). At the beginning of their classic text on the psychology and physiology of hearing, Stevens and Davis (1938) remarked that the development of the vacuum tube removed the principal impediment to the study of acoustics: the ability to produce sounds of any frequency, intensity, and complexity. No longer did researchers need to rely on tuning forks, sirens, and reeds to produce acoustic stimuli. The desired frequency and intensity could now be presented with electric signal generators, amplifiers, and loudspeakers. However, Stevens and Davis could not have known that the remarkable development that removed such a major impediment would also constrain psychoacoustic research for some time to come. Even with the advances of the day in electronics, it was still somewhat of a task to present listeners with simple static acoustic stimuli. More realistic sounds that exhibited dynamic changes in frequency, intensity, and spectrum were even more difficult to generate and were rarely used in experiments. Thus, most psychoacoustic experiments were conducted with static sine wave tones or complexes and in some cases bursts of noise. Although these types of sounds are rarely encountered in a natural listening environment, the limited instrumentation of the day dictated that these were the only types of experiments that could be performed under controlled conditions. Thus, researchers "looked where the light was better" and for the most part examined the perception of single-source, unchanging pure tones and noise.

The results of many of these studies have since become widely accepted classical models of auditory perception. The obvious problem is that they are based largely on sounds that rarely occur in a natural listening environment. Prior to the widespread use of the vacuum tube, realistic, complex sounds were generated manually. However, the level of precision and experimental control often suffered. Early electronics offered greater control but at the cost of dynamic complexity. Advances in computer technology have given researchers the best of both worlds, enabling the presentation of complex, dynamic stimuli under highly controlled conditions.

This more recent work is beginning to show that that under many circumstances, the perception of dynamic, ecologically valid stimuli is not predicted well by the results of many traditional stimuli experiments using static stimuli. If one accepts the position that our perceptual abilities have evolved specifically to deal with the stimuli that occur in a natural environment, perhaps it is not surprising that there are differences in processing naturally occurring stimuli and those that are more artificial. In this respect, auditory researchers are clearly not alone. Differences between static and dynamic perception have been shown not only in audition (Canévet & Scharf, 1990; Iverson, 1995; Neuhoff & McBeath, 1996; Perrott & Musicant, 1981; Spitzer & Semple, 1993) but also in vision (Kleiss, 1995; Muise, LeBlanc, Blanchard, & de Warnaffe, 1993; Spillmann & Kurtenbach, 1992; Verstraten, Fredericksen, van Wezel, Lankheet, & Van de Grind,

1996), haptics (Menier, Forget, & Lambert, 1996; Rochat & Wraga, 1997), and categorization (Arterberry & Bornstein, 2002). The growing consensus among many perception researchers is that using the results of static-stimuli experiments to make broad generalizations about dynamic perception is often an untenable proposition.

DOMINANT PSYCHOLOGICAL PARADIGMS

Another historical influence on the development of psychoacoustic research was the dominant theoretical perspective in the psychology of the day. The classical conditioning work of Pavlov and Watson in the early part of the 20th century gave way to operant conditioning and the rise of radical behaviorism. According to the behaviorist approach, the reinforcing consequences of behavior are the causes of subsequent behavior. One of the strengths of this approach was that it posited no internal cognitive mechanisms in explaining behavior. Previous approaches, such as those of James and Freud, required the use of ill-defined and unobservable phenomena. James and Freud both posited that instincts were the driving forces behind behavior. Freud suggested that a few instincts (primarily having to do with sexuality) were responsible for behavior. James suggested that there were many instincts that drove behavior. Many in the scientific community bristled at the proposals because of the obvious problem of operationally defining or observing an "instinct."

Part of the strength of behaviorism was that operational definitions were easy to come by. Behavior and reinforcers could be easily observed and quantified. The approach did not need to appeal to any internal mechanisms to explain behavior. As the behaviorist movement grew, it became less and less fashionable for researchers to examine internal mechanisms such as thought processes, prior knowledge, expectations, or beliefs. Thus, psychoacoustic research of the time was conducted under the dominance of a theoretical perspective in psychology that essentially renounced any type of cognitive or internal process as a means of explaining behavior. Although many psychoacousticians were keenly aware that cognition influenced behavior and action in response to an acoustic signal, it was more common to control for this influence and factor it out than to study the phenomenon to investigate its relationship with sensation and physiology.

Finally, it should be noted that the study of audition was, and is, an interdisciplinary endeavor involving physicists, engineers, physiologists, biologists, and psychologists, to name only a few. The direction that auditory research took as a result of World War II probably did little to draw more psychologists into hearing research (Schubert, 1978). Much of the work became focused on the physics of the signal and the physiological response of the peripheral auditory system. Students in psychology found that in order to study the psychology of audition, they were often presented with the daunting task of first tackling the physics and physiology (Schubert, 1978). Thus, the limitations in technology and the general avoidance of anything cognitive, coupled with growing avoidance of audition by psychologists, resulted in many investigations of auditory function that, although rigorous and well defined, often brushed only the surface of true listening behavior.

EVOLUTION AND AUDITION

The ability to acquire and process acoustic information about the environment has no doubt evolved because it provides a selective advantage. The abilities to localize sound sources, communicate with conspecifics, and heed auditory warnings are all crucial to survival. In the biological sciences it is generally accepted that physiological structures often evolve because they provide advantages that allow more successful survival and reproduction. What is no less true, but is less emphasized, is that the behaviors that are supported by these physiological structures are also products of evolution. So, for example, if one agrees that the complex shape of the outer ear has evolved because it provides a selective advantage in source localization, one must also concede that the behavior of localizing a sound source using input from the acoustic filtering performed by the pinnae has also evolved. Although the evolution of specific behaviors is met with skepticism by some, the point was not lost on Charles Darwin. In 1859 he predicted that the impact of evolutionary theory would reshape how we thought about behavior:

> In the distant future I see open fields for far more important researches. Psychology will be based on a new foundation, that of the necessary acquirement of each mental power and capacity by gradation. (Darwin, 1859, p. 449).

The impact of evolutionary theory on the behavioral sciences clearly has not lived up to Darwin's prediction. Cognitive scientist Steven Pinker (a strong proponent of evolution in the study of cognitive science) has summed up the current status of evolutionary theory in psychology in this way:

> ... the study of the mind is still mostly Darwin-free. Evolution is said to be irrelevant, sinful, or fit only for speculation over a beer at the end of the day. (Pinker, 1997, pp. 22–23).

Nonetheless, evolutionary theory has clearly influenced the thinking of a growing number of psychologists. The interaction between behavioral and biological scientists has recently flowered with the explosion of the neurosciences. Still, the dominant trend among those who study human audition has been to focus on psychoacoustic questions per se, leaving the often "wooly" evolutionary origins of the psychoacoustic phenomena unaddressed. It is interesting to note that this is in contrast to much of the bioacoustic research on animals, where the role of evolution in shaping the auditory system and listening behaviors of organisms is often stressed.

ECOLOGICAL, EXTERNAL,
AND INTERNAL VALIDITY

In any type of experimental setting, the validity of the findings is crucial to interpreting the results and drawing reasonable conclusions about the data. There are various types of validity, most of which have been extensively outlined by Campbell and Stanley (1963). The focus of traditional psychoacoustic research has been on internal validity, assuring that the experimental manipulations or independent variables are really responsible for any changes in the dependent variable. Typically, researchers have gone to great lengths to assure that experiments are conducted in a quiet, controlled environment, that stimuli are presented in precisely the same manner on every trial, and that a small number of well-practiced participants receive a large number of trials. All of these precautions are requisites from the standpoint of maintaining the internal validity of the research and the practicality of actually conducting the experiments. For example, the practice of using a small number of listeners with a large number of trials has several advantages. First, the resources required to recruit and compensate participants are minimal. It is certainly easier to convince 2 or 3 graduate students to sit in a sound booth for 45 minutes and press a key in response to a sound than it is to entice 30 undergraduates to do the same. Second, because of the small number of participants, extraneous variability due to individual differences is minimized. Finally, presenting a large number of trials to well-practiced listeners minimizes the effects of learning and practice on the results.

However, when it comes to drawing reasonable conclusions about the data, a telescopic focus on internal validity to the exclusion of other types of validity can be as detrimental as ignoring internal validity altogether. External validity is the degree to which the results of an experiment would apply in other settings with other populations. For example, how might an auditory effect discovered by conducting an experiment in a sound booth hold up in a concert hall or a living room? The experimental control afforded by the booth increases internal validity at the cost of external validity. The small number of participants typical of many psychoacoustic experiments can also reduce external validity. How might the findings of a study conducted with authors and graduate assistants differ from one conducted with naïve listeners? If the critical question is one that involves using psychophysics to make inferences about the physiology of the peripheral auditory system, these questions become less of a concern. However, if one is interested in listening behavior, how listeners perceive and use acoustic information to guide action, then these questions are crucial.

Campbell and Stanley (1963) have proposed that the ideal design is one in which both internal and external validity are maximized, thereby yielding tightly controlled designs from which real-world conclusions can be drawn. However, others have suggested that the relative importance of internal versus external validity depends on the questions and goals of the investigation. In defending external "invalidity," Mook (1983) has suggested that the terms "validity" and "invalidity" connote inherent value judgments and that in some cases experiments that lack external validity are quite valuable and informative. For example, if the goal of the investigation is to determine the limits of the perceptual system under ideal conditions, a tightly controlled experimental environment is critical, even if this environment never exists outside the laboratory. The insights gained from such experiments can lead to a greater understanding of perceptual systems even though the laboratory conditions may never match those experienced in the real world. On the other hand, if the goal is to examine how auditory phenomena generalize across situations and populations, an investigation with greater external validity is clearly called for.

A final validity issue is that of ecological validity, essentially how the results of an experiment might apply in an environment in which similar conditions might be encountered. The precise meaning of ecological validity has been the subject of considerable debate. However, Schmuckler (2001) has suggested a dimensional analysis that specifies ecological validity as the extent to which the laboratory setting, stimuli, and task of the participant are representative of those experienced in everyday life. For example, almost any experiment that uses isolated sine wave tones has suspect ecological validity because isolated pure sine waves almost never occur in a natural listening environment.

It is interesting to note that before the widespread development of reliable electronic signal generating instrumentation, many ecologically valid psychoacoustic experiments were conducted with "real-world" stimuli. For example, after a conversation about the generality of Weber's law, Fechner and Volkman fashioned a makeshift apparatus to examine the validity of Weber's law in loudness perception.

> After Volkman had carried out his photometric experiments, I spoke to him about the great importance of a general validation of Weber's Law. He improvised on the spot the following apparatus for a preliminary proof of the law applied to loudness, which was built the same day at a cost hardly worth mentioning.
>
> It consists simply of a free-swinging hammer, which knocks against a plate made of some substance that either does or does not give off a tone. A strong knitting needle served as the axis for this pendulum. . . . The sound produced is understandably stronger or weaker, physically speaking if the hammer is made heavier or lighter, if it is allowed to drop from a greater or lesser height against the plate, or if one stands closer or further away from the apparatus. (Fechner, 1966, p. 147).

The pendulum apparatus was used by Fechner, Volkman, and many others to investigate loudness perception and even to investigate auditory pathology (Fechner, 1966, p. 149). This illustrates the somewhat ironic and circular historical course that ecological validity has taken in psychoacoustic investigations. Fechner used real sounds with rich harmonic structure that were heard binaurally in a natural listening environment. It is difficult to imagine an experimental setting with better ecological validity. The drawback of the methodology was a certain lack of precision (or internal validity). Releasing the pendulum from exactly the same point from trial to trial was problematic. Producing sounds of fractional intensity by releasing the pendulum from correspondingly lower heights was compounded by differences in friction at the axis and even differences in air resistance. The characteristics of the room and the listener could also affect the results.

When it became practical to present acoustic signals electronically through headphones, the internal validity of psychoacoustic experiments was increased dramatically. The intensity of tones could be produced reliably from trial to trial. Fractional intensities could be presented accurately. The drawback now, however, was that the types of sounds that could easily be presented electronically rarely, if ever, occurred in a natural listening environment. However, the rise of behaviorism with its emphasis on rigorous operational definitions and the backlash against the ill-defined Freudian psychology probably convinced psychoacoustic researchers that the precision and convenience of the available electronics outweighed the drawbacks. Advances in computer technology have now given researchers the best of both worlds. Realistic, harmonically rich, dynamic stimuli can now be presented with great precision.

It is clearly not the case that any one type of validity is somehow more valuable than any other. A variety of experimental approaches and techniques are required to gain a better understanding of auditory function and listening behavior. Different approaches should emphasize different types of validity. If convergent evidence from these different approaches can be obtained, we can have greater confidence in the theories and models derived from them.

PSYCHOACOUSTICS VERSUS AUDITORY COGNITION

Traditional psychoacoustic research has focused on the sensory impressions of an acoustic stimulus and determining the physiological structures that mediate these experiences. In comparison, the cognitive and ecological components of auditory perception have been studied somewhat less and are often treated by psychoacousticians as extraneous variables that need to be controlled. The classic technique that exemplifies this approach is signal detection theory. Essentially, the goal of signal detection theory is to separate a listener's sensitivity to a stimulus from the listener's decision criterion for responding. The goal is to separate the lower level physiological and sensory characteristics of a response from the higher order cognitive influence on deciding how to respond to the stimulus. Clearly, this is a necessary technique if we are to fully understand auditory processing. However, this type of approach alone is not *sufficient*.

The relationship of sensory and physiological investigations to ecological and cognitive investigations should be one of synergy. Physiological discoveries of structures that are implicated in specific auditory functions give rise to specific predictions about perception and listening behavior. Thus, psychological investigations can test the limits of the relationship between the structure and the function. Conversely, discoveries in perception and listening behavior can provide direction for physiological investigations of the structures that mediate the behavior. The relationship is synergistic because advances in one area spur research in the other.

However, at best there has been relatively little dialogue between traditional psychoacousticians and the researchers who do study nonspeech auditory cognition. At worst, there is a clear rift between the two types of researchers. The extreme traditional view is that if a phenomenon does not have a readily identifiable physiological structure that mediates it, the effect is somehow less important. After presenting a finding about a particular listening behavior at a recent professional meeting, a psychologist was asked by a more physiologically inclined colleague, "Yes, but what cells or tissues are responsible for the effect?" The psychologist sheepishly responded that he did not know. The physiologist nodded, as if this lack of a known neural basis for the effect somehow diminished the results of the experiment. On the contrary, psychological findings that flow well from what we currently know about the physiology of the auditory system are often less interesting than those that are surprising. It is the phenomena that lack a clear physiological explanation that illustrate what we do not know about physiology and drive physiological investigations. A complete understanding of auditory function will require cooperation between physiology and psychology. It will require more than just a description of cellular form and function from cochlea to cortex. Although this level of cellular analysis is necessary, it is not sufficient. Physiology is the basis for perception, cognition and behavior. It is interesting to note that in vision, the synergistic relationship between research in physiology, psychophysics, and cognition is widely accepted and advocated by such notable figures as Nobel Laureate David Hubel (Livingstone & Hubel, 1988).

This is not to say that relationships between physiology and perception as well as the study of complex real-world auditory phenomena have been ignored, only that further development of this integrative approach might yield greater understanding. This idea was pointed out in an address by the eminent psychoacoustician Reinier Plomp. His comments were given at the March 1999 meeting of the Acoustical Society of America in a session honoring the Plomp's lifetime of achievement and contributions to the field.

> The exceptional honor of this session gives me the opportunity to introduce some questions usually not discussed in conference papers. My point of departure is that the function of our hearing is to inform us as reliably as possible about the world of sounds around us. It is the task of hearing research to find the laws involved. In carrying out this task, we are permanently confronted with several temptations. Their common origin is the scientific rule to keep the number of variables as small as possible. In this way, parts get more attention than structure. Hence, many essential aspects of everyday sounds had to wait surprisingly long before they got proper scientific attention. (Plomp, 1999, p. 1239)

Hearing usually takes place in the presence of complex stimuli in complex acoustic environments. The neural mechanisms and processes responsible extend beyond the peripheral auditory system and in some cases beyond the auditory system itself. For example, the auditory researcher would be hard pressed to explain things such as the McGurk effect (McGurk & MacDonald, 1976), where visual speech can influence what is heard, or the visual effect of vocal effort on loudness (Rosenblum & Fowler, 1991) using only physiological structures solely devoted to audition. It is understanding the complex interaction of acoustics, physiology, sensation, perception, cognition, and behavior that is the puzzle of audition.

SUMMARY

Auditory perception and cognition are the result of complex physical, physiological, and cognitive factors. However, the cognitive characteristics and perception–action relationships of early psychoacoustic research were limited by the technology of the day, the dominant theoretical perspectives in psychology, and perhaps reluctance on the part of psychologists to engage in the more cumbersome physical and physiological modeling of acoustic signals and responses. Thus, influential models of auditory processing were developed using sounds that are not frequently encountered in a natural listening environment. Although this approach was useful in developing models of the function of the peripheral auditory system, it was less so in developing models of auditory cognition and behavior. However, technical innovations and paradigmatic shifts in psychology have spawned more ecologically valid investigations of complex auditory perception–action relationships and auditory cognition. These efforts complement more traditional psychoacoustic research in furthering our understanding of audition.

REFERENCES

Arterberry, M. E., & Bornstein, M. H. (2002). Infant perceptual and conceptual categorization: The roles of static and dynamic stimulus attributes. *Cognition, 86*(1), 1–24.

Campbell, D. T., & Stanley, J. C. (1963). *Experimental and quasi-experimental designs for research.* Boston: Houghton Mifflin.

Canévet, G., & Scharf, B. (1990). The loudness of sounds that increase and decrease continuously in level. *Journal of the Acoustical Society of America, 85,* 2136–2142.

Darwin, C. (1859). *On the origin of species.* London: John Murray.

Fechner, G. (1966). *Elements of psychophysics (vol. I).* New York: Holt, Rinehart and Winston.

Iverson, P. (1995). Auditory stream segregation by musical timbre: Effects of static and dynamic acoustic attributes. *Journal of Experimental Psychology: Human Perception and Performance 21*(4), 751–763.

Kleiss, J. A. (1995). Visual scene properties relevant for simulating low-altitude flight: A multidimensional scaling approach. *Human Factors, 37*(4), 711–734.

Livingstone, M., & Hubel, D. (1988). Segregation of form, color, movement, and depth: Anatomy, physiology, and perception. *Science, 240,* 740–749.

McGurk, H., & MacDonald, J. W. (1976). Hearing lips and seeing voices. *Nature 264*, 746–748.

Menier, C., Forget, R., & Lambert, J. (1996). Evaluation of two-point discrimination in children: Reliability, effects of passive displacement and voluntary movement. *Developmental Medicine and Child Neurology, 38*, 523–537.

Mook, D. G. (1983). In defense of external invalidity. *American Psychologist, 38*, 379–387.

Muise, J. G., LeBlanc, R. S., Blanchard, L. C., & de Warnaffe, A. (1993). Discrimination of the shape of the masked inducing figure perception of the illusory triangle. *Perception, 22*, 623–628.

Neuhoff, J. G., & McBeath, M. K. (1996). The Doppler illusion: The influence of dynamic intensity change on perceived pitch. *Journal of Experimental Psychology: Human Perception and Performance, 22*, 970–985.

Perrott, D. R., & Musicant, A. D. (1981). Dynamic minimum audible angle: Binaural spatial acuity with moving sound sources. *Journal of Auditory Research, 21*, 287–295.

Pinker, S. (1997). *How the mind works.* New York: Norton.

Plomp, R. (1999). Fifty years in (psycho) acoustics: Some conclusions. *Journal of the Acoustical Society of America, 105*, 1238.

Rochat, P., & Wraga, M. (1997). An account of the systematic error in judging what is reachable. *Journal of Experimental Psychology: Human Perception and Performance, 23*, 199–212.

Rosenblum, L. D., & Fowler, C. A. (1991). Audiovisual investigation of the loudness effort effect for speech and nonspeech events. *Journal of Experimental Psychology: Human Perception and Performance, 17*, 976–985.

Schmuckler, M. A. (2001). What is ecological validity? A dimensional analysis. *Infancy 2*, 419–436.

Schubert, E. D. (1978). History of research on hearing. In E. Carterette and M. Friedman (Eds.), *Handbook of perception* (vol. 4, pp. 40–80). New York: Academic Press.

Spillmann, L., & Kurtenbach, A. (1992). Dynamic noise backgrounds facilitate target fading. *Vision Research, 32*, 1941–1946.

Spitzer, M. W., & Semple, M. N. (1993). Responses of inferior colliculus neurons to time-varying interaural phase disparity: Effects of shifting the locus of virtual motion. *Journal of Neurophysiology, 69*, 1245–1263.

Stevens, S. S., & Davis, H. (1938). *Hearing: Its psychology and physiology.* Oxford, England: Wiley.

Verstraten, F. A. J., Fredericksen, R. E., Van Wezel, R. J. A., Lankheet, M. J. M., & Van de Grind, W. A. (1996). Recovery from adaptation for dynamic and static motion aftereffects: Evidence for two mechanisms. *Vision Research, 36*, 421–424.

Wever, E. G., & Bray, C. W. (1936a). Hearing in the pigeon as studied by the electrical responses of the inner ear. *Journal of Comparative Psychology, 22*, 353–363.

Wever, E. G., & Bray, C. W. (1936b). The nature of bone conduction as shown by the electrical response of the cochlea. *Annals of Otology, Rhinology, and Laryngology, 45*, 822–830.

Wever, E. G., & Bray, C. W. (1937). A comparative study of the electrical responses of the ear. *Proceedings of the American Philosophical Society, 78*, 407–410.

2

AUDITORY PERCEPTUAL ORGANIZATION INSIDE AND OUTSIDE THE LABORATORY

RHODRI CUSACK AND ROBERT P. CARLYON

Often, the sound arriving at our ears is a mixture from several different sources, but we are interested in only a subset of them. The ears perform analysis by frequency, segregating the incoming sound into many channels, and the auditory system then extracts many other acoustic features. From this vast array of sensory information we must then select the parts that are important. If we have prior knowledge of the exact acoustic characteristics of the source(s) we wish to listen to, we may be able to select the appropriate parts. However, in many circumstances we may not have this *a priori* knowledge, or there may be several sources with similar characteristics. Fortunately, there is another useful type of information, which is exploited to structure the vast incoming array of information. There are certain regularities to sounds in the world, and these can be used by the auditory system to partition the incoming sound prior to selection—a process usually referred to as *auditory scene analysis*. The automaticity and proficiency with which we usually perform this task belie its complexity, as sources often produce sounds spread over time and frequency, making their separation anything but trivial. Perhaps only when our ability to separate sounds fails in noisy environments or as a result of hearing loss do we catch a glimpse of the importance of this hidden skill. The extent of the challenge is apparent from computational models of auditory scene analysis, which, despite their high complexity, do not approach human performance (e.g., Ellis, 1996).

Auditory scene analysis depends entirely upon regularities in the sound from sources in the world. The physics of common sources are such that they often produce sounds with a regular harmonic spectral structure, where many different frequencies start and stop together, and they have a pitch that changes only slowly over time. These regularities and many others are used to organize the incoming jumbles perceptually. Given the intimate connection between the kinds of sounds that are out in the world and the best way in general for the auditory system to organize them, maintaining an ecological perspective on scene analysis is crucial. Where possible, we have focused on ecological aspects of grouping. Auditory scene analysis affects how we perceive the acoustic world in many ways. Our ability to judge timing, rhythm, pitch, and timbre or even attend to a particular subset of sounds can be affected by it. In an initial section, we discuss the effects that auditory scene analysis has on our percept and in a second section the cues used for grouping. We then discuss the interaction of selective attention and perceptual organization (vital in situations with many sound sources). Statistical methods that might be used to extract regularities for corpuses of real world sounds are presented next. We then discuss some computational models of streaming and discuss the kinds of neural system we should be looking for. Finally, we discuss grouping of degraded stimuli and multimodal grouping.

HOW DOES PERCEPTUAL ORGANIZATION AFFECT WHAT WE HEAR?

Many features of sound can affect perceptual organization, but, conversely, it is also true that perceptual organization strongly affects what we hear. It affects our ability to select any particular subset of sounds and can affect the pitch and timbre of sounds. It can also affect the rhythm we hear and our ability to make temporal judgments. In this section we discuss possible ways in which perceptual organization affects what we hear, mention some ways in which tasks have been developed that exploit these changes, and discuss how it has been used in music.

EFFECT ON EASE OF SELECTION

There are several ways in which the current state of perceptual organization affects what we hear. Auditory scene analysis is usually thought of as the generation of a number of "auditory streams," each of which corresponds to a single source. (We refine what we mean by a source later.) The most obvious effect of stream formation is that it makes it easy for us to attend to only a subset of sounds that are grouped into a single stream. If one of the streams generated by scene analysis corresponds to a source we wish to listen to, it is relatively easy to attend selectively to this stream. Where the stream containing the source we wish to listen to also contains other sounds—or worse, the source we wish to listen to is split over different streams—it is much harder to attend to it. Note that there are parallels between this kind of model and a dominant model of visual selective attention (Duncan, 1984) in which selective attention acts to select *objects* that have been formed by perceptual organization processes. This contrasts with other models, which propose that we selectively attend around a particular point in the visual field—so called spotlight models of attention (e.g., Posner, Snyder, and Davidson, 1980). In audition, an equivalent of the spotlight model might be one in which we were able to focus our attention to sounds in a particular frequency region, even if they do not form a separate stream.

There has been some debate about the degree to which unattended auditory streams are processed (early versus late selection). People often report hearing very little of unattended stream, and can be unaware if a different language or even backward speech is presented to them (Cherry, 1953). Several neuro-imaging studies suggest that the response to unattended stimuli is attenuated even in early cortical stages of auditory processing (e.g., Alho *et al.*, 1999; Jancke, Mirzazade, Shah, 1999; Hugdahl *et al.*, 2003), mirroring findings in vision (e.g., Hillyard, Vogel & Luck, 1998). This suggests that to some extent, even fairly early stages of auditory processing are withdrawn from unattended stimuli. However, in counterpoint, there is evidence that some fairly high-level processing can happen to stimuli in unattended streams, such as that shown by Von Wright, Anderson, and Stenman (1975), who conditioned subjects by pairing a mild electric shock with the presentation of a particular word. They then took galvanic skin response (GSR) measurements and found a response to these words, even when they were in an unattended stream.

How we hear a piece of music is strongly affected by perceptual organization. Music played on more than one instrument can often be heard in an analytic manner, in which, for example, a melodic line carried by a bass guitar can be separated from that played on the lead guitar. Composers of such polyphonic music often take care to keep different melodic lines separate by ensuring that there are good cues that will lead to stream segregation at all times. Conversely, there are composers who use the fusion of several instruments into a single perceptual stream to create effects otherwise unavailable—such as the example of African drumming on Bregman's demonstration CD (http://www.psych.mcgill.ca/labs/auditory/bregmancd.html) in which two drummers interleave their notes to produce a single melodic line with beats twice as frequent as any one drummer is playing. The emergence of a melody from a mixture when streaming takes place has been used in an experimental setting by Dowling (1973). He interleaved two melodies so that alternate notes come from different melodies (i.e., first note from melody one then first note from melody two then second note from melody one, second note from melody two, and so on). If alternate notes were made different in some way that led them to separate into different streams, recognition of the melodies improved.

Another important related question concerns the extent to which the organization of sounds is affected by attention. That is, does auditory scene analysis act merely to partition sound into a number of objects from which attentional mechanisms can choose, or does attention actually affect that organization? There is evidence that some degree of perceptual organization can take place even when subjects are not fully focusing their attention on the sounds in question (Bregman

& Rudnicky, 1975; Macken *et al.*, 2003). However, as we discuss later, it now seems clear that attention does indeed facilitate the mechanisms underlying one form of perceptual organization, namely auditory streaming (Carlyon, Cusack, Foxton, & Robertson, 2001; Carlyon, Plack, Fantini, & Cusack, 2003; Cusack, Deeks, Aikman, & Carlyon, in press).

EFFECT ON PITCH AND TIMBRE

Perceptual organization can have a strong effect on pitch and timbre. Many physical sources of sounds, such as those that involve vibrating solids or air in a resonant cavity, produce sound with a spectrum that has energy at a basic frequency (the *fundamental frequency*, F_0) and at integer multiples of it (e.g., frequencies of $2F_0$, $3F_0$, $4F_0$ . . .).[1] This regularity in natural sounds is exploited by the auditory system to group together different simultaneously occurring frequency components with such a structure. There are some salient changes in the percept we hear when perceptual organization of harmonic complexes takes place. When the components are grouped together, the pitch of the higher harmonics (e.g., $3F_0$) is not perceived, but rather the entire harmonic complex is heard with the pitch of the fundamental frequency (F_0). The most striking example of this is perhaps when the fundamental frequency is not actually present, but because of the harmonic relationship between the higher components, this is still heard as the pitch. In these cases, if perceptual grouping breaks down—for example, by shifting the components out of exactly harmonic spacing or by making the different components start asynchronously—the pitch of the components can return. This has been used in the design of some experiments, discussed later.

Timbre is similarly affected by perceptual organization. In the preceding example, the timbre of the complex as a whole when it is grouped together is very different from that of each of the single components. Indeed, complex timbres can only exist when many components of a sound are perceptually grouped together. Where large numbers of components fuse together into a single sound, a richer and more complex timbre is heard, and this has been used as one way of rating the degree of perceptual grouping (e.g., Bregman and Pinker, 1978). Composers such as Debussy and Ravel have carefully designed some pieces to ensure that there is perceptual fusion of many different orchestral instruments, so creating a rich novel timbre.

The pitch of sounds can also be affected by the fusion or segregation of sequential as well as simultaneous sounds. The discrimination of the pitch of a harmonic complex can be impeded by flanking sounds, but this effect can be reduced if these flankers are drawn into a different stream by differences in pitch or perceived location (Gockel, Carlyon, & Micheyl, 1999; Micheyl & Carlyon, 1998).

---

[1] Actually, there are small deviations from this rule in some situations (see http://www.phys.unsw.edu.au/~jw/harmonics.html).

EFFECT ON TEMPORAL ORDER
JUDGMENT AND RHYTHM

Stream segregation can alter the ease with which temporal judgments can be made and affect the perceived rhythm of sound sequences. This phenomenon was reported by Broadbent and Ladefoged (1959) and Warren, Obusek, Farmer, and Warren (1969) and then used by Bregman and Campbell (1971) to investigate some of the characteristics that influence segregation. They played a repeating sequence of three tones chosen from a high-frequency region and three tones chosen from a low-frequency region, interleaved. They found that although listeners could accurately report the relative order of the three low tones or the three high tones, they were very poor at reporting the order across the low and high regions. Some listeners even reported hearing all of the high tones and then all of the low tones. Bregman and Campbell concluded that the low and high tones were falling into different streams and that order judgments could not be made between streams.

A related effect is that when the perceptual grouping of sequences changes, a change in perceived rhythm can also occur. As an example, a task used first by Van Noorden (1975) to investigate many aspects of streaming is shown in Fig. 1. When the low- and the high-pitched tones are grouped together into a single stream, a "galloping" rhythm is heard (Fig. 1, A). When they separate into different streams, this rhythm is lost and two regular isochronous rhythms are heard instead. This salient change in stimuli can be readily described to experimental participants and has been used in many studies (e.g., Anstis & Saida, 1985; Carlyon et al., 2001; Cusack & Roberts, 1999, 2000; Van Noorden, 1975). A common procedure is to present to listeners sequences of a few tens of seconds and have them rate what percept they hear at each moment by pressing one of two buttons.

A performance measure of stream segregation with a task requiring finer judgment of temporal discrimination has been used by Cusack and Roberts (2000) and Roberts, Glasberg, and Moore (2002). The stimuli used by Cusack and

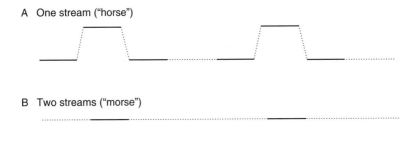

A One stream ("horse")

B Two streams ("morse")

FIGURE 1   Stimuli used by Van Noorden (1975) and many subsequent researchers to investigate sequential auditory grouping. A change in perceptual organization leads to a salient change in rhythm that participants find easy to report.

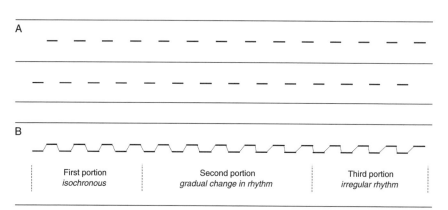

FIGURE 2   The "drunken horse" stimuli, which give a performance measure of stream segregation. Subjects have to discriminate trials in which the tones remain isochronous throughout from those in which there is a gradual drift in the synchrony of the high relative to the low tones. **A,** A trial in which the high and low tones form separate perceptual streams, so preventing temporal comparisons between them. This makes the task harder than when the sounds form a single stream (*B*).

Roberts (2000) are shown in Fig. 2. Each trial consists of three parts. In an initial period, the upper and lower tones make an isochronous rhythm. In half of the trials, the tones remained in this rhythm throughout the rest of the trial. In the other half of the trials, the interstimulus interval of the higher tones was increased slightly so that over time they drifted relative to the lower tones. In the third period the spacing of the tones remained as reached at the end of the second period. The subjects' task was to judge whether the tones maintained their isochronous rhythm or not. If the lower and higher frequency tones fell into a single stream, this judgment was relatively easy (Fig. 2, *B*). If, however, the sequence segregated into separate streams during the first period, then as the within-stream timing changes are small, the task was hard. Roberts *et al.* (2002) used similar stimuli but with a two-alternative forced-choice task structure.

In music, the perceptual grouping of notes in a sequence can have a strong effect on where a beat is perceived. For example, if every 16th note is differentiated in some way from the others, perhaps by being more intense, or by having a different pitch or timbre, this higher level temporal structure may emerge as a beat. In all sorts of music, the perceptual organization evoked has a strong effect on the rhythmic structure that emerges.

EFFECT ON PERCEIVED SPATIAL DISTRIBUTION

Perceptual grouping can also affect the perceived spatial distribution of sounds. For example, Carlyon, Demany, and Deeks (2001) presented subjects with the dichotic click trains shown in Fig. 3, filtered into the frequency region 3900–5400 Hz in order to eliminate place-of-excitation cues. When the pulses were presented at a low overall rate (e.g., 2 and 4 Hz), subjects heard a sequence of clicks alternating between the left ear and the center of the head. However, at

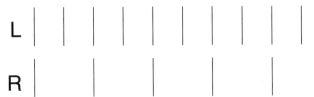

FIGURE 3   Perceptual organization can affect where we hear sounds. At low rates, the simultaneous clicks in the two ears fuse together and are heard as a sound in the middle of the head, accompanied by the remaining clicks in the left ear. At higher rates, however, the binding between the clicks in the left ear is tighter than that across the two ears, and one sound in each ear is heard with nothing in the middle of the head.

higher rates (e.g., 100 and 200 Hz), they heard two buzzes of different pitches, one on each side of the head. They noted that this finding was consistent with the temporal binding between successive clicks in each ear inhibiting the formation of a centered binaural image, produced by the fusion of two simultaneous clicks.

Deutsch (1975) presented a compelling illusion illustrating the effect of the grouping of sequential sounds on where they are heard. A rising scale was played with alternate notes arriving at alternate ears, interleaved with a falling scale with the opposite pattern. Grouping by pitch prevails, and subjects actually report hearing in each ear sequences that only gradually change in pitch—as if every other note had shifted from one ear to the other (see http://psy.ucsd.edu/~ddeutsch/psychology/deutsch_research3.html).

REGULARITIES USED BY THE AUDITORY SYSTEM FOR SCENE ANALYSIS

Here we briefly survey the main cues to perceptual organization that have been identified, giving examples where possible that have used more complex, ecological sounds. For more detailed reviews the reader is referred to Bregman (1990) or Darwin and Carlyon (1995). A summary of the factors influencing sequential stream segregation is given in Moore and Gockel (2002). In this section, some of the factors correspond to physical acoustic factors (e.g., harmonicity) and others correspond to higher level percepts generated in the auditory system (e.g., pitch and timbre). This is discussed further in a later section.

HARMONICITY

As mentioned earlier, sources often produce sounds that have a harmonic structure. This regularity is used by the auditory system as an organizational principle. Experiments with speech found that it is easier to separate two speakers when the fundamental frequencies of their voices are very different. In an early study, Ladefoged and Broadbent (1957) played two speech formants with the same or different F_0s, and found that listeners reported hearing two voices only when the F_0s differed. Brokx and Nooteboom (1982) resynthesized speech with monotonous pitch and found that when two voices were presented simultaneously, intelligibility increased as the separation of the fundamental frequencies of the voices was increased. This was attributed to the perceptual grouping of simultaneous components with harmonic relationships and perceptual tracking of sounds with the same harmonic frequency over time. A similar effect as been shown for vowel sounds alone (Assmann & Summerfield, 1990; Scheffers, 1983), although performance was somewhat above chance even when there was no difference in fundamental frequency.

The loss of pitch of the individual components when a harmonic complex is grouped together (described earlier) has been ingeniously used to probe this kind of grouping. If a single harmonic in a complex is mistuned from its correct frequency, it begins to segregate, and two sounds are heard. Moore, Glasberg, and Peters (1986) asked subjects to identify on each trial which of two harmonic complexes contained a mistuned harmonic and investigated the amount of mistuning required to make harmonics stand out. Mistuning of only 2% was enough for the pitch of a low harmonic to emerge; although they found that greater mistuning was required for higher harmonics. In another experiment (Moore, Peters, & Glasberg, 1985), they found that mistuning a harmonic by a modest amount caused it to shift the pitch of the complex but that once it was mistuned by about 8% it ceased to have an effect. Interestingly, this reveals the existence of a duplex region, where, for mistunings between 3% and 8%, a mistuned harmonic is heard out as a separate tone, yet still contributes to the pitch of the complex.

AMPLITUDE VARIATIONS OVER TIME

For many sound sources, changes in amplitude at one frequency co-occur with changes in amplitude at another frequency. For example, many sounds have abrupt onsets, and the onsets are roughly simultaneous across a range of frequencies. This provides a potential cue for the auditory system to use to group together different components across frequency. Later, we investigate some of the regularities that are present in corpuses of real world sounds, but in this section we discuss some psychoacoustic measurements.

Psychoacoustic studies have shown that synchronous onset is indeed a strong cue to grouping. For example, Bregman and Pinker (1978) asked subjects to rate the timbre of a two-component complex (which was actually part of a sequence containing other sounds) and found that when the components were presented with asynchronies of either 29 or 58 ms, the timbre became less rich, suggesting that they were no longer grouping the two components together into a complex sound. Darwin (1984) showed that modifying the onset time of a single harmonic of a vowel could reduce its effect on the vowel identity. Offset differences also had an effect, albeit a smaller one. In another study using speech sounds, Cutting (1975) found that if the first and second formants of a syllable were played to opposite ears, listeners could still fuse them together. However, when there were onset asynchronies of more than 20–40 ms, the fusion broke down and they could no longer identify the syllable correctly. In general, onsets provide a strong grouping cue, whereas offsets provide only a weak one. A possible ecological source of this asymmetry is presented later.

There has been some work on the grouping of "simultaneously" played notes in music. Rasch (1979) studied the synchrony of different players in ensemble music and found asynchronies of 30–50 ms for simultaneous notes. This might be sufficient to induce some segregation. He noted that the order of onset of the instruments cannot be judged, and two of the arguments he puts forward could easily be reframed as effects of grouping. He argued that comparisons might be difficult because the quality of the instruments is different and also that attention is directed to horizontal (e.g., melodic) rather than vertical (e.g., synchrony) aspects.

As well as onsets and offsets, sounds contain amplitude variations on many other scales. For example, speech contains both rapid oscillations in amplitude due to the opening and closing of the vocal folds (at the fundamental frequency) and slower modulations due to movement of the mouth and vocal tract. There is evidence that these amplitude modulations may also be important for grouping sounds across frequency.

Rhythmic temporal structure can also have an important effect on grouping. For example, in a piece of music, if a rhythm is set up it may influence the grouping of subsequent sounds, so that components on the beat may be pulled into a stream with other notes on this beat. The effect of rhythmic expectancy on attention and grouping is discussed further by Jones (this volume).

LOCATION

Sounds that come from a similar direction are more likely to be allocated to the same stream. The effect tends to be more prominent for the streaming of sequences of sounds rather than those played simultaneously. Norman (1966, reported in Bregman, 1990, p.75) noted that "the continuous up-and-down movement of the pitch in a trill does not occur when the alternate tones are presented to different ears." Furthermore Norman argued that "dichotic presentation of the two tones could never lead to perceptual continuity because the tones could never be attended to simultaneously." Further evidence comes from Van Noorden (1975), who played a sequence of tones that alternated in their ear of presentation. He found that it was difficult to judge when the tones formed an isochronous sequence.

Location does have an effect on the perceptual organization of sounds, but it is not as dominant as in vision. In vision, spatial information has a strong effect on the perceptual organization. Because of differences in the wavelengths of the information carrier, the precision of localization in the auditory domain is very much worse (around 1^0 to 10^0, Moore, 1997, p. 218). Moreover, sound can be reflected and diffracted by objects. In a process known as the *precedence effect* (Campbell and Greated, 1987; Wallach, Neumann, and Rosenzweig, 1949), echoes of sounds arriving after the initial sound (up to 40 ms later for complex sounds) have a reduced effect upon the perceived locale of a sound. In fact, the pattern of echoes might be used by the auditory system to separate different sources. A processing strategy that would exploit this information is described in Blauert (1997, section 5.3).

FREQUENCY

Frequency has a strong effect on the perceptual organization of sounds. Sounds that are more similar in frequency are more likely to be allocated to the same stream. An early demonstration of this in an experimental setting was by Miller and Heise (1950), who played a sequence comprising low- and high-frequency pure tones alternating repeatedly. For smaller frequency separations between the tones, listeners heard a single sequence, with its pitch "moving up and down continuously." However, they reported that when the frequency separation was increased above a critical value, the sequence appeared to "break," and two unrelated and interrupted streams of different pitch were heard. Miller and Heise called this critical value the "trill threshold." Their results can be described in terms of auditory streaming. When the frequency separation between the tones is large enough, they split into two different streams.

As mentioned earlier, Bregman and Campbell (1971) used the property that it is difficult for participants to judge temporal order across streams to investigate the effect of pitch differences on streaming. Subsequent work has confirmed and extended this work. In particular, in his widely cited thesis, Van Noorden (1975) further investigated the segregation of tone sequences as a function of frequency separation and presentation rate. Higher presentation rates and larger frequency differences were both found to increase segregation. Van Noorden also investigated the role of attention in streaming. Figure 4 shows the effects of frequency separation and presentation rate on the percepts possible. Between the two boundaries, either one or two streams can be heard. The "fission boundary" marks the smallest frequency separation at which the tones can be segregated and the "temporal coherence boundary" the largest separation for which the tones can be heard as a single stream, when deliberate listening strategies are employed by the listener.

PITCH

For complex sounds, their pitch (primarily defined by their fundamental frequency) and the frequency region in which they have energy can be varied independently. For example, a complex sound that contains no energy at the frequency of its fundamental can still have a clear pitch corresponding to this frequency ("residue pitch": Schouten, 1940). Several experiments have been done to inves-

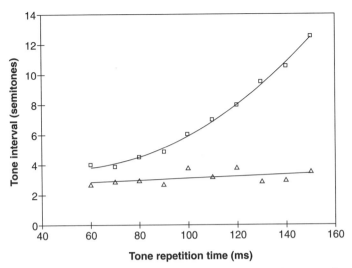

FIGURE 4   The effect of frequency separation and repetition rate on the perceptual grouping of a sequence comprising higher and lower frequency pure tones. Below the fission boundary, only one stream is heard, but above the temporal coherence boundary, two streams are heard. Between the two boundaries, both percepts can be heard.

tigate whether segregation is determined by the pitch or the actual spectral region in which there is energy. Experiments in which only pure tones have been used cannot differentiate these two, as the pitch of a pure tone cannot be manipulated without also changing its spectral region. Van Noorden (1975) used alternating complexes with the same fundamental frequency but different selections of harmonics (3–5 and 8–10). He found that the tones in the sequence segregated, despite having the same pitch. He found no evidence for a role of the fundamental frequency in segregation. However, subsequent experiments have shown that pitch differences can lead to streaming in the absence of differences in the long-term pattern of excitation in the cochlea. For example, Vliegen and Oxenham (1999) generated harmonic complexes and filtered them into a high frequency region that would ensure that the harmonics were unresolved. The pattern of excitation across frequency in the ear was the same for all of their stimuli, but a pitch difference was heard because of differences in the temporal structure of the response. They found that this pitch difference could induce stream segregation, although other work has shown that it had only a weak effect on obligatory segregation (Vliegen, Moore, & Oxenham, 1999).

Singh (1987) has also investigated the relative importance of spectral region and fundamental frequency in perceptual segregation. She played sequences of sounds that could group either by pitch (fundamental) or by timbre (spectral region). Both factors were shown to influence grouping, and a trade-off was demonstrated: the increase in segregation from a greater pitch difference could be counteracted by a reduction in timbre difference and vice versa. These experiments are discussed in more detail below.

Composers of polyphonic music use the effects of pitch differences and tempo to manipulate perceptual organization (Huron, 1991). When making music with multiple parts, they may take care to ensure that different parts do not become to close in pitch. At slower rates, they ensure that a greater frequency separation is maintained between parts. In an experimental setting, several researchers have investigated the effect of pitch on grouping using "interleaved melodies," in which alternate notes come from different melodies. Listeners find it much easier to segregate interleaved melodies that have a distinct pitch difference between them (Dowling, 1973; Hartmann & Johnson, 1991).

TIMBRE

Sounds that differ in timbre are more likely to segregate. In music, melodic lines are often kept separate by using different musical instruments to carry them. Experimentally, there have been many studies illustrating the effect of timbre on perceptual organization. For example, Dannenbring and Bregman (1976) found that listeners rate an alternating sequence of pure tones and narrowband noises as segregating more than one of either timbre alone. Smith, Hausfield, Power, and Gorta (1982) found that sequences of synthetic musical instrument sounds were more likely to segregate when the timbre varied.

In a study using speech sounds, Culling and Darwin (1993) played two synthetic diphthongs simultaneously. Each "diphthong" was calculated from two synthetic vowels. It began with one vowel and ended with the other, and the transition was generated using linear interpolation over time of the formant frequencies. The fundamental frequencies of the diphthongs followed one of two sets of trajectories, which are shown in Fig. 5. The task was to determine whether the pitches "crossed" or "bounced" away from each other. Culling and Darwin (p. 303) reported that "Despite the changing timbres of the two sounds, the subjects were able to discriminate crossing and bouncing F_0s, provided that the timbres of the vowels differed at the moment when their F_0s were the same. When the timbres were the same, the subjects could not make the discrimination and tended to hear a bouncing percept." Their results suggest that continuity of timbre is used in perceptual grouping.

Cusack and Roberts (2000) used two different paradigms to quantify the effect of timbral differences on stream segregation. In one experiment they found that subjects found it easier to identify changes in a melody that had been interleaved with another when the tones of the two melodies had different timbres. Differences in timbre provided a cue that enabled the listener to segregate the two melodies. In another experiment, they used the procedure described earlier and shown in Fig. 2. They found that subjects were worse at detecting temporal differences within sequences when the timbre of the sounds varied. This second

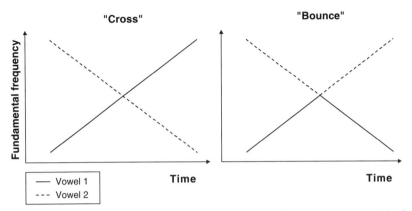

FIGURE 5   The time course of the fundamental frequencies of two vowels presented simultaneously by Culling and Darwin (1993). Listeners had to distinguish between the "cross" and "bounce" percepts. To do so, the sounds that are most similar just before and after the pitches meet must be grouped together.

experiment shows something rather different from the first. Differences in timbre within a sequence led to stream segregation, even though this segregation made performance worse by preventing temporal comparisons across groups of tones. Some or all of the segregation induced by timbral differences must therefore be compulsory, and the listener has no conscious access to representations at a pre-segregated level.

Singh (1987) investigated the role of timbre and fundamental frequency in the grouping of sequences of complex tones. Listeners were asked to describe the grouping in each trial using the response labels shown in Fig. 6. The results showed a trade-off between pitch and timbre, indicating competition between them in determining the perceptual organization of the sequence. When there was a large difference in timbre and a small difference in pitch, the percept heard was that of grouping by timbre, but when there was a large difference in pitch, and a small difference in timbre, the percept heard was that of grouping by pitch. For intermediate difference in each, the percept heard was ambiguous.

There is no obvious way to identify acoustic properties that have a strong effect on timbre. However, several attempts have been made, and some authors have tested whether each of these acoustic properties has an effect on stream segregation. One aspect that has already been discussed is that of the effect on segregation of the spectral region in which a sound has energy. Van Noorden (1975) found that sounds with energy in a more similar spectral region were less likely to segregate from one another. A related feature of timbre is that of brightness, which has also been found to induce segregation (Bregman & Levitan and Bregman & Liao [both reported in Bregman, 1990, p. 83]; Iverson, 1995; Wessel, 1979). Another property that might affect timbre, the shape of the temporal amplitude envelope, has been found in some studies to affect segregation (Cusack &

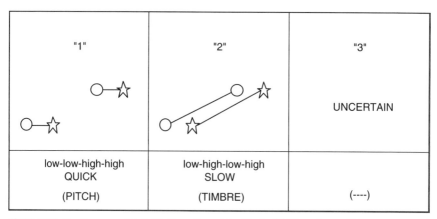

FIGURE 6 Response labels (*1, 2,* or *3*) used by Singh (1987) to denote different perceptual groupings.

Roberts, 2000; Dannenbring & Bregman, 1976; Iverson, 1995) but not in others (Hartmann & Johnson, 1991). Other dynamic properties affecting timbre have also recently been shown to affect stream segregation (Cusack & Roberts, In press).

SIMILARITY OF LEVEL

There is some evidence that differences in level can induce or enhance segregation. Dowling (1968, reported in Hartmann & Johnson, 1991) reported that listeners were able to segregate a sequence on the basis of differences in intensity. This was confirmed by Van Noorden (1975), who played a sequence comprising two alternating sounds. The frequency separation between the two sounds was swept up and down cyclically, and listeners were asked to indicate continuously whether they heard the sequence as one or two streams. Van Noorden found more segregation when the intensities of the sounds differed than when they did not. Hartmann and Johnson (1991) used a different task in which two familiar melodies were interleaved with each other. The effect on performance of various acoustic differences between the two melodies was studied. The task was designed to be easier when the melodies showed greater stream segregation. A difference in intensity of 8 dB was found to improve performance for all subjects. No data were given about whether there was a difference in performance on the quieter and louder melodies. The improvement in performance related to differences in loudness was significant but small in comparison with many of the other conditions they ran.

Another example of segregation by loudness comes from the "roll" effect, first reported by van Noorden (1975). He presented subjects with a sequence of brief tones, which alternated between a lower and a higher intensity. He reported that, for a range of intensity differences and repetition rates, subjects heard a sequence of soft tones, every other one of which was accompanied by an additional louder tone. In other words, the soft tones were not only heard when they were present but also "perceptually extracted" from the louder tones.

More recently, Stainsby, Moore, Medland, and Glasberg (submitted) investigated the effect of intensity differences on streaming using a paradigm with stimuli similar to those of Cusack and Roberts (2000) as described earlier and shown in Fig. 2. Stainsby *et al.* found that an intensity difference between the higher and lower frequency tones made the temporal discrimination harder, reflecting an enhancement in stream segregation.

HIGHER ORDER COMMONALITIES

Many of the commonalities described in the preceding sections are quite easy to specify in a simple way. For example, harmonicity is simply described mathematically, and pitch is a percept that is phenomenologically easy to identify and therefore easy to measure. However, there are commonalities in common sounds that are not so easy to describe. Some of these are complex and correspond to the same kinds of commonalities on which we can perform pattern recognition, such as vowel or word sounds. Other regularities may exist of intermediate complexity between that which can be described by simple mathematical rules and obvious percepts and high-level auditory objects.

We can use these high level regularities for selection. For example, Scheffers (1983, as cited by Bregman, 1990, p. 396) showed that if two synthetic vowel sounds are played with the same fundamental frequencies and onset and offset times, listeners can still separate them, presumably by comparison with stored internal "templates" or schemas. Bregman (1990) refers to this process as "schema-driven selection," and differentiates it from "primitive stream segregation." Bregman sees these as processes that are different in character, with primitive stream segregation as a bottom-up process and schema-driven selection a top-down one. However, such a simple dichotomy may not be appropriate. We would like to argue that it is likely that more complex regularities play a role in perceptual grouping. As we discuss later, there is good evidence that perceptual grouping is influenced by representations at several different stages of processing in the auditory pathway. This could naturally include influence from systems that identify higher order patterns. Given extensive repeated exposure to a particular complex sound (such as some of those in speech), it seems likely that the auditory system will learn to use this regularity for grouping.

These higher order commonalities depend intimately on the particular sounds present in the real world. An ecological approach is therefore important for either modeling or empirical work. A problem, however, is that the regularities may be intrinsically difficult to describe because they do not have simple mathematical or perceptual correlates. One approach that we think is promising is to apply statistical models to analyze regularities in natural sounds. This approach is discussed in detail later.

GROUPING AND SELECTIVE ATTENTION

Selective attention and perceptual grouping differ in character. To be able to select, we need knowledge of the characteristics of the target of interest and, indeed, we need to know which target we are interested in. It is a top-down process, primarily under conscious control of the listener. It will be context dependent in that performance will depend upon the degree of experience the listener has in selecting sounds from a particular source and on many other factors. A simple schematic of this is shown in Fig. 7, *A*. Similar models have been proposed as either the whole story (Jones, 1976) or as one mechanism at our disposal (schema-driven selection; Bregman, 1990). Some authors have argued that perceptual grouping, on the other hand, is an invariant process, exploiting probabilities of co-occurrences in natural sounds to group acoustic elements together into streams, regardless of the particular context of the listener. Once streams have been formed, they might then be selected or rejected as a whole. A schematic of this is shown in Fig. 7, *B*.

The simplest model, which has been popular in the absence of evidence to the contrary (e.g., Bregman, 1990), is that perceptual grouping processes are automatic. However, there is growing evidence that, in fact, perceptual grouping is affected by attention. Carlyon, Cusack, Foxton, and Robertson (2001) looked at the buildup of stream segregation using repeating triplet sequences such as those described earlier (see Fig. 1). For intermediate frequency separations between the high and low tones, these tone sequences are generally heard as a single stream to begin with but, over the course of a few seconds, stream segregation builds up

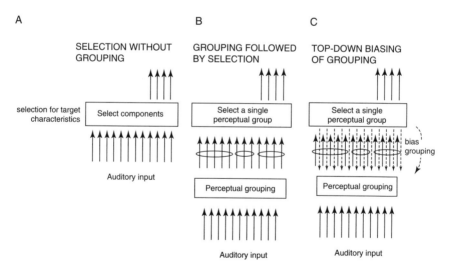

FIGURE 7   Three possible models showing the relationship between perceptual grouping and selection.

and they are more likely to be heard as two streams near the end. They played 21-second-long tones sequences to one ear and, for the first 10 seconds, a set of noises to the other ear. If attention was focused on the tone sequence throughout, stream segregation built up over the first 10 seconds. If, instead, attention was directed to a distracting noise in the opposite ear for the first 10 seconds and then attention switched to the tones, subjects reported an amount of stream segregation that was similar to that which would occur if the sequence had just started. Hence, a phenomenon previously thought to reflect primitive automatic stream segregation processes is in fact dependent on the focus of selective attention. A schematic of the model we proposed is shown in Fig. 7, *C*. In other experiments, we controlled for the effect of switching tasks and showed that patients with brain damage leading to an attentional deficit showed the predicted shift in grouping.

THE HIERARCHICAL DECOMPOSITION MODEL

The stimuli that are used in the laboratory to investigate streaming are, for simplicity, usually designed with only a few possible perceptual organizations (e.g., one or two). In the real world, tens or hundreds of possible ways to perceptually organize an auditory scene may be possible and, indeed, may happen in particular contexts. When faced with these complex auditory scenes, a way for the auditory system to limit the complexity of the incoming input is to select only part of it. As described in the last section, Carlyon, Cusack, Foxton, and Robertson (2001) found that when listeners were attending to some distracting noises in a different frequency region and the opposite ear to a tone sequence, the buildup of streaming of the tone sequence was reduced. Cusack *et al.* (in press) investigated the domain of which streaming is reduced. They suggested that it might be reduced either:

1. In the *opposite ear* to that currently being attended;
2. In *distant frequency regions* from those being attended;
3. Or, after some initial streaming, in *unattended streams.*

They found that the reduction in the buildup of streaming due to a distracting noise did not depend strongly on whether it was presented to the same or opposite ear to the tone sequence and could even have a frequency spectrum that encompassed the tones. They concluded that rather than an effect of ear or frequency region, it was *unattended streams* that showed no further fragmentation. A *hierarchical decomposition model* was proposed, which is illustrated in Fig. 8 using a real-world example. In this model, initially (and perhaps automatically) grouping forms three streams of music, speech, and traffic noise. When attention is focused upon one of these (the music), this then fragments and several further streams become available for attention. If one of these is then attended, further fragmentation takes place and so on. In a further experiment, they showed that if attention is withdrawn from a sequence and then switched back, its

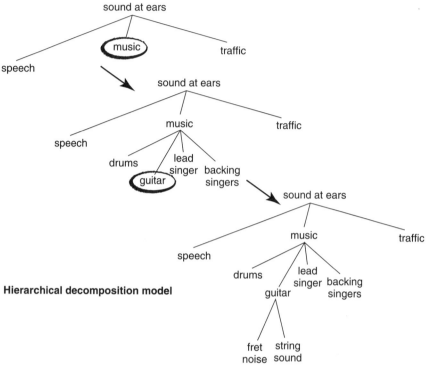

FIGURE 8 In the hierarchical decomposition model, there is some initial stream segregation. Then, when one of these streams is attended to (e.g., music, as shown by the highlighting) this object fragments into a range of substreams.

segregation is reset. In our example, if attention is switched to the traffic, the fragmentation of the music hierarchy collapses.

Preventing the further perceptual fragmentation of unattended parts of the auditory scene provides an ecological advantage. If, for example, a listener is attending to a speaker against a background of music and some traffic noise, it may not be advantageous for the auditory system to segregate the two backing singers or the sounds of different car engines. If perceptual organization itself is a limited-capacity process, then using resources to organize unattended parts of the scene is a waste. However, even if perceptual organization is not capacity limited, we know that some of the subsequent processes are. On arrival in an auditory scene, the listener may wish not to be bombarded with many small components of sounds (e.g., fret noise from guitar), but rather to perceive a few large-scale objects (e.g., speech, music). A hierarchy of perceptual grouping has been proposed before (e.g., Bregman, 1990; Darwin & Carlyon, 1995)—what we are adding here is that unattended branches are not elaborated: when we are attending to speech, we are not fragmenting the music.

This view contrasts with a more general interpretation of Bregman (1990) and Rogers and Bregman (1998), who argued that unattended streams were "well formed" and that you do not "wrap up all your garbage in the same bundle" (Bregman, 1990 p. 193). However, it is in line with the conclusions of Brochard, Drake, Botte, and McAdams (1999). They presented sequences of tones that comprised four subsequences. Within each subsequence, the tone frequency was fixed and the stimulus onset asynchrony (SOA) regular. The four different sequences had different rates (SOAs of 300, 400, 500, and 700 ms). In each trial, subjects were cued to attend to one of the four subsequences and asked to detect which of two intervals contained temporal irregularities in this subsequence. This was easy if the target subsequence fell in a separate stream from the others but very hard if it did not. They found that performance was not dependent on the number of interfering subsequences and concluded that the unattended subsequences were not segregated into separate perceptual groups.

MISMATCH NEGATIVITY USING ELECTROENCEPHALOGRAPHY AND MAGNETOENCEPHALOGRAPHY

Some mismatch negativity (MMN) experiments have led to the conclusion that streaming can occur when participants are not attending to the to-be-streamed sounds. Sussman, Ritter, and Vaughan (1999) played participants a tone sequence that alternated regularly between a high-frequency and a low-frequency range, with the tones in each range playing a simple melody. On a minority of trials, they altered the order of tones in the low range and argued that this should elicit an MMN only when the interfering high-frequency tones were pulled into a separate auditory stream. They observed an MMN when the SOA between successive tones was 100 ms, at which behavioral experiments suggest that streaming should occur. In contrast, when the SOA was 750 ms, for which streaming should be much weaker, no MMN was observed. They attributed the difference in MMN between the two conditions to differences in streaming, which, as subjects were reading a book, they described as occurring outside the focus of attention. However, it should be noted that even when the low tones were omitted, the MMN to the higher frequency deviants was very weak at the 750-ms SOA, indicating that the observed effects of repetition rate may not have been entirely due to its effects on streaming.

Yabe *et al.* (2001) used magnetoencephalography (MEG) to measure the magnetic MMN (MMNm) produced by the omission of an occasional high (3000 Hz, "H") tone in a sequence of alternating high and low (L) tones (i.e., HLHLHL_LHL). Previous work had suggested that stimulus omissions elicit an MMN only when the SOA between successive tones is less than 160–170 ms. Using an SOA of 125 ms, they observed an MMN when the lower tone frequency was 2800 Hz but not when it was 500 Hz. They attributed the lack of an MMN in the latter condition to the high and low tones being pulled into separate auditory streams, so that the SOA in the high stream was now too long (250 ms) to elicit the MMN. Their finding provides a clear demonstration that the omission MMN operates on a frequency-selective basis and, as described earlier, so does auditory streaming. However, a demonstration that the MMN difference is due to streaming would be more compelling if it could be shown that it varies with other parameters known to affect streaming. Indeed, the results of Shinozaki *et al.* (2000) show that size of the frequency separation between pairs of tone sequences can affect the MMN even when participants hear all pairs of sequences as a single stream.

One general limitation of the preceding approach is that, although subjects were instructed to ignore the sounds, one can never be sure that they did not "sneak a little listen." An alternative approach is to manipulate the amount of attention paid to the sounds and see whether this affects the MMN response. This approach was adopted by Sussmann *et al.*, using a paradigm similar to that in their 1999 experiment described earlier. They used an SOA of 500 ms and observed an MMN only when subjects were attending to the tones, and they concluded that, for this stimulus, attention did indeed modulate streaming.

The presence of some stream segregation in the absence of attention does not preclude there being an effect of attention on stream segregation. In the hierarchical decomposition model, for example, the initial decomposition into a few large-scale streams may well be automatic, but further fragmentation may require the application of selective attention.

STATISTICAL ANALYSIS OF
NATURAL SOUNDS

CORRELATION

As described in an earlier section, the auditory system may be sensitive to higher order commonalities in sets of sounds. However, unlike the case with simple commonalities such as harmonicity and onset synchrony, it is not obvious *a priori* what these commonalities are likely to be. One possible approach is to use more model-free statistical analysis methods to find commonalities that are present in the sounds encountered in everyday life. The reasoning here is that the auditory system may have, through either evolution or experience, developed strategies to deal with the commonalities that it needs to process. Cusack (2003) searched for correlations in four different sets of sounds (speech, environmental sounds, and orchestral and solo instrument music). The sounds were processed using a simple auditory gammatone filterbank using components from Cooke and Brown (http://www.dcs.shef.ac.uk/~martin/MAD/docs/mad.htm). The resulting spectrograms were then cut into 400-ms fragments, and correlations across fragments were calculated between energy at one time and frequency with the occurrence of energy at other times and frequencies. This was also done for the temporal derivative of energy in each frequency band, which will identify coherent patterns of change across different frequency. Some results are shown in Fig. 9.

Each of the six panels in Fig. 9 shows a correlation map between energy at a particular reference time and frequency (in the center of the map at 231 Hz, shown by the circle) and each other frequency and time. This is the correlation across different samples of sound, so a bright patch shows that when the feature usually occurs at the reference time/frequency it also occurs at the time/frequency indicated by the bright patch. Note the range of times, from 200 ms before to 200 ms after the reference. The frequency scale used was one that characterizes the width of the auditory filters across the equivalent rectangular bandwidth scale (ERB, Glasberg and Moore, 1990). The frequency bins were equal ERB spaced from

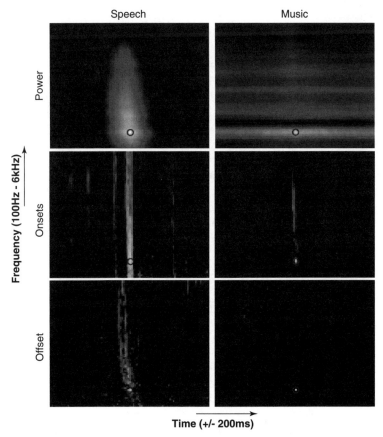

FIGURE 9   The correlation (black r = 0; white r = 1.0) between acoustic characteristics at a reference frequency (indicated by the *circle*) and a range of other frequencies, for two collections of sounds (left column speech; right column music). The top row shows correlations in energy; the middle row correlations in onset, and the bottom row correlations in offset. Common onset across frequency provides an excellent grouping cue for both types of sounds.

100 to 6 kHz. White corresponds to a correlation of +1 and black to a correlation of 0. There were few negative correlations. The left three panels are for a set of speech sounds (taken from the TIMIT database), the right three for the "single musical instrument" set (Bach lute music). The top two panels show correlations in energy. There are strong correlations, but the pattern of those correlations is quite different across the two different classes. The speech correlates much more heavily across frequency for a short period of time, whereas the music correlates to a greater degree across time within frequency range. The complex frequency structure of the music is evident. This suggests that synchronous changes across time may be more useful for perceptual grouping of the components of speech, but continuity across frequency might be more useful for grouping the components of music.

The middle two panels show patterns of correlations in onset and the bottom two panels correlations in offset. These were generated by calculating the temporal derivatives of the power within each frequency band and then setting to zero of all bins above or below a particular threshold to select only onsets or only offsets. For both the speech and music, strong synchronous coherence in onset across frequency can be seen. This would provide a useful grouping cue. Interestingly, as can be seen in the bottom left panel, for speech the correlation in offset is less strong and more diffuse across time. For music, as shown on the bottom right, there is very little correlation in offsets across time or frequency. From these data sets, onset seems to hold much more useful information for grouping than offset. As discussed earlier, onsets have indeed been shown to be a more powerful segregation cue than offsets. This result is encouraging because it suggests that, by measuring the commonalities present in everyday sounds, one can identify cues that could prove useful for auditory scene analysis. The hope is that further statistical analysis will reveal more complex regularities, whose psychological validity can then be tested in a laboratory setting.

INDEPENDENT COMPONENT ANALYSIS

The correlation method just described will find only simple first-order regularities in which a feature at one time/frequency is correlated to another. However, it is likely that there will be higher order regularities. Independent component analysis (ICA) provides a mathematical tool for the identification of underlying components present in a mixture of sounds. It uses an iterative procedure to optimize a set of basis functions so that they can be combined to represent a set of input data as accurately as possible. In the variant we applied, we also optimized the functions so that as few basis functions as possible were necessary to provide a high-fidelity representation of each item in the input set. ICA is attractive in particular because there are simple biologically plausible neural models that can implement its learning and activation stages (Harpur & Prager, 2000).

To test an ICA model, we generated a set of 10-second-long mixtures comprising each of four types of sounds that were randomly distributed in time.

Although in due course we hope to apply this model to ecologically valid stimuli, for simplicity we initially used simple synthesized sounds. The four types were 1-kHz pure tones, three-component harmonic complexes ($F_0 = 400\,\text{Hz}$), eight-component harmonic complexes ($F_0 = 600\,\text{Hz}$), and a digitally generated noise band (1500–2499 Hz). The ICA model was then trained to generate a set of basis functions that can be used to represent the data. Some sample input to the model is shown in Fig. 10, A and B. It can be seen that the density of the sounds in the mixture was such that each of the sounds was rarely presented alone but was usually mixed with others. This input was fed through a gammatone filterbank (http://www.dcs.shef.ac.uk/~martin/MAD/docs/mad.htm) of 80 filters and the spectral energy averaged (RMS) over 4-ms bins. The input was then decomposed into 9980 windows each 40 ms in duration (i.e., 10 time points × 80 frequencies). The sparse coding ICA procedure and implementation of Olshausen and Field (1996) was then used to decompose the data into six basis functions analogous to six neurons each with a different "receptive field."[2] A small number of basis functions were used as, for this simple stimulus, this leads to more easily interpretable individual functions.

The results are shown in Fig. 10, C and D. Figure 10, D shows the "receptive fields" of the six neurons, and Fig. 10, C shows their activation in response to the mixture stimulus. Some of the neurons are obviously responding to the underlying stimuli. For example, neuron 2 (second from the top in panel C; second from left in panel D) fires whenever the 8 component complex is present. Neuron 4 responds to the tone, and neurons 5 and 6 both fire when the noise is present. The firing of each neuron is dependent only on whether its preferred stimulus is present and not on what other stimuli are present. In the process of representing the data, segregation is being performed. This demonstration is particularly impressive because the stimuli were not usually presented alone in the original mixtures: the ICA process has exploited the statistical regularities in the data to learn the underlying components. Given the simplicity of neural implementations of ICA, this is a candidate mechanism for the process in the brain. Neurons in the thalamus and auditory cortex show receptive fields that might be appropriate (monkey: deCharms *et al.*, 1998; cat: Miller *et al.*, 2001, 2002; bird: Theunissen *et al.*, 2000; Gehr *et al.*, 2000; ferret: Depireux *et al.*, 2001; Kowalski, Depireux, & Shamma, 1996a, 1996b; Kowalski, Versnel, & Shamma, 1995) and so might be candidate loci for such a process.

There are several extensions to this model that would extend its scope. In our example, for easy interpretability, we presented only a few types of sound, and so the model learned each of the individual types (compare "grandmother cells"). However, if presented with input stimuli that cover a range of exemplars with

---

[2] Note that calculating the activation to a particular stimulus is more involved for ICA than it is for other systems such as principal components analysis (PCA). Neurally plausible mechanisms have been demonstrated, but for speed of implementation on a serial computer we used a conjugate gradient convergence algorithm.

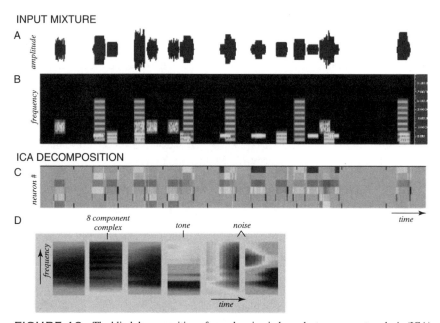

FIGURE 10 The blind decomposition of sounds using independent component analysis (ICA). (A and B) A mixture of four different types of sound (tone, two harmonic complexes, and a noise burst) randomly distributed in time. Each sound usually overlaps with at least one other. An iterative ICA learning scheme was then employed to develop the optimum "receptive fields" for a set of six neurons that will most accurately and efficiently represent the data. The firing of the neurons is shown in *C*, and their receptive fields in *D*. The ICA neurons perform a substantial part of the job of segregating the sounds.

some common aspect (e.g., harmonic complexes with different numbers of components), this type of model should be able to generalize. For example, given a sufficiently wide mixture some "neurons" would be expected to code common features such as harmonic structure or common spectral shapes. Another interesting test of the model would be to take two sets of mixtures (e.g., set A and set B) and compare the performance of models trained on A to each of the sets with the response of models trained on B to each of the sets. It would be expected that the models would better segregate sounds that they have been trained on.

COMPUTATIONAL MODELS

There have been several computational models of auditory streaming. Beauvois and Meddis (1991, 1996) and McCabe and Denham (1997) both modeled the stream segregation of simple tone sequences using models based on interactions between processing of auditory frequency channels. These models match the effect on streaming of frequency separation and the effect of rate of presentation. They can also model the "old-plus-new" heuristic that new sounds added to a scene tend to form their own stream. There is also a model that attempts to mirror the findings in vision that neurons representing parts of the visual scene that are in the same perceptual group tend to fire in synchrony (Engel, Konig, Gran, & Singer, 1990). Wang and Brown have produced models of auditory streaming based on sets of oscillators that either fire in synchrony or not depending on the degree of grouping (Brown & Wang, 1996; Wang, 1996). It is possible that even if oscillatory synchrony does not participate in the formation of perceptual groups, it may still code the output of processes that do. Other models that incorporate higher level regularities have been designed (Cooke & Ellis, 2001; Ellis, 1996). There are also nonauditory models of scene analysis, purely based on the statistical properties of signal mixtures. Blind deconvolution works extremely well when there are multiple simultaneous recording channels (i.e., multiple linear mixtures, Bell and Sejnowski, 1995) but it can also work well on a single channel (van der Kouwe, Wang, & Brown, 2001). A related literature that connects too rarely with the psychological and neuroscientific ones is that of artificial intelligence. For example, Sarkar and Boyer (1994) wrote a volume on perceptual organization in computer vision, which contains some useful formalizations such as the use of a Bayesian framework for grouping in the introduction.

NEURAL SUBSTRATE OF GROUPING

MULTIPLE NEURAL LEVELS?

Is it the case that a single neural substrate at a particular level in the processing stream is responsible for stream segregation? Or do processes at several levels contribute? And, are these different levels qualitatively different, or do the different levels modify the resultant organization in the same way?

Some authors have argued that auditory streaming can be explained by interactions early in the auditory processing stream. For example, Hartmann and Johnson (1991) proposed that *peripheral channeling*—channeling by frequency and ear in the early auditory system—is the dominant factor in determining stream segregation. As mentioned before, there are computer models that explain some streaming effects using information present in the periphery. Rose and Moore (1997) investigated the frequency separation necessary for a particular degree of stream segregation as a function of the center frequency of the sounds. They found that the separation was constant across frequency when expressed in equivalent rectangular bandwidths (ERBs, Glasberg & Moore, 1990), which is a measure of auditory filter width. Certainly for simple sounds, the degree of peripheral overlap in the filters that are activated is a good predictor of their segregation. Taken alone, these data might suggest a neural locus for auditory streaming at some point in the brainstem.

Subsequent experiments have shown that streaming can happen in the absence of peripheral channeling (Cusack, 1998; Glasberg & Moore, 2002; Grimault, Micheyl, Carlyon, Arthaud, & Collet, 2000; Moore & Gockel, 2002; Roberts, Vliegen, & Oxenham, 1999; Vliegen, Moore and Oxenham, 1999). For example, Vliegen & Oxenham (1999) generated harmonic complexes and filtered them into a high-frequency region that ensured the harmonics were unresolved. The pattern of excitation across frequency in the ear was the same for all of their stimuli, but a pitch difference is heard because of differences in the temporal structure of the response. They found that this pitch difference could induce stream segregation. Rose and Moore (1997) investigated sequential stream segregation in people with unilateral hearing loss that led to broadening of their auditory filters in one ear. According to the peripheral channeling model, we might expect that if the peripheral activation generated by two stimuli overlaps to a greater extent they are more likely to be grouped together. Interestingly, Rose and Moore found that the frequency separation required for stream segregation was similar in the hearing-impaired ear and the normal ear even though the broader filters in the former will have led to a greater overlap in the activation produced. The following effects of many other higher order perceptual factors on stream segregation have already been discussed: pitch (even in the absence of spectral differences), timbre, and perceived location (Cusack & Roberts, In press). Indeed, in an interesting review Moore and Gockel (2002) proposed that a general principle behind sequential streaming is that any sufficiently salient perceptual differences may enhance segregation.

As described earlier, other authors have highlighted that even these "primitive" stream segregation effects can be modified by high-level functions such as the focus of selective attention or by high-level deficits such as unilateral neglect (Carlyon, Cusack, Foxton, & Robertson, 2001). They suggest that this supports a view that stream segregation is likely to be a higher level cortical process or at the very least, that it is affected by these higher level cortical processes. Cusack *et al.* (in press) collected evidence for the involvement of higher level cortical areas in stream segregation using functional magnetic resonance imaging. I presented sequences of sounds such as those in Fig. 1, which could be heard either as one stream or as two streams. Listeners were asked to rate throughout which of the two percepts they heard. We found more activity when listeners perceived two streams than when they perceived one, in both auditory cortex and a region in the intraparietal sulcus that is associated with binding in vision.

In an earlier section, we discussed some studies using the mismatch negativity paradigm with EEG and MEG. Sussman, Ritter, and Vaughan (1999) argue that stream segregation is well formed at the level of the generator of the MMN. The mismatch negativity is thought to arise from around auditory cortex (e.g., see references from Ulanovsky, Las, & Nelken, 2003), and this suggests that streaming affects processing at this level. Other authors have focused on the extent to which high-level learned schemata may affect grouping. Scheffers (1983, as cited by Bregman, 1990, p. 396) showed that if two synthetic vowel sounds are played with the same fundamental frequencies and onset and offset times, listeners can still separate them, presumably by comparison with a stored internal "template" or schema.

It seems that differences at a wide range of levels in the auditory system affect streaming (see Fig. 11). It is possible that there is convergence of information of many different kinds at a single locus in auditory processing that leads to grouping. However, here we propose that grouping takes place at many levels in the auditory system in the form of competition within and between those levels and that it is the combination of the results of competition at these individual levels that leads to what we call perceptual grouping.

NEURAL INSTANTIATION: SYNCHRONY OF FIRING

A framework that has gained great popularity in vision may form a practical instantiation of the cognitive mechanism we propose in the preceding section. In vision, neurophysiologists have shown that perceptual grouping across visual cortex correlates with the synchrony of firing of neurons. When neurons in different regions of space are coding the same object, they tend to fire together. Such a coding system has also been suggested in audition and even implemented in the form of a computer model (Wang, 1996). If there are reciprocal connections between different layers in auditory processing, a spread in the timing of firing between layers might lead to a spread in synchrony and provide a mechanism by which the different layers can interact and influence the grouping.

Single locus or interactive multiple levels?

- Peripheral channelling (e.g., Hartmann & Johnson, 1991)

- ITD: (e.g., Rogers & Bregman, 1998)

- Pitch: (e.g., Vliegen & Oxenham, 2001)

- Timbre: (e.g., Cusack & Roberts, 2000; Roberts, Glasberg & Moore, 2002)

- Higher-level representations (schemas) (e.g., Scheffers, 1983)

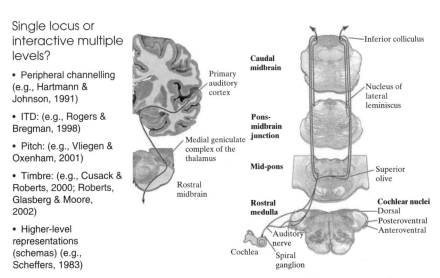

FIGURE 11   Multiple neural levels are probably involved in stream segregation.

AUTOMATICITY AND INNATENESS

Bregman (1990) has suggested a dichotomy between primitive auditory processes, which he defines as being automatic and innate, and schema-based selection, which he argues is likely to be learned and consciously applied. However, the distinction between Bregman's categories is now less than clear. Nonautomatic processes of selective attention have been shown to affect "primitive" stream segregation. Another example of dissociation between automaticity and innateness is suggested by work on feature detectors situated in primary auditory cortex. Processing at this level is often thought to be automatic, but learning has been shown to play a part. The organization of the auditory cortex is heavily dependent on input during development and can even organize to detect visual features (orientation) if "rewired" to receive visual input during early development (Sharma, Angelucci, & Sur, 2000).

PERCEPTUAL GROUPING OF DEGRADED SIGNALS

In some ways, perceptual grouping processes are robust. For example, often one might listen to a mixture of sound sources with all spatial information removed, on a mono television, radio, or telephone, but simultaneous talkers may still be separated. In a reverberant room, much of the fine temporal structure of different sounds will be smoothed out, reducing the usefulness of amplitude variations such as abrupt onsets. Frequency filtering through bad reproduction (e.g., telephone) may reduce pitch strength. Masking noise in many environments may effectively remove several cues.

As well as external degradation, hearing loss may degrade the signal internally. As mentioned in the preceding section, Rose and Moore (1997) tested the degree of stream segregation in patients with unilateral hearing loss leading to broadened auditory filters and found that in some subjects, stream segregation was not affected. However, the reduced frequency selectivity will lead to a reduced ability to resolve different sounds, and so in noisy environments background noise will interfere to a greater extent. Carlyon, Cusack, Foxton, and Robertson (2001) looked at neuropsychological deficit called unilateral neglect that results from damage to the parietal and/or frontal lobes. In this deficit, attention is biased away from one side of space (in right brain–damaged patients, from the left to the right). They found reduced stream segregation on the side in which attention was reduced, in line with behavioral findings on the relationship between attention and grouping.

A particularly extreme form of degradation occurs when speech is presented through a stream of electrical impulses, applied an electrode array that is implanted in the inner ear of a profoundly deaf patient. The preprocessing used to transform speech into this pattern of impulses greatly degrades cues to pitch perception (Moore & Carlyon, in press), but some patients nevertheless understand speech very well in quiet surroundings. However, when a competing voice is present performance drops precipitously, and patients are unable to take advantage of gender differences between the target and interfering speaker (Nelson & Jin, 2002)

MULTIMODAL GROUPING

As noted by Van Valkenburg and Kubovy (this volume), objects in the real world are not just unimodal. Real objects can often be seen, smelled, and touched as well as heard. We perceive coherent objects with all of these properties. Sometimes the combination of information across modalities may be on the basis of higher level knowledge about the world (e.g., identifying that it is the fish on a plate of food in front of you that smells of fish). However, as within a modality, at other times we will be able to exploit regularities in the world to help us form appropriate perceptual objects.

A compelling example of this is that our percept of what is happening in one modality can be affected by what is happening in another. A classic example of this is the "McGurk effect" (McGurk & McDonald, 1976; http://www.media.uio.no/personer/arntm/McGurk_english.html) in which talking faces are shown on a screen. The lip movements are, for example, those of someone saying "ga" and the soundtrack that of someone saying "ba." Subjects are asked to watch the video clip but report only what they *hear*. Almost everyone reports *hearing* the syllable "da", a fusion of the incongruent information coming from the auditory and visual modalities. As with other forms of perceptual grouping, multimodal binding can be so powerful that we are unable to report the parts alone (i.e., one modality).

Perceptual grouping in one modality can also be affected by perceptual grouping in another (e.g., O'Leary & Rhodes, 1984). O'Leary and Rhodes used alternating low- and high-frequency tones that can form a single stream or fragment into two, and visual sequences of alternating low- and high-position squares that can group or fragment similarly. They found that the state of grouping in one modality influenced that in the other, although it is possible that these results were influenced by some high-level response bias. There is a significant literature on the neurobiological processes underlying multimodal integration. A review of the imaging literature and some theoretical framework was presented by Calvert (2001), and we will not repeat this here.

However, it should be noted that there are strong parallels between identifying regularities within a modality and identifying regularities across them, and so many of the techniques of each field may be applicable to the other.

SUMMARY

It is vital to maintain an ecological perspective when considering auditory perceptual organization, as it is only because there are general regularities in real sounds that it is possible at all. In this chapter, we have surveyed a number of the findings on perceptual grouping and, where possible, have related them to their ecological origins. We have also reviewed some of the topics we think are vital to making the connection between segregation as studied in the literature and that which happens in our day-to-day lives, such as the influence of selective attention, statistical analysis and computer modeling, and multimodal grouping and the grouping of degraded signals. Given our increasingly sophisticated understanding of early auditory system, we are now in a position to tackle these exciting questions.

ACKNOWLEDGMENTS

The authors thank Jessica Grahn and Brian C. J. Moore for their helpful comments on earlier versions of the manuscript.

REFERENCES

Alho, K., Medvedev, S. V., Pakhomov, S. V., Roudas, M. S., Tervaniemi, M., Reinikainen, K., Zeffiro, T., & Naatanen, R. (1999). Selective tuning of the left and right auditory cortices during spatially directed attention. *Brain Research Cognitive Brain Research, 7*, 335–341.
Anstis, S., & Saida, S. (1985). Adaptation to auditory streaming of frequency-modulated tones. *Journal of Experimental Psychology: Human Perception and Performance, 11*, 257–271.
Assmann, P. F., & Summerfield, Q. (1990). Modeling the perception of concurrent vowels: vowels with different fundamental frequencies. *Journal of the Acoustic Society of America, 88*, 680–697.
Beauvios, M. W., & Meddis, R. (1991). A computer model of auditory stream segregation. *Quarterly Journal of Experimental Psychology, 43*, 517–541.
Beauvois, M. W., & Meddis, R. (1996). Computer simulation of auditory stream segregation in alternating-tone sequences. *Journal of the Acoustic Society of America, 99*, 2270–2280.
Bell, A. J., & Sejnowski, T. J. (1995). An information-maximization approach to blind separation and blind deconvolution. *Neural Computation, 7*, 1129–1159.
Blauert, J. (1997). *Spatial hearing.* Cambridge, MA: MIT Press.
Bregman, A. S. (1990). *Auditory scene analysis.* Cambridge, MA: MIT press.
Bregman, A. S., & Campbell, J. (1971). Primary auditory stream segregation and perception of order in rapid sequences of tones. *Journal of Experimental Psychology, 89*, 244–249.
Bregman, A. S., & Pinker, S. (1978). Auditory streaming and the building of timbre. *Canadian Journal of Psychology, 32*, 19–31.
Bregman, A. S., & Rudnicky, A. I. (1975). Auditory segregation: stream or streams? *Journal of Experimental Psychology: Human Perception and Performance, 1*, 263–267.
Bregman, A. S., Liao, C., & Levitan, R. (1990). Auditory grouping based on fundamental frequency and formant peak frequency. *Canadian Journal of Psychology, 44*, 400–413.
Broadbent, D. E., & Ladefoged, P. (1959). Auditory perception of temporal order. *Journal of the Acoustic Society of America, 31*, 1539–1540.

Brochard, R., Drake, C., Botte, M. C., & McAdams, S. (1999). Perceptual organization of complex auditory sequences: Effect of number of simultaneous subsequences and frequency separation. *Journal of Experimental Psychology: Human Perception and Performance, 25,* 1742–1759.

Brokx, J. P. L., & Nooteboom, S. (1982). Intonation and the perceptual separation of simultaneous voices. *Journal of Phonetics, 10,* 23–36.

Brown, G. J., & Wang, D. L. (1996). Modelling the perceptual segregation of double vowels with a network of neural oscillators. Technical report CS-96-06. Sheffield University Computer Science Department.

Campbell, M., & Greated, C. A. (1987). *The musicians' guide to acoustics.* New York: Schirmer Books.

Carlyon, R. P., Cusack, R., Foxton, J. M., & Robertson, I. H. (2001). Effects of attention and unilateral neglect on auditory stream segregation. *Journal of Experimental Psychology: Human Perception and Performance, 27,* 115–127.

Carlyon, R. P., Demany, L., & Deeks, J. (2001). Temporal pitch perception and the binaural system. *Journal of the Acoustic Society of America, 109,* 686–700.

Carlyon, R. P., Plack, C. J., Fantini, D. A., & Cusack, R. (2003). Cross-modal and non-sensory influences on auditory streaming. *Perception, 39,* 1393–1402.

Calvert, G. A. (2001). Crossmodal processing in the human brain: Insights from functional neuroimaging studies. *Cerebral Cortex, 11,* 1110–1123.

Cherry, E. C. (1953). Some experiments on the recognition of speech with one and two ears. *Journal of the Acoustic Society of America, 11,* 45–54.

Cooke, M., & Ellis, D. P. W. (2001). The auditory organization of speech and other sources in listeners and computational models. *Speech Communication, 35,* 141–177.

Culling, J. F., & Darwin, C. J. (1993). The role of timbre in the segregation of simultaneous voices with intersecting F_0 contours. *Perception and Psychophysics, 54,* 303–309.

Cusack, R. (2003). Parieto-occipital cortex and non-spatial auditory perceptual organisation. Presented at the 9th International Conference on Functional Mapping of the Human Brain, June 19–22, 2003, New York, NY. Available on CD-Rom in *NeuroImage, 19*(2), Abstract 387.

Cusack, R., & Roberts, B. (1999). Effects of similarity in bandwidth on the auditory sequential streaming of two-tone complexes. *Perception, 28,* 1281–1289.

Cusack, R., & Roberts, B. (2000). Effects of differences in timbre on sequential grouping. *Perception and Psychophysics, 62,* 1112–1120.

Cusack, R., & Roberts, B. (In press). Effects of differences in the pattern of amplitude envelopes across harmonics on auditory stream segregation, *Hearing Research.*

Cusack, R., Deeks, J., Aikman, G., & Carlyon, R. P. (In press). Effects of location, frequency region, and time course of selective attention on auditory scene analysis. *Journal of Experimental Psychology: Human Perception and Performance.*

Cutting, J. E. (1975). Aspects of phonological fusion. *Journal of Experimental Psychology: Human Perception and Performance, 104,* 105–120.

Dannenbring, G. L., & Bregman, A. S. (1976). Stream segregation and the illusion of overlap. *Journal of Experimental Psychology: Human Perception and Performance, 2,* 544–555.

Darwin, C. J. (1984). Perceiving vowels in the presence of another sound: Constraints on formant perception. *Journal of the Acoustic Society of America, 76,* 1636–1647.

Darwin, C. J., & Carlyon, R. P. (1995). Auditory grouping. In: B. C. Moore (Ed.), *Hearing.* (pp. 387–423) San Diego, CA: Academic Press.

deCharms, R. C., Blake, D. T., & Merzenich, M. M. (1998). Optimizing sound features for cortical neurons. *Science, 280,* 1439–1443.

Depireux, D. A., Simon, J. Z., Klein, D. J., & Shamma, S. A. (2001). Spectro-temporal response field characterization with dynamic ripples in ferret primary auditory cortex. *Journal of Neurophysiology, 85,* 1220–1234.

Deutsch, D. (1975). Musical illusions. *Scientific American, 233,* 92–104.

Dowling, W. J. (1973). The perception of interleaved melodies. *Cognitive Psychology, 5,* 322–337.

Duncan, J. (1984). Selective attention and the organization of visual information. *Journal of Experimental Psychology: General, 113,* 501–17.

Ellis, D. (1996). *Prediction driven computational scene analysis.* Ph.D. thesis, Massachusetts Institute of Technology.

Engel, A. K., Konig, P., Gray, C. M., & Singer, W. (1990). Stimulus-dependent neuronal Oscillations in cat visual cortex: Inter-columnar interaction as determined by cross-correlation analysis. *European Journal of Neuroscience, 2,* 588–606.

Gehr, D. D., Hofer, S. B., Marquardt, D., & Leppelsack, H. (2000). Functional changes in field L complex during song development of juvenile male zebra finches. *Brain Research. Developmental Brain Research, 125,* 153–165.

Glasberg, B. R., & Moore B. C. (1990). Derivation of auditory filter shapes from notched-noise data. *Hearing Research, 47,* 103–138.

Gockel, H., Carlyon, R. P., & Micheyl, C. (1999). Context dependence of fundamental-frequency discrimination: Lateralized temporal fringes. *Journal of the Acoustic Society of America, 106,* 3553–3563.

Grimault, N., Micheyl, C., Carlyon, R. P., Arthaud, P., & Collet, L. (2000). Influence of peripheral resolvability on the perceptual segregation of harmonic complex tones differing in fundamental frequency. *Journal of the Acoustic Society of America, 108,* 263–271.

Harpur, G., & Prager, R. (2000). Experiments with low-entropy neural networks In: R. Baddeley, P. J. B. Hancock, and P. Földiák (Eds.), *Information theory and the brain* (pp. 84–100) New York: Cambridge University Press.

Hartmann, W. M., & Johnson, D. (1991). Stream segregation and peripheral channeling. *Music Perception, 9,* 155–183.

Hillyard, S. A., Vogel, E. K., & Luck, S. J. (1998). Sensory gain control (amplification) as a mechanism of selective attention: Electrophysiological and neuroimaging evidence. *Philosophical Transactions of the Royal Society of London. Series B: Biological Sciences, 353,* 1257–1270.

Hugdahl, K., Thomsen, T., Ersland, L., Morten Rimol, L., & Niemi, J. (2003). The effects of attention on speech perception: An fMRI study. *Brain and Language, 85,* 37–48.

Hukin, R. W., & Darwin, C. J. (1995). Effects of contralateral presentation and of interaural time differences in segregating a harmonic from a vowel. *Journal of the Acoustic Society of America, 98,* 1380–1387.

Huron, D. (1991). Tonal consonance versus tonal fusion in polyphonic sonorities. *Music Perception, 9,* 135–154.

Iverson, P. (1995). Auditory stream segregation by musical timbre: Effects of static and dynamic acoustic attributes. *Journal of Experimental Psychology: Human Perception and Performance, 21,* 751–763.

Jancke, L., Mirzazade, S., & Shah, N. J. (1999). Attention modulates activity in the primary and the secondary auditory cortex: a functional magnetic resonance imaging study in human subjects. *Neuroscience Letters, 266,* 125–128.

Jones, M. R. (1976). Time, our lost dimension: Toward a new theory of perception, attention, and memory. *Psychological Review, 83,* 323–355.

Kowalski, N., Depireux, D. A., & Shamma, S. A. (1996a). Analysis of dynamic spectra in ferret primary auditory cortex. II. Prediction of unit responses to arbitrary dynamic spectra. *Journal of Neurophysiology, 76,* 3524–3534.

Kowalski, N., Depireux, D. A., & Shamma, S. A. (1996b). Analysis of dynamic spectra in ferret primary auditory cortex. I. Characteristics of single-unit responses to moving ripple spectra. *Journal of Neurophysiology, 76,* 3503–3523.

Kowalski, N., Versnel, H., & Shamma, S. A. (1995). Comparison of responses in the anterior and primary auditory fields of the ferret cortex. *Journal of Neurophysiology, 73,* 1513–1523.

Ladefoged, P., & Broadbent, D. E. (1957). Information conveyed by vowels. *Journal of the Acoustic Society of America, 29,* 98–104.

Macken, W. J., Tremblay, S., Houghton, R. J., Nicholls, A. P., & Jones, D. M. (2003). Does auditory streaming require attention? Evidence from attentional selectivity in short-term memory. *Journal of Experimental Psychology: Human Perception and Performance, 27*, 115–127.

McCabe, S. L., & Denham, M. J. (1997). A model of auditory streaming. *Journal of the Acoustic Society of America, 101*, 1611–1621.

McGurk, H., & MacDonald, J. (1976). Hearing lips and seeing voices. *Nature, 264*, 746–748.

Micheyl, C., & Carlyon, R. P. (1998). Effects of temporal fringes on fundamental-frequency discrimination. *Journal of the Acoustic Society of America, 104*, 3006–3018.

Micheyl, C., Carlyon, R. P., Pulvermuller, F., Shtyrov, Y., Hauk, O., & Dodson, T. (2003). Neurophysiologyogical correlates of a perceptual illusion: A mismatch negativity study. *J Cognitive Neuroscience, 15*, 747–758.

Miller, G. A., & Heise, G. A. (1950). The trill threshold. *Journal of the Acoustic Society of America, 22*, 637–638.

Miller, L. M., Escabi, M. A., Read, H. L., & Schreiner, C. E. (2001). Functional convergence of response properties in the auditory thalamocortical system. *Neuron, 32*, 151–160.

Miller, L. M., Escabi, M. A., Read, H. L., & Schreiner, C. E. (2002). Spectrotemporal receptive fields in the lemniscal auditory thalamus and cortex. *Journal of Neurophysiology, 87*, 516–527.

Moore, B. C. (1997). *An introduction to the psychology of hearing*, 4th ed.. San Diego: Academic Press.

Moore, B. C., Peters, R. W., & Glasberg, B. R. (1985). Thresholds for the detection of inharmonicity in complex tones. *Journal of the Acoustic Society of America, 77*, 1861–1867.

Moore, B. C., Glasberg, B. R., & Peters, R. W. (1986). Thresholds for hearing mistuned partials as separate tones in harmonic complexes. *Journal of the Acoustic Society of America, 80*, 479–483.

Moore, B. C., Peters, R. W., & Glasberg, B. R. (1990). Auditory filter shapes at low center frequencies. *Journal of the Acoustic Society of America, 88*, 132–140.

Moore, B. C. J., & Gockel, H. (2002). Factors influencing sequential stream segregation. *Acta Acustica, 88*, 320–333.

Moore, B. C. J., & Carlyon, R. P. (In press). Perception of pitch by people with cochlear hearing loss and by cochlear implant users. In: C. J. Plack, A. J. Oxenham (Eds.), *Springer handbook of auditory research*. Berlin: Springer-Verlag.

Nelson, P. B., & Jin, S.-H. (2002). Understanding speech in single-talker interference: Normal-hearing listeners and cochlear implant users. *Journal of the Acoustic Society of America, 111* (Pt. 2), 2429.

O'Leary, A., & Rhodes, G. (1984). Cross-modal effects on visual and auditory object perception. *Perception and Psychophysics, 35*, 565–569.

Olshausen, B. A., & Field, D. J. (1996). Emergence of simple-cell receptive field properties by learning a sparse code for natural images. *Nature, 381*, 607–609.

Posner, M. I., Snyder, C. R., & Davidson, B. J. (1980). Attention and the detection of signals. *Journal of Experimental Psychology, 109*, 160–174.

Rasch, R. A. (1979). Synchronization in performed ensemble music. *Acustica, 43*, 121–131.

Roberts, B., Glasberg, B. R., & Moore, B. C. (2002). Primitive stream segregation of tone sequences without differences in fundamental frequency or passband. *Journal of the Acoustic Society of America, 112*, 2074–2085.

Rogers, W. L., & Bregman, A. S. (1998). Cumulation of the tendency to segregate auditory streams: resetting by changes in location and loudness. *Perception and Psychophysics, 60*, 1216–1227.

Rose, M. M., & Moore, B. C. (1997). Perceptual grouping of tone sequences by normally hearing and hearing- impaired listeners. *Journal of the Acoustic Society of America, 102*, 1768–1778.

Sarkar, S., & Boyer, K. L. (1994). *Computing perceptual organization in computer vision*. Singapore: World Scientific.

Scheffers, M. T. M. (1983). *Sifting vowels: Auditory pitch analysis and sound segregation*. Groningen University.

Schouten, J. F. (1940). The perception of pitch. *Philips Technology Review, 5,* 286–294.

Sharma, J., Angelucci, A., & Sur, M. (2000). Induction of visual orientation modules in auditory cortex. *Nature, 404,* 841–847.

Shinozaki, N., Yabe, H., Sato, Y., Sutoh, T., Hiruma, T., Nashida, T., & Kaneko, S. (2000). Mismatch negativity (MMN) reveals sound grouping in the human brain. *Neuroreport, 11,* 1597–1601.

Singh, P. G. (1987). Perceptual organization of complex-tone sequences: A tradeoff between pitch and timbre? *Journal of the Acoustic Society of America, 82,* 886–899.

Smith, J., Hausfeld, S., Power, R. P., & Gorta, A. (1982). Ambiguous musical figures and auditory streaming. *Perception and Psychophysics, 32,* 454–464.

Stainsby, T. H., Moore, B. C. J., Medland, P. J., & Glasberg, B. R. (Submitted). Sequential streaming and effective level differences due to phase-spectrum manipulations.

Sussman, E., Ritter, W., & Vaughan, H. G., Jr. (1999). An investigation of the auditory streaming effect using event-related brain potentials. *Psychophysiology, 36,* 22–34.

Theunissen, F. E., Sen, K., & Doupe, A. J. (2000). Spectral-temporal receptive fields of nonlinear auditory neurons obtained using natural sounds. *Journal of Neuroscience, 20,* 2315–2331.

Ulanovsky, N., Las, L., & Nelken, I. (2003). Processing of low-probability sounds by cortical neurons. *Nature Neuroscience, 6,* 391–398.

van der Kouwe, A. J. W., Wang, D. L., & Brown, G. J. (2001). A comparison of auditory and blind separation techniques for speech segregation. *IEEE Transactions on Speech and Audio Processing, 9,* 189–195.

Van Noorden, L. P. A. S. (1975). *Temporal coherence in the perception of tone sequences.* Eindhoven University of Technology.

Vliegen, J., & Oxenham, A. J. (1999). Sequential stream segregation in the absence of spectral cues. *Journal of the Acoustic Society of America, 105,* 339–346.

Vliegen, J., Moore, B. C., & Oxenham, A. J. (1999). The role of spectral and periodicity cues in auditory stream segregation, measured using a temporal discrimination task. *Journal of the Acoustic Society of America, 106,* 938–945.

Von Wright, J. M., Anderson, K., & Stenman, U. (1975). Generalisation of conditioned GSR's in dichotic listening, *Attention and Performance.* New York: Academic Press.

Wallach, H., Neumann, E. B., & Rosenzweig, M. R. (1949). The precedence effect in sound localization. *American Journal of Psychology, 52,* 315–336.

Wang, D. L. (1996). Primitive auditory segregation based on oscillatory correlation. *Cognitive Science, 20,* 409–456.

Warren, R. M., Obusek, C. J., Farmer, R. M., & Warren, R. P. (1969). Auditory sequence: confusion of patterns other than speech or music. *Science, 164,* 586–587.

Wessel, D. L. (1979). Timbre space as a music control structure. *Computer Music Journal, 3,* 45–52.

Yabe, H., Winkler, I., Czigler, I., Koyama, S., Kakigi, R., Sutoh, T., Hiruma, T., & Kaneko, S. (2001). Organizing sound sequences in the human brain: the interplay of auditory streaming and temporal integration. *Brain Research, 897,* 222–227.

Yu, S. (2003). *Computational models of perceptual organization.* Ph.D. thesis, Pittsburgh: Carnegie Mellon University.

3

ATTENTION AND TIMING

MARI RIESS JONES

My goal in this chapter is to convey some thoughts about attention and timing. The chapter comprises two main sections. In the first section, I outline general theoretical assumptions about attending that have shaped my thinking since 1975. These assumptions reveal an ecological orientation with similarities to the approach advocated by Gibson (1979), although they differ importantly with regard to my emphasis upon the rhythmicity of organisms. In the second section, I consider research relevant to these assumptions drawn from three categories of tasks: time estimation, time discrimination, and target sound identification tasks.

THEORETICAL OVERVIEW: A BIOLOGICAL ORIENTATION

At an elementary level, a theorist is faced with a choice when conceiving of the ways in which an organism might relate to its environment. One can rely on a machine metaphor that is largely nonbiological, or one can espouse a system that is inherently biological. An important distinction concerns whether a living system operates as a more or less passive receptacle of environmental information, powered solely by external energy inputs, much as a hardwired computer, or whether it displays a participatory quality supported by an internal energy source, which allows for the possibility of active energy exchanges with the surrounding environment. The latter characterizes biological systems that are capable of growth and self-organization. In the following assumptions, I subscribe to the latter, biological, framework (Jones, 1976; Kelso, 1995).

BASIC ASSUMPTIONS

1. *Time in event structure.* The world comprises events having extension in time. An event is an environmental happening arising from animate or inanimate activities; it has temporal shape with a distinctive rate and time structure that includes quasi-periodicities. Events project into optic and/or acoustic flows as dynamic patterns, which are taken to be *driving rhythms*.

2. *Time in an organism's structure.* Among other things, the internal structure of animate things is inherently rhythmical, comprising diverse biological oscillations ranging from small (milliseconds) to large (days, years) periodicities (Jones, 1976). In nonlinear dynamical systems, physiological oscillations function as *driven rhythms*.

3. *Interactions of an organism's time with event time.* Animate things connect with and adapt to their environment through the common medium of time. Rhythmic organisms interact, more or less effectively, with dynamic flow patterns of events via *entrainment*: An event's driving rhythm shapes an organism's driven rhythm through adaptations of period and phase. This entrainment process extends to rhythms that reflect the ebb and flow of attending energy.

ENTRAINMENT AND ATTENDING

Attending happens in real time. As listeners, we engage our acoustic environment as it unfolds; we actively track a speaker's utterance, monitor a child's playful noises, and notice as a kitten purrs. Each sound-making event leads to a characteristic flow pattern (e.g., Boltz, 1994; Li *et al.*, 1991; Repp, 1987; Warren & Verbrugge, 1984). Our engagement with these patterns is a continuous interaction of an internal activity with a to-be-attended stimulus. Consider one well-examined case, that of the pianist whose multiple key presses send a series of sounds into the medium (Palmer, 1997; Palmer and Pfordresher 2003). We experience the resulting music in real time, where its structure affords both anticipations and surprise as we interact with the acoustic flow.

How might we explain real-time attending to such sound patterns? I build my theory on the principle of *synchrony*. Attending entails a synchronization of many internal attending periodicities with corresponding time spans within an event (assumption 3). Distal events, as happenings, project time-varying acoustic arrays; as proximal stimuli, such arrays convey spectral information changes over time either continuously (e.g., unbroken speech utterances) or discretely (e.g., music, natural sounds). Attending is engaged by such arrays; thus, attending resources must be distributed in time. It is tempting to assume that this distribution is uniform over event time, but I suggest that attending energy waxes and wanes over time. That is, for a listener to focus on some portions of a distal event, and not others, requires a selective allocation of attending energy at critical points in time, points that temporally coincide with relevant portions of the acoustic array. In this way, we become connected to the distal event itself. Especially in arrays transmitted by a series of discrete sounds, the succession of sound onsets marks out recurrent time spans that define an event's rate and rhythm. In many cases, such events project a time structure that facilitates at once, a periodic pacing of attending and a synchronization of this activity.

At a general level, the synchronization of attending is promoted by nonrandomness in event timing. A few examples of nonrandom time patterns appear in Fig. 1 (see Boltz, 1994). Event rhythms are often described in terms of *inter onset intervals* (IOIs), where IOI refers to the time between the onset of one discrete sound and that of the next. Thus, fast and slow patterns have, respectively, short and long IOIs. Such event rates are rarely constant in our world; rather, they modulate in characteristic ways. Small rate modulations, shown in Fig. 1, *A, C,* and *D,* may permit component IOIs to approximate simple ratio relationships (1 : 1, 1 : 2, etc.). By contrast, larger rate modulations (e.g., pattern lb) complicate simple ratio relationships as they shape the whole sequence over time. Modest rate modulations often convey meaningful and expressive information (Palmer, 1989; 1997; Repp, 1998, 1999), while not violating a listeners' sense of the underlying rhythm (see Fig. 1, *E*) (Drake *et al.*, 2000; Large & Palmer, 2002; Penel & Drake, 1998). Of course, many rhythms comprise patterns of distinctly different IOIs as in Fig. 1, *C-E* (London, 2002; Povel & Essens, 1985). These patterns illustrate events that convey a high degree of rhythmic regularity. I maintain that the degree of rhythmic regularity of an event's time structure affects how and how effectively we attend to it (e.g., Jones & Boltz, 1989).

Events with much rhythmic regularity can promote synchrony of attending in various ways. I consider the following two aspects of attending: (1) *anticipatory*

Examples of Rhythmic Sequences

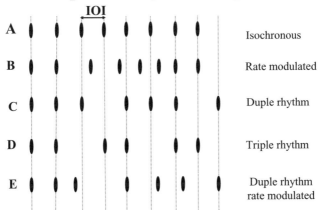

FIGURE 1   Examples of sequences of discrete sounds with rhythms determined by interonset intervals (IOIs). Panels a through e reflect stationary rhythms, either isochronous (**A**) or metrically grouped (**C, D**); panels **B** and **E** illustrate systematic modulations of local rate of, respectively, **A** and **C**.

attending, which entails periodic shifts of attending that are timed to coincide with expected sound onsets, and (2) *reactive attending*, which entails rapid attentional shifts associated with unexpected sound onsets. Both aspects of attending depend on event time structure and both ultimately serve the principle of synchrony.

Synchrony is achieved through anticipatory attending when it ensures that attention is allocated *just before* the onset of an expected sound. Anticipations are more likely when an event's time structure projects a simple regular rhythm (e.g., Fig. 1). By contrast, reactive attending ensures synchrony by rapidly shifting attention *just after* the temporal occurrence of something unexpected. In some cases, reactive attending resembles the automatic attending elicited by a single distinctive (exogenous) sound cue that precedes an auditory target in spatial cuing designs (e.g., Spence & Driver, 1994; Experiment 1). But instead of a shift of attention *in space* to the location of an exogenous cue, reactive attending is a rapid shift that occurs *in real time*, producing an accommodation to an unexpected sound's temporal position. Of course, such distinctions do not *explain* anticipatory and reactive attending. One explanation is considered next.

AN EXEMPLAR ENTRAINMENT MODEL

Attempts to explain attending dynamics include descriptions of both anticipatory and reactive attending. Anticipatory attending is viewed as a dynamic expectancy, based on internal timing, whereas reactive attending is a response that is contingent upon an expectancy violation. Various models rely on basic assumptions of *entrainment*, where entrainment refers to the way a driven rhythm adapts to and synchronizes with a driving rhythm (Large, 1994; Large & Jones, 1999; Large & Kolen, 1995; McAuley 1995; McAuley & Jones, 2003). Although different in detail, these models assume that attending is inherently oscillatory. Important properties involve period and phase of the postulated oscillations. The *period* of an oscillator refers to the duration of single cycle of its activity; *phase* refers to a time point within a given cycle. Entrainment models posit internal *oscillations in which period and phase change in real time in response to external timing*. In short, these oscillations are adaptive.

Entrainment models are dynamical systems; they realize assumptions 1 to 3. The construct of a *driving rhythm* corresponds to a proximal flow pattern that originates from an environmental event; a *driven rhythm* corresponds to an entrainable internal oscillation. The simplest of these models typically involve a single internal oscillator. For these, the system comprises one driving stimulus and one driven oscillation. Entrainment, then, is the process by which a system (driving-plus-driven rhythm) moves toward certain attractor states. An attractor is a state to which a system converges over time. Specifically, attractors involve states of phase synchrony and period matching between driving and driven rhythms. Attractors instantiate the principle of synchrony. Essentially, the driven rhythm (the oscillator) is "tuned" by the driving rhythm (the event).

One Entraining Oscillator

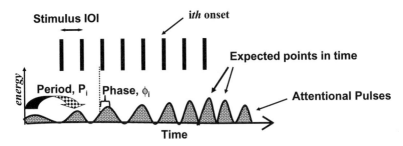

Period and phase govern attunement of an internal oscillator to stimulus timing

FIGURE 2   Schematic of a single oscillator's timed pulse (*dotted portions*) entraining in real time to an isochronous rhythm (*bars*). Over time, period, P_i, and relative phase, φ_i, change to align peaks of the periodic attending pulse with successive tone onsets ($i = 1$ to n). The oscillator continues this attuned rate, for a brief time, after tones cease, revealing only the persistence of period.

Consider a model developed by Edward Large (Large & Jones, 1999). In the single-oscillator version of this model, an internal oscillation is interpreted as a periodic fluctuation in attentional energy. Thus, attending waxes and wanes within a given time span. A single oscillator becomes active with an initial period denoted P_0 and it carries this energy pulse forward in time.[1]

The peak of this energy pulse determines the phase point, denoted $\varphi_i = 0$ ($-0.5 < \varphi_i < 0.5$) (i indexes onset times of discrete markers, e.g., tones). This point of maximal excitatory energy (or amplitude) is the expected point in time. When considered with respect to stimulus onsets (i.e., constituting a driving rhythm), φ_i is, technically, a *relative phase* and $\varphi_i = 0$ becomes an attractor in a system comprising a driving plus a driven rhythm. If a sound occurs at a time that *does not coincide* with this internal peak of attending energy, by definition this sound is unexpected and has relative phase of $\varphi_i \neq 0$. The system responds to unexpected onsets by moving toward the phase attractor state, that is, by shifting the attentional pulse toward phase synchrony. In this model, theoretical variables (so-called state variables) correspond to attentional pulse, relative phase, and period, all of which change over a series of stimulus onsets that mark n-1 IOIs ($i = 1$ to n).

Figure 2 illustrates real-time attending. A listener interacts from moment to moment with a series of discrete sounds that constitute a regular rhythm. Shown here is an oscillator that adjusts its period and phase to align with successive

---

[1] The energy pulse is formalized as a circular probability density function wrapped onto the limit cycle oscillation as suggested in Fig. 3 (see equation 5 in Large & Jones, 1999).

System Components

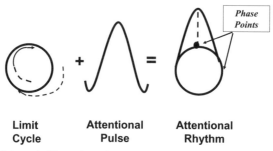

Limit	Attentional	Attentional
Cycle	Pulse	Rhythm

FIGURE 3   Schematic illustration of the three main components of a one-oscillator model: *period* (limit cycle oscillation), *attentional focus* (pulse), and *phase* (points within a cycle). A temporally expected point (•) corresponds to the phase of a pulse peak.

sound onsets. Although the temporal trajectory of the energy peak is basically periodic, an underlying adaptive process corrects phase and period by continually modifying these two variables. Here we see attending as a participatory process: the oscillator engages in a continual interplay with an event's rhythm such that each correction of the oscillator moves it closer to synchrony. The dynamics of this interplay include both anticipatory and reactive attending. At any instant in time, i, the state of this system, is associated with an oscillator's pulse peak, period, and phase. These three system components can be found in the schematic of Fig. 3.

Attentional Pulse

The attentional pulse functions as an attentional *focus in time*. As such, it is analogous to constructs in visual attention that involve an attentional focus *in space* (e.g., Erickson & St. James, 1986; Posner, Snyder, & Davidson, 1980).[2] In this model, the pulse reflects a concentration of attending energy that varies not only in temporal location but also in width. All other things equal, pulse width widens as attentional synchrony declines (i.e., with increased variability in φ_i). When an event is rhythmically regular (i.e. very coherent) phase synchrony tends to be high and a narrow attentional pulse develops, indicating precise temporal expectancies. However, with a rhythmically irregular event, a wide attentional pulse occurs, indicating poor attentional synchrony and imprecise temporal expectancies (Large, 1994; Large & Jones, 1999).

Oscillator Period

An oscillator's period is mainly responsible for carrying an attending pulse into the future as *anticipatory attending*. It plays an important role in anticipa-

---

[2] One might generalize this idea to attentional focus in pitch space and time to address auditory streaming (e.g., as in Jones, 1976).

tory attending. The oscillator is a *endogenous self-sustaining oscillation* (ESSO in biology). A self-sustaining biological oscillation, or limit cycle, is generated by internal, potentially renewable, energy sources that characterize living organisms. The term "limit cycle" refers to a limiting, or asymptotic, path of a dynamical system in a space defined by state variables, that is, a state space[3] (Glass & Mackey, 1988; Kaplan, 1995; Pikovsky *et al.*, 2001). For instance, a limiting circular path can be described by coordinates corresponding to state variables of position and velocity as shown in Fig. 3 (heavy line); the limit path represents the stable period of a period-matching oscillator.

Assume that some event, with a characteristic rate, projects an acoustic flow with a nearly isochronous driving rhythm (i.e., all IOIs are virtually equal). The IOI of such a rhythm, in the limit, determines the final goal path for a period-matching oscillator. The limit cycle oscillation changes its initial period to one that matches a recurrent IOI within an event. For instance, an oscillator with an initial period that is briefer than an event's average time span has a $P_i < IOI_i$; this oscillator "runs faster" than the event's rate. However, in a system forced by periodic onsets of a slower external rhythm, the angular velocity of such an oscillator would decelerate (within limits). In an entraining system, namely one with periodic attractors, the difference between P_i and IOI_i is continually reduced such that $P_i \rightarrow IOI_i$ over time.[4] In this way, event timing can "tune" an attending oscillator. The self-sustaining properties of such an oscillator contribute to appropriately timed anticipations. Moreover, as a self-sustaining oscillation, its "beat" can continue, as an extrapolation of a stable period, even in the absence of a driving rhythm. This persistence reveals the sustaining quality of anticipatory attending; we see this in Fig. 2 where an entrained period persists, for a while, after tones cease.

Oscillator Phase

Oscillator phase also contributes to temporal expectancies. At any given point, i, relative phase, φ_i, gauges the disparity between a driven and a driving rhythm. It is defined as the time difference between an expected (driven) and observed (driving) onset divided by the current oscillator period. Thus, when a disparity between expected and observed timing is absent, relative phase connotes an expected time, $\varphi_i = 0$; however, when a disparity is present, relative phase also connotes an unexpected time, $\varphi_i \neq 0$, that is, an *expectancy violation*. In the latter case, φ_i values have direction and magnitude. For instance, large negative φ_i values (up to -0.5) indicate unexpected sounds that occur very early, whereas small positive φ_i values indicate slightly late sounds. Note that the variance of φ_i, taken over i, can index the precision of a temporal expectancy.

---

[3] A state space is the space of all possible combinations of values of state variables that are possible over time; it is parameterized by time.
[4] A state space is the space of all possible combinations of values of state variables that are possible over time; it is parameterized by time.

Finally, an important construct in dynamical systems is an *order variable*. An order variable summarizes the combined state of a dynamical system having several interacting state variables. In this framework, relative phase, which gauges expectancy violations, is an order variable. In a given task, it provides a means of predicting performance as function of the joint influence of several state variables. At any moment relative phase is affected by: (1) attentional focus (where attending energy is concentrated at an expected, i.e., peak, point), (2) period (which defines the time of an expected onset in cycle), and (3) phase (which defines the time of an expected onset within cycle). Finally, because the system comprises both a driving and a driven rhythm, relative phase necessarily also reflects properties of the environmental context through its definition as relative asynchrony between an observed and expected time.[5] For these reasons, relative phase becomes important to understanding of task demands.

ADAPTIVE ORGANISM

A key property for survival of an organism is the ability to change appropriately in response to environmental demands. This property forms the core of a true biological entrainment theory. It is also important in describing how we cope with our increasingly complex sound environment. Ideally, as any sound pattern unfolds, anticipatory attending is associated with fallible expectancies about the future course of some environmental event. But these expectancies can change in real time as a listener reacts to surprisingly timed portions of the event's sound pattern. Although surprises may cause transitory errors, they also can contribute to a tuning of a listener's attention. Attunement refers to adaptation of an oscillator's phase and period. This adaptive process is clearly a functional one because it describes how an expectancy violation leads to a new expectancy. Because this is a critical part of the theoretical story, I consider phase correction first and then period correction.

Phase Correction and Reactive Attending

Phase adaptation immediately follows an expectancy violation. Thus, when an expectancy violation ($\varphi_i \neq 0$) happens at time i, it is followed by a new phase (φ_{i+1}), which differs from it by $\Delta\varphi$. This is phase correction. To preview, shortly I will claim that phase correction involves *reactive attending*, which entails a transitory increment in attending that involves a temporal shift of focus away from an expected point in time in response toward an unexpected onset.

The difference equation describing phase correction (in Large & Jones, 1999) is

$$\varphi_{i+1} = \varphi_i + IOI_{i+1}/P_i - \eta \tfrac{1}{2}\pi \sin\{2\pi\varphi_i\} \qquad (1)$$

---

[5] A state space is the space of all possible combinations of values of state variables that are possible over time; it is parameterized by time.

In this expression, the order variable, φ_{i+1}, is a function of prior phase, φ_i, oscillator period, P_i, at the ith onset, and the following IOI. The final portion of Eq. (1) does the adaptive work. It comprises a *control parameter*, η_φ (coupling strength), and a nonlinear *coupling term*, $\frac{1}{2}\pi \sin\{2\pi\varphi_i\}$. The coupling term can be either nonlinear (as in Eq. 1) or linear. This term predicts the phase correction, $\Delta\varphi$, resulting from a response to an expectancy violation, φ_i, at the ith onset.

Phase Response Curves

Figure 4 is a theoretical phase response curve (PRC) (adapted from Large & Jones, 1999). Effectively, it hypothesizes how phase correction occurs. Thus, it shows phase change, $\Delta\varphi$ (from Eq. 1), by plotting $-\eta_\varphi\frac{1}{2}\pi \sin\{2\pi\varphi_i\}$ as a function of φ_i, for $\eta_\varphi = 1.0$. Figure 4 illustrates the two-part relationship of an expectancy violation (abscissa) and a subsequent phase correction (ordinate). The ordinate gives amounts and direction of a *phase change* arising from different φ_i values (between -0.5 and $+0.5$) associated with the ith onset. Thus, if a sound happens unexpectedly early, by 25% of the oscillator's period ($\varphi_i = -0.25$ on abscissa), this PRC predicts a corrective attenuation of this disparity, through an expectancy adjustment of $-\Delta\varphi = 0.15$, that will change relative phase at a

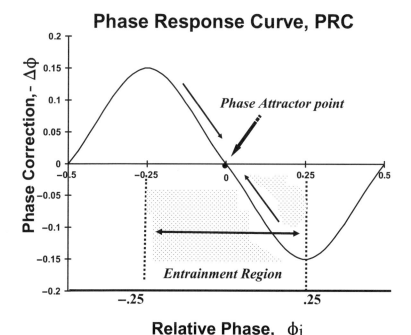

FIGURE 4 The phase response curve (PRC) predicted by the Large & Jones (1999) model (Eq. 1). A PRC plots the amount and direction of a phase change (ordinate) to be applied to relative phase of $i + 1$ in response to a relative phase at instant i (abscissa). Also shown is a hypothetical phase entrainment region.

subsequent point in time. Thus, when inserted into Eq. (1), a new expectancy in the next cycle for the $i + 1$ onset produces $\varphi_{i+1} = -0.10$. Similarly, an unexpectedly late sound, with $\Delta_i = 0.10$, yields a change in the opposite direction, with $\Delta\varphi = -0.09$; the latter expresses a quick approach to a zero phase point (i.e., an attractor) because one's expectancy is corrected to yield a new phase of 0.01.

A theoretical PRC not only illustrates how expectancy correction might work but also posits two important aspects of this process. First, Fig. 4 shows that phase synchrony functions as an attractor point (i.e., where $\varphi_i = \Delta\varphi = 0$; see arrows in Fig. 4). Second, Fig. 4 implies that phase adjustment is nonlinear and symmetrical about the attractor point. A strong prediction is that the greatest (absolute) amount of phase correction will occur for $/\varphi_i / = 0.25$. This means that the system coherently copes with *only so much deviation* from an expected point. An unexpected sound arriving *very* early, with $\varphi_i = -0.40$, sparks a disproportionately small corrective response of $\Delta\varphi = +0.05$. By contrast, if the PRC involved a linear function, with a slope of -1.0, full phase correction would occur ($\Delta\varphi = +0.40!$). But note that Eq. (1) (Fig. 4) predicts an *almost linear* function for φ_i near zero (within ± 0.15). One implication of this is that it may be difficult, empirically, to differentiate linear from nonlinear functions with small relative phase values.

Equations such as Eq. (1) are useful because they offer a theoretical PRC that can be tested empirically by examining phase correction in dynamic attending. Empirical PRCs are rare in psychological research; however, they are common in biology, where data-driven plots express observed phase changes in a variety of biological activities as a function of the application time (φ_i) of a potentially entraining signal (a Zeitgeber) in the biological cycle (P_i). Much is known about phase correction from biological research, where the most commonly studied activity cycles involve circadian rhythms, tidal rhythms, heart beats, respiratory rhythms, and so on (e.g., Moore-Ede, Sulzrnon, & Fuller, 1982; J. D. Palmer, 1976; Winfree, 2001). In addition, Repp has presented empirical PRCs, of the kind considered here, for finger tapping (Repp, 2002a,b). An important commonality among these empirical studies is that the most effective phase correction is observed for φ values near the expected phase ($\varphi = 0$). Such findings suggest that limits may exist for phase entrainment.

The Entrainment Region

A region of *phase entrainment* covers values of φ_i on the abscissa (of the PRC) that correspond to significant adaptive phase corrections. Limiting values of φ_i identify this region. Theoretically, these limits correspond to extrema of a PRC function. For instance, the extrema points of the PRC in Fig. 4 are endpoints of a nearly linear segment of the function, a portion with slope between 0 and -2 (and determined by η_φ). Projecting these extrema points onto the abscissa, the limit values of φ for the phase entrainment region are $-0.25 \leq \varphi_i \leq 0.25$. The phase entrainment region, which is symmetrical about $\varphi_i = 0$, corresponds to expectancy violations for which phase correction is most efficient. In this region, attending energy is most concentrated (as a pulse), that is, expectancies are less variable and one's focus of attending is narrow and sharply tuned. The width of an entrainment region co-varies with the width of an attentional pulse; both are a function of the η_φ parameter in Large's model: As $|\eta_\varphi|$ decreases, the region widens. Finally, in some circumstances, where entrainment breaks down, values of η_φ are near zero and a flat PRC function specifies virtually no phase correction over a wide region. These theoretical limits have broad implications. They not only suggest the degree to which listeners can correct their expectancies to monitor changes in an event rate's or rhythm but they also suggest that in certain situations (e.g., highly variable temporal contexts) entrainment becomes erratic.

Finally, the symmetry of the PRC in Fig. 4 implies that early and late expectancy violations are corrected with equal efficiency. This is probably not the case. With an early violation, a tone onset arrives prior to its expected time and therefore is first signaled by the *presence* of stimulation; by contrast, with a correspondingly late onset, the expectancy violation is first signaled by the *absence* of expected stimulation and only subsequently does stimulation occur. In absolute magnitude, both yield the same expectancy violation, $\varphi_i = |\Delta \tau_i| / P_i$ where $\Delta \tau_i$ = an observed – expected interval. However, they have different implications for reactive attending. Earlier I defined reactive attending as engaging a translatory shift of an attentional *focus* that accompanies a phase correction from an expected point in time *toward* an unexpected one. The time shift can be expressed as traversing all or part of the interval defined by an expectancy violation, $\Delta \tau_i$. That is, a shift of $\Delta \tau_i$ corresponds to *full* phase correction at $i+1$. Also, underlying Fig. 4 is the implication that a given shift does not always realize full phase correction, particularly when $\varphi_i \geq 0.25$. Figure 4 also suggests that reactive attending is equally effective in phase correction for early and late time violations. Both these predictions are testable, as we shall see in a later section. In short, Fig. 4 suggests limits on phase correction and it also predicts symmetry with respect to phase correction with tone onsets that are unexpectedly early and late.[6] This raises interesting questions for future research.

To sum up, for a listener attending to a rhythmic sound pattern, the incongruity of some temporally unexpected sound is gauged by relative phase (expectancy violation). In response to an expectancy violation, the listener engages in reactive attending, thus briefly reorienting attending; this leads to phase correction. The nature of the stimulus sequence itself (i.e., the driving rhythm) is, of course, critical; it determines the degree to which a given expectancy is precise and whether a sequence contains a potentially surprising element. Outlining the nature of phase correction is the domain of a theory. Here one model is described that presents theoretical predictions in the form of a PRC along with entrainment limits and reactive attending. Together they suggest how ongoing expectancies are corrected and attending keeps "on track."

[6] Issues of involuntary versus voluntary aspects of attending and phase correction are also relevant (e.g., Repp, 2002a).

Period Correction

Events often manifest global changes in rate. Clearly, we must be able to explain a listener's ability to adjust to such changes. However, empirically and theoretically, less is known about period correction than about phase correction in both biological and psychological research. I limit my discussion to two issues. The first issue concerns adaptation of the period of a single oscillator to a global rate change. The second concerns the role of multiple oscillators in responding to several IOI changes that, together, convey a truly rhythmic event as in Fig. 1, *C-E*.

One approach to rate change relies on the period-matching properties of a single limit cycle oscillation. Earlier in this chapter, I suggested that the period of an oscillator may change to match a new event rate. But, is this adaptation slow or rapid or is it simply a response that depends on some abstract intention of a listener to match a particular rate, as some recent evidence suggests (see Repp, 2001b; Barnes, 1998)? I have suggested that different neural entrainment frequencies, each tuned to a respectively different intrinsic time period, respond to such time changes but only within narrow limits (Jones, 1976). At the micro-time level (e.g., periods less than 1 ms), some support for this idea is found in frequency tuning curves and characteristic firing rates of neural units that respond maximally to a narrow range of periodicities of similar sinusoids (e.g., Liberman, 1982b; A. R. Palmer, 1987). If relatively stable tuning units exist, this implies that the period of a single internal oscillation adapts, within limits, only to IOIs near its *preferred period*. Boltz (1994) and McAuley (1995) offer related ideas in the context of internal periods of 300 to 1500 ms.

Another hypothesis about period correction is not mutually exclusive with the idea of frequency tuning limits. Large proposed that period adaptation to any time change is slow; moreover, he suggested that it depends on phase correction (see equation 4 in Large & Jones, 1999). Thus, the period change of an oscillator may piggyback on phase correction by incorporating a proportion of the phase change. In this case, period correction will necessarily follow phase correction; it will be slower and constrained by limits on phase entrainment, that is, by the phase entrainment region (Fig. 4). In this view, adapting to small (expressive) rate changes found in rhythms such as Fig. 1, *B* and *E*, does not necessarily entail period correction; instead, the expressive feelings we might experience in these cases are merely responses to expectancy violations that accompany quick shifts in reactive attending. Reactive attending shifts are transitory experiences that effectively "fly by" against the more gradually shifting backdrop provided by a slow modulating period.

Both these proposals about period correction raise related questions such as, "How far can a single oscillator 'stretch' its intrinsic period to accommodate patterns of arbitrarily large changes in IOIs?" The key phrase here is "arbitrarily large." A single attending oscillator with a period matched to the smallest IOI in driving rhythms of Fig. 1 would probably persist through most of these patterns with little difficulty. This is because the oscillator period is essentially harmonically compatible with different sequence IOIs that are multiples of its period. However, unruly rhythms, namely those containing large IOIs that are not compatible (i.e., not harmonically related), would require rapid, substantive, period adjustment of a single oscillator to accommodate such IOIs. This is a daunting undertaking for one oscillator. It raises the second issue related to period correction, namely the role of multiple oscillations. Rapid adaptations to dramatic rate changes or to rhythms with significantly different IOIs (as in Fig. 1, *C* and *D*) probably require the activity of collections of specifically tuned oscillators. Multiple oscillator models offer the potential for entrainment to complex rhythmic sequence that embed distinctly different IOIs (see Large & Jones, 1999; Large & Palmer, 2002; for examples of two-oscillator models). This topic is beyond the scope of this chapter.

SUMMARY OF THEORETICAL OVERVIEW

I have sketched major aspects of an entrainment approach to attending with sound patterns. Using dynamical systems terms, these involve a driving rhythm provided by an acoustic flow and a driven rhythm expressed as an attending oscillation. An attending oscillation comprises three basic components: an attentional pulse, an oscillator period, and oscillator phase. Entrainment is the process by which the oscillator adjusts its pulse, period, and phase to attune to the time structure of a driving rhythm. Fig. 5 summarizes a real-time (vertical arrow) sequence of the three main activities outlined in this section, beginning with (1) *anticipatory attending*, which initially involves a targeting of attending energy, carried by a driven rhythm, toward future (expected) points in time; it is indexed by oscillator period when relative phase is zero, next (2) an *expectancy violation* may occur, contingent on a disparity of expected and observed times; it is indexed by relative phase, and finally (3) *reactive attending*, which is a translatory time shift of attentional focus that is associated with phase correction and which occurs in response to an expectancy violation.

DYNAMIC ATTENDING IN DIFFERENT TASKS

The remainder of this chapter reviews behavioral data in the context of the proposals of the preceding section. I draw from three categories of task in which sound sequences are presented to listeners: time estimation, time discrimination, and target identification. I attempt to show that these tasks, respectively, offer insight into anticipatory attending, expectancy violations, and reactive attending. In the present framework, the order variable (i.e., relative phase) inevitably plays a major role in predictions for each task. Because it summarizes the combined influence of the three theoretical components (attentional pulse, oscillator period, phase), relative phase specifies the state of the whole system at the instant a listener produces a response. The real challenge, then, is to understand how various tasks differentially weight the contribution of each state variable to the yield ultimate value of relative phase that determines a response.

In time estimation tasks, I will try to show that the order variable is weighted heavily by the role of oscillator period in periodically pacing anticipatory attending. In time discrimination, I suggest that the order variable is reflecting the task demand that a listener respond to time differences, as such; hence this task weights more heavily violations of expectancies (i.e., than the expectancy itself). Finally, in target identification tasks, where people judge nontemporal dimensions of targets, I argue that the order variable weights reactive attending more heavily than in other tasks because this task forces people to shift their attentional focus, following an expectancy violation, to identify a target sound.

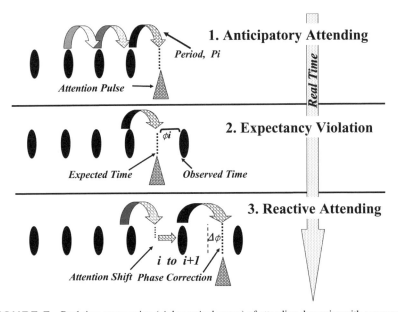

FIGURE 5   Real-time progression (*right vertical arrow*) of attending dynamics with a sequence of sounds (*solid ovals*). Anticipatory attending (time 1), which involves oscillator period, P_i, and phase, φ_i, is followed by an expectancy violation (time 2) elicited by a shifted tone onset; reactive attending to follow this (time 3) involves an immediate attention shift in time (arrow expresses time translation that approximates $\Delta\tau$), which is ultimately incorporated into phase correction.

TIME ESTIMATION AND ANTICIPATORY ATTENDING

Anticipatory attending, as depicted in Fig. 5 (top), depends heavily on the period of an entrained oscillator. An attentional pulse is recurrently targeted to occur at points in the future that are consistent with the time period of an oscillator's limit cycle. For these points, the order variable, φ_i, is mod 0, namely the expected phase, and because of this it is possible to glimpse "pure" anticipatory attending as a function of an internal periodicity. Two relevant tasks are (1) productions of sequence time intervals (where φ_i is zero) and (2) relative duration judgments about a pair of time intervals (standard, comparison) that follow a context sequence (where φ_i is both zero and nonzero). In both tasks, I assume that a rhythmically coherent sequence of tones is presented at a fixed rate and that it induces in listeners' synchronization (entrainment) of one or more limit cycle oscillations. Anticipatory attending, then, is an extrapolation of an induced period; the persistence of this periodicity is assumed to underlie time estimation in both sequence production and duration judgment tasks.

Reproduction/Production Tasks

The overt reproduction of a recurrent stimulus time interval that defines the rate of presented sequence forms a popular production task known as the synchronization–continuation task. Listeners hear a (usually) isochronous tone sequence in an initial synchronization phase, where they tap in synchrony with tone onsets. When the tones cease, listeners must continue tapping at the same rate. Thus, each continuation tap offers an estimate of the expected point in time associated with the entrained oscillator's period.[7]

The literature on this task is significant. Much of it derives from a prominent approach to the synchronization–continuation task that is based on an interval timer theory (Repp, 2001a; Vorberg & Wing 1996; Wing 2002; Wing & Kristofferson, 1973a,b). The interval timer approach to timing differs from an entrainment one. At the heart of interval timer theories is a governing internal timekeeper (a pacemaker) with properties unlike those of an entraining oscillator. A pacemaker framework assumes that (1) physical markers (tones) automatically trigger the pacemaker's activity, (2) the triggering switch allows a pacemaker to fill a marked stimulus time interval with ticks (distributed deterministically or stochastically), and (3) duration is coded as an accumulated count (of ticks) and placed in a memory store; when retrieved, this code enables reproduction of a given interval. Various timing models spring from the interval timer approach, and many apply to time estimation as well as production tasks (for reviews, see Allan, 1979; Grondin, 2001; Killeen & Weiss, 1987; Meck, 1996). The interval timer approach is an important one because it offers plausible alternative predictions about some of the phenomena I discuss in this chapter. Specifically, with regard to the motor production task, interval timer models have been developed to explain both response-based asynchronies (in synchronization) and coding of time intervals (in continuation) (e.g., Schulze & Vorberg, 2002; Vorberg

---

[7] Each tap is biased estimate of expectancy because of motor ("implementation") delays. Inter-tap-intervals tend to be less biased estimates of an oscillator's period because successive implementation delays are negatively correlated and hence cancel.

& Wing, 1996). Synchronization is achieved by reducing the time difference between a tap and a sound onset, whereas continuation tapping is accomplished using a time interval code that triggers a series of timed motor responses (with fixed motor delays).

Entrainment and interval timer accounts predict similar outcomes for many synchronization–continuation paradigms. Here I mention two significant differences in these approaches. The first concerns stationarity and period correction. Different pacemaker models incorporate period but few of these have been tested in synchronization tasks that present to listeners nonstationary rhythmic contexts, namely ones wherein rate and rhythm drift and change in complex ways. Entrainment models differ from the interval timer models in their potential for tracking such time-varying contexts; as models of an adaptive organism, they were designed to respond to non-stationarity (e.g., Large & Kolen, 1995; Large & Palmer, 2002; Large et al., 2002; Palmer & van de Sande, 1995; Palmer & Pfordresher, 2003). A second difference between the two approaches involves the role of attention in synchronization. Interval timer models emphasize acquisition of motor synchronization: Adaptation to a sound pattern entails linear reductions of the time difference between a *response and a sound*, (i.e., response asynchrony). By contrast, entrainment theories emphasize convergence to attentional synchrony: Synchronous performance depends on reducing the time difference between *expected and observed times of successive sounds*.

In light of the preceding distinction, I consider a few time estimation tasks that require attentional synchrony but only minimal motor activity. What happens when people merely attend to a rhythmical event? Can they extrapolate certain event-related time intervals? It appears they can. Jones & Boltz (1989) used folk tunes to illustrate this point. Listeners heard truncated monophonic melodies in a binary meter. They had to extrapolate event timing to estimate the time of a (missing) final tone using a single button press. Temporal expectancies about the final tone were manipulated through prior accent patterns in the folk tunes; in some melodies, accents implied an early ending time whereas in others, accents implied a late ending. As predicted, listeners extrapolated event-specific time spans, producing early, on-time, or late ending times contingent on accent condition. Such findings suggest that listeners selectively monitored interaccent time intervals and extrapolated related periodicities to perform the task.

Other research is consistent with the idea of rhythmic extrapolation in attention tasks (e.g., Jones et al., 1993; Pashler, 2001; Experiment 2). Converging physiological data reveal the presence of persisting internal periodicities in response to stimulus rhythms, oscillations that cannot be attributed to motor activity (Osman & Albert, 2000; Snyder & Large, 2003). Finally, other selective attending tasks offer related evidence for timed, event-specific anticipations (Boltz 1991, 1993). In sum, it appears that simply monitoring rhythmical events, without overtly responding, can induce in listeners an event-specific periodicity that persists.

Time Judgments in Sequential Contexts

Attending can also be assessed in time judgment tasks that minimize motor responding. As we shall see shortly, time estimation theories pertinent to these tasks, derived from both interval timer and entrainment assumptions, offer distinctly different pictures of internal timing. Figure 6 outlines some tasks that allow evaluation of these views by requiring people to compare two time intervals in different contexts.

This task was first used by McAuley and Kidd (1998). A listener encounters a series of context IOIs, followed by a standard, then a yoked comparison IOI and must judge whether the comparison interval is "shorter," "same," or "longer" than the standard. Although various aspects of this task, such as sequence length, structure and rate, are of interest, the most important variable involves the ending time of the standard (Fig. 6, *A*). Sometimes a standard ends as expected, given preceding IOIs (i.e., $\varphi_i = 0$ for the standard's ending) and sometimes it ends unexpectedly ($\varphi_i \neq 0$). Both entrainment and interval timer models can address this task.

An entrainment approach approaches this task with the assumption that internal timing depends, in large part, upon a sustained internal periodicity acquired via entrainment of a limit cycle oscillation to induction IOIs. Moreover, the periodicity is assumed to persist through a standard to permit judgments about the comparison. Of concern is what the oscillator does when standards end unexpectedly (versus expectedly). If listeners fail to correct the oscillator's period when an unexpected standard occurs, they will, nonetheless, rely on the prevailing period as an internal referent when they judge the subsequent comparison. The result will be a systematic pattern of errors, involving over- and under-

Comparative Time Judgments

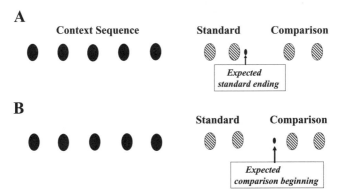

FIGURE 6 Two common comparative time judgment tasks are shown that incorporate sequential context. **A,** The main independent variable involves the ending time of the standard (hence the standard interval's duration). **B,** The main independent variable involves the beginning time of a comparison time interval.

estimations of the comparison, with best performance for the rhythmically expected standard duration. Specific predictions are based on values of the order variable φ_{final}, which is final relative phase; this specifies the relative difference between an expected and observed comparison ending time, given a sustained oscillator period.

A pacemaker approach offers a different perspective. As interval timers, these models assume that in this task the internal representation of a standard is stored as a discrete interval code that can be compared with the code for a comparison interval. This view stresses the importance of comparing discrete memories for numerically coded time intervals that are established by a pacemaker-accumulator (see, e.g., Block & Zakay, 1997; Grondin, 2001; Killeen & Weiss, 1987). It has successfully explained judgments of isolated pairs of time intervals, where it is assumed that physical markers of intervals automatically trigger the pacemaker. Adaptations to accommodate sequential contexts (e.g., as in Fig. 6) assume an internal averaging of interval codes for context IOIs with a code for the standard IOI; this average then provides an internal referent for the standard (Drake & Botte, 1993; McAuley & Jones, 2003; Schulze, 1989).

In this section, I focus upon entrainment models of time estimation and their potential for explaining effects of *sequence length*, *context*, and *rate*. Nevertheless, the contrasting predictions of the other models, particularly from the interval timer perspective, are important and useful.

Sequence Length

Barnes and Jones (2000) used the task of Fig. 6a to manipulate the ending times of standards in isochronous sequences of various lengths. Overall, people were best with standards that ended as expected given the preceding rhythm. This pattern was most pronounced with longer induction sequences where judgment errors were especially common with unexpected standards that ended very early or very late. A significant quadratic trend in proportion correct (PC) found with longer (seven IOIs) sequences and across different standard ending times is shown in Fig. 7 (for an isochronous context).

The accuracy profile of Fig. 7 is termed an *expectancy profile* because people do best with the rhythmically expected standard. Typically, confusion errors are systematic. For instance, when a standard ends unexpectedly early (relative to the context), people incorrectly remember it as longer than it was. Converging evidence that sequence length influences performance comes from research of Schulze (1989), who found that a timer based on an internal periodicity[8] (i.e., an internal beat) explained data better than an interval timer model based on an average of context intervals. This beat-based model has a fixed internal beat and detects phase asynchronies.

---

[8] Schulze found length advantages mainly when sequences of different lengths were randomized (not blocked) in a session.

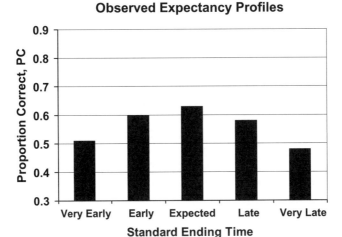

FIGURE 7   A typical expectancy profile observed by Barnes & Jones (2000) using the design of Figure 6, *A*, in which standard ending times are varied. Standard durations ranged from ones ending very early (524 ms) through an expected duration (600 ms) to ones ending very late (676 ms) on the abscissa. Accuracy, measured by average proportion of correct "shorter," "same," and "longer" responses, is shown on the ordinate.

Beat-based models resemble entrainment models because they incorporate an internal period; for this reason the two approaches are sometimes confused. But beat-based models do not entrain; rather, they represent a third way of expressing internal timing (e.g., Povel & Essens, 1985; Schulze, 1989). A true beat-based model adapts neither period nor phase in response to an expectancy violation. Therefore, it cannot predict certain errors observed in time judgments (e.g., Ivry & Hazeltine, 1995; Keele *et al.*, 1989; McAuley & Jones, 2003). Thus, entrainment models differ not only from interval models but also from beat-based timers in positing one or more adaptive oscillators that adjust, more or less adequately, period and phase to nonstationary time patterns. Nevertheless, in some circumstances (e.g., isochronous sequences), all three types of timing models (entrainment, interval, and beat-based) correctly predict the symmetric expectancy profile of Fig. 7.

We have seen that the entrainment model predicts a symmetric expectancy profile because it assumes that anticipatory attending in this task weights heavily the role of a sustained oscillator period. As the length of an isochronous sequence increases, the attentional pulse carried by this oscillator narrows, due to entrainment; this yields the prediction that attending is narrowly focused on those standard ending times that are compatible with a preceding rhythm. However, this interpretation raises the question, "How do we *know* that the symmetric expectancy profile arises from a persisting oscillator period and not from the oscillator's failure to correct phase?" For example, a beat-based model also predicts a sharp and symmetrical expectancy profile, due to a phase asynchrony. In this respect an entrainment model, with poor period correction, renders predictions similar to those of the beat-based model. This presents an apparent dilemma: Is phase or period critical?

In dynamical systems models, the order variable summarizes the current states of several variables. In this case, the states of *both* oscillator period and phase are captured by φ_{final} at the time of a judgment. Therefore, a failure of *either* phase *or* period to correct (i.e., to an unexpected standard) may be responsible for systematic errors in judgments. For example, an entrainment model with a low value of the phase coupling strength parameter η_φ predicts systematic errors consistent with an inverted U expectancy profile due to phase correction failures. These predictions imply that lasting effects accrue to phase asynchronies associated with unexpected standard endings. But the same inverted U expectancy profile (e.g., Fig. 7) will arise if lasting effects are due to a failure to correct period; this happens when η_p is low. Thus, the order variable can predict the observed expectancy profile based either on period or phase! So, what is the answer? This is where modeling is critical. Modeling efforts of both Large and McAuley have been crucial in providing an answer because an entraining oscillator exhibits intricate interactions of period with phase over time. Models can assess these interactions, fit data from many experiments, and provide estimates of parameters that reflect the relative strengths of period and phase correction during entrainment (Barnes & Jones, 2000; Large & Jones, 1999; McAuley & Kidd, 1998; McAuley & Jones, 2003). From these assessments we learn that the symmetrical expectancy profile is mainly due to a failure to fully correct period; that is, period correction appears to be sluggish (Large & Jones, 1999; McAuley & Jones, 2003). Time judgment errors are explained best by entrainment models with low values of η_p (poor period correction) and relatively high values of values of η_φ (good phase correction).

To sum up, given an entrainment interpretation, we can rule out interpretations that phase differences alone explain the symmetric expectancy profiles in data that result from modest variations in standard durations. These profiles are strongly affected by an oscillator's failure to correct its period in response to an unexpected standard. We conclude that a contextually established oscillator period persists, somewhat imperviously, through unexpected standards.

Context Structure

Various manipulations of context structure have been employed, using the task in Fig. 6, *A*, with the aim of evaluating different timing models. In this task, interval timer models assume an internal code for the standard based on a running average of context-plus-standard IOI codes; by contrast, entrainment models assume that "memory" for a standard is carried forward by the momentary period of an oscillator. In several experiments designed to compare predictions of these two accounts, McAuley and Jones (2003) found that both models performed well in response to isochronous context rhythms in the task of Fig. 6; however, interval models performed less well than entrainment models in other contexts that included a single lengthened context IOI.

One reason that an interval timer fails to adequately describe certain context effects is that, in averaging context IOIs, it weights an IOI according to its absolute interval (not ratio) value. Thus, a large time interval that is twice the duration of other IOIs greatly inflates the average interval serving as a memory code for context structure. The oscillator, by contrast, chugs right through any context IOI that is harmonically related to its period. Of course, it is always possible to construct an interval timer that selectively "ignores" a lengthened or (other undesirable) IOI, but this entails an ad hoc interpretation that violates a key assumption of timer operation, namely the assumption that homogenous markers (tones) *automatically* trigger the accumulator switch for any arbitrary IOI. Thus, strategically ignoring a lengthened IOI implies an override of this automatic trigger due to foreknowledge of a forthcoming (e.g., long) IOI.

In sum, variations in rhythm provide data that challenge interval timer models. At least for the simple rhythmic variations examined thus far, oscillator models equipped with weak period correction and strong phase correction do a reasonable job. These models correctly predict symmetrical expectancy profiles that occur when certain lengthened time intervals are introduced into a context sequence.

Sequence Rate

Sequence rate can have curious effects on time judgments and these provide another challenge for various timing models. Using the task of Fig. 6, *A*, Barnes & Jones (2000) sought to induce oscillator entrainments to isochronous sequences where it was predicted that an internal oscillator period should match one of three different sequence rates (e.g., based on IOIs of 300, 500, or 600 ms). Each of these three different sequence rates was followed by the same set of standard IOIs (524, 600, or 676 ms) plus yoked comparisons. If three different oscillator periods are induced, respectively, for these rates, then the oscillator should persist through various standard endings. The oscillator based on 600-ms periodicity was predicted to yield a symmetrical expectancy profile as in Fig. 7. So also was an oscillator with a 300-ms period (an harmonic ratio of 600); it should guide anticipatory attending to "expect" a standard to end at either 300 or 600 ms. By contrast, the 500-ms oscillator should *not* permit anticipation of the standard ending. Thus, the fast, 300-ms, rate condition and the slow, 600-ms, rate should both produce symmetric expectancy profiles whereas the 500 ms rate, by contrast, should produce a linear trend in accuracy over the three standard endings. Accuracy profiles (Ag) consistent with these predictions appear in Fig. 8 (cf. McAuley & Jones, 2003). Such findings can be explained either by a sophisticated beat-based model or by an entrainment model, both of which permit a continuation of an induced periodicity as an internal referent for judgments. However, such findings are difficult for current interval timer models which assume that context IOIs are coded to yield a fixed mean IOI as an internal referent.

Observed Expectancy Profiles
Three Time Judgment Conditions

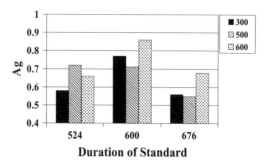

Duration of Standard

FIGURE 8   The nonparametric ROC measure, Ag, is plotted as function of the duration of the standard (524, 600, 676 ms) given 300-, 500-, and 600-ms IOIs in isochronous context sequences. (From Barnes & Jones, 2000.)

In sum, models that posit internal periodicities provide reasonably parsimonious descriptions of data in which rates vary. They naturally assume that an oscillator will realize harmonic relationships among various sequential IOIs. Interval timer models that do not incorporate a persisting periodicity have problems with these particular rate manipulations.

Summary of Time Estimation Tasks

A running theme is that time estimation in sequential contexts is a task that elicits anticipatory attending due to entrainment. Two types of time estimation tasks were considered. First, the production task induces an internal attentional periodicity to an isochronous sound sequence that persists when sounds cease; during continuation tapping, a persisting oscillator period is revealed by intertap intervals (i.e., $\varphi_i = 0$). Second, certain time judgment tasks encourage a reliance on persisting oscillator period when listeners must judge a comparison interval relative to an expected or unexpected standard, given a context rhythm. In experiments that vary sequence length, sequence context, and sequence rate, people are best judging rhythmically expected time intervals; overall accuracy patterns as a function of standard durations, indicate that most judgment errors follow a rhythmically unexpected standard. One explanation involves an entraining oscillator that is sluggish in correcting period but highly efficient in correcting phase. Relative to prominent alternative views (e.g., beat-based and interval timers), this entrainment hypothesis fares reasonably well.

TIME DISCRIMINATION AND EXPECTANCY VIOLATIONS

Classically, time discrimination is studied using highly trained listeners in order to ascertain the smallest perceivable time change (ΔT) between two isolated intervals, T and $T + \Delta T$. It is important to remember that, unlike time estimation tasks, discrimination tasks orient listeners to *differences*, namely to deviations from a referent time interval. Usually, participants are not even offered the choice of a "same" response, for example. In this section I consider this activity in settings that more closely approximate everyday situations encountered by average listeners. These settings engage events that unfold in time and they can embed one or more to-be-detected time changes. I propose that in these situations, the surrounding acoustic pattern induces anticipatory attending, namely a temporal expectancy, and that when listeners are encouraged to attend to time differences they comply by overtly responding to violations of this induced expectancy (Fig. 5, middle).

In this scenario, the magnitude of a time change is typically a variable of interest; it calibrates threshold levels. The order variable, relative phase, conveniently expresses the contribution of this variable in terms of an expectancy violation. I claim that the real impact of an arbitrary time change is calibrated by relative phase, φ_i; that is, a listener essentially determines: "Is φ_i nonzero?" In terms of prior notation, this describes reliance on an expectancy violation. Accordingly, we can identify two implications: (1) the perceived magnitude of a time change will vary with the momentary value of $\Delta\tau_i$ (*before* phase correction; cf. Figure 4) where $\Delta\tau_i$ = (observed − expected time); and (2) this perceived time difference, $\Delta\tau$, is an estimate of ΔT. Normalizing by the current oscillator period, P_i, we have: $\varphi_i = \Delta\tau_i/P_i$.

I focus upon two general cases in which sequence monitoring and time discrimination converge using paradigms such as that outlined in Fig. 9. The first case concerns discrimination of time changes in rhythmically coherent sequences

Relative Phase, ϕi,
as an Expectancy Violation

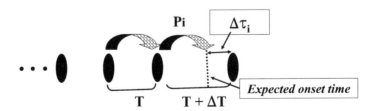

$$\phi i \;=\; \Delta\tau_i \,/\, Pi$$

FIGURE 9   The final portion of a sequence of sounds (*solid ovals*) with IOIs of duration T is objectively lengthened by ΔT. For a precise expectancy of the last IOI, $P_i = T$, the subjective time change, $\Delta\tau$, equals ΔT. This permits specifying expectancy violation with relative phase: $\varphi_i = \Delta\tau/P_i$ (temporal contrast/oscillator period), which (averaged over i) yields $\varphi = \Delta T/T$.

where we expect to find monitoring guided by fairly precise temporal expectancies. The second case concerns time discrimination in rhythmically incoherent contexts where we predict that imprecise temporal expectancies will occur.

Time Discrimination in Rhythmically Coherent Contexts

For simplicity, consider a rhythmically coherent context as in an isochronous sequence. The recurrence of a fixed IOI establishes a standard time interval, such that $T = \text{IOI}$ ms. As indicated in Fig. 9, such tasks require that people respond to a time change, ΔT, that is within or terminates a sequence.

Weber Fractions. An entrainment approach naturally lends itself to an expression of a Weber fraction for discrimination of a time change embedded within a sequence. This rests on the assumption that the magnitude of a momentary phase asynchrony and the ensuing expectancy violation determines performance. Given a stationary rate and strong phase correction, then an oscillator's entrained period, P_i, will quickly come to match T, reflecting a precisely tuned expectancy. Thus, listeners synchronize attending over intervals of T for all sequence time intervals (IOI_i). Moreover, a rhythmic deviation of a single IOI, by ΔT, can be assessed as $\Delta \tau \cong \Delta T$. Clearly, as $\Delta \tau$ increases, the likelihood of detecting a time change should increase; larger expectancy violations are more likely to elicit "different" responses. Finally, $|\varphi_i| = |\Delta\tau|/P_i \cong |\Delta T|/T$. In psychophysical tasks, where $|\Delta T|$ is typically averaged,[9] this is estimated by a mean of absolute $\Delta\tau_i$ values; similarly, the T of a Weber fraction is taken to represent the average oscillator period, P_i. In short, by assuming precisely tuned expectancies, we find that a threshold Weber fraction, based on a just noticeable difference (JND) is simply $\varphi_{\text{JND}} = \text{JND}/T$.

Classically, a major concern in time discrimination concerns Weber's law: Is $\text{JND}/T = \text{constant}$ when T is varied? This question has been largely addressed in two interval tasks where the answers are mixed, at best (Allan, 1979; Grondin, 2001). In sequence monitoring situations, the issue of Weber's law is relevant mainly in situations where sequences have different, but fixed, rates (i.e., different T values); in these situations, we also find mixed support for Weber's law holding over variations in rate (e.g., Drake & Botte, 1993; Halpern & Darwin, 1982). Drake and Botte (1993) asked how well listeners perceived a rate change between two sequences where the base rate, T, was varied; the task resembled that of Fig. 10, A. Although they found that the tempo JND decreased with sequence length and with rhythmic coherence, they did not find clear support for Weber's law. They relied on an averaging model of context time intervals to explain these effects of rate discrimination. I note that these findings may also be explained if listeners respond to the phase difference between two successive sequences. This is suggested in Fig. 10, under the assumption that an oscillator

---

[9] Typically, the standard deviation of responses in psychometric functions yields an estimate of JND as a mean difference score; conceptually this corresponds to the standard deviation of $\Delta\tau$.

Three Types of Time-Change

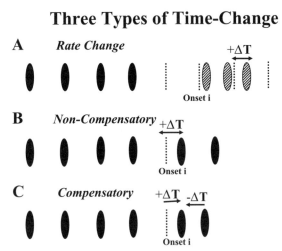

FIGURE 10   Three common time changes to isochronous sequences of a given IOI. **A,** A step change in rate from the first sequence (*solid ovals*) to the second (*striped ovals*), with *dotted lines* reflecting the continued extrapolation of preceding IOI to show an objective time change. **B,** A non-compensatory change is a single lengthened IOI with dotted line indicating the objective disparity from the preceding IOI. **C,** A compensatory change; the first IOI is lengthened and the second compensates by shortening.

entrained to the first sequence (filled ovals in Fig. 10, *A*) persists for while during the second sequence (striped ovals).

Relative Phase, and PRC Hypothesis

In the remainder of this section, I do not address Weber's law and variations in rate. Instead, I concentrate more specifically on the hypothesis that time discrimination entails a response to an expectancy violation, φ_i. If this is so, then certain situations should systematically affect listeners' responses to a given time change. Here we rely on the PRC hypothesis to predict what may influence the perception of a time difference, $\Delta\tau_i$ (numerator of a Weber fraction) when the oscillator's period, P_i (denominator of a Weber fraction) is constant and a preceding disruption occurs in a sequential context. Specifically, does the noticeability of a time change, at some point *i* in a sequence, depend on whether or not it was preceded by an expectancy violation? The PRC hypothesis, outlined earlier (cf. Figure 4), suggests ways to answer this question. That is, the PRC hypothesis proposes that unless phase coupling is very strong (i.e., a large value of η_φ), a preceding expectancy violation indeed can perturb performance and lower temporal acuity of an immediately following time change.

Here we evaluate the PRC hypothesis using sequences containing two different types of time changes. These changes, identified by Michon (1976) and Schulze (1978), appear in Fig. 10, labeled as noncompensatory (*B*) and compensatory (C) time changes. The *noncompensatory change*[10] embeds a single shortened or lengthened IOI into an isochronous rhythm; the *compensatory time change* introduces a local onset time shift that lengthens (shortens) one IOI and shortens (lengthens) the next IOI, reciprocally. Repp (2000; 2001a,b; 2002a; 2002b) has studied effects of such time changes in synchronized tapping, but here we consider their implications for sequence monitoring and time discrimination tasks. In particular, the timing models, discussed earlier, differ in their respective portrayals of the impact of these time changes.

We consider how listeners may respond to each kind of time change (Fig. 10, *B* and *C*) within an otherwise isochronous sequence. To address this using the PRC hypothesis, we assume that a listener relies on a constant sustained oscillator period: $P_i \cong T$ in both sequence conditions. We raise the following questions: (1) do people correct phase in response to a single time change? and (2) does the correction of phase to *i*th onset (if it occurs) have any effect on the discrimination of *another* time change associated with the $i + 1$ onset?

To answer these questions, we begin by considering phase responses to time changes given by hypothetical oscillator. Two extreme cases exist (see Eq. 1). They are special cases of a general entrainment model in that each represents an extreme value of the phase coupling strength term, η_φ; it turns out that values of this term capture defining assumptions of pacemaker and beat-based timing models regarding phase. At one extreme, complete phase resetting occurs; a listener fully phase corrects to any time change ($\eta_\varphi \gg 1$). This reflects an assumption generic to pacemaker models, namely that an interval timer is automatically reset by any marker. At the other extreme, no phase correction occurs to any time change ($\eta_\varphi = 0$). This reflects an assumption of beat-based timers, namely that they produce a fixed phase with each beat (Schulze, 1978; see also Keele *et al.*, 1989).

Beat-based and interval timers provide very different answers to the two questions we have posed. Accordingly, they offer contrasting predictions about time discrimination for the sequences in Fig. 10, *B* and *C*. In the case of an interval timer a listener is predicted to experience only one expectancy violation to the noncompensatory time change (Fig. 10, *B*) but should experience two violations to the compensatory change (Fig. 10, *C*). Hence, detection should be better for the compensatory change condition, if the interval timer model is correct.[11] By contrast, the beat-based model predicts the reverse. Because no phase correction exists, a beat-based listener should find the first sequence (Fig. 10, *B*) highly disruptive; the single deviant IOI initiated by the *i*th onset will permanently throw off her attentional tracking. However, a compensatory time change, at the $i + 1$ onset (Fig. 10, *C*), allows this listener to resynchronize quickly without phase

---

[10] The noncompensatory change has also been termed a pulse shift (Michon, 1967), the compensatory one an event-onset shift (Repp, 2002a,b).

[11] It may be advantageous to suppress responding to the first deviant IOI of a compensatory change (if one knows in advance that it is compensatory), but Repp has shown that this reaction, insofar as a motor response (tapping) gauges attending, cannot be completely suppressed (Repp, 2002a,b).

correction. Thus, the beat-based model predicts that listeners will be more likely to notice a time change in the noncompensatory sequence than in the case of Fig. 10, *C*.

So what happens? It appears that time change detection thresholds do not greatly differ for the two types of time changes. This finding is difficult for both of these models because it favors the idea that *some* phase correction occurs (e.g., Repp, 2001a, 2002a,b). In other words, the answer lies somewhere between these two extreme cases. A middle ground is supplied by the general entrainment model, which proposes partial phase correction. Predictions from an exemplar entrainment model are shown in Fig. 4; following the PRC hypothesis, this curve specifies the degree of partial phase correction that should occur in response to an expectancy violation by the *i*th onset (abscisa); in turn, this change can affect the discriminability threshold for a time change at i + 1 onset.

McAuley and colleagues (McAuley & Jones, 2003; McAuley & Kidd, 1998) pursued this issue. They used the task of Fig. 6b with an isochronous sequence in which the standard (*T*) is always identical to context IOIs (McAuley & Kidd, 1998; McAuley & Jones, 2003).[12] That is, no standard could end unexpectedly (as in Fig. 6, *A*) and thus $P_i \approx T$. Instead, a noncompensatory time change was associated with the *i*th onset, which marked the arrival of a comparison IOI. Specifically, a comparison could arrive early, on time, or late, relative to the preceding rhythm, meaning that an expectancy violation could occur at this *i*th location; depending on whether or not this is phase corrected, it will affect a listener's time judgments of the comparison's ending. In this task, the order variable, which summarizes the state of system when judging the comparison (at i + 1) is again final relative phase here denoted as $\varphi_{i+1} = \varphi_{final}$. The latter is predicted to register any *immediately prior* effects of phase correction on the time discrimination thresholds. Thus, McAuley and Jones asked, "Does a prior expectancy violation, elicited by a noncompensatory time change of the *i*th onset, affect a listener's discrimination of a duration difference (ΔT) between the standard and the comparison's ending (i + 1 onset)?"

Again different outcomes are possible, given the different theoretical perspectives we have identified. If *full* phase correction to the unexpected arrival of a comparison happens at *i*, as interval resetting models imply, time discrimination should be quite good for all three φ_i values. If *no* phase correction occurs, as a beat-based model implies, time discrimination should be quite poor for the two unexpected arrival times but very good for an on-time comparison arrival. The results fit neither of these predictions. Although small changes (φ_i of ±0.10) in comparison arrival times appeared to have little impact on performance, the picture changed with larger ones ($\varphi_i = ±0.30$). Here JNDs were significantly greater for comparisons arriving very early ($\varphi_{JND} \approx 0.10$) than for other comparison onset times ($\varphi_{JND} \approx 0.04$). In short, time discrimination thresholds in

---

[12] In conditions where a lengthened IOI immediately preceded the standard, it was always twice the context IOI.

coherent rhythmic contexts suggest that some phase correction occurs, but it is neither full phase correction nor null phase correction. Rather, partial phase correction is implied.

These data permit us to return to the two questions earlier posed regarding phase information with the following conclusions: (1) people do correct phase, but partially, in response to a single time change, and (2) phase correction does carry over to influence a subsequent time discrimination threshold. The findings of McAuley and colleagues are useful in several respects. First, they are consistent with the interpretation that people render judgments in discrimination tasks based on expectancy violations as these are summarized by relative phase. Second, they illustrate the fluidity of studying time discrimination in real-time contexts; people appear to base judgments on relative phase at one point in time that are influenced by responses (phase corrections) to prior time changes. As such, they speak to the PRC hypothesis in that two successive expectancy violations were examined in this task. Third, although phase corrections occur, contrary to a beat-based account, they appear to be more efficient with small time changes than large ones. This is clear evidence for limits on phase correction, and this is a problem for interval timer models. Fourth, the threshold differences McAuley and Jones found were *asymmetrical* with respect to arrival time; larger thresholds occur when the preceding expectancy violation was a very early one than when it was a very late one. This is a problem for a symmetrical phase correction process such as depicted in Fig. 4.

The finding of an asymmetrical phase response function is interesting. According to the PRC hypothesis of Fig. 4, phase corrections of an expectancy violation are symmetrical about the phase attractor state; comparable entrainment limits are hypothesized for early and late violations. The McAuley and Jones data provide only partial support for this prediction. Although phase correction limits (i.e., an entrainment region) are clearly suggested, the predicted symmetry of the PRC was not found. Indeed, the observed asymmetry of time discrimination thresholds over early, on time and late onsets of a comparison (Fig. 6, *B*) must be contrasted with the symmetric expectancy profiles (Figure 7) based on early, on time and late endings of standards (Fig. 6, *A*). Recall that I attributed the symmetry of the latter profiles to the consequences of failures in period correction to an unexpected standard ending. In the task of Fig. 6, *B*, where we find asymmetry, lower temporal acuity appears to result from a failure to correct phase when a comparison arrives unexpectedly early.[13] That is, phase correction is more

---

[13] These findings converge with findings of corrective shifts of overt taps to a phase-shifted tone in motor synchronization tasks (e.g., Repp, 2001a,b, 2002a, 2002b). Repp suggests that such corrections involve a significant involuntary component (but he also shows effects due to task and instructions, suggesting voluntary influences too). Efficient motor phase corrections following small time changes appear to increase linearly with $|\varphi|$ to around $\pm\varphi \leq 0.15$, but for larger time changes, phase correction is nonlinear. Findings on motor phase correction in synchronization converge in some ways with parallel tasks requiring phase synchronization of attending (e.g., McAuley & Jones, 2003; McAuley & Kidd, 1998).

effective following a late expectancy violation than an early one. In short, the asymmetrical accuracy profile associated with variation in arrival times of the comparison interval raises the intriguing possibility that boundaries of the phase entrainment region are not symmetrically located about a phase attractor of $\varphi = 0$.

Time Discrimination in Rhythmically Variable Contexts

It is less common to study time discrimination in nonstationary situations, where rate and rhythm vary. Not surprisingly, we assume that expectancies are less precise in such contexts. Nevertheless, the entrainment theory continues to imply that an internal referent, now a changing oscillator period, is used to generate anticipations and support temporal acuity. But entrainment becomes "looser" in these environs; at any instant the period is unlikely to match precisely the current IOI ($P_i \neq IOI = T$), and the degree of mismatch increases monotonically with rhythmic irregularity. Thus, temporal expectancies are less precise and one's attentional pulse widens and fluctuates. Accordingly, temporal acuity will change from moment to moment due to contextual influences on both oscillator period and pulse width. Only a few studies address these situations.

Monahan and Hirsh (1990) varied rhythmic structure and found evidence for local influences on temporal acuity. To explain their findings, they proposed that the average of IOIs surrounding a time change, ΔT, determined the functional T value listeners used. Although this approach accommodates local context effects, Large and Jones (1999) found threshold changes that were due to variability in remote context as well (Jones & Yee, 1997; Pashler, 2001; Yee *et al.*, 1994). Large and Jones (1999) describe an entrainment model in which the width of an attentional pulse fluctuates with remote rhythmic irregularities. We held local context constant in a two alternative forced choice (2AFC) monitoring task: listeners identified which of two isochronous test regions in longer sequences contained a compensatory time change where the time change varied in magnitude. The primary variable involved temporal irregularity in regions surrounding the test regions; some conditions contained no timing irregularities (were isochronous), others contained varying amounts of irregularity. Contextual irregularities were predicted to affect the width of an attentional pulse. Thus, better discrimination should occur with (1) larger time changes, $\Delta T/T$, due to correspondingly larger expectancy violations, φ_i, and (2) lower context irregularity, as measured by standard deviation of context IOIs. Both predictions received support. Figure 11 shows observed and predicted mean PC values for the four context conditions as a function of time change magnitude. Furthermore, although the estimated φ_{JND} increased with context variability, overall fits of an entrainment model were again consistent with the hypothesis that listeners engage in substantial (but not complete) phase correction ($\eta_\varphi = 0.60$) and minimal period correction ($\eta_p = 0.10$). Large's entrainment model implies that greater rhythmic coherence narrows a listener's attentional focus. Thus, the rhythmically coherent contexts induce

Time Discrimination Experiment

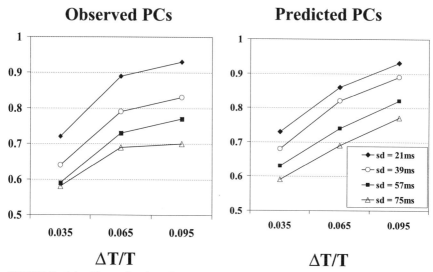

FIGURE 11   Observed and predicted mean PC scores in a task in which a to-be-detected compensatory time change ($\Delta T/T = .035$ to .095) was embedded within isochronous test regions of longer sequences (mean IOI = 600 ms). Four context conditions (coded lines) corresponded to rate-modulated context segments surrounding the test regions with standard deviation (sd) of IOIs varied from 21 to 75 ms (experiment 1; Large & Jones, 1999).

more precise temporal expectancies and hence heightened acuity for small time-changes.

Summary of Time Discrimination Tasks

Time discrimination in sequence monitoring requires that listeners pay attention to change within an unfolding sequence. This encourages an entrainment activity in which listeners rely on dynamic expectancies to supply a referent period, but they overtly respond only to violations of these expectancies. In this theoretical frame, an expectancy violation is summarized as relative phase.

Two general cases involved time change detection in rhythmically coherent and in rhythmically variable sequences. These cases differ in the degree to which a sequential context affords precise expectancies (e.g., stable periodicity; narrow attentional pulse). In rhythmically coherent sequences, precise expectancies permit heightened temporal acuity. Here issues raised by the PRC hypothesis permit comparisons of different hypotheses about phase correction and its immediate impact on acuity thresholds for subsequent time changes. It appears that partial phase correction occurs in monitoring for time changes and this affects subsequent acuity levels. Furthermore, in contrast to symmetrical expectancy profiles based on standard ending times, which were attributed to failures in period correction, an asymmetrical pattern of temporal JNDs occurred when the arrival of times of comparisons varied, suggestive of partial failures in phase correction. Finally, in the second case, involving rhythmically variable contexts, I reported that overall temporal acuity declines with increases in rhythmic irregularity.

TARGET IDENTIFICATION TASKS
AND REACTIVE ATTENDING

Do oscillators really guide attention, or do they merely calibrate time perception? The evidence cited in favor of attentional entrainment theory derives mainly from time judgment tasks. Although it would be incorrect to assume that the act of judging time does not require attention (see Brown & Boltz, 2002), a stronger case comes from target identification tasks in which listeners identify some nontemporal feature of a target sound such as its pitch or timbre. In these tasks, time is technically both an irrelevant and unreported dimension (Yantis & Egeth, 1999).

If attending is inherently temporal, then in spite of its formal irrelevance, a rhythmic context may guide an attentional focus to when a target sound occurs, thereby facilitating target identification. If so, then event timing remains relevant, at least to the listener. Both anticipatory and reactive attending are involved in such situations. Good identification of an unexpected target requires both effective entrainment to event rhythm (i.e., anticipatory attending) and efficient shifts of attending to temporally deviant targets (i.e., reactive attending). Anticipatory attending relies on entrainment of the periods of (one or more) oscillators, whereas reactive attending entails both a shift of attending energy and corrective time change in response to an expectancy violation (Fig. 5; bottom).

Early research generally demonstrated that in melodies rhythmically predictable pitch targets tend to be better identified than unpredictable ones (e.g., Jones, et al., 1982; Boltz, 1989). Kidd (1993) found that frequency discrimination thresholds increased systematically as a to-be-discriminated tone departed in time (early or late) from its expected temporal location in a sequence rhythm. Klein and Jones (1996), using a sustained attending task in which listeners monitored long rhythmic sequences, found that both the complexity of the rhythm and listeners' attentional set affected detection of targets (timbre changes).

Recently, we adapted a task from Deutsch's (1972) study to address rhythmic influences on pitch identification of target sounds placed at the end of a sequence (Jones et al., 2002). This task is outlined in Fig. 12, A. It consists of presenting two tones, a standard and comparison, separated by a sequence of interpolated tones which varied haphazardly in pitch. Interpolated tones were less than half the duration of standard and comparison tones. Equally often, the comparison tone frequency was the same, higher or lower (by one semitone) than the standard; the listener identified which alternative occurred. We introduced two changes from the task used by Deutsch. First, the interpolated rhythm was

A   **Target Identification Task**

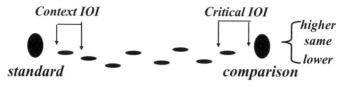

B   **Observed Expectancy Profile**

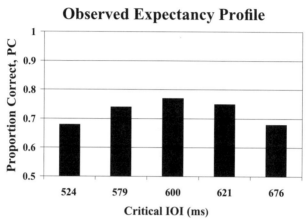

FIGURE 12   Task and data from a pitch target identification task. **A,** The procedure for a single trial; interpolated tones always formed an isochronous context rhythm; the critical IOI varied over trials. **B,** Proportion correct pitch identification (chance is 0.33) as a function of critical IOI.

isochronous and the IOI (critical IOI) between the final interpolated tone and the comparison tone was varied. A comparison occurred very early, early, on time, late, and very late (equally often). The second change involved adapting Deutsch's practice of repeating the standard within the interpolated tones; we repeated the standard once as the final interpolated tone. A series of experiments revealed the following:

1. Overall accuracy was greatest for comparison tones that occurred at the expected point in time (critical IOI = context IOI) and lowest for the very unexpected comparison tones (very early, very late), as shown in Fig. 12, *B*. In some cases, a tendency emerged for better performance with late than early targets.

2. This observed accuracy profile holds up even when the expected point in time follows a missing beat (critical IOI = two context IOIs), suggesting a persistence of the induced rhythm.

3. The significant quadratic trends in PC observed in experiments using an isochronous interpolated rhythm disappeared when the interpolated tones were randomly distributed in time (with same average IOI).

These target identification experiments suggest that the rhythmic context that either surrounds or precedes a target sound is not irrelevant to the listener performing the task. This is true in spite of the fact that, formally, the task defines a sound's pitch, and not its timing, as the relevant and reported dimension. Our interpretation builds on a combination of anticipatory and reactive attending. When the final IOI deviates from an expected point in time, given by anticipatory attending to a preceding context sequence, reactive attending is engaged after a comparison sound occurs. This entails a translatory time shift that moves a listener's attentional focus toward synchrony with the surprising tone; this time span is related to $\Delta\tau$, which is associated with an expectancy violation. Reactive attending is most efficient with relatively small phase shifts within the entrainment region and in some few cases it is more efficient with late than early onsets (see also Barnes, 2002).

Summary of Target Identification Task

Only recently has evidence surfaced to indicate that listeners rely on anticipatory attending, established by a rhythmic context, to facilitate allocating attending energy to identify the pitch of target tones occurring at an expected time. To shift an attending pulse to identify the pitch of a temporally unexpected tone requires reactive attending. The relationship of reactive attending to the attentional pulse, limits on phase correction, and conventional approaches to attentional capture remain topics of future research.

ACKNOWLEDGMENTS

The author is indebted to Heather Moynihan, Noah Mackenzie, J. Devin McAuley, Amandine Penel, and Jennifer K. Puente for comments on earlier versions of this chapter. Special thanks are due to Bruno Repp, who offered many helpful suggestions and comments on an earlier draft. The research reported here was supported by National Science Foundation grant BCS-9809446. Correspondence should be directed to Marl Riess Jones, Department of Psychology, 137 Townshend Hall, The Ohio State University, Columbus, Ohio 43210; jones.80@osu.edu.

REFERENCES

Allan, L. G. (1979). The perception of time. *Perception and Psychophysics 26*, 340–354.

Barnes, H. J. (1998). *Concurrent processing during sequenced finger tapping.* In D. A. Rosenbaum and C. E. Collyer (Eds.), Timing of Behavior: Neural, Psychological, and Computational Perspectives. (pp. 145–164). Cambridge, MA: MIT Press.

Barnes, R. M. (2002). *Attentional capture in sequential auditory arrays.* Unpublished doctoral dissertation, The Ohio State University.

Barnes, R. M., & Jones, M. R. (2000). Expectancy, attention, and time. *Cognitive Psychology 41*, 254–311.

Block, R. A., & Zakay, D. (1997). Prospective and retrospective duration judgments: A meta-analytic review. *Psychonomic Bulletin and Review 4*, 184–197.

Boltz, M. (1991). Time estimation and attentional perspective. *Perception and Psychophysics 49*, 422–433.

Boltz, M. (1993). The generational of temporal and melodic expectancies during musical listening. *Perception and Psychophysics 53*, 585–600.

Boltz, M. (1994). Changes in internal tempo and effects on learning and remembering of event durations. *Journal of Experimental Psychology: Learning, Memory and Cognition 20*, 1154–1171.

Boltz, M. (1989). Perceiving the end: Effect of tonal relationships on melodic completion. *Journal of Experimental Psychology: Human Perception and Performance 15*, 749–761.

Bregman, A. (1990). *Auditory scene analysis*. Cambridge, MA: MIT Press.

Brown, S., & Boltz, M. (2002). Attentional processes in time perception: Effects of mental workload and event structure. *Journal of Experimental Psychology; Human Performance and Perception 28*, 600–615.

Deutsch, D. (1972). Effect of repetition of standard and comparison tones on recognition memory for pitch. *Journal of Experimental Psychology 93*, 156–162.

Drake, C., & Botte, M. (1993). Tempo sensitivity in auditory sequences: Evidence for a multiple-look model. *Perception and Psychophysics 54*, 277–286.

Drake, C., Penel, A., & Bigand, E. (2000). Tapping in time with mechanically and expressively performed music. *Music Perception 18*, 1–23.

Ericksen, C. W., & St. James, J. D. (1986). Visual attention within and around the field of focal attention: A zoom lens model. *Perception and Psychophysics 40*, 225–240.

Gibson, J. (1979). *The ecological approach to visual perception*. Boston: Houghton Mifflin.

Glass, L., & Mackey, M. C. (1988). *From clocks to chaos: The rhythms of life*. Princeton, NJ: Princeton University Press.

Grondin, S. (2001). From physical time to first and second time moments of psychological time. *Psychological Bulletin 127*, 22–44.

Halpern, A. R., & Darwin, C. J. (1982). Duration discrimination in a series of rhythmic events. *Perception and Psychophysics 32*, 86–89.

Ivry, R., & Hazeltine, R. E. (1995). Perception and production of temporal intervals across a range of durations: Evidence for a common timing mechanism. *Journal of Experimental Psychology: Human Performance and Perception 21*, 3–18.

Jones, M. R. (1976). Time, our lost dimension: Toward a new theory of perception, attention and memory. *Psychological Review 83*, 323–335.

Jones, M. R., & Boltz, M. (1989). Dynamic attending and responses to time. *Psychological Review 96*, 459–491.

Jones, M. R., & Boltz, M., et al. (1982). Controlled attending as a function of melodic and temporal context. *Perception and Psychophysics 32*, 211–218.

Jones, M. R., Boltz, M., & Klein, J. (1993). Duration judgments and expected endings. *Memory and Cognition 21*, 646–665.

Jones, M. R., Jagacinski, R. J., Yee, W., Floyd, R. L., & Klapp, S. (1995). Tests of attentional flexibility in listening to polyrhythmic patterns. *Journal of Experimental Psychology: Human Perception and Performance 21*, 293–307.

Jones, M. R., Moynihan, H., MacKenzie, N., & Puente, J. (2002). Temporal aspects of stimulus-driven attending in dynamic arrays. *Psychological Science 13*, 313–319.

Jones, M. R., Yee, W. (1997). Sensitivity to Time Change: The role of context and skill. *Journal of Experimental Psychology: Human Perception and Performance 23*, 693–709.

Kaplan, D. G. L. (1995). *Understanding nonlinear dynamics*. New York: Springer-Verlag.

Keele, S., Nicolette, R., Ivry, R. I., & Pokorny, R. A. (1989). Mechanisms of perceptual timing: Beat-based or interval-based judgments? *Psychological Research 50*, 251–156.

Kelso, S. J. A. (1995). *Dynamic patterns: The self-organization of brain and behavior*. Cambridge, MA: MIT Press.

Kidd, G. R. (1993). *Temporally directed attention in the detection and discrimination of auditory pattern components.* Poster presented at the Acoustical Society of America, Toronto.

Killeen, P. R., & Weiss, N. A. (1987). Optimal timing and the Weber function. *Psychological Review 94*, 455–468.

Klein, J. M., & Jones, M. R. (1996). Effects of attentional set and rhythmic complexity on attending. *Perception and Psychophysics 58*, 34–46.

Large, E. W. (1994). *Dynamic representation of musical structure.* Ohio State University.

Large, E. W., & Jones, M. R. (1999). The dynamics of attending: How people track time-varying events. *Psychological Review 106*, 119–159.

Large, E. W., & Kolen, J. (1995). Resonance and the perception of musical meter. *Connection Science 6*, 177–208.

Large, E. W., & Palmer, C. (2002). Perceiving Temporal Regularity in Music. *Cognitive Science 26*, 1–37.

Large, E. W., Fink, P., & Kelso, J. A. Scott. (2002). Tracking simple and complex sequences. *Psychological Research 66*(1), 3–17.

Li, X., Logan, R. J., & Pastore, R. E. (1991). Perception of acoustic source characteristics: Walking sounds. *Journal of the Acoustical Society of America 90*, 3036–3049.

Liberman, M. C. (1982b). The cochlear frequency map for the cat: Labeling auditory-nerve fibers of known characteristic frequency. *Journal of the Acoustical Society of America 72*, 1441–1449.

London, J. (2002). Cognitive constraints on metric systems: some observations and hypotheses. *Music Perception 19*, 529–550.

Mates, J. (1994a). A model of synchronization of motor acts to a stimulus sequence. I. Timing and error corrections. *Biological Cybernetics 70*(5), 463–473.

Mates, J. (1994b). A model of synchronization of motor acts to a stimulus sequence. II. Stability analysis, error estimation and simulations. *Biology Cybern 70*(5), 475–484.

McAuley, J. D. (1995). *Perception of time phase: Toward an adaptive oscillator model of rhythmic pattern processing.* Bloomington: Indiana University.

McAuley, J. D., & Jones, M. R. (2003). Modeling effects of rhythmic context on perceived duration: A comparison of interval and entrainment approaches to short-interval timing. *Journal of Experimental Psychology: Human Perception and Performance 29*, 1102–1125.

McAuley, D. J., & Kidd, G. R. (1998). Effect of deviations from temporal expectations on tempo discrimination of isochronous tone sequences. *Journal of Experimental Psychology: Human Perception and Performance 24*, 1786–1800.

Meck, W. H. (1996). Neuropharmacology of timing and time perception. *Cognitive Brain Research 3*, 227–242.

Michon, J. A. (1976). *Timing in temporal tracking.* Assen, The Netherlands: van Gorcum & Co.

Monahan, C., & Hirsh, I. (1990). Studies in auditory timing: 2. Rhythm patterns. *Perception and Psychophysics 47*, 227–242.

Moore-Ede, M. C., Sulzrnan, F. M., & Fuller, C. A. (1982). *The clocks that time us.* Cambridge, Massachusetts: Harvard University Press.

Osman, A., & Albert, R. (2000). *The beat goes on: Rhythmic modulation of cortical potentials by imagined tapping.* Poster presented at the Annual Meeting of the Cognitive Neuroscience Society, San Francisco.

Palmer, A. R. (1987). *Physiology of the cochlear nerve and cochlear nucleus.* In M. P. Haggard and E. F. Evans (Eds.), Hearing. Churchill Livingston, Edinburgh.

Palmer, C. (1989). Mapping musical thought to musical performance. *Journal of Experimental Psychology: Human Perception and Performance 15*, 331–346.

Palmer, C. (1997). Music performance. In J. T. Spence, J. M. Darley, and D. J. Foss (Eds.), *Annual review of psychology* (vol. 48, pp. 115–138). Palo Alto, CA: Annual Reviews.

Palmer, C., & Pfordresher P. Q. (2003). Incremental planning in sequence production. *Psychological Review 110*, 683–712.

Palmer, C., & van de Sande, C. (1995). Range of planning in music performance. *Journal of Experimental Psychology: Human Perception and Performance 21*, 947–962.

Palmer, J. D. (1976). *An introduction to biological rhythms.* New York: Academic Press.

Pashler, H. (2001). Perception and production of brief durations: Beat based versus interval-based timing. *Journal of Experimental Psychology: Human Perception and Performance 27*, 485–493.

Pikovsky, A., Rosenblum, M., & Kurths, J. (2001). *Synchronization: A universal concept in nonlinear sciences.* Cambridge University Press, Cambridge.

Posner, M. I., Snyder, C. R. R., & Davidson, B. J. (1980). Attention and the detection of signals. *Journal of Experimental Psychology: General 109*, 160–174.

Povel, D. J., & Essens, P. (1985). Perception of temporal patterns. *Music Perception 2(4)*, 411–440

Repp, B. H. (1987). The sound of two hands clapping: An exploratory study. *Journal of the Acoustical Society of America 81*, 1100–1109.

Repp, B. H. (1995). Detectability of duration and intensity increments in melody tones: A partial connection between music perception and performance. *Perception and Psychophysics 57*, 1217–1232.

Repp, B. H. (1996). Patterns of note onset asynchronies in expressive piano performance. *Journal of the Acoustical Society of America 100*, 3917–3932.

Repp, B. H. (1998). Obligatory "expectations" of expressive timing induced by perception of musical structure. *Psychological Research 61*, 33–43.

Repp, B. H. (1999). Detecting deviations from metronomic timing in music: Effects of perceptual structure on the mental timekeeper. *Perception and Psychophysics 61*, 529–548.

Repp, B. H. (2000). Compensation for subliminal timing perturbations in perceptual-motor synchronization. *Psychological Research 63*, 106–128.

Repp, B. H. (2001a). Phase correction, phase resetting, and phase shifts after subliminal timing perturbations in sensorimotor synchronization. *Journal of Experimental Psychology: Human Perception, and Performance 27*, 600–621.

Repp, B. H. (2001b). Processes underlying adaptation to temp changes in sensori-motor synchronization. *Human Movement Science 20*, 277–312.

Repp, B. H. (2002a). Automaticity and voluntary control of phase correction following event onset shifts in sensorimotor synchronization. *Journal of Experimental Psychology: Human Perception and Performance 28*, 410–430.

Repp, B. H. (2002b). Phase correction in sensorimotor synchronization: Nonlinearities in voluntary and involuntary responses to perturbations. *Human Movement Science 21*, 1–37.

Repp, B. H. (2002). Phase correction following a pertubation in sensorimotor synchronization depends on sensory information. *Journal of Motor Behavior 34*, 291–298.

Schulze, H. H. (1978). The detectability of local and global displacements in regular rhythmic patterns. *Psychological Research 40*, 173–181.

Schulze, H. H. (1989). The perception of temporal deviations in isochronic patterns. *Perception and Psychophysics 45*, 291–296.

Schulze, H. H., & Vorburg, D. W. (2002). Linear phase correction models for synchronization: parameter identification and estimation of parameters. *Brain and Cognition 48*, 80–97.

Snyder, J., & Large, E. W. (2003). Neurophysiological correlates of meter perception: Evoked and induced gamma-band (20–60 HZ) activity. Manuscript submitted for publication.

Spence, C. J., & Driver, J. (1994). Covert spatial orienting in audition: exogenous and endogenous mechanisms. *Journal of Experimental Psychology: Human Perception and Performance 20*, 555–574.

van Noorden, L. P. A. S. (1975). *Temporal coherence in the perception of tone sequences.* Eindhoven: University of Technology.

Vorberg, D. W., & Wing, A. (1996). Modeling variability and dependence in timing. In H. K. Heuer and S. W. (Ed.), *Handbook of perception and action* (Vol. 2, pp. 181–262). London: Academic Press.

Warren, W. H., & Verbrugge, R. R. (1984). Auditory perception of breaking and bouncing events: A case study in ecological acoustics. *Journal of Experimental Psychology: Human Perception and Performance 10*, 704–712.

Winfree, A. T. (2001). *The geometry of biological time* (ed. 2; Vol. 12). New York: Springer-Verlag.

Wing, A. M. (2002). Voluntary timing and brain function: an information processing approach. *Brain and Cognition 48*, 7–30.

Wing, A. M., & Kristofferson, A. B. (1973a). Response delays and the timing of discrete motor responses. *Perception & Psychophysics 14*, 5–12.

Wing, A. M., & Kristofferson, A. B. (1973b). The timing of interresponse intervals. *Perception and Psychophysics 13*, 455–460.

Yantis, S., & Egeth, H. G. (1999). On the distinction between visual salience and stimulus-driven attentional capture. *Journal of Experimental Psychology: Human Perception and Performance 25*, 661–676.

Yee, W., Holleran, S., & Jones, M. R. (1994). Sensitivity to event timing in regular and irregular sequences: Influences of musical skill. *Perception and Psychophysics 56*, 461–471.

4

AUDITORY MOTION AND LOCALIZATION

JOHN G. NEUHOFF

By almost any measure, determining the spatial location and path of movement of objects in the environment is a primary task of most perceptual systems. The ability to localize acoustic sources is considered by many to be the most important task of the vertebrate auditory system (Popper & Fay, 1997). Accurate estimates of spatial location facilitate proper navigation through the environment and precise interaction with objects and organisms. In the visual system there is a relatively isomorphic correspondence between spatial positions in the environment and equivalent points on the retina. This correspondence is well preserved through cellular organization throughout much of the physiology of the visual pathway. There is a tonotopic organization in the auditory system that corresponds to an ordered *frequency* scale, and some early work was suggestive of place coding in the auditory cortex for spatial position (Coleman, 1959). However, the correspondence between spatial position and neuronal representation is not nearly as detailed as that of the visual system.

Instead, spatial position is calculated using a number of different sources of information, including differences in the characteristics of a sound as it arrives at each ear. These differences are both temporal and spectral and are created by the spatial separation of the two ears and the influence of the head, torso, and pinnae. Rather than neurons tuned to a single spatial position or region, there is evidence to suggest that single neurons in the auditory cortex are panoramic and respond to source locations through 360° of azimuth. Spatial position appears to be represented in these cells by the pattern rather than the rate of neuronal firing (Fitzpatrick, Batra, Stanford, & Kuwada, 1997; Middlebrooks, Clock, Xu, & Green, 1994; Middlebrooks, Xu, Clock, & Green, 1998).

Perhaps as a result of the different means of coding spatial information in the auditory and visual systems, the spatial resolution of the visual system is much better than that of the auditory system and the temporal resolution of the auditory system generally exceeds that of the visual system. Thus, the two systems complement each other as well as one might expect given the millions of years that that evolutionary processes have had to shape the respective systems. Some of the deficits of the visual system, for example, not being able to perceive 360° of azimuth at a time or to sense around corners, are compensated for by the auditory system, which accomplishes both of these tasks nicely. From an evolutionary perspective, it is perhaps no accident that the perceptual systems have evolved to take advantage of these particular characteristics of the environment. For example, the wavelength of visible light makes it such that very good spatial resolution is physically possible. The characteristics of sound waves are such that they are less susceptible than light to the influence of obstacles, corners, or shadows (Griffin, 1959). Thus, the respective sensory systems have evolved to take advantage of the available information in the physical environment.

Yet, it is interesting to note that much of the research on auditory localization has been conducted with stationary static sounds. Often listeners in the laboratory are asked to choose the source location of a presented sound from an array of several loudspeakers. However, the number and position of the loudspeakers, and thus the number of possible response choices, are typically quite restricted. This setup differs from listening in a natural environment in several ways. First, in the laboratory, there is usually an equal probability of a sound coming from any given speaker in the array, regardless of whether the source is in front, behind, or even above or below the listener. This is often not the case in a natural listening environment, particularly when the space directly above the head is investigated. Sounds more often emanate from somewhere on or near the horizontal plane than from above or below the listener. Unlike those in the laboratory setup, on the other hand, the *potential* locations in a natural environment from which a sound could emanate are unlimited. The importance of the number and placement of available responses was manifest in a study by Perrett and Noble (1995) that showed that the available response choices in a localization task can influence localization performance significantly. Thus, investigations with highly constrained response choices are somewhat limited in their ability to inform us about localization in a more natural listening environment (Middlebrooks & Green, 1990). Furthermore, identifying the location of static sound sources from a fixed listening location is a condition that probably occurs less often than more dynamic examples of localization tasks. In addition to presenting static stimuli in anechoic environments, investigators sometimes even limit head movements of the listeners by either immobilization or instruction (Blauert, 1997).

To be fair, however, the primary goal of such investigations is usually to test hypotheses about particular mechanisms and processes that allow listeners to localize sound sources, not to develop ecological theories of how listeners use acoustic information under more natural listening conditions. Furthermore, the experimental control and internal validity afforded by these types of investigations are of great value in determining the particular cues with which listeners can identify source location as well as in defining the limitations of localization abilities under any conditions. Such studies continue to provide important information about how listeners localize and have also laid the groundwork for more recent investigations with dynamic stimuli. Even so, much of the work on dynamic localization has not used actual sound sources in motion. More often, studies employ auditory "apparent motion." For example, a typical experimental setup might include a linear array of loudspeakers. If a signal is sent to each speaker in succession with the appropriate interstimulus interval, listeners report the perception of auditory motion. Still other work has employed headphone presentation of stimuli to produce auditory apparent motion, usually varying only one cue to localization at a time such as monaural intensity change or interaural level difference. In evaluating these various approaches, it is clear that many of the findings with stationary static stimuli do not predict well the results of experiments with dynamic stimuli (see later). The difference between studies that use apparent motion and actual motion appears to be smaller. However, the number of experiments that use real auditory motion is probably to small to evaluate this comparison properly.

There are several advantages to using apparent motion to investigate localization and motion perception. First, any mechanism that produces real motion also generates some sound itself that may interfere with the target signal. Second, using apparent motion, especially in headphones, allows the researcher to present different auditory motion cues selectively and examine the relative contribution of each while factoring out the effects of the others.

STATIONARY LOCALIZATION

There are a considerable number of studies that examine the ability of listeners to localize sounds in the horizontal plane (roughly defined as the plane that passes through the head at ear level). There is less work that investigates localization in the median (or sagittal) plane and still less on the ability of listeners to determine the distance of a sound's source (Scharf & Houtsma, 1986). It is likely that the preponderance of work done in the horizontal plane is due to the fact that this plane can be easily simulated in headphones. Although there are clearly differences between horizontal localization of external sounds and what has been called "lateralization" of sounds in headphones, the two methodologies have provided a reasonably clear picture of the physical cues that are used to localize sounds in the horizontal plane.

One of the earliest studies to examine localization in the horizontal plane and the physical cues that listeners use to localize was conducted by Stevens and Newman (1936). Listeners were seated in a tall chair on a rooftop to avoid reflected sound and were asked to identify the angular position of a loudspeaker that could circle the listener on the end of a boom. Stevens and Newman are credited as being the first to provide empirical evidence for the "duality theory" of localization, an idea that had been proposed by Rayleigh as early as 1907. By the time Stevens and Newman presented their data, duality theory was generally accepted on logical grounds alone (Scharf & Houtsma, 1986). Duality theory proposes that listeners use both interaural intensity differences (IIDs) and interaural phase differences (IPDs) to localize sound sources in the horizontal plane. Using pure tone stimuli that ranged in frequency from about 400 to 10,000 Hz, they found that listeners used IPDs to localize sounds below about 1500 Hz and IIDs to localize sounds above about 4000 Hz. As one might expect, localization performance was worst between 1500 and 4000 Hz.

Whereas Stevens and Newman primarily examined localization *accuracy*, Mills (1958) employed a different methodology to examine localization *precision*. Essentially, Mills was interested in the smallest amount of source displacement that could be reliably detected. He seated listeners in an anechoic chamber and played sounds from a loudspeaker mounted on the end of a boom. The initial sound was followed by a second sound that was played after the boom had been moved to the left or right. The task of the listener was to determine the direction in which the sound source had been moved. The angle at which listeners achieved an accuracy rate of 75% was termed the minimum audible angle (MAA). Mills found that the MAA was dependent upon both frequency and azimuth. Performance was best at 0° azimuth (directly in front of the listener) and deteriorated as azimuth was increased to 75°. At 0° azimuth the MAA was less than 4° for all frequencies tested between 200 and 4000 Hz.

Perrott and his colleagues have conducted extensive work on MAAs and how they differ from minimum audible movement angles (MAMAs). For example, Mills (1958) showed that a 500-Hz stationary tone can be localized to within plus or minus 1° of azimuth. Thus, we might predict that the listeners would be able to detect the motion of a sound source once it has traveled at least 2°. Nonetheless, a sound source in motion can travel up to 10 times this distance before the motion can be detected, and the velocity of the source influences the distance required for detection (Harris & Sergeant, 1971; Perrott & Musicant, 1981). Other work has examined how MAAs interact with the precedence effect (Perrott, Marlborough, Merrill, & Strybel, 1989; Saberi & Perrott, 1990) and differences between MAAs in horizon and azimuth (Perrott & Saberi, 1990).

The MAA paradigm has also been used to examine the ability of listeners to determine the "facing angle" of a directional sound source. An audible facing angle is formally defined by a line between a source and a listener and a ray in the direction in which the source is radiating (see Fig. 1). Under certain conditions, listeners can discriminate between facing angles that differ by as little as 9° (Neuhoff, Rodstrom, & Vaidya, 2001). In this study, a burst of broadband noise was played in an anechoic room through a small loudspeaker that directly faced the listener. After the stimulus was presented, the loudspeaker silently rotated on

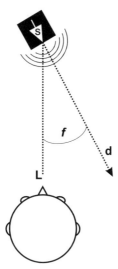

FIGURE 1 The audible facing angle *f* is defined by a line between the source *s* and listener *L* and the ray *d* in the direction in which the source is radiating.

its axis to either the left or the right. The same burst of noise was then played again. The task of the blindfolded listener was to determine the direction of rotation. The minimum audible facing angle (MAFA) was found to be dependent on the distance between the source and the listener and also on the directivity (or pattern of acoustic dispersion) of the source. The closer the listener was to the source and the narrower the pattern of directivity, the better listeners could discern differences between facing angles.

From an ecological perspective, localizing filtered pure tones in one plane on a reflectionless rooftop or detecting source displacement in an anechoic chamber leaves much to be desired. However, Stevens and Newman also found that if presented with broader spectrum sounds, for example, unfiltered pure tones that produced an audible click, or broadband noise, listeners could localize with less error. Presumably, for sounds with sufficient bandwidth, listeners could use both IPD and IID information in addition to interaural time differences (ITDs). Mills found an effect of source frequency that showed that localization precision was best for frequencies between about 200 and 1000 Hz. More recently, researchers have shown that auditory localization for some listeners is comparable in real environments and virtual auditory environments in which interaural differences in the signal are synthesized to simulate virtual auditory sources in space (Loomis, Hebert, & Cicinelli, 1990). These findings are particularly encouraging to those involved in developing devices to provide navigation information to the visually impaired.

HORIZON AND AZIMUTH

In several studies, researchers have asked listeners to locate sounds in the near space around the head. In these studies the location of the stimulus varied freely in elevation and azimuth, although distance from the listener was held constant. Makous and Middlebrooks (1990) used a head-pointing technique to examine the ability to localize sounds in both the vertical and horizontal planes. Listeners were seated in the center of a coordinate sphere with a radius of 1.2 m, and the stimuli were presented in 340° of azimuth and 100° of elevation in 10° increments. The task was simply to orient toward or face the perceived location of the sound source. After extensive training with feedback, listeners typically showed errors of less than 5° in both the horizontal and vertical dimensions directly in front of the listener. Accuracy diminished as sounds were presented from more peripheral locations.

Oldfield and Parker (1984) conducted a similar study in which listeners indicated the perceived location of a sound source on a coordinate sphere whose radius was 0.92 m. Perceived location was specified by using a special pointing "gun." The results were largely concordant with those of Makous and Middlebrooks (1990). Listeners showed better performance in front of the head than behind. Both Makous and Middlebrooks (1990) and Oldfield & Parker (1984) have argued that the use of pointing or orienting responses may be superior to other methods for indicating spatial position. For example, Makous and Middlebrooks cited better performance for listeners using the head-pointing technique over a similar study by Wightman and Kistler (1989) that used a verbal response technique, despite the fact that the characteristics of the stimuli used by Wightman and Kistler should have made localization easier.

One common element among all three of these studies is the extensive practice that participants engaged in prior to the actual recording localization performance. Oldfield and Parker's listeners were given at least 2 hours of training prior to data collection. Makous and Middlebrooks' (1990) listeners engaged in 10 to 20 training sessions. The authors of both studies provided extensive feedback during these practice sessions. Typically, training and feedback are provided in order to acquaint participants with the apparatus and to reduce the variability of responses. From the standpoint of traditional psychoacoustics, this practice makes sense because it better informs us of the limits of localization abilities by reducing variation. However, from an ecological perspective this practice is perhaps questionable because, although it may give us some insight into the limits of localization abilities, it tells us little of how listeners localize sounds under more novel conditions.

ELEVATION

The localization of sound sources in the vertical midline cannot be accomplished by analysis of any interaural differences in the arriving signal because a source in the median plane is equidistant from the two ears (excluding any differences caused by head asymmetry or facing angle). However, listeners are reasonably good at localizing sounds in the median plane provided that the sounds have a relatively broad spectrum. In fact, it appears that spectral information is critical to accurate localization in the median plane. Blauert (1969) found that when narrowband stimuli are presented in the median plane, judgments of location (either front, back, or above) are almost entirely dependent upon frequency, rather than amplitude or actual location (see also Pratt, 1930; Roffler & Butler, 1968a, 1968b; Trimble, 1934). Blauert has termed the frequency ranges that produce this effect "directional bands." Other work has shown that median plane localization suffers when pinnae cues are eliminated by occlusion (Roffler & Butler, 1968a). The experiments of Blauert and others were typically conducted in an anechoic environment, and listeners were restrained so that head movements were eliminated. Thus, in a natural environment the errors in localization reported are unlikely to occur for several reasons. First, many naturally occurring sounds contain broader spectra, thereby eliminating spatial ambiguity. Second, head movements can create interaural differences that would help resolve spatial position. Still, this finding is important in that it gives some insight into the physical cues that the auditory system uses to localize sounds in the median plane.

These findings also provided a framework for more recent work that attempts to tie these psychophysical results to specific physiological structures in the auditory system that are implicated in the localization of median plane sound sources. For example, using single-cell and cluster recordings, Xu, Furukawa, and Middlebrooks (1999) have identified cortical neurons in cats that accurately identify the median plane location of broadband signals. These are signals that both cats and humans can localize reasonably well. Furthermore, when narrowband stimuli were used, the output of the cortical responding specified incorrect spatial locations, much like those found in the psychophysical studies such as those conducted by Blauert (1969).

DISTANCE

Much as with the perception of visual distance, there are several sources of information that listeners can use to determine the distance of sound sources. Two of the most informative cues are intensity change and reverberation (Bronkhorst & Houtgast, 1999; Zahorik, 2002). Others have to do with source familiarity and the increased atmospheric damping of high frequencies as source distance increases (Little, Mershon, & Cox, 1992). Mershon and colleagues (Mershon, Ballenger, Little, McMurtry et al., 1989; Mershon & Bowers, 1979; Mershon & King, 1975) have shown that differences in intensity do not necessarily serve as an absolute cue to auditory distance. However, such differences do provide strong cues to changes in source distance, and greater reverberation is typically associated with more distant sources. Source familiarity can influence distance perception, with some work showing that more errors occur when listeners are asked to judge the distance of familiar "real-world" sounds such as those created by vehicles than when asked to judge the distance of white noise (Barnecutt & Pfeffer, 1998).

Much of the work on auditory distance perception has focused primarily on the perception of sources that are greater than 1 m from the listener. However, more recent work has highlighted special acoustic circumstances that occur when sources are close to the listener (Shinn-Cunningham, Santarelli, & Kopco, 2000). One might even argue that sources closer to the listener have greater importance from an evolutionary and ecological perspective. There is some work that shows that listeners are particularly sensitive to auditory distance for near sources. In a set of experiments on "auditory reachability," blindfolded listeners heard a rattle that was shaken by a mechanical device at various distances from the listener (Rosenblum, Wuestefeld, & Anderson, 1996). Rosenblum and his colleagues found that listeners could readily discriminate between source locations that were within their reach and those that were not. They also found that listeners were sensitive to the advantage provided by bending at the hip when reaching versus simply extending an arm. Furthermore, when estimates of reachability were scaled to account for differences in reach between individuals due to arm and torso length, differences in reachability estimates between individuals disappeared. Thus, the auditory perception of what is within one's reach appears to be scaled to one's body dimensions.

There does appear to be some corroborating physiological evidence to support the claim the listeners can discriminate between sources that are reachable and those that are not. Graziano, Reiss, and Gross (1999) examined ventral premotor cortex neurons in the frontal lobe of macaque monkeys. They identified cells that had spatial receptive fields extending only a limited distance outward from the head. In addition to auditory stimuli, these cells responded to tactile and visual stimul. Graziano *et al.* examined distance limitations in auditory receptive fields by manipulating the distance between a loudspeaker and the head. They found that the ventral premotor cortex neurons would respond to sounds presented 10 cm from the head but not to sounds presented 30 or 50 cm away, even though stimuli at all distances covered the same range of amplitudes. Visual representation in PMv is primarily limited to the space within reaching distance. Thus, these "trimodal" cells appear to process auditory spatial information only at distances that are within the reach of the listener.

DEVELOPMENT

A limited ability to localize sounds is present at birth. However, it appears that the ability becomes worse before it becomes better. Muir, Clifton, and Clarkson (1989) demonstrated a U-shaped function in localization performance for infants who ranged in age from 3 days to 7 months. The pattern of development is probably due to a maturational shift in locus of control from subcortical to cortical structures (Muir *et al.*, 1989). Morrongiello, Fenwick, Hillier, and Chance (1994) found that newborns could could differentiate between hemifields in localizing sources and showed some ability to localize within hemifields. Infants made head-turning adjustments to ongoing sounds that moved within a hemifield, suggesting that the infants used more than simple onset differences to determine the hemifield of the source. Ashmead, Clifton, and Perris (1987) examined localization precision in infants 26 to 30 weeks old and found minimum audible angles of about 19°, performance considerably poorer that that of adults, whose MAAs are generally 1 to 2°. These results suggest developmental trends in localization that subsequent work has investigated.

Morrongiello (1988) found a steady increase in localization precision as infants increased in age from 6 to 18 months. Performance increased almost linearly from MAAs of about 12° at 6 months to those of about 4° at 18 months. Between 6 and 18 months, infants (like adults) also showed better localization precision in the horizontal plane than the vertical plane. Morrongiello suggested that localization improvement with age may be the result of anatomical and neurological development, particularly in the auditory cortex, where development lags lower structures in the human auditory system (Clifton, Morrongiello, Kulig, & Dowd, 1981; Hecox, 1975).

In addition to developmental investigations of directional hearing, some work has examined the development of auditory distance perception. Typically, this methodology involves the infant making a distinction between sounds that are reachable and those that are not. Work has shown that infants as young as 6 months can use auditory information alone to make accurate judgments about the reachability of sources of sound (Clifton, Rochat, Litovsky, & Perris, 1991; Clifton, Rochat, Robin, & Bertheir, 1994). However, their strategy for determining auditory distance appears to be somewhat different from that of adults. Infants tend to weight cues to distance more equally, whereas adults in the same task rely more heavily on sound pressure level (Litovsky & Clifton, 1992). A comprehensive discussion of development and ecological psychoacoustics by Werner and Liebold can be found in Chap. 8.

MOTION PERCEPTION

The specific mechanisms that allow human listeners to process auditory motion are a matter of considerable debate. There are two general competing theories about how auditory motion is processed. The first theory suggests that listeners perceive auditory motion by simply comparing static "snapshots" of an auditory source in time and space (Grantham, 1985). Thus, according to snapshot theory, the mechanism behind the processing and of detection and processing of auditory motion is the same that is used to detect sources that are not in motion. The auditory system simply samples the auditory source at different points in time and makes a comparison of the samples in order to detect motion.

Velocity information could be obtained by comparing the distance traveled and the time elapsed during the motion.

Alternatively, the auditory system may respond directly to the motion of acoustic sources. Evidence for this position comes from both psychophysical studies that show that listeners are sensitive to motion information between the starting and ending points of auditory motion and physiological studies that show cellular responding to specific types of auditory motion. Perrott, Costantino, and Ball (1993) showed that listeners could discriminate between accelerating and decelerating auditory motion that traversed the same distance in the same elapsed time. The snapshot theory of motion detection runs into difficulty in accounting for these results. Acceleration discrimination could not be accomplished by simply comparing the endpoints of the path of motion and using the time between the two to determine acceleration because these factors were held constant in both conditions.

Grantham (1997) has suggested that both snapshot theory and direct perception of auditory motion may be at work in perceiving moving sounds. Grantham presented listeners with both dynamic and stationary sound sources. The task was to say whether sources in the dynamic condition were moving or stationary and whether the sounds in the static condition came from the same or different spatial locations. Essentially, the experiments investigated whether the middle of a source's trajectory provided any advantage to listeners in processing auditory motion. Snapshot theory would predict that listeners need only the endpoints of travel (such as those provided in the stationary condition) to make accurate estimates of sources motion. However, improved performance in the dynamic condition could not be accounted for by snapshot theory alone. The results suggested that for slow moving targets (20°/s) in the horizontal plane, the dynamic portion of a sound source's travel provides improved performance in processing auditory motion. The advantage provided by dynamic information was slight. Nonetheless, it cannot be accounted for by snapshot theory alone. At higher velocities (60°/s) the advantage afforded by dynamic cues disappeared. Thus, if the auditory system does use dynamic information in processing auditory motion, it may only do so within a restricted range of velocities. In examining thresholds for velocity discrimination, Carlile and Best (2002) have suggested that listeners may use both true motion perception and displacement detection simultaneously when both cues are available. Their listeners could discriminate well between auditory stimuli at different velocities. However, the highest thresholds for discrimination occurred when the duration of the motion was varied randomly. Thus, velocity discrimination was best if aided by displacement cues.

The study of the neural basis of auditory motion perception has seen great advances with the advent of brain imaging techniques that can investigate auditory perception. Specific neural mechanisms that process auditory motion have been identified (Baumgart, Gaschler-Markefski, Woldorff, Heinze, & Scheich, 1999; Griffiths, Bench, & Frackowiak, 1994; Griffiths, Green, Rees, & Rees, 2000; Warren, Zielinski, Green, Rauschecker, & Griffiths, 2002). These areas of activation often include premotor cortices, indication of a preparation for action in response to the moving source. Moreover, brain imaging in combination with virtual spatial displays has identified a common cortical substrate composed of the planum temporale, superior parietal cortex, and premotor cortex that appears to process auditory motion in both vertical and horizontal directions (Pavani, Macaluso, Warren, Driver, & Griffiths, 2002).

AUDITORY LOOMING

A host of acoustic variables support the perception of sound sources in motion (see Jenison, 1997, for an excellent review). Jennison has shown that the motion of sound sources structures that acoustic array such that higher order variables such as interaural delay, Doppler shift, and average sound intensity specify the kinematics of the source. There is some evidence that suggests that listeners may rely more heavily on some of these cues than others. Rosenblum, Carello, and Pastore (1987) examined the relative contribution of each of these cues in estimating time to contact with a simulated approaching source. They found that when interaural differences, monaural loudness change, and the Doppler effect are manipulated so that they specify different arrival times within the same stimulus, listeners rely most heavily on loudness change, followed by interaural time differences and, to a lesser extent, the Doppler effect.

Given the relative salience of a clear physical cue to the time of closest approach in both interaural time difference and monaural intensity change, perhaps the findings of Rosenblum *et al.* (1987) are not surprising. Both interaural time differences and monaural intensity change have salient physical characteristics that mark the point of closest passage for a sound source. Assuming that the listener is facing the straight-line path of the source perpendicularly (see Fig. 2), interaural differences shrink to zero when the source is at its closest point, and monaural intensity change is at its peak. The Doppler shift has no such salient characteristic. The change in frequency produced by the Doppler follows the formula

$$f_{obs} = f_{src} \left(\frac{v_{snd}}{v_{snd} - v_{src} \cos \theta} \right)$$

where f_{obs} = frequency observed, f_{src} = frequency of source, v_{src} = velocity of source, v_{snd} = velocity of sound, and θ = approach angle of source. For a constant-frequency approaching source, the frequency that arrives at the observation point is initially higher than the frequency that is emitted by the source. The observed frequency remains essentially constant at first, falls at a successively increasing rate as the source approaches, drops rapidly as the source passes, and finally drops at a successively decreasing rate as the source recedes (Fig. 2). The rate of the frequency drop depends on the distance from the observer to the path of the source. The magnitude of the frequency drop depends on the speed of the source.

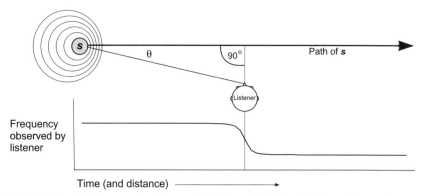

FIGURE 2 For a listener whose interaural axis is parallel to the path of a moving sound source, interaural differences shrink to zero when the source is at its closest point, and monaural intensity change is at its peak. The frequency at the listening point remains essentially constant at first, falls at a successively increasing rate as the source approaches, drops rapidly as the source passes, and finally drops at a successively decreasing rate as the source recedes.

At the point of closest passage, the frequency of the source is in the midst of a dramatic drop.

However, despite the drop in frequency, listeners tend to report hearing a rise in pitch as acoustic sources approach. The apparent paradox between falling frequency and the perception of rising pitch on approach has been termed the "Doppler illusion" (Neuhoff & McBeath, 1996). The effect is so pervasive that it has even worked itself into the physics literature. Many texts erroneously imply that approaching sources produce a rise in frequency on approach (McBeath & Neuhoff, 2002; Neuhoff & McBeath, 1996).

The pattern of rising intensity produced by an approaching source is particularly salient information on source approach. Shaw, McGowan, and Turvey (1991) have termed this pattern of change "acoustic tau," after the visual variable tau that specifies time to contact by the pattern of optical expansion produced by visual approaching objects. The derivation of acoustic tau by Shaw *et al.* shows that the acoustic change in intensity produced by a sound source moving rectilinearly toward a listener at a constant velocity specifies the time to contact with the listener.

However, whether listeners actually use this information to predict arrival time accurately is an issue of some debate. When asked to predict arrival time on the basis of auditory cues, listeners often err on the side of safety, expecting contact before the source actually arrives (Rosenblum, Wuestefeld, & Saldana, 1993; Schiff & Oldak, 1990). Alternatively, listeners have also been asked to estimate time to contact with a sound source while using intensity change to guide their locomotion toward a stationary source. Performance is slightly more accurate in this condition (Ashmead, Davis, & Northington, 1995; Rosenblum, Gordon, & Jarquin, 2000). However, the tendency to err on the side of safety is still apparent, with listeners stopping well short of the stationary target location.

Guski (1992) has suggested that perhaps this type of "error" should not be interpreted as such. He proposed that when a sound source and a listener are coming closer together, the primary role of the auditory system in localizing the source is that of warning, either to direct the visual system toward the object if time allows or to initiate appropriate behaviors to avoid the object. In this view, precise judgments about time to contact are not as important as a categorical decision about whether the listener has time to turn to look or must simply jump out of the way. This idea is echoed by Popper and Fay (1997), who suggested that the primary function of auditory localization may not be to provide exact estimates of source location but rather to provide input to the listener's perceptual model of the environment. Thus, under some circumstances distortions, errors, or biases in auditory localization may prove to be adaptive.

The relationship between monaural loudness change and auditory approach has received some attention. However, there is some debate about whether loudness change per se (for example, rising and falling intensity tones presented in headphones) can be equated with localizing approaching and receding sources. In one set of experiments, listeners reliably overestimated the change in intensity of rising loudness tones relative to equivalent falling intensity tones (Neuhoff, 1998). Listeners were presented with equivalent rising and falling intensity signals and asked to rate the amount of loudness change that occurred in each case. Despite an identical amount of loudness change (falling intensity signals were simply rising intensity signals played backward), listeners judged rising intensity tones to change more than falling tones. In a natural environment in the context of approaching and receding sources, this overestimation could provide a selective advantage because rising intensity can signal movement of the source toward a listener. The bias was found to be stronger at higher levels, suggesting that rising loudness is even more critical when a sound source is either close or loud. The bias was also specific to tones and did not occur with broadband noise. Tonal sounds are produced by a wide variety of single sound sources and in a natural environment are produced almost exclusively by biological organisms. Thus, anticipating such a source's approach is an important environmental event. However, tonal sounds are almost never produced by simultaneously sounding dispersed sources. Multiple sounding sources in a natural environment often result in the production of broadband noise. Thus, tonality can act as a reliable marker for single-source identity and can help listeners distinguish important signals from background noise. These results suggested a privileged status of dynamic rising loudness for harmonic tones and an asymmetry in the neural coding of harmonic dynamic intensity change that provides a selective advantage.

However, Canevet and colleagues have challenged the evolutionary implications of these findings. Simple loudness change in headphones is vastly different from the kind of acoustic change produced by an approaching source in a natural environment (Canévet, Scharf, Schlauch, Teghtsoonian, & Teghtsoonian, 1999). First, the intensity change produced by an approaching source follows the inverse-square law, whereby changes in intensity occur at a faster and faster rate as the source draws closer to the listener. The rate of intensity change used by Neuhoff (1998) was linear, thus specifying decelerating approaching sources and accelerating receding sources. Second, the sounds were heard through headphones, but the inferences made concerned free-field auditory motion. Consistent differences have been shown between both loudness and localization estimates with sounds heard in headphones and those heard in a free-field setting (e.g., (Hartley & Carpenter, 1974; Stream & Dirks, 1974; Wightman & Kistler, 1989)). Finally, listeners were asked simply to make estimates of loudness change. Although it is likely that monaural loudness change is a primary cue that listeners use to judge auditory source approach (Rosenblum, Carello, & Pastore, 1987), it is possible that the estimates of loudness change do not correspond well to estimates of distance change in a natural listening environment (but see Warren, 1958, 1963, for an alternative view).

To address these concerns, Neuhoff (2001) conducted three subsequent experiments. If listeners have indeed evolved to be more sensitive to approaching sounds than receding sounds based on intensity change, several predictions could be made. First, given equal change in intensity, rising intensity sounds should be perceived to change in loudness more than falling intensity sounds. Similarly, given equal stopping points in a natural environment, approaching sounds should be perceived as being closer than receding sounds. This would provide a margin of safety on approach that could provide a selective advantage. Second, at higher intensity levels, the disparity between rising and falling loudness change should be greater. A bias for rising intensity would be more advantageous for loud (close) sounds than for soft (distant) sounds. Finally, the bias for source approach should be greater for tones than for noise.

In the subsequent experiments, listeners heard approaching and receding sounds in an open field and indicated the perceived starting and stopping points of the auditory motion (see Fig. 3). Results showed that approaching sounds were perceived as starting and stopping closer than receding sounds despite the fact that all sounds had equal starting and stopping points (see Fig. 4). The effect was greater for tones than for noise. The evidence suggests that an asymmetry in the neural coding of approaching and receding auditory motion is an evolutionary adaptation that provides advanced warning of approaching acoustic sources. However, theories regarding the evolution of a perceptual characteristic must be evaluated carefully. It is, to say the least, difficult to do experiments that directly test evolutionary hypotheses in humans. Thus, converging evidence from different methods and perspectives is required.

Currently, there is psychophysical, physiological, and phylogenetic converging evidence that supports the role of the auditory system as a warning mechanism in processing approaching sources and the adaptive characteristics of the rising intensity bias. First, Schiff and Oldak (1990) examined accuracy in judging time to arrival in both the auditory and visual modalities. They specifically examined the effects of gender and source trajectory in each modality. In one

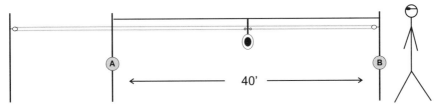

FIGURE 3   In Neuhoff (2001), blindfolded listeners heard approaching and receding sounds that had a common terminus. Approaching sounds began 40 feet from the listener (point A) and stopped at a distance of 20 feet. Receding sounds started at the listener (point B) and moved away 20 feet.

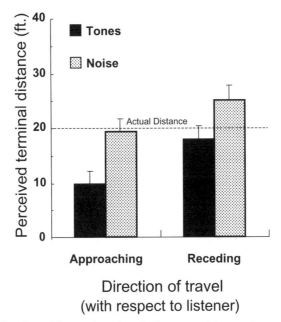

FIGURE 4   Despite equidistant points of termination, approaching sounds were perceived to stop significantly closer than receding sounds. Harmonic tones were perceived as stopping significantly closer than broadband noise.

condition the source was on a collision course with the listener. In another the source traveled a path that would bypass the listener at a safe distance. From an evolutionary perspective one would predict greater underestimation of time to contact when the source is on a collision course. Indeed, this is exactly what Schiff and Oldak found. Listeners underestimated arrival time across all conditions. However, the underestimation was greater when the source was on a collision course with the observer. Furthermore, the further the angle of approach was from a collision course, the more accurate time-to-arrival estimates were (Schiff & Oldak, 1990). Schiff and Oldak also found that females tended to underestimate arrival time more than males. It is unclear whether this underestimation is due to greater risk-taking behavior by males than females or better spatiotemporal skills. However, it should be noted that these results are consistent with hunter–gatherer theories of sex-specific spatial ability (Eals & Silverman, 1994; Silverman & Eals, 1992; Silverman & Phillips, 1998). In either case, the authors suggested that such cautious estimates of arrival time would provide survival benefits, particularly in situations in which judgment errors are likely.

Ashmead *et al.* (1995) investigated the case in which a listener is in motion toward a stationary sound source. They asked listeners to make auditory distance judgments as they listened to the source while walking toward it or while standing still. The information provided by the relative motion between the source and observer yielded better estimates of source location. However, walking to the source yielded estimates of source location that were closer to the listener than estimates made while listening in place. Ashmead *et al.* also manipulated the level of the source in order to make it appear nearer or farther from the listener. For example, as the listener approached, the intensity level of the source was either increased to make it sound nearer or decreased to make it sound farther. They found that increases in intensity produced appropriate undershooting of the target but that decreases did not produce the expected overshooting. This robust resistance to overshooting auditory targets supports the idea that the auditory system in localizing sources errs on the side of safety and acts as a warning system.

At the physiological level, there is evidence that cells in the auditory system are selective in processing directional motion and that neural firing rates in response to auditory motion can vary asymmetrically based on direction of travel (Doan & Saunders, 1999; Kautz & Wagner, 1998; Rauschecker & Harris, 1989; Wagner, Kautz, & Poganiatz, 1997; Wagner & Takahashi, 1992; Wilson & O'Neill, 1998). Evidence also comes from electrophysiological recordings, which show that a greater proportion of primary auditory cortical neurons are selective for rising intensity than for falling intensity (Lu, Liang, & Wang, 2001). Furthermore, the human brain mechanisms that process this perceptual bias have also been identified. Functional magnetic resonance imaging has demonstrated that specific motion-sensitive neural streams show anisotropic responses to rising versus falling intensity tones (Seifritz *et al.*, 2002). Rising intensity tones preferentially activate a neural network responsible for attention allocation, motor planning, and the translation of sensory input into ecologically appropriate action. All of these processes suggest preparation for the arrival of a looming acoustic source (see Fig. 5).

Finally, if the bias for rising intensity is truly a product of evolution, we would expect to see the same phenomenon in a closely related species. To test this hypothesis, rhesus monkeys were presented with equivalent rising and falling intensity tones and noise from a hidden loudspeaker (Ghazanfar, Neuhoff, & Logothetis, 2002). The duration of an orienting response (a head turn toward the loudspeaker) was measured after each stimulus presentation. The results showed that nonhuman primates exhibit a strikingly similar spectrum-specific bias for

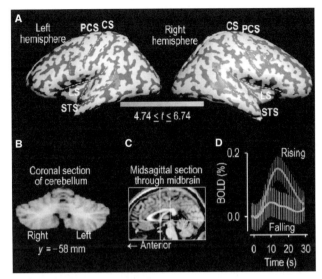

FIGURE 5   Cortical activation by "looming" compared with "receding" tones. (A) The general linear contrast "rising versus falling" intensity tones yielded a neural network comprising bilaterally the superior temporal sulci and the middle temporal gyri, the right temporoparietal junction encompassing the inferior portion of the angular gyrus, the right motor and lateral premotor cortices mainly on the right hemisphere, the left frontal operculum and discrete areas (B) in the left superior posterior cerebellar cortex and (C) in the midbrain (possibly representing the reticular formation). (D) Condition specific averaged (and standard errors; linear interpolation to one sample per second) blood oxygen level–dependent (BOLD) signal responses in all areas shown in (A)–(C). CS, central sulcus; LS, lateral sulcus; PCS, precentral sulcus; STS, superior temporal sulcus. The results indicate a preferential treatment of looming sounds and preparation for actions in response to auditory looming. (From Seifritz *et al.*, 2002.)

rising intensity. Subjects oriented over twice as long to rising intensity tones than to falling intensity tones (see Fig. 6). However, analogous to the human data, there was no difference in the duration of orienting to rising and falling intensity noise.

ECHOLOCATION

The human ability to use the auditory system to localize objects in the environment is perhaps most acute (and probably has the greatest ecological validity) in the case of blind listeners who use echolocation. In the strict sense of the term, echolocation is determining the location of objects in the environment on the basis of how they reflect sounds produced by the listener. However, some researchers have used the term to include the use of ambient reflected sound that is not produced by the listener (Ashmead & Wall, 1999; Ashmead *et al.*, 1998). Bats are perhaps the most proficient echolocating species, listening to reflected vocalizations for navigational guidance in three-dimensional flight as well as the

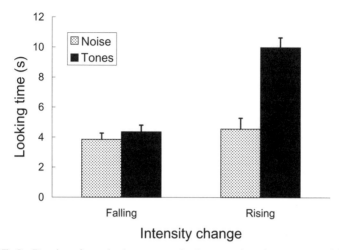

FIGURE 6   Duration of an orienting response in rhesus monkeys in response to rising versus falling intensity tones and noise. The results mirror the pattern of auditory looming results in humans. Rising intensity tones are given priority over falling intensity tones. However, there is no difference between rising and falling intensity noise (Ghazanfar, Neuhoff, & Logothetis, 2002).

tracking and capture of prey (Griffin, 1958). Humans rely predominantly on vision for localization, tracking, and navigation. Yet, despite the dominance of the visual system, humans have also been show to be able to use echolocation (for a review see Stoffregen & Pittenger, 1995).

Much of the work on human echolocation has involved blind participants. Early investigations examined what had been termed "facial vision," wherein blind participants could detect objects and obstacles that were at close range (Dallenbach, 1941; Supa, Cotzin, & Dallenbach, 1944). Prior to this work, there was some question about the modality that was actually used to detect obstacles. Many blind participants in earlier less systematic work insisted that they "felt" the presences of obstacles in their path. Many hypothesized that the ability of the blind to avoid obstacles was based on a tactile sense, perhaps based on changes in air pressure detected by the face (thus, the term facial vision).

However, Dallenbach and his colleagues (Dallenbach, 1941; Supa et al., 1944) showed unequivocally that the key to successful navigation around obstacles for the blind was echolocation. Several of these studies examined the ability of blind and blindfolded sighted listeners to detect a large obstacle as they approached it. The experiment was conducted indoors, and it was found that, in general, blind listeners could perform the task better than sighted listeners. Furthermore, performance was better when the motion of the listener produced sound. For example, performance was better when listeners made estimates while wearing shoes on a hardwood floor than when in stocking feet on carpet. The unequivocal evidence for acoustic rather than tactile cues was provided when a microphone was mechanically moved toward the obstacle, the output of which was fed through headphones to a listener in another room. Performance was equal to that which occurred when the listener approached the obstacle personally. Covering the skin and otherwise interfering with tactile senses decreased performance only slightly (presumably because the ears were also covered). However, preventing acoustic input by plugging the listener's ears resulted in an absolute failure to sense the obstacle on all trials. These main findings were replicated outdoors under conditions of higher ambient noise (Ammons, Worchel, & Dallenbach, 1953).

One case study examined the ability of a blind 11-year-old boy to ride a bicycle while avoiding obstacles (McCarty & Worchel, 1954). The boy rode a bicycle over a course in which two obstacles had been placed. He detected the obstacles by making a clicking sound with his mouth and listening for a difference in the pitch of the echo. After 40 trials without a collision, the boy was instructed to ride as swiftly as possible through the course. A similar level of performance was maintained at increased rates of speed. This particular ability has also been documented anecdotally elsewhere (Griffin, 1959). Other studies have shown that some listeners can use echolocation with remarkable accuracy to estimate object size and distance and as a general tool for mobility (Boehm, 1986; Rice & Feinstein, 1965a, 1965b; Rice, Feinstein, & Schusterman, 1965; Taylor, 1966).

With some exceptions, blind listeners have generally been shown to echolocate better than sighted listeners. In an effort to examine the psychoacoustic underpinnings of this finding, Arias and colleagues (1993) compared the peripheral and central auditory functioning of blind listeners who were good obstacle detectors with that of sighted listeners. Audiological tests and brainstem evoked responses showed that blind listeners were faster than sighted listeners in auditory processing. In addition, it was found that echolocating signals were processed more slowly than standard stimuli and that they may be processed in the superior olivary complex of the midbrain. Blind listeners have also been show to have improved spatial tuning in the auditory periphery when compared with sighted listeners (Roeder, Teder-Saelejaervi, Sterr, Hillyard, & Neville, 1999). Electrophysiological recordings suggest that this behavioral advantage stems from compensatory reorganization of brain areas.

Initially, it was thought that there was a relationship between high-frequency hearing and echolocation abilities. However, several investigations have brought this idea into question. Carlson-Smith and Weiner (1996) developed a battery of audiometric tests to examine what particular auditory skills are correlated with good echolocation abilities. In their examination of nine echolocators there was no relationship between high-frequency hearing and the ability to echolocate. Furthermore, Ashmead and colleagues (1998) found that blind children used primarily ambient low-frequency sounds to navigate successfully through artificially constructed hallways and walking paths.

It does appear that motion cues produced by movement of the echolocator improve localization estimates. Rosenblum et al. (2000) had listeners estimate the location of a wall by echolocating in a stationary condition or while walking.

There was a slight advantage in the walking condition, suggesting that listeners may use echoic time-to-contact information. Reflected sound can also be used to some extent to determine whether there is sufficient room between a sound source and a wall to permit unimpeded passage for the listener (Russell, 1997). Other work has shown that listeners can detect the presence of occluding objects between a sound source and the listener (Ader, 1935; Russell, 1997). However, in some cases occluding objects can make the source sound as though it is simply farther away.

It should be noted that echolocation is probably not a task that is used exclusively by the blind. Stoffregen and Pittenger (1995) have presented a detailed exposition of the types of information that are available to listeners via echolocation. In addition to distance and azimuth information about objects in the environment, there is within a reflected signal information that can specify characteristics of shape, material, size, motion, and time to contact. Stoffregen and Pittenger (1995) suggested that echolocation is used far more often than one might suppose and that a research focus on echolocating bats coupled with the dominance of the human visual system may obscure the often used but perhaps unnoticed echolocation skills of sighted listeners. Work showing that listeners can indeed discern shape, length, and material characteristics from objects that generate sound provides indirect support for this proposition (Carello, Anderson, & Kunkler-Peck, 1998; Kunkler-Peck & Turvey, 2000; Lakatos, McAdams, & Causse, 1997; Lutfi, 2001).

REFERENCES

Ader, H. (1935). Ein neues Hoerphaenomen. *Monatsschrift fuer Ohrenheilkunde* (5), 7.

Ammons, C. H., Worchel, P., & Dallenbach, K. M. (1953). "Facial vision": The perception of obstacles out of doors by blindfolded and blindfolded-deafened subjects. *American Journal of Psychology, 66,* 519–553.

Arias, C., Curet, C. A., Moyano, H. F., Joekes, S., *et al.* (1993). Echolocation: A study of auditory functioning in blind and sighted subjects. *Journal of Visual Impairment and Blindness, 87*(3), 73–77.

Ashmead, D. H., Clifton, R. K., & Perris, E. E. (1987). Precision of auditory localization in human infants. *Developmental Psychology, 23,* 641–647.

Ashmead, D. H., Davis, D. L., & Northington, A. (1995). Contribution of listeners' approaching motion to auditory distance perception. *Journal of Experimental Psychology: Human Perception and Performance, 21,* 239–256.

Ashmead, D. H., & Wall, R. S. (1999). Auditory perception of walls via spectral variations in the ambient sound field. *Journal of Rehabilitation Research and Development, 36,* 313–322.

Ashmead, D. H., Wall, R. S., Eaton, S. B., Ebinger, K. A., Snook-Hill, M.-M., Guth, D. A., & Yang, X. (1998). Echolocation reconsidered: Using spatial variations in the ambient sound field to guide locomotion. *Journal of Visual Impairment and Blindness, 92,* 615–632.

Barnecutt, P., & Pfeffer, K. (1998). Auditory perception of relative distance of traffic sounds. *Current Psychology: Developmental, Learning, Personality, Social, 17*(1), 93–101.

Baumgart, F., Gaschler-Markefski, B., Woldorff, M. G., Heinze, H. J., & Scheich, H. (1999). A movement-sensitive area in auditory cortex. *Nature, 400,* 724–726.

Blauert, J. (1969). Description of hearing experiments by means of a simple, system-theoretical model. *Kybernetik, 6*, 45–49.

Blauert, J. (1997). *Spatial hearing.* Cambridge, MA: MIT Press.

Boehm, R. (1986). The use of echolocation as a mobility aid for blind persons. *Journal of Visual Impairment and Blindness, 80*, 953–954.

Bronkhorst, A. W., & Houtgast, T. (1999). Auditory distance perception in rooms. *Nature, 397*, 517–520.

Canévet, G., Scharf, B., Schlauch, R. S., Teghtsoonian, M., & Teghtsoonian, R. (1999). Perception of changes in loudness. *Nature, 398*, 673.

Carello, C., Anderson, K. L., & Kunkler-Peck, A. J. (1998). Perception of object length by sound. *Psychological Science, 9*, 211–214.

Carlile, S., & Best, V. (2002). Discrimination of sound source velocity in human listeners. *Journal of the Acoustical Society of America, 111*, 1026–1035.

Carlson-Smith, C., & Weiner, W. R. (1996). The auditory skills necessary for echolocation: A new explanation. *Journal of Visual Impairment and Blindness, 90*, 21–35.

Clifton, R. K., Morrongiello, B. A., Kulig, J. W., & Dowd, J. M. (1981). Newborns' orientation toward sound: Possible implications for cortical development. *Child Development, 52*, 833–838.

Clifton, R. K., Rochat, P., Litovsky, R. Y., & Perris, E. E. (1991). Object representation guides infants' reaching in the dark. *Journal of Experimental Psychology: Human Perception and Performance, 17*, 323–329.

Clifton, R. K., Rochat, P., Robin, D. J., & Bertheir, N. E. (1994). Multimodal perception in the control of infant reaching. *Journal of Experimental Psychology: Human Perception and Performance, 20*, 876–886.

Coleman, P. D. (1959). Cortical correlates of auditory localization. *Science, 130*, 39–40.

Dallenbach, K. M. (1941). Facial vision: The perception of obstacles by the blind. *Psychological Bulletin, 38*, 610–611.

Doan, D. E., & Saunders, J. C. (1999). Sensitivity to simulated directional sound motion in the rat primary auditory cortex. *Journal of Neurophysiology, 81*, 2075–2087.

Eals, M., & Silverman, I. (1994). The hunter-gatherer theory of spatial sex differences: Proximate factors mediating the female advantage in recall of object arrays. *Ethology and Sociobiology, 15*(2), 95–105.

Fitzpatrick, D. C., Batra, R., Stanford, T. R., & Kuwada, S. (1997). A neuronal population code for sound localization. *Nature, 388*, 871–874.

Ghazanfar, A. A., Neuhoff, J. G., & Logothetis, N. K. (2002). Auditory looming perception in rhesus monkeys. *Proceedings of the National Academy of Sciences USA, 99*, 15755–15757.

Grantham, D. W. (1997). Auditory motion perception: Snapshots revisited. In R. H. Gilkey & T. R. Anderson (Eds.), *Binaural and spatial hearing in real and virtual environments* (pp. 295–313). Hillsdale, NJ: Lawrence Erlbaum Associates.

Grantham, W. D. (1985). Auditory spatial resolution under static and dynamic conditions. *Journal of the Acoustical Society of America, Suppl. 1, 77*, S50.

Graziano, M. S. A., Reiss, L. A. J., & Gross, C. G. (1999). A neuronal representation of the location of nearby sounds. *Nature, 397*, 428–430.

Griffin, D. R. (1958). *Listening in the dark: The acoustic orientation of bats and men.* New Haven, CT: Yale University Press.

Griffin, D. R. (1959). *Echoes of bats and men.* New York: Anchor Books.

Griffiths, T. D., Bench, C. J., & Frackowiak, R. S. (1994). Human cortical areas selectively activated by apparent sound movement. *Current Biology, 4*, 892–895.

Griffiths, T. D., Green, G. G., Rees, A., & Rees, G. (2000). Human brain areas involved in the analysis of auditory movement. *Human Brain Mapping, 9*(2), 72–80.

Guski, R. (1992). Acoustic tau: An easy analogue to visual tau? *Ecological Psychology, 4*, 189–197.

Harris, J. D., & Sergeant, R. L. (1971). Monaural/binaural minimum audible angles for a moving sound source. *Journal of Speech and Hearing Research, 14*, 618–629.

Hartley, L. R., & Carpenter, A. (1974). Comparison of performance with headphone and free-field noise. *Journal of Experimental Psychology, 103*, 377–380.

Hecox, K. (1975). Electro-physiological correlates of human auditory development. In L. B. Cohen and P. Salapatek (Eds.), *Infant perception: From sensation to cognition*. New York: Academic Press.

Jenison, R. L. (1997). On acoustic information for motion. *Ecological Psychology, 9*(2), 131–151.

Kautz, D., & Wagner, H. (1998). GABAergic inhibition influences auditory motion-direction sensitivity in barn owls. *Journal of Neurophysiology, 80*, 172–185.

Kunkler-Peck, A. J., & Turvey, M. T. (2000). Hearing shape. *Journal of Experimental Psychology: Human Perception and Performance, 26*, 279–294.

Lakatos, S., McAdams, S., & Causse, R. (1997). The representation of auditory source characteristics: Simple geometric form. *Perception and Psychophysics, 59*, 1180–1190.

Litovsky, R. Y., & Clifton, R. K. (1992). Use of sound-pressure level in auditory distance discrimination by 6-month-old infants and adults. *Journal of the Acoustical Society of America, 92*(2, Pt 1), 794–802.

Little, A. D., Mershon, D. H., & Cox, P. H. (1992). Spectral content as a cue to perceived auditory distance. *Perception, 21*, 405–416.

Loomis, J. M., Hebert, C., & Cicinelli, J. G. (1990). Active localization of virtual sounds. *Journal of the Acoustical Society of America, 88*, 1757–1764.

Lu, T., Liang, L., & Wang, X. (2001). Neural representations of temporally asymmetric stimuli in the auditory cortex of awake primates. *Journal of Neurophysiology, 85*, 2364–2380.

Lutfi, R. A. (2001). Auditory detection of hollowness. *Journal of the Acoustical Society of America, 110*, 1010–1019.

Makous, J. C., & Middlebrooks, J. C. (1990). Two-dimensional sound localization by human listeners. *Journal of the Acoustical Society of America, 87*, 2188–2200.

McBeath, M. K., & Neuhoff, J. G. (2002). The Doppler effect is not what you think it is: Dramatic pitch change due to dynamic intensity change. *Psychonomic Bulletin and Review, 9*, 306–313.

McCarty, B., & Worchel, P. (1954). Rate of motion and object perception in the blind. *New Outlook for the Blind, 48*, 316–322.

Mershon, D. H., Ballenger, W. L., Little, A. D., McMurtry, P. L., et al. (1989). Effects of room reflectance and background noise on perceived auditory distance. *Perception, 18*, 403–416.

Mershon, D. H., & Bowers, J. N. (1979). Absolute and relative cues for the auditory perception of egocentric distance. *Perception, 8*, 311–322.

Mershon, D. H., & King, L. E. (1975). Intensity and reverberation as factors in the auditory perception of egocentric distance. *Perception and Psychophysics, 18*, 409–415.

Middlebrooks, J. C., & Green, D. M. (1990). Directional dependence of interaural envelope delays. *Journal of the Acoustical Society of America, 87*, 2149–2162.

Middlebrooks, J. C., Clock, A. E., Xu, L., & Green, D. M. (1994). A panoramic code for sound location by cortical neurons. *Science, 264*, 842–844.

Middlebrooks, J. C., Xu, L., Clock, A. E., & Green, D. M. (1998). Codes for sound-source location in nontonotopic auditory cortex. *Journal of Neurophysiology, 80*, 863–881.

Mills, A. W. (1958). On the minimum audible angle. *Journal of the Acoustical Society of America, 30*, 237–246.

Morrongiello, B. A. (1988). Infants' localization of sounds along the horizontal axis: Estimates of minimum audible angle. *Developmental Psychology, 24*, 8–13.

Morrongiello, B. A., Fenwick, K. D., Hillier, L., & Chance, G. (1994). Sound localization in newborn human infants. *Developmental Psychobiology, 27*, 519–538.

Muir, D. W., Clifton, R. K., & Clarkson, M. G. (1989). The development of a human auditory localization response: A U-shaped function. *Canadian Journal of Psychology, 43*, 199–216.

Neuhoff, J. G. (1998). Perceptual bias for rising tones. *Nature, 395*, 123–124.

Neuhoff, J. G. (2001). An adaptive bias in the perception of looming auditory motion. *Ecological Psychology, 13*, 87–110.

Neuhoff, J. G., & McBeath, M. K. (1996). The Doppler illusion: The influence of dynamic intensity change on perceived pitch. *Journal of Experimental Psychology: Human Perception and Performance, 22*, 970–985.

Neuhoff, J. G., Rodstrom, M. A., & Vaidya, T. (2001). The audible facing angle. *Acoustic Research Letters Online, 2*, 109–114.

Oldfield, S. R., & Parker, S. P. (1984). Acuity of sound localisation: A topography of auditory space: I. Normal hearing conditions. *Perception, 13*, 581–600.

Pavani, F., Macaluso, E., Warren, J. D., Driver, J., & Griffiths, T. D. (2002). A common cortical substrate activated by horizontal and vertical sound movement in the human brain. *Current Biology, 12*, 1584–1590.

Perrett, S., & Noble, W. (1995). Available response choices affect localization of sound. *Perception and Psychophysics, 57*, 150–158.

Perrott, D. R., Costantino, B., & Ball, J. (1993). Discrimination of moving events which accelerate or decelerate over the listening interval. *Journal of the Acoustical Society of America, 93*, 1053–1057.

Perrott, D. R., Marlborough, K., Merrill, P., & Strybel, T. Z. (1989). Minimum audible angle thresholds obtained under conditions in which the precedence effect is assumed to operate. *Journal of the Acoustical Society of America, 85*, 282–288.

Perrott, D. R., & Musicant, A. D. (1981). Dynamic minimum audible angle: Binaural spatial acuity with moving sound sources. *Journal of Auditory Research, 21*, 287–295.

Perrott, D. R., & Saberi, K. (1990). Minimum audible angle thresholds for sources varying in both elevation and azimuth. *Journal of the Acoustical Society of America, 87*, 1728–1731.

Popper, A. N., & Fay, R. R. (1997). Evolution of the ear and hearing: Issues and questions. *Brain, Behavior and Evolution, 50*, 213–221.

Pratt, C. C. (1930). The spatial character of high and low tones. *Journal of Experimental Psychology, 13*, 278–285.

Rauschecker, J. P., & Harris, L. R. (1989). Auditory and visual neurons in the cat's superior colliculus selective for the direction of apparent motion stimuli. *Brain Research, 490*, 56–63.

Rayleigh, L. (1907). On our perception of sound direction. *Philosophical Magazine, 13*, 214–232.

Rice, C. E., & Feinstein, S. H. (1965a). The influence of target parameters on a human echo-detection task. *Proceedings of the Annual Convention of the American Psychological Association* (pp. 65–66).

Rice, C. E., & Feinstein, S. H. (1965b). Sonar system of the blind: Size discrimination. *Science, 148*, 1107–1108.

Rice, C. E., Feinstein, S. H., & Schusterman, R. J. (1965). Echo-detection ability of the blind: Size and distance factors. *Journal of Experimental Psychology, 70*, 246–251.

Roeder, B., Teder-Saelejaervi, W., Sterr, A., Roesler, F., Hillyard, S. A., & Neville, H. J. (1999). Improved auditory spatial tuning in blind humans. *Nature, 400*, 162–166.

Roffler, S. K., & Butler, R. A. (1968a). Factors that influence the localization of sound in the vertical plane. *Journal of the Acoustical Society of America, 43*, 1255–1259.

Roffler, S. K., & Butler, R. A. (1968b). Localization of tonal stimuli in the vertical plane. *Journal of the Acoustical Society of America, 43*, 1260–1266.

Rosenblum, L. D., Carello, C., & Pastore, R. E. (1987). Relative effectiveness of three stimulus variables for locating a moving sound source. *Perception, 16*, 175–186.

Rosenblum, L. D., Gordon, M. S., & Jarquin, L. (2000). Echolocating distance by moving and stationary listeners. *Ecological Psychology, 12*, 181–206.

Rosenblum, L. D., Wuestefeld, A. P., & Anderson, K. L. (1996). Auditory reachability: An affordance approach to the perception of sound source distance. *Ecological Psychology, 8*, 1–24.

Rosenblum, L. D., Wuestefeld, A. P., & Saldana, H. M. (1993). Auditory looming perception: Influences on anticipatory judgments. *Perception, 22*, 1467–1482.

Russell, M. K. (1997). Acoustic perception of sound source occlusion. In M. A. Schmuckler and J. M. Kennedy (Eds.), *Studies in perception and action IV: Ninth International Conference on Perception and Action* (pp. 92–94). Mahwah, NJ: Erlbaum.

Saberi, K., & Perrott, D. R. (1990). Lateralization thresholds obtained under conditions in which the precedence effect is assumed to operate. *Journal of the Acoustical Society of America, 87,* 1732–1737.

Scharf, B., & Houtsma, A. J. M. (1986). Audition II: Loudness, pitch, localization, aural distortion, pathology. In K. R. Boff, L. Kaufman, and J. P. Thomas (Eds.), *Handbook of perception and human performance.* New York: John Wiley.

Schiff, W., & Oldak, R. (1990). Accuracy of judging time to arrival: Effects of modality, trajectory, and gender. *Journal of Experimental Psychology Human Perception and Performance, 16,* 303–316.

Seifritz, E. ••.

Seifritz, E., Neuhoff, J. G., Bilecen, D., Scheffler, D., Mustovic, H., Schächinger, H., Elefante, R., & Di Salle, F. (2002). Neural processing of auditory "looming" in the human brain. *Current Biology, 12,* 2147–2151.

Shaw, B. K., McGowan, R. S., & Turvey, M. T. (1991). An acoustic variable specifying time-to-contact. *Ecological Psychology, 3,* 253–261.

Shinn-Cunningham, B. G., Santarelli, S., & Kopco, N. (2000). Tori of confusion: Binaural localization cues for sources within reach of a listener. *Journal of the Acoustical Society of America, 107,* 1627–1636.

Silverman, I., & Eals, M. (1992). Sex differences in spatial abilities: Evolutionary theory and data. In J. H. Barkow, L. Cosmides, *et al.* (Eds.), *The adapted mind: Evolutionary psychology and the generation of culture* (pp. 533–549). New York: Oxford University Press.

Silverman, I., & Phillips, K. (1998). The evolutionary psychology of spatial sex differences. In C. B. Crawford and D. L. Krebs (Eds.), *Handbook of eolutionary psychology: Ideas, issues, and application* (pp. 595–612). Mahwah, NJ: Erlbaum.

Stevens, S. S., & Newman, E. B. (1936). The localization of actual sources of sound. *American Journal of Psychology, 48,* 297–306.

Stoffregen, T. A., & Pittenger, J. B. (1995). Human echolocation as a basic form of perception and action. *Ecological Psychology, 7,* 181–216.

Stream, R. W., & Dirks, D. D. (1974). Effect of loudspeaker position on differences between earphone and free-field thresholds (MAP and MAF). *Journal of Speech and Hearing Research, 17,* 549–568.

Supa, M., Cotzin, M., & Dallenbach, K. M. (1944). "Facial vision"; the perception of obstacles by the blind. *American Journal of Psychology, 57,* 133–183.

Taylor, J. G. (1966). Perception generated by training echolocation. *Canadian Journal of Psychology, 20,* 64–81.

Trimble, O. C. (1934). Localozation of sound in the anterior-posterior and vertical dimensions of "auditory" space. *British Journal of Psychology, 24,* 320–334.

Wagner, H., Kautz, D., & Poganiatz, I. (1997). Principles of acoustic motion detection in animals and man. *Trends in Neurosciences, 20,* 583–588.

Wagner, H., & Takahashi, T. (1992). Influence of temporal cues on acoustic motion-direction sensitivity of auditory neurons in the owl. *Journal of Neurophysiology, 68,* 2063–2076.

Warren, J. D., Zielinski, B. A., Green, G. G., Rauschecker, J. P., & Griffiths, T. D. (2002). Perception of sound-source motion by the human brain. *Neuron, 34,* 139–148.

Warren, R. M. (1958). A basis for judgments of sensory intensity. *American Journal of Psychology, 71,* 675–687.

Warren, R. M. (1963). Are loudness judgments based on distance estimates? *Journal of the Acoustical Society of America, 35,* 613–614.

Wightman, F. L., & Kistler, D. J. (1989). Headphone simulation of free-field listening: II. Psychophysical validation. *Journal of the Acoustical Society of America, 85,* 868–878.

Wilson, W. W., & O'Neill, W. E. (1998). Auditory motion induces directionally dependent receptive field shifts in inferior colliculus neurons. *Journal of Neurophysiology, 79,* 2040–2062.

Xu, L., Furukawa, S., & Middlebrooks, J. C. (1999). Auditory cortical responses in the cat to sounds that produce spatial illusions. *Nature, 399,* 688–691.

Zahorik, P. (2002). Assessing auditory distance perception using virtual acoustics. *Journal of the Acoustical Society of America, 111,* 1832–1846.

5

FROM GIBSON'S FIRE

TO GESTALTS

A BRIDGE-BUILDING THEORY OF
PERCEPTUAL OBJECTHOOD

DAVID VAN VALKENBURG AND
MICHAEL KUBOVY

Two kinds of rifts separate perceptual researchers: theoretical and modality specific. Theoretical rifts divide modality-specific communities, and modality-specific rifts divide theoretical communities. Each group seeks to understand perception, but each uses such different approaches that synthesis into one coherent theory has been impossible. Here, we examine the fissures and propose a theory of perceptual objecthood that closes them.

Neuhoff (Chap. 1) discusses theoretical rifts in audition. He distinguishes the *constructivist psychoacousticians*, who use simple stimuli and well-controlled artificial environments to explore lower level sensory processes, from the *ecologists*, who use real-world stimuli and less controlled environments to explore higher level sensation, cognition, and behavior. Both groups have learned a great deal about auditory perception, but the lack of a unified framework makes it difficult for them to share their knowledge.

The gap between types of modality specificity is even wider. Most researchers work within a modality-specific community which has its own theories and terminology. Gibson (1966) illustrated this problem with his description of a fire,

> [A] terrestrial event with flames and fuel. It is a source of four kinds of stimulation, since it gives off sound, odor, heat and light. . . . One can hear it, smell it, feel it, and see it, or get any combination of these detections, and thereby perceive a fire. . . . For this event, the four kinds of stimulus information and the four perceptual systems are *equivalent*. If the perception of fire were a compound of separate sensations of sound, smell, warmth and color, they would have had to be associated in past experience in order to explain how any one of them could evoke memories of all the others, But if the perception of fire is

---

simply the pickup of information the *perception* will be the same whatever system is activated, although, of course, the conscious sensations will not be the same. (pp. 54–55)

Gibson understood, as is now commonly recognized (Spence & Driver, 1997, 1998, 1999; Stein & Meredith, 1993), that a theory of perception should have something to say about all modalities (see also Rosenblum, Chap. 9). Unfortunately, even Gibson focused his theories on visual perception and made no attempt to include other modalities.

In this chapter, we seek to solve this problem. The key to our solution is the development of a modality-neutral theory of objecthood that captures perceptual commonalities between the modalities. First, we point out the importance of perceptual objecthood. Second, we move from a discussion of the historical and modern perspectives on auditory objecthood, audition being our primary focus, to our modality-neutral theory of perceptual objecthood. We demonstrate how modality-neutral objecthood can be applied and discuss the implications for auditory perception. Third, we describe how our theory, combined with new methodology, begins to create a unified theory. Finally, we discuss the problem of ecological validity and future research directions.

THE IMPORTANCE OF OBJECTHOOD

To bridge the chasms between the variety of theoretical and modality-specific approaches, we need to assess what they have in common: perceptual organization.

Gibson (1966) provides a starting point in the passage we quoted previously, where he says of his ecological theory:

> In this theory the problem of perception is not how sensations get associated; it is *how the sound, the odor, the warmth, or the light that specifies fire gets discriminated from all the other sounds, odors, warmths, and lights that do not specify fire.* (p. 55)

In vision, the input to our eyes is a constantly changing, two-dimensional array of light, but what we *see* is organized. We experience our ecology grouped into separable, three-dimensional wholes, or *objects*. Likewise, in audition, even though the input to our ears is an undifferentiated stream of variation of pressure, what we *hear* is organized. We experience our *echology* grouped into voices, sources, or *auditory objects*.

Perceptual organization is thus common to all modalities. This fundamental basis is too often overshadowed by debates over such issues as the basic function of perception (i.e., reconstructing perceptual objects from deconstructed elements vs. picking up affordances) or the "correct" way to study perceptual systems (i.e., with contrived sounds in a laboratory or with naturally occurring sounds in a natural environment). Rather than being treated as a unifying concept, issues of perceptual organization and subsequent theories of perceptual objecthood have become the basis for theoretical rifts among researchers.

According to Gibson, there are two obstacles to understanding perceptual organization: (1) how does the system know how many groups to form and (2) how does the system know which components belong to which group? If we can surmount these obstacles, we will understand grouping. And if we can understand grouping, we will better understand perception.

In audition, a variety of approaches have been tried. Here again, approaches have varied so widely that reconciling results has proved difficult. Here, we review some of these approaches and show why each is insufficient for the purpose of linking the various modalities.

THE GESTALT PERSPECTIVE

Traditional Gestalt theories of grouping and objecthood have relied on demonstrations (Fig. 1) and have therefore been vague and qualitative. Furthermore, they were often formulated from a visuocentric point of view and not much heed was paid to their auditory counterparts. There is, however, little doubt that Gestalt grouping principles apply to audition. Bregman (1990) lists numerous examples, including grouping by frequency proximity, spectral similarity, and common fate. Yet, just as with the visual counterparts, even Bregman's analysis is primarily qualitative.

Aside from the qualitative nature of the traditional Gestalt approach, it does have merits. Gibson (1982) says:

> There is a need to study the perception of surfaces with a realistic attitude as well as a phenomenological attitude. What we need is a theory that can relate conscious sensation to the pickup of information. The approach advocated is much closer to Gestalt theory than it is to input processing theory. It is a sort of ecological Gestalt theory. (p. 156)

In other words, because the Gestalt approach is rooted in phenomenology, it is concerned with conscious perception. Gibson's work, on the other hand, was primarily concerned with the pickup of information. Here we see Gibson recognizing that a full account of perception must be adequate to deal with both of these aspects. The approach that we suggest here is not incompatible with either the Gestalt or the Gibsonian approach.

FIGURE 1   Grouping partitions a set of discrete entities into mutually exclusive subsets, called *blocks*. (Top) Grouping by proximity. (Bottom) Grouping by similarity. (From Wertheimer, 1923/1938.)

THE SPATIAL METAPHOR

In the past, theorists and researchers often conceived of audition as a spatial phenomenon—they explicitly or implicitly assumed that the primary function of the auditory system was to analyze the spatial aspects of sound and that auditory objects were spatial entities. This bias stems from a general presupposition that all reality is contained in space and time, which can be traced at least back to Newton (1726/1999), who said, "Absolute, true, and mathematical time, in and of itself and of its own nature, without reference to anything external, flows uniformly. . . . Absolute space, of its own nature without reference to anything external, always remains homogeneous and immovable. . . . times and spaces are, as it were, the places of themselves and of all things" (pp. 408–410). In his *Critique of Pure Reason*, Kant (1787/1996) took Newton's idea further: "Space is not an empirical concept that has been abstracted from outer experiences. For the presentation of space must already lie at the basis in order for certain sensations to be referred to something outside of me . . ." (p. 77, B 38).[1] "Time is not an empirical concept that has been abstracted from any experience. For simultaneity or succession would not even enter our perception if the presentation of time did not underlie them a priori" (p. 85, B 46).

The spatial conception of audition emerged in the mid-20th century. How do we segregate one voice from others at a cocktail party? According to Cherry (1959), the problem is spatial. His experiments involved dichotic listening: the listener hears a different message in each ear and has to report something from one or both. The implicit primacy of space is even clearer in Broadbent (1958): "Sounds reaching the two ears are of course often perceived as coming from different directions . . . and such sounds we will regard as arriving by different 'channels' " (p. 15).

There are two reasons why the spatial conception of objecthood does not apply to auditory perception:

1. According to the *Oxford English Dictionary*, *object* means "Something placed before the eyes, or presented to the sight or other sense; an individual thing seen or perceived, or that may be seen or perceived; a material thing" ("object," 1993). The word's Latin roots are *ob-*, "before" or "toward," and *iacere*, "to throw." It used to mean, "Something 'thrown' or put in the way, so as to interrupt or obstruct the course of a person or thing; an obstacle, a hindrance" ("object," 1993). Language itself implies that objects are visible, and that they exhibit opacity. Auditory objects are, of course, not visible—but, more important, there is no auditory analog of opacity. Bregman (1990), in his discussion of the auditory continuity illusion, explains why this is true. When one deletes part of a signal and replaces it with a louder sound, one hears auditory continuity: the signal is perceived to continue uninterrupted "behind" the sound.

---

[1] This denotes p. 38 in the second edition (B) of the *Critique*.

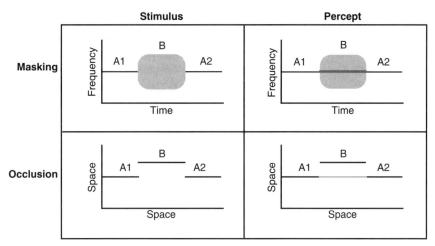

FIGURE 2   The auditory continuity illusion (top) compared with the visual effect of continuity behind an occluder (bottom).

Bregman compares this illusion with the visual experience of continuity behind an occluder (Fig. 2): "Let us designate the interrupted sound or visual surface as A, and consider it to be divided into A1 and A2 by B, the interrupting entity. . . . [In vision one] object's surface must end exactly where the other begins and the contours of A must reach dead ends where they visually meet the outline of B. In the auditory modality, the evidence for the continuity occurs in the properties of B itself as well as in A1 and A2; B must give rise to a set of neural properties that contain those of the missing part of A. In vision, on the other hand, if objects are opaque, there is no hint of the properties of A in the visual region occupied by B" (p. 383).

2. There is a fundamental difference between the primary types of information with which the visual and auditory systems are concerned. The auditory system is generally concerned with *sources* of sound (such as speech or music), not with *surfaces* that reflect the sound (Bregman, 1990, pp. 36–38). Indeed, the auditory system compensates for the distortion of spectral envelope (the major determinant of the perceived identity of many sounds) caused by factors such as room reverberation (Watkins, 1991, 1998, 1999; Watkins & Makin, 1996). For the visual system the opposite is true: it is generally concerned with *surfaces* of objects, not with the *sources* that illuminate them. As Mellon (1995) points out (giving credit to Monge, 1789),

> our visual system is built to recognize . . . permanent properties of objects, their spectral reflectances, . . . not . . . the spectral flux. . . . (pp. 148–149.)

MODERN THEORIES OF AUDITORY OBJECTHOOD

"Nearly 50 years after Cherry (1959) described the cocktail party problem, his most important question remains unanswered: How do humans listen to and understand what one person is saying when there are many people speaking at the same time?" (Feng & Ratnam, 2000, p. 717). It is clear that the spatial conception of objecthood, while it does apply to visual objects and it has become central to the study of visual perception, is not sufficient to account for the perception of auditory objects (Feng & Ratnam, 2000; Kubovy & Van Valkenburg, 2001; Van Valkenburg & Kubovy, 2003; Wightman & Jenison, 1995). Many modern researchers acknowledge the shortcomings of this spatial conception, but few have attempted to offer an alternative. So the notion of auditory objecthood has remained vague or undefined in modern research.

Based on a review of modern perspectives in auditory theory and research, we differentiate three nonspatial approaches to the notion of object: auditory events, auditory streams, and products of figure–ground segregation. In the following, we briefly discuss the merits and pitfalls of each approach.

Some researchers believe only in auditory "events," not in auditory "objects" (Blauert, 1997; Fowler, 1994; Gaver, 1993; also see Rosenblum, Chap. 9). This preference for the term "event" in auditory perception is often associated with an ecological perspective. For example, Fowler (1994) proposes that we explore auditory perception as the direct perception of events, in a manner analogous to Gibson's theory of direct perception of layouts in vision. The reasoning behind this approach is straightforward: sound is the result of an abrupt change in the environment (i.e., there must be an interaction between solid objects to produce the atmospheric disturbance that propagates to the observer), therefore the perception of sound is the perception of events.

Rosenblum, in this volume (Chap. 9), presents a compelling argument for the event perspective. He is also trying to find a cross-modal conception of perceptual operations, but he offers a radically different solution. Whereas we advocate dropping the term *event* in favor of *object* across modalities, his solution is to drop *object* in favor of *event* across modalities. His position has a distinguished pedigree: Socrates (in Plato's *Cratylus* 402A) says,

> Heraclitus of Ephesus[2] says somewhere that "everything gives way and nothing stands fast," and likening the things that are to the flowing of a river, he says that "you cannot step into the same river twice." (Cooper, 1997, p. 120.)

It might seem then that Rosenblum is a follower of Heraclitus. But Aristotle's more explicit presentation (in the *Physics*, Θ3, 253b9) aligns Heraclitus with our position:

> And some say that some existing things are moving, and not others, but that all things are in motion all the time, but that *this escapes our perception*. (Emphasis ours, Kirk & Raven, 1962, p. 197.)

---

[2] Active before 480 BCE.

Although the *physical* world is properly understood as a dynamical system, expressible as a massive collection of differential equations, phenomenologically speaking, the world is a collection of objects, not events or processes.

Those who believe that events are fundamental are committing the *stimulus error* (Boring, 1921; Savardi & Bianchi, 1999): they are confusing our phenomenological ecology, with what we—as scientists—know about our ecology. Most events do manifest themselves in more than one medium: the hammer hitting the nail is visible, audible, and tactile. Furthermore, the information conveyed in these different media is about the same event. This, however, is an account of information *outside* the experiencing individual. Because we are concerned with explaining perceptual phenomenology, our modality-neutral theory of objecthood (see later) is about linking modality-specific phenomenology *within* an observer.

We cannot attempt to argue our stand in detail in this chapter. It is not an easy argument to defend. Indeed, some philosophers hold that the analogies between objects and events are so strong as to make them interchangeable (Casati & Varzi, 1999, §10.1). In many ways they are *duals*. A striking example of duality can be found in projective geometry, where all the theorems can be arranged in pairs: if a theorem is true, then its dual—obtained by interchanging the terms "point" and "line"—is also true (Figs. 3 and 4).

Mayo (1961) presents a thoroughgoing analysis of the duality of objects and events (see also Casati & Varzi, 1999, Chap. 10), which he calls the "complementarity hypothesis." He offers five statements about objects and their duals about events (Table 1). He takes the fact that both statements in each pair make sense as evidence in favor of his hypothesis.

The event conception is appealing, but it does not help us to address questions about perceptual organization. Consider the act of plucking a guitar string: the sound *event* consists of a mechanical disturbance that forces a nylon string to

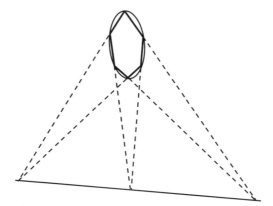

FIGURE 3   Pascal's theorem: If a hexagon is inscribed (*vertices* touch the curve) in a conic section (an ellipse, a parabola, or a hyperbola), the three pairs of the continuations of *opposite sides* meet on a *straight line*, called the *Pascal line*. Each pair of *lines* share a *point*; the three points of incidence of the three pairs of *opposite sides* share a line.

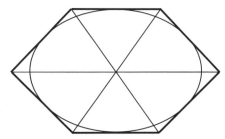

FIGURE 4   Brianchon's theorem: If a hexagon is circumscribed (*lines* touch the curve) in a conic section, the three lines joining *opposite vertices* meet in a *single point*. Each pair of *points* share a line; the three lines that connect pairs of *opposite vertices* share a *point*. This is the dual of Pascal's theorem.

TABLE 1   Evidence for Mayo's complementarity hypothesis

An object	An event
1 (a) Has a limited *extension* and an unlimited *duration*;	Has a limited *duration* and an unlimited *extension*;
(b) It cannot take up the whole of *space*, but it could take up the whole of *time*;	It cannot take up the whole of *time*, but it could take up the whole of *space*;
(c) There must be room in *space* for the many *objects*, which may or may not overlap *temporally*.	There must be room in *time* for the many *events*, which may or may not overlap *spatially*.
2 Can, at different *times*, take up the same *space* (rest, endurance) or different *spaces*, normally of the same *size* (locomotion, endurance).	Can, at different *places*, take up the same *time* (occurrence, extension) or different *times*, normally of the same *length* ("propagation," extension).
3 Cannot be at different *places* at the same *time*, unless its *spatial* size is greater than the interval between the *places*.	Cannot be at different *times* at the same *place*, unless its *temporal* size is greater than the interval between the *times*.

vibrate at 440 Hz; the sound *percept* is the note *A*. It seems logical to equate *event* with *percept* in this context because the percept, *A*, corresponds directly to one event. The story is more confusing, however, when we consider more complex cases. If the guitarist (or a group of guitarists) begins to play multiple notes in succession, we may perceive a melody rather than a collection of individual notes. Is the perception of a melody, which is caused by multiple physical events, to be labeled as multiple perceptual events—even though the phenomenological percept is that of one melody? There is a numerical correspondence problem here—there is not necessarily a one-to-one correspondence between the number of sound events and the number of sound percepts. So, even if we were to adopt "event" as a formal characterization of sound perception, it does not help us to solve Cherry's cocktail party problem. We would still need to address the problem of how the system knows how many events there are, which events should be grouped together, and which events should not.

A second conception of auditory objecthood relies on Bregman's (1990) notion of *stream* (Alain, Arnott, & Picton, 2001; Brochard, Drake, Botte, & McAdams, 1999; Darwin & Hukin, 1999; Izumi, 2002). Perceptual elements are extracted from the auditory signal on the basis of features (or, put another way, the auditory system analyzes the incoming signal for features) and then these elements are combined following Gestalt-like principles (grouping by physical similarity, temporal proximity, good continuity, etc.) into perceptual streams, or auditory objects, to form the auditory scene (Bregman, 1990; see Cusak & Carlyon in this volume). A classic demonstration of streaming is illustrated in Fig. 5A (Bregman, 1990; van Noorden, 1975). Observers listen to two-tone patterns in which two mutually exclusive organizations can be heard: (1) If the two tones are close in frequency, or the listener has little experience with such patterns, an unambiguous galloping rhythm is heard (Fig. 5B), in which the high and the low tones form a single stream; (2) If the two tones are sufficiently different *and* some time has elapsed from the beginning of the pattern, it splits into two streams. These two streams are ambiguous because one can focus on the high-frequency stream or the low-frequency stream. The high-frequency stream consists of a regularly

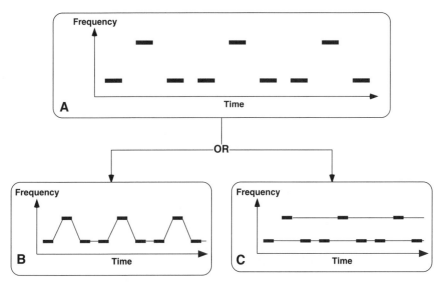

FIGURE 5   An example of auditory streaming. The sequence in panel *A* is perceived by a listener either as in panel *B* or as in panel *C*.

repeating double beat. The low-frequency stream sounds like a $\frac{3}{4}$ time signature with two quarter-notes followed by a rest (Fig. 5C).

There is much that is attractive about the stream conception of auditory object-hood. To anyone who has listened to demonstrations like the one depicted in Fig. 5, the experience of streaming is convincing. Also, the appeal to Gestalt principles is attractive because it suggests a direct analogy with vision. It implies that the mechanisms by which perceptual entities are formed in vision and audition might have commonalities. However, this approach suffers from the same flaw as the "event" approach: it separates auditory objects from other kinds of objects. For example, it does not help solve the problems posed by Gibson's fire; we are left trying to correlate visual objects and auditory streams using vague principles (the Gestalt grouping principles).

A third way to define auditory objecthood is as follows: it is the end result of the process of figure–ground segregation. For example, Carrell and Opie (1992) characterize the process of auditory object formation as "separating the auditory foreground from its background" (p. 437). Figure 6 is an example of visual figure–ground segregation: either the faces or the vase are seen in the foreground at any given time; they cannot be perceived simultaneously. An auditory analog is a stream; when the sequence in Fig. 5A splits into two streams (Fig. 5C), a listener can listen to only the high stream or the low stream at any given time; they cannot be perceived simultaneously. This is best exemplified in a demonstration by Bregman and Campbell (1971). They interleaved three high-frequency notes (*ABC*) with three low-frequency notes (123), to produce . . . *A1B2C3* . . . . When played for an observer, they report hearing . . . *ABC123A* . . . . In other words, because the tones grouped into two streams based on their frequency proximity, either stream was available for selection as figure, but they were not available simultaneously—otherwise, observers should have been able to report the correct order. Note that both the auditory and visual examples follow the *principle of exclusive allocation* (Bregman, 1990)—an edge cannot be simultaneously assigned to more than one object. This point is vital to the theory and research that we discuss later.

FIGURE 6   The Rubin vase/face follows the principle of the exclusive allocation of edges.

The figure–ground segregation approach is consistent with idea that objects are the "units of attention" (Scholl, 2001; Scholl & Pylyshyn, 1999). With respect to vision, there is indeed evidence (reviewed by Driver & Baylis, 1998) that attention is directed at and bound to objects rather than spatial locations. Another way to say that the faces and vase in Fig. 6 cannot be *perceived* concurrently is to say that they cannot be *attended to* concurrently—figures *are* the "units of attention." In other words, saying that objects are the units of attention is equivalent to saying that objects are the product of figure–ground segregation.

As with Bregman's concept of streaming, there is much that is appealing about the figure–ground conception of auditory objecthood. It is better than the idea of "stream" because it overcomes that term's modality specificity. Figure–ground segregation is a phenomenon that happens in all the modalities. However, Gibson (1982), addressing the notion of figure–ground segregation, warns us that "(a)n object . . . is only a surface that stands out from the rest of the surface layout, the ground. . . . This is an ecological fact, to which figure ground segregation is incidental" (p. 151). Gibson is pointing out that there may be multiple "objects" in the environment, only one of which becomes figure. Characterizing objecthood as the end result of the figure–ground segregation process carries with it a danger of being too narrow a viewpoint—it neglects the fact that a "figure" is often chosen from a number of alternatives. We believe that each of these alternatives should also rightly be called an object. This is a point to which we will return when we describe our theory of objecthood.

SUMMARY: COMPETING PERSPECTIVES

Some of the most important concepts of psychology (e.g., attention, consciousness) are among the most poorly defined. Attention, for example, has been operationally defined in some experiments by performance on a dichotic listening task and in other experiments by performance on a visual search task. Add these definitions to colloquial expressions (e.g., to pay attention), and one quickly becomes mired in semantic problems. These are *vague* terms that are used consistently within experimental paradigms but seldom across experimental paradigms (Parasuraman & Davies, 1997).

"Auditory object" has become a vague term of this sort. Wightman and Jenison (1995), for example, conclude that a good formal definition of auditory objecthood is difficult. Like us, they reject the notion of "event" or of "stream" as an adequate definition and point out that unlike vision there is "no straightforward mapping of object features to stimulus features" on something like a retina. However, they conclude: "Nevertheless, the fact that auditory percepts in daily life are so naturally and immediately associated with the objects that produced the sounds is undeniable and gives currency, if not clarity, to the term *auditory object*" (p. 371). They then proceed to define two classes of auditory object: concrete (emitted by real objects in the environment) and abstract (not real objects in the environment); this is their departure point for the rest of the book, which is about the spatial layout of concrete auditory objects. Wightman and Jenison have convinced us what an auditory object *is not*, that such a thing must surely exist, and that there may be different kinds; but we are still left wondering what an auditory object *is*.

HOW TO THINK ABOUT OBJECTHOOD

We combine elements of the preceding theories into one formal framework. *We define a* perceptual object *as that which is susceptible to figure–ground segregation.* Early processing in any modality produces elements that require grouping. This grouping follows the principles described by the Gestalt psychologists (Fig. 1, further developed by Kubovy, Holcombe, & Wagemans, 1998). The grouping produces gestalts or perceptual organizations (POs), that is, *elements*. Attention selects one PO (or a small set of them) to become a figure (Fig. 6; Peterson & Gibson, 1994) and relegates all other information to ground (Fig. 7;

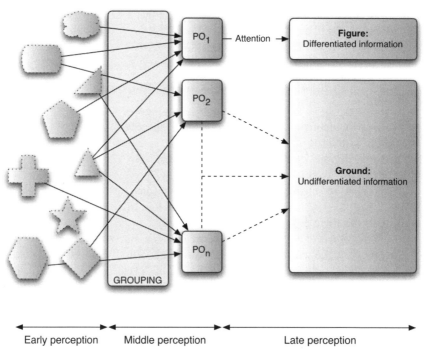

FIGURE 7   The formation of perceptual objects. Early processing produces elements that undergo grouping to produce PO_1, PO_2, . . . , PO_n, a set of perceptual organizations (or POs). Attention produces figure–ground segregation, which allocates processing capacity to the figure and leaves the ground undifferentiated (Kubovy & Van Valkenburg, 2001).

Kubovy & Van Valkenburg, 2001; Brochard *et al.*, 1999 provide evidence that the ground remains undifferentiated in audition).

We define objecthood in terms of *susceptibility* to figure–ground segregation rather than as the end product because we, like Gibson, believe that "figure ground segregation is incidental"—in any environment, there are many possibilities concerning what is perceptually segregated from the ground. Consider the example of driving on the freeway. As you drive, what you attend to becomes figure: the sight of the car in front of you, its broken tail light, or a road sign; the sound of a song on the radio, its bass line, or the voice of your passenger. Which of these becomes figure is indeed incidental, but the possibilities are constrained to the surfaces, or auditory streams, that *can* become figure. In the way that we have formulated our theory, the song, bass line, and talking passenger are to be considered objects (POs in the model), not just the arbitrary choice of which is currently attended.

We have good reason to believe that grouping takes place in the absence of attention. A study of streaming by Bregman and Rudnicky (1975) provides persuasive evidence. They presented pairs of target tones, A and B (Fig. 8), whose order the observers could easily report. But when they bracketed the target tones with interference tones (*X*, Fig. 8A), observers had trouble reporting their order. They had chosen the frequency and timing of the interference tone so that the four tones would form a single stream, *XABX*, which begins and ends on the same note, depriving the observer of onset or termination cues to support the discrimination. However, when they added captor tones whose frequency was close to that of the interference tones, the perception of the order of the target tones was restored (Fig. 8B). When the captor tones were far from the interference tones (Fig. 8C), they did not help. As noted by Bregman and Rudnicky (1975), this seemingly paradoxical effect[3] demonstrates two important things:

1. Perceptual grouping is not mediated entirely by attention. Even though observers were trying to listen for the *AB* tones in Fig. 8A, they could not ignore the *X* tones.
2. Attention is an act of selecting from *already organized* alternatives. The *AB* tones in Fig. 8A are difficult to discriminate because the results of perceptual grouping produced only one putative object (*XABX*). With the addition of the *C* tones in Fig. 8B, the results of perceptual grouping produced two POs (*AB* and *CCCXXCC*), and observers were able to select one of them. If the *C* tones are too far from the *X* tones, however (Fig. 8C), the results of perceptual grouping produce two different POs (*XABX* and *CCCCC*) and once again observers are unable to make the discrimination.

---

[3] Paradoxical in the sense that adding more tones acts to reduce interference.

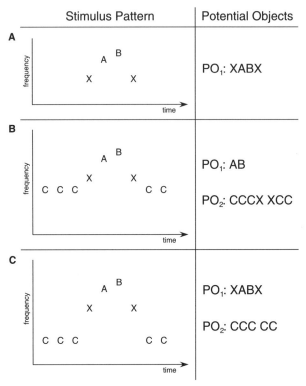

FIGURE 8 (Left) Stimulus patterns used by Bregman and Rudnicky (1975). (Right) The putative objects (POs) available for selection. In A, observers are *not* able to report the direction of the *AB* pair; in B, observers *are* able to report the direction of the *AB* pair; in C, observers are *not* able to report the direction of the *AB* pair.

PERCEPTUAL NUMEROSITY AND THE THEORY
OF INDISPENSABLE ATTRIBUTES

The theory of indispensable attributes (TIA; Kubovy, 1981; Kubovy & Van Valkenburg, 2001; Van Valkenburg & Kubovy, 2003) provides a principled heuristic for the mapping of modality-specific perceptual phenomena onto each other. Consider the problem of grouping. In vision, grouping in space is a perceptual operation that produces a phenomenal partition of a set of discrete elements into mutually exclusive subsets, called *blocks* (Fig. 1). For this to occur, (1) the subsets must share some properties, or features, on which the visual system bases the phenomenal partition, and (2) the elements must be distributed over a medium (in this case, space). The TIA points out that Gestalts occur where discrete entities can be distributed over a medium—an indispensable attribute (IA).

To discover these media the TIA asks, Which object features (attributes) are indispensable for perceptual numerosity? In other words, TIA asks what needs to be different between different physical entities for an observer to perceive that there is more than one entity? An attribute is considered *indispensable* if and only if it is necessary for perceptual numerosity. We develop our argument by offering some thought experiments.

Spatial separation is an IA for vision (Fig. 9, left). Imagine presenting to an observer two spots of light on a surface (i). The wavelength of both lights is 580 nm and they coincide; the observer will report one yellow light. Now suppose we change the wavelengths of the lights so that the wavelength of one light is 480 nm (seen as blue when alone) and the other is 580 nm (seen as yellow when alone), but they still coincide (ii); the observer will report one white light. For the observer to see more than one light, they must occupy different spatial locations (iii). (Time is another IA. We will not concern ourselves with it here. See Jones, Chap. 3, this volume, for discussion of the role of time in auditory object formation.)

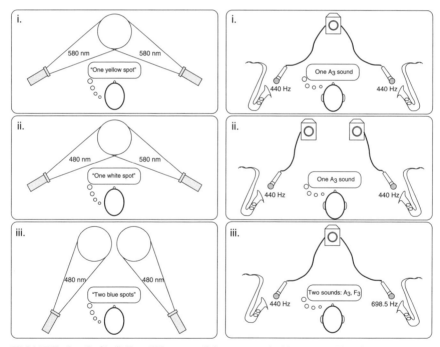

FIGURE 9   (Left) (i) Two 580-nm spotlights create coincident spots. The observer sees one yellow spot, (ii) One 580-nm spotlight and one 480-nm spotlight (seen as blue when alone) create coincident spots. The observer sees one white spot, (iii) Two spotlights create separate spots. Regardless of their color, the observer sees two spots. (Right) (i) One loudspeaker plays two sounds with frequency 440 Hz. The listener hears one A_3 tone, (ii) One loudspeaker plays a 440-Hz tone while another speaker plays a 440-Hz tone. The listener hears one A_3 tone, (iii) A 400-Hz tone and a 698.5-Hz tone are played. Regardless of whether they are played over one loudspeaker or two, the listener hears two sounds, an A_3 and an F_3.

Frequency separation is an IA for audition (Fig. 9, right). Imagine concurrently playing two 440-Hz sounds for a listener (i). If both are played over the same loudspeaker, the listener will report hearing one sound. Now suppose we play these two sounds over two loudspeakers (ii); the listener will still report hearing one sound. For the listener to report more than one sound, they must be separated in frequency (iii).

We conclude from our thought experiments that space acts as a container for visual objects and that frequency acts as a container for auditory objects. Our conclusions mirror those of Attneave and Olson (1971), who claimed that both spatial location (for vision) and frequency (for audition) are *morphophoric*, or form bearing (from the Greek *morphe*, form; and *phoros*, the act of carrying). Attneave and Olson (1971) based their conclusions on the observation that a visual object always maintains its perceptual identity regardless of spatial location, and auditory an object, such as a "melodic phrase . . . is transposable: the pattern as a whole may be raised or lowered in frequency without destroying its perceptual identity. The corollary of this statement is that frequency is a medium, in which the same pattern may have different locations." (p. 148).

THE IMPLIED MAPPING

Kubovy and Van Valkenburg (2001) used the TIA to argue for a mapping between the auditory and visual modalities: experiments and theories of objecthood in the respective modalities are comparable in terms of the media over which the objects are distributed. In other words, the IAs in vision (space and time) should map onto on the IAs in audition (frequency and time). We call this the TIA mapping paradigm. Our position on this matter is not unique. Belin and Zatorre (2000) argue for the same sort of mapping based on the fact that that auditory spectral motion (SM) and visual spatial motion are "both related to changes of energy across the sensory epithelium" (p. 965). In other words, instead of mapping based on functional characteristics of the two systems (where auditory space is analogous to auditory space), they too prefer to map between modalities based on physiological–sensory characteristics.

We can take well-developed procedures for the study and manipulation of visual objecthood and create their auditory analogs by mapping them with respect to their IAs. This means that if a visual experiment involves the manipulation of spatial aspects of the stimuli, an auditory analog would involve the manipulation of frequency aspects of the stimuli. We call this the TIA *mapping*. This has been successfully done in the past with research on concurrent pitch segregation (Kubovy, 1981; Kubovy, Cutting, & McGuire, 1974; Kubovy & Daniel, 1983; Kubovy & Jordan, 1979). Another example comes from Woods, Alain, Diaz, Rhodes, and Ogawa (2001), who conducted four experiments designed to assess the role of space and frequency cuing in auditory selective attention. They concluded that auditory frequency plays a role analogous to visual space. In fact, they proposed an auditory version of Treisman's (1993) feature integration theory

(FIT), which they called the frequency-based feature integration theory (FB-FIT). This is exactly the kind of theory mapping that we are proposing. In the next section, we will show how we are using the TIA to quantify Gestalts in auditory perception.

THE QUANTIFICATION OF OBJECTS

Our method for quantifying auditory objects comes directly from applying the TIA mapping paradigm onto work in vision. Therefore, in order to better understand our techniques for quantifying auditory objects, it will be useful to take a brief foray into the world of vision to discuss the quantification of visual objects.

In some dot patterns in Fig. 10 the dots appear organized horizontally, and in others they appear organized vertically. The visual system imposes order on otherwise ambiguous displays, following principles of grouping. Until recently, researchers who studied Gestalt phenomena such as these did little more than illustrate the principles.

A grouping *principle* suggests a rule that does not allow exceptions. For example, the *ceteris paribus* principle runs "*all* other things being *equal*," not "*most* other things being equal, and a few other things being *almost* equal." This is not the spirit in which we have been investigating grouping. That is

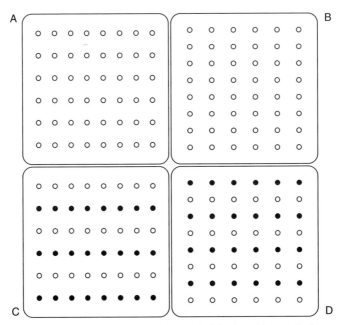

FIGURE 10   Examples of Gestalt principles in ambiguous displays.

why, for the remainder of this chapter, we will avoid locutions such as "the strength of grouping by principle ξ." Instead, if we let π stand for a property on which two entities α and β can be compared, we will talk about "the strength of π-attraction between entities α and β." This has the advantage of distinguishing the observable (i.e., grouping) from an inferred construct (i.e., attraction).

We would expect the proximity attraction between dots in columns (Fig. 10a) to be stronger if the distance between adjacent dots in columns were smaller, and the color-similarity attraction to be stronger if the colors of the dots in Fig. 10c differed less. When properties π_1 (e.g., spatial proximity) and π_2 (e.g., similarity) are in mutual opposition (Fig. 10d), one of them may prevail; but this can be made to change by weakening the π_1-attraction or strengthening the π_2-attraction. We will call the net effect of all the attractions between two entities α and β the *attraction* between α and β.

Visual research by Kubovy and his colleagues (Kubovy, 1994; Kubovy & Wagemans, 1995; Kubovy *et al.*, 1998; Kubovy, Cohen, & Hollier, 1999; Kubovy & Gepshtein, 2000) has overcome an important obstacle: the assumption that one could not measure a π_1-attraction without reference to a π_2-attraction (Hochberg & Silverstein, 1956). Hochberg, for example, thought that one could measure only the *relative strengths of two attractions* and that the only way to do this was to pit a π_1-attraction against a π_2-attraction. He and his associates used 6×6 rectangular lattices of squares (Hochberg & Silverstein, 1956) and 4×4 rectangular lattices of dots (Hochberg & Hardy, 1960). They studied the relation between proximity attraction and luminance-similarity attraction. For instance, while the luminance difference between dots in adjacent rows and the spacing between dots within rows were held constant, observers adjusted the distance between rows (Fig. 10d) until they found a spacing between rows that was the point of subjective equality (PSE) between the tendency for the stimulus to group by columns and by rows. The PSE is the spacing for which observers report that their tendency to see rows and columns is equal.

Using this method, Hochberg and Hardy (1960) plotted what microeconomists call an *indifference curve* (Krantz, Luce, Suppes, & Tversky, 1971). Imagine a consumer who would be equally satisfied with a market basket consisting of 4 lb of meat and 2 lb of potatoes and another consisting of 2 lb of meat and 3 lb of potatoes. In such a case, we say that the $\langle$meat, potato$\rangle$ pairs $\langle 4, 2 \rangle$ and $\langle 2, 3 \rangle$ are said to lie on one indifference curve. As Hochberg reduced the luminance difference between dots in adjacent rows, the distance between rows that observers reported to be a PSE increased (Fig. 11). We call this a *grouping-indifference curve* because the observer—whose task is to find the point of subjective equality between grouping by rows and grouping by columns—is indifferent among the $\langle$luminance-difference, row-distance$\rangle$ pairs that lie on it: each member of these pairs is a point of subjective equality for the other.

Kubovy and his colleagues have found an exception to Hochberg's claim: the strength of spatial-proximity attraction *can* be measured without recourse to other

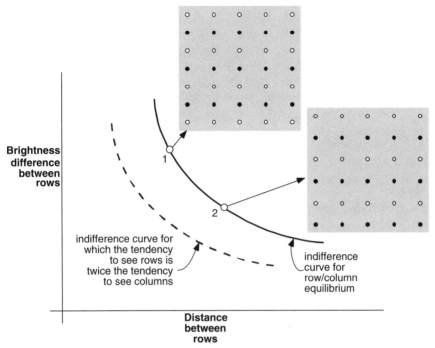

FIGURE 11 Two grouping-indifference curves. Only the solid curve is achievable by methods such as Hochberg's (for the trade-off between spatial-proximity attraction and luminance-similarity attraction in static grouping) and Burt & Sperling's (for the trade-off between spatial-proximity attraction and temporal-proximity attraction in apparent motion). The method described here allows us to plot a *family* of indifference curves.

principles of grouping.[4] In the visual domain techniques have been developed to measure spatial attraction, using ambiguous dot patterns (Kubovy, 1994; Kubovy & Wagemans, 1995; Kubovy *et al.*, 1998, 1999; Kubovy & Gepshtein, 2000). The key was the use of two-dimensional arrays of dots, called *dot lattices*, similar to those used by the Gestalt psychologists in their classic demonstrations. The need to measure one form of attraction by comparing it to another was circumvented because dot lattices are multistable. By varying the distances between dots in a lattice, we can manipulate the proximity attraction between these dots. In other words we figured out how to measure proximity attraction by pitting it against another proximity attraction. As we will show, this allows us to measure the attraction between dots in the lattice and attraction between tones played in a cyclical sequence.

[4] Henceforth we will refer to spatial-proximity attraction as "spatial attraction."

VISUAL QUANTIFICATION

A dot lattice is a collection of dots in the plane that is invariant under two translations. Figure 12 shows the main features of a dot lattice. A lattice is specified by its two shortest translations in the orientations AB and AC, that is, a pair of translation vectors $\mathbf{a}$ and $\mathbf{b}$, and the angle between them, γ. We call the short and long diagonals of the basic parallelogram of a dot lattice $\mathbf{c}$ and $\mathbf{d}$, respectively. The distance of any dot from its eight nearest neighbors is $|\mathbf{a}|$, $|\mathbf{b}|$, $|\mathbf{c}|$, and $|\mathbf{d}|$. Because a lattice's basic parallelogram (and hence the lattice itself) is specified by $|\mathbf{a}|$, $|\mathbf{b}|$, and $\gamma = \angle(\mathbf{a}, \mathbf{b})$, if $|\mathbf{a}|$ is held constant, any lattice can be located in a two-parameter space whose coordinates are $|\mathbf{b}|$ and $\gamma = \angle(\mathbf{a}, \mathbf{b})$.

Methods

On each trial Kubovy and Wagemans (1995) briefly (300 ms) presented a dot lattice, randomly rotated, and seen through a circular aperture. Each lattice consisted of a large number of dots. After the lattice was removed, observers were shown a four-alternative response screen that offered the choice among four orientations, and they were asked to choose the orientation that corresponded to the organization of the dots. Thus, the task was a four-alternative forced-choice task without a correct response.

The Law

The Kubovy and Wagemans (1995) data consist of two independent variables—$|\mathbf{b}|/|\mathbf{a}|$ and γ, and four dependent variables—$p(a)$, $p(b)$, $p(c)$, and $p(d)$. (We use $\mathbf{v}$ to refer to a vector, $|\mathbf{v}|$ to refer to its length, and v to refer to the corresponding response. $p(a)$ refers to the probability of an a response.) Because there are only three degrees of freedom in these data the Kubovy et al. (1998) analysis reduced the data to three dependent variables by calculating $p(b)/p(a)$, $p(c)/p(a)$, and $p(d)/p(a)$. Let $\mathbf{V} = \{\mathbf{b}, \mathbf{c}, \mathbf{d}\}$, with generic element $\mathbf{v} \in \mathbf{V}$, and the corresponding set of responses $V = \{b, c, d\}$, with generic element $v \in V$. Thus,

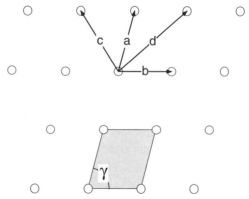

FIGURE 12　The main features of a dot lattice.

$p(v)/p(a)$ means $p(b)/p(a)$ for some data points, $p(c)/p(a)$ for others, and $p(d)/p(a)$ for the remaining ones. In addition, because in the data the range of these probability ratios is large, they used the natural logarithms of the dependent variable(s), $\ln[p(v)/p(a)]$ (which is a log-odds measure).

Figure 13 shows the data. This linear function, called the *proximity attraction function*, accounts for more than 95% of the variance. Notice the three different data symbols; they represent the data for the log odds of choosing, b, c, or d relative to a.

Kubovy *et al.* (1998) found empirically that:

$$\ln \frac{p(b)}{p(a)} = s\left(\frac{|\mathbf{b}|}{|\mathbf{a}|} - 1\right) \tag{1}$$

$$\ln \frac{p(c)}{p(a)} = s\left(\frac{|\mathbf{c}|}{|\mathbf{a}|} - 1\right) \tag{2}$$

$$\ln \frac{p(d)}{p(a)} = s\left(\frac{|\mathbf{d}|}{|\mathbf{a}|} - 1\right) \tag{3}$$

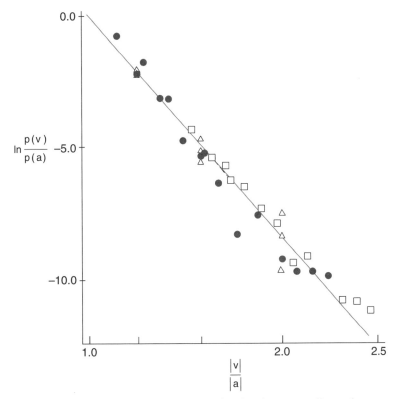

FIGURE 13   The proximity attraction function obeys a pure distance law.

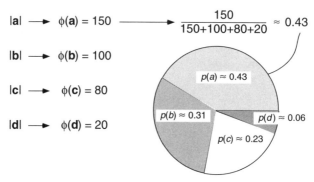

FIGURE 14   Model of proximity attraction.

More concisely,

$$\ln \frac{p(v)}{p(a)} = s\left(\frac{|\mathbf{v}|}{|\mathbf{a}|} - 1\right) \tag{4}$$

or

$$\phi(v) = \frac{p(v)}{p(a)} = e^{s\left(\frac{|\mathbf{v}|}{|\mathbf{a}|} - 1\right)}, \quad \text{where} \quad s < 0 \tag{5}$$

This is a quantitative law of proximity attraction. Proximity attraction follows a decaying exponential function of relative interdot distances. We refer to this empirical relationship as a law because it is invariant over lattices of all shapes. Because proximity attraction in these lattices is based solely on interdot distances, we call this law a *pure distance law.*

The pure distance law has an important implication: *the pure distance law allows us to measure proximity attraction on a ratio scale* (Luce, 1959; Suppes, Krantz, Luce, & Tversky, 1989). Such results are rare and precious. For example, economists and psychologists have always looked for scales of cardinal utility because they want to say of an indifference curve that it represents commodity bundles that have, for example, twice the utility of the commodity bundles falling on another indifference curve.

The full import of this result will become clear when we discuss the auditory analogs. For the moment, we should like to state one consequence of this finding. We have described the competition among the four principal organizations of a dot lattice—the four vectors **a**, **b**, **c**, and **d**—as the competition among four independent scalar quantities—$\phi(a)$, $\phi(b)$, $\phi(c)$, and $\phi(d)$ (Fig. 14). According to the model, the only dependence among responses is due to the mutual exclusivity that reigns among them.[5] Because we can model our data with four independent

---

[5] We assume that a lattice can be organized in only one way at a time. There is nothing in the model that forces us to make that assumption.

scalars, we think of proximity attraction as being a *non-Gestalt phenomenon*. We could hypothesize that the underlying visual subsystem consists of multiple units, each with an orientation-tuned receptive field (RF). A unit whose RF is tuned to the orientation of **w** would respond to the dots that fall within its RF with a strength $\phi(w)$ (which could be interpreted as a firing rate), *independently* from the responses of other units. The probability that an observer would see the lattice organized in the orientation **w**, $p(w)$, is the normalized value of $\phi(w)$.

AUDITORY QUANTIFICATION

In the previous section, we described a methodology for quantifying visual Gestalts. In order to adapt this to the auditory domain, the TIA mapping suggests to us that we use frequency instead of space to create perceptually ambiguous auditory stimuli (circular tone flows or CTFs; see Fig. 16) in our research. By manipulating the frequencies of the tones in these patterns, we can predict the probability that the pattern will be organized in one or another way. The functions we obtain are *attraction functions*, which specify the *strength of grouping*. Once we have found the attraction function for grouping by proximity in frequency for temporally regular patterns, we can examine the effects of other auditory features on grouping. If, in addition to varying frequency proximity, we vary amplitude, phase, space, rhythm, and timbral qualities, we can obtain new attraction functions from which we can infer the strength of grouping by these features.

Figure 15 is a hypothetical generator of CTFs. It is a set of linked concentric wheels that rotate around an axle and share n (in this case, five) spokes. As the generator spins, the spokes ($T1, \ldots, T5$) touch a stylus periodically, causing a sound to be played. Each wheel (labeled **a**, . . . , **e**) produces a sound frequency proportional to its radius ($f_a, \ldots, f_e$). Rotating the generator counterclockwise produces a pattern of sound (Fig. 16), a CTF. Our CTFs contain five tones, with onsets separated by a constant inter stimulus interval (ISI). The duration of a cycle is the *period* of the CTF. The frequencies of the five tones are **a**, . . . **e**.

Our CTFs resemble stimuli used by van Noorden (1975) and Bregman (1990) to study streaming. As in Fig. 5, our CTFs (Fig. 16) break into two streams: in ours they are a two-tone stream and a three-tone stream. The two-tone stream forms a high–low–high . . . sequence; the three-tone stream is heard as a cyclical descending sequence (Fig. 17). There is a frequency of the target **c**, f_c^*, at which it has an equal chance of joining either stream. It cannot join both streams—it is *exclusively allocated*. The more we raise the frequency of **c**, the more likely it is to join the high stream. We will find the *frequency-proximity attraction function* in a manner analogous to the way we found spatial-proximity attraction functions in dot lattices.

We assume that the target **c** is attracted to the other tones in the sequence and that it is the balance of these attractions that determines the streaming of the pattern. Consider a tone w, whose distance from **c** in frequency is $\mathcal{F} = f_w - f_c$, and

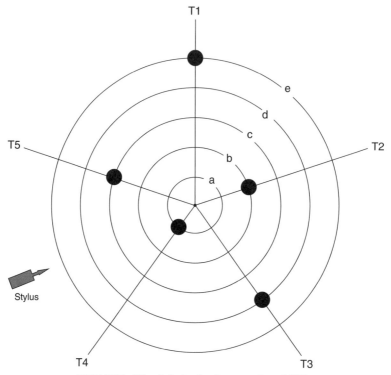

FIGURE 15   A device for the generation of CTFs.

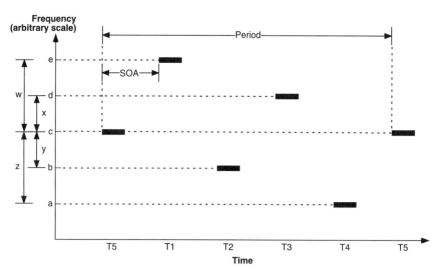

FIGURE 16   A five-element CTF. Six elements (**a**, . . . **e**) are shown, as well as the distances of the target tone **c** to the other tones.

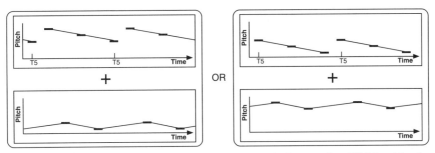

FIGURE 17 Two possible percepts of the CTF in Fig. 16. The target (**c** at $T5$) joins either the high or the low stream.

stream	tone	frequency difference	c attracted to tone:	attraction strength	c attracted to stream:	attraction strength	probabilities	
high	e d c	} x w	e	$\phi(w)$	high	$\phi(x) \cdot \phi(w)$	$p(high) = \dfrac{\phi(x) \cdot \phi(w)}{\phi(x) \cdot \phi(w) + \phi(y) \cdot \phi(z)}$	p(high) p(low)
low	b a	} y z	d b a	$\phi(x)$ $\phi(y)$ $\phi(z)$	low	$\phi(y) \cdot \phi(z)$	$p(low) = \dfrac{\phi(y) \cdot \phi(z)}{\phi(x) \cdot \phi(w) + \phi(y) \cdot \phi(z)}$	

FIGURE 18 A model of grouping in the five-element CTF. Assume that the frequency differences have been scaled, so that if $x = y$ and $w = z$, then $\phi(x) = \phi(y)$ and $\phi(w) = \phi(z)$, from which it follows that the probability of **c** joining the high stream is $p(h) = .5$. In the present case, $x < y$ and $w < z$, therefore $\phi(x) > \phi(y)$ and $\phi(w) > \phi(z)$. Hence, $p(h) > .5$.

whose distance from **c** in time is $T = t_w - t_c$. In close analogy with Eq. (5), we assume that the strength of the attraction of **c** to w is

$$\phi(\mathcal{F}, T) = \phi_0 e^{k_{\mathcal{F}} \mathcal{F}} e^{k_T T} \tag{6}$$
$$= \phi_0 e^{k_{\mathcal{F}} \mathcal{F} + k_T T}$$

where ϕ_0 is the hypothetical attraction of two tones that are separated in neither frequency nor time and $k_{\mathcal{F}}, k_T < 0$ are coefficients. In other words, the attraction between **c** and w is a decaying exponential function of the distance in frequency between them.

Let us suppose that the listeners' task is to decide whether **c** has joined the high or the low stream and that the corresponding responses are h, with probability $p(h)$, and l, with probability $1 - p(h)$. We assume, in analogy with our work on grouping in vision, that

$$p(h) = \frac{\phi(\mathbf{x}, 2t)\phi(\mathbf{w}, t)}{\phi(\mathbf{x}, 2t)\phi(\mathbf{w}, t) + \phi(\mathbf{y}, 2t)\phi(\mathbf{z}, t)} \tag{7}$$

where we take into account the temporal distances between **c** and the other tones (letting $t = $ ISI). Taking odds and substituting Eq. (6):

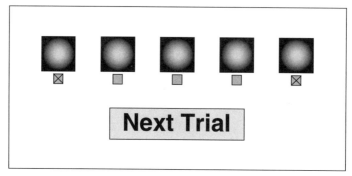

FIGURE 19 The response screen for the preliminary experiments. The large boxes on top are *off boxes*. Each of them turns off one of the tones in the sequence. The smaller boxes below them are response boxes. Here the user has selected the first and the last box.

$$\frac{p(h)}{p(l)} = \frac{\phi(\mathbf{x}, 2t)\phi(\mathbf{w}, t)}{\phi(\mathbf{y}, 2t)\phi(\mathbf{z}, t)} \tag{8}$$

$$= \frac{e^{k_{\mathcal{F}}(\mathbf{x}+\mathbf{w})}}{e^{k_{\mathcal{F}}(\mathbf{y}+\mathbf{z})}}$$

Taking natural logarithms, we obtain the auditory attraction function:

$$\ln \frac{p(h)}{p(l)} = k_{\mathcal{F}}(\mathbf{x}+\mathbf{w}-\mathbf{y}-\mathbf{z}) \tag{9}$$

AN EXPERIMENT

During a training session, we demonstrated to observers how CTFs split into two streams; then during the experiment we asked them to listen for the two-tone stream, and indicate these tones using the response screen (Fig. 19). Each of the five *off boxes* on the screen corresponded to one of the tones in the sequence. When observers clicked on one of them, the corresponding tone was silenced until they released the mouse button. They silenced each tone in turn and decided whether it was a member of the two-tone stream. If it was, they clicked the small response box under the off box; when they had identified both tones in the two-tone stream, they clicked on Next Trial to continue the experiment. Each CTF played for four seconds before observers were allowed to respond.[6] This method allows us to infer which stream the target tone joined, that is, whether the listener's response was low (*l*) or high (*h*).

---

[6] This allowed time for the perceptual system to group the stimuli because streaming is known to "build up" (Bregman, 1990).

Data

Table 2 shows the critical-band number (in Bark) of the flanking tones, **a**, **b**, **d**, and **e**. As Table 3 shows, we used two different sets of flanking tones. For each set we chose four values of f_c, producing four values of our independent variable, $R = x + w - y - z$, suggested by our predicted attraction function derived in Eq. (9).

Figure 20 shows the results of this experiment. The data fit the predictions of Eq. (9) well because the attraction function is linear. However, the intercept is

TABLE 2   Pilot experiment: critical-band number (in Barks) of the flanking tones

Tones	Set 1	Set 2
a	4.0	5.5
b	5.0	6.5
d	8.0	9.5
e	9.0	10.5

TABLE 3   Pilot experiment data: critical-band number (in Bark) of the target tone **c** with the corresponding values of $R = x + w - y - z$

Set 1	Set 2	R
6.00	7.50	−2.00
6.33	7.83	−0.66
6.66	8.17	0.66
7.00	8.50	2.00

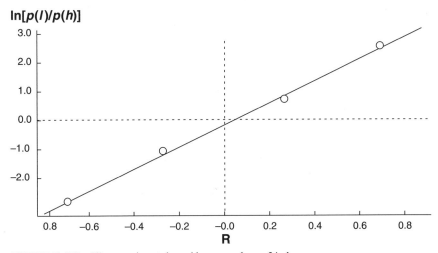

FIGURE 20   Pilot experiment: log-odds averaged over 24 observers.

different from 0 (−0.13 ± 0.015), as we would expect if by using the Bark scale we had placed the tones symmetrically. The data from individual observers were quite variable; we had to reject the data of some observers because of floor and ceiling effects.

An Alternative Method

Bregman and Rudnicky (1975) suggest an alternative method for the quantification of auditory gestalts (Fig. 8). In their experiment, they used only three different frequency values for the C tones. At the lowest frequency there was no effect; at the medium frequency there was a medium effect; and at the highest frequency there was the greatest effect. Presumably, if one were to sample many more frequencies, one could construct a function similar to the ones that we are proposing with our technique. We hope that these functions would be similar to the ones that we will generate—but we have no a priori reason to believe that they would be. In their paradigm, because streaming is being measured as operationalized by the discrimination of the two-tone pair (AB), we feel that observers' performance on this task might tell only part of the tale. In Bregman and Rudnicky (1975), it could be argued that attention was possibly a confound because observers were always listening for the AB tones. Results from studies of spontaneous grouping, which is what we are proposing, might be different. Any differences between the results of these two paradigms might reveal interesting things about the nature of attention.

A COMPUTATIONAL MODEL OF AUDITORY GROUPING

As mentioned previously, a major advantage of this methodology is that the data afford quantitative modeling. To demonstrate this, we have created a simple, physiologically plausible, computationally deterministic model that can spontaneously produce patterns of grouped tones without invoking subjective, Gestalt-like rules of grouping. Because our model parallels those we are developing in the visual domain and the concept of "object" is consistent between the two, it is our intention eventually to be able to describe the perception of modality-neutral, Gibsonian-like objects using this formulation. What follows is a description of our model.

The Conceptual Model: One-Armed Tones

Perhaps the easiest way to conceptualize the model is as follows: imagine that there are, say, five people standing in a circle and that each person is allowed to use one arm to grab any one other person, including themselves. Depending on who grabbed whom, the end result of this exercise could lead to any number of combinations, or *groupings*, ranging from everyone choosing themselves (five groups of one) to, for example, everyone choosing the person on their left (one group of five).

Now, instead of people, imagine that these are "one-armed tones," each of which can *"grab"* or link to one other tone. It turns out that, for five tones, there are 3125 different ways in which this exercise could conclude ($5^5 = 3125$)—we call these *linkage patterns* (LPs).[7] There are, however, only 52 possible perceptually distinguishable partitions of five elements—POs.

Consider the LP examples in Fig. 21. The direction of an arrow signifies a one-way linkage between elements—in each LP there are five elements and thus five arrows. Let us first see how two different LPs can have the same PO. In Fig. 21a, *A* is linked to *B*, *B* is linked to *C*, etc. We represent this LP as $\{(A \rightarrow B),$ $(B \rightarrow C), (C \rightarrow A), (D \rightarrow E), (E \rightarrow D)\}$. This is a 3–2 grouping of the form $\{(A, B, C), (D, E)\}$ (one of the 52 POs). The LP in Fig. 21b is $\{(A \rightarrow B),$ $(B \rightarrow A), (C \rightarrow A), (D \rightarrow E), (E \rightarrow E)\}$. It has the same PO as the one in Fig. 21a: $\{(A, B, C), (D, E)\}$.

Figure 21c and d are examples of LPs that lead to different POs. Figure 21c has the LP $\{(A \rightarrow D), (B \rightarrow D), (C \rightarrow E), (D \rightarrow A), (E \rightarrow E)\}$, which corresponds to the PO $\{(A, B, D), (C, E)\}$. Figure 21d has the LP $\{(A \rightarrow C), (B \rightarrow B), (C \rightarrow D), (D \rightarrow A), (E \rightarrow A)\}$, which corresponds to the PO $\{(A, C, D, E), (B)\}$.

Calculating and Combining Strengths

Each of the linkages depicted in Fig. 21 has a strength associated with it. Following our work in vision, the strength of attraction between two elements (e.g., $\phi_{(A \rightarrow B)}$) is defined as a decaying exponential function:

$$\phi_{AB} = e^{-k(|AB|/\min)}, \tag{10}$$

where |**AB**| is the distance between *A* and *B* (in frequency or time). We calculate strengths relative to all the possible linkage candidates; the **min** term is the smallest distance in a given five-tone sequence. The *k* term is a free parameter in the model, which is analogous to the slope of the attraction function in our visual research. If we are calculating attraction for frequency, we use k_f; if we are calculating attraction for time, we use k_t.

Within frequency and time, we calculate five linkage strengths for each of 3125 possible LPs. In Fig. 21a the five strengths are ϕ_{AB}, ϕ_{BC}, ϕ_{CA}, ϕ_{DE}, and ϕ_{ED}.

To keep the model tractable (until the data tell us otherwise), we assume that the individual linkage strengths are independent. We therefore compute the strength of any particular LP (within each domain) as the product of the individual linkage strengths. In this case, for the *i*th LP (where $i = 1, \ldots, 3125$) and the *d*th domain (where $d = 1$ for frequency, and $d = 2$ for time):

$$\phi_{LP_{id}} = \phi_{AB_{id}} \times \phi_{BC_{id}} \times \phi_{CA_{id}} \times \phi_{DE_{id}} \times \phi_{ED_{id}} \tag{11}$$

The end result of this set of calculations in the frequency domain is a list of 3125 strengths, one for each of the possible LPs. We follow the same procedure to cal-

---

[7] Note: LPs are the end result of hypothetical, hidden processes. This is different from a grouping pattern, which is a phenomenological percept.

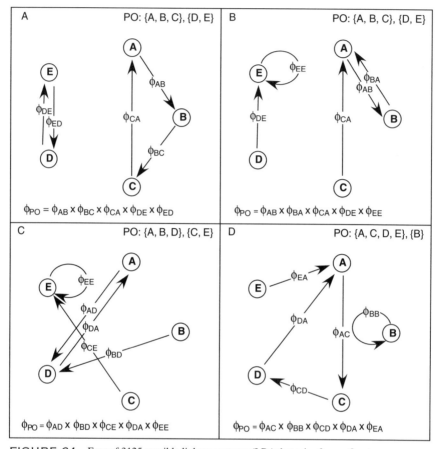

FIGURE 21   Four of 3125 possible linkage patterns (LPs) that arise from a five-tone sequence.

culate the relative strengths of attraction in the time domain—this gives us a second column of 3125 LP strengths.

The total strength of a particular LP is the product of the frequency attraction strength and the time attraction strength:

$$\phi_{LP_i} = \phi_{LP_{i1}} \times \phi_{LP_{i2}} \qquad (12)$$

This operation collapses the frequency attraction strength column and the time attraction strength column into one column of 3125 total strengths. It is analogous to the way in which we combined the strength of grouping by proximity with grouping by similarity.

Recall that each these 3125 LPs belongs to one of 52 perceptually discriminable categories, or POs. Therefore, we partition the LP strengths into their respective 52 PO categories and then determine the overall PO strengths by multiplying together the appropriate LP strengths (where $j = 1, \ldots , 52$):

$$\phi_{PO_j} = \prod_{LP_i \in PO_j}$$ (13)

We normalize the 52 resulting LP strengths to create a probability distribution. The values in this probability distribution are meant to correspond to the probabilities that an observer will hear a given five-tone sequence in each of the 52 POs. Keep in mind, however, that the probability of most of these POs is infinitesimal. In our work on grouping in vision we faced a similar phenomenon: one can show that a dot lattice can be organized as a collection of parallel strips in an infinite number of ways. Nevertheless, only three or four of these (the ones that correspond to small interdot distances) are ever reported by observers.

Our simulation produces attraction functions similar to those of our actual observers when presented with the same stimulus sequences. We have found parameters for which the slopes of the attraction functions are of the correct order of magnitude ($k_f = 1.7$ and $k_t = 0.726$). We are therefore confident that a thorough exploration of the parameter space will yield the expected attraction functions. The value of these parameters does not tell us anything about the relative importance of frequency and time because they are dependent on the units of measurements we happen to have chosen (Barks for frequency differences and milliseconds for time intervals).

Until we have found these parameters, we do not yet know which qualitative predictions the model will make that we will be able to test. For example, streaming *is* time scale dependent—as you increase the interval between tones, the likelihood of streaming decreases. Because our model has two parameters, we will be able to study the way streaming changes as we diminish or increase the interval between successive tones.

THE ECOLOGY OF CIRCULAR TONE FLOWS

It may seem odd to be speaking of Gestalts, computational models, and ecology in the same breath, and yet our theory embraces all three. "Until now," argues the ecologist, "you have been talking about research and models that walk like psychoacoustics, look like psychoacoustics, and sound like psychoacoustics. Where is the ecology?" The answer is simple: our approach is not strictly ecological. There are aspects of our approach, however, that resonate to the ecological perspective:

1. Our modality-neutral perceptual model and our framework allow us to understand how the "pickup of information" (about, for example, Gibson's fire) can be the same across modalities while the "sensory stimulation" (e.g., smell, sight, sound) is different. Figure–ground segregation (which we consider to be the pickup of information) is, as Gibson points out, common to all modalities and so any ecological theory should try to account for it. By defining objects in terms of figure–ground segregation,

we have a common language for all modalities, which allows us to create a truly ecological theory. Such a common language results from the cross-modal mapping paradigm (the TIA), which enables us to apply well-understood paradigms to all modalities.

2. Our theoretical framework accounts for the multimodal perception that Gibson had in mind in his description of fire. Gibson thought this was the key to understanding perception. We agree, and our theory provides a solution to the problem that he set. Contrary to Gibson, however, we believe that "incidental" figure–ground segregation *can* give insights into "how sensations get associated."

But does our use of artificial pure tones reduce the ecological relevance of our theory and model? Not at all:

1. Any sound that occurs in the environment (including the laboratory) comes to an observer as an undifferentiated stream. The origin of the sound and the content of the sound are to be determined by the system. It does not govern the operation of the system. From this point of view, there is nothing particularly artificial about our stimuli.
2. Our methodology does not *require* the use of pure tones. We chose them for convenience. From them we can build stimuli in multiple ways.

Progress rarely occurs in isolation—it usually happens when experts share information. We have offered the motivation and some tools for this sharing. Perhaps the time has come when there is no need to distinguish between ecologists and psychoacousticians or between auditory and visual researchers; we are all perceptual researchers.

ACKNOWLEDGMENT

We would like to thank John Neuhoff, Lawrence Rosenblum, Bill Epstein, and Judith Shatin for insightful comments on an earlier draft. Our work is supported by NEI grant No. R01 EY 12926-06. Correspondence: Department of Psychology, PO Box 400400, University of Virginia, Charlottesville, VA 22904-4400 (e-mail: dlv6b@virginia. edu or kubovy@virginia. edu).

REFERENCES

Alain, C., Arnott, S. R., & Picton, T. W. (2001). Bottom-up and top-down influences on auditory scene analysis: Evidence from event-related brain potentials. *Journal of Experimental Psychology: Human Perception and Performance, 27*, 1072–1089.

Attneave, R, & Olson, R. K. (1971). Pitch as a medium: A new approach to psychophysical scaling. *The American Journal of Psychology, 84*, 147–166.

Belin, P., & Zatorre, R. J. (2000). "What", "where", and "how" in auditory cortex. *Nature Neuroscience, 3*(10), 965–966.

Blauert, J. (1997). *Spatial hearing: The psychophysics of human sound localization* (rev. ed.). Cambridge, MA: MIT Press.

Boring, E. G. (1921). The stimulus error. *American Journal of Psychology, 32*, 449–471.

Bregman, A. (1990). *Auditory scene analysis: The perceptual organization of sound.* Cambridge, MA: MIT Press.

Bregman, A. S., & Campbell, J. (1971). Primary auditory stream segregation and perception of order in rapid sequences of tones. *Journal of Experimental Psychology, 89,* 244–249.

Bregman, A., & Rudnicky, A. (1975). Auditory segregation: Stream or streams? *Journal of Experimental Psychology: Human Perception and Performance, 1,* 263–267.

Broadbent, D. E. (1958). *Perception and communication.* New York: Pergumon Press.

Brochard, R., Drake, C., Botte, M., & McAdams, S. (1999). Perceptual organization of complex auditory sequences: Effects of number of simutaneous subsequences and frequency separation. *Journal of Experimental Psychology: Human Perception and Performance, 25,* 1742–1759.

Carrell, T. D., & Opie, J. M. (1992). The effect of amplitude comodulation on auditory object formation in sentence perception. *Perception and Psychophysics, 52,* 437–445.

Casati, R., & Varzi, A. C. (1999). *Parts and places: The structures of spatial representation.* Cambridge, MA: MIT Press.

Cherry, C. (1959). *On human communication.* Cambridge, MA: MIT Press.

Cooper, J. M. (Ed.). (1997). *Plato: Complete works.* Indianapolis: Hackett.

Darwin, C. J., & Hukin, R. W. (1999). Auditory objects of attention: The role of interaural time differences. *Journal of Experimental Psychology: Human Perception and Performance, 25,* 617–629.

Driver, J., & Baylis, G. (1998). Attention and visual object segmentation. In R. Parasuraman (Ed.), *The attentive brain* (pp. 299–325). Cambridge, MA: MIT Press.

Feng, A. S., & Ratnam, R. (2000). Neural basis of hearing in real-world situations. *Annual Review of Psychology, 51,* 699–725.

Fowler, C. A. (1994). Auditory "objects": The role of motor activity in auditory perception and speech perception. In K. H. Pribram (Ed.), *Origins: Brain and self-organization* (pp. 594–603). Hillsdale, NJ: Lawrence Erlbaum Associates.

Gaver, W. W. (1993). What in the world do we hear? An ecological approach to auditory event perception. *Ecological Psychology, 5,* 1–29.

Gibson, J. J. (1966). *The senses considered as perceptual systems.* Boston: Houghton Mifflin.

Gibson, J. J. (1982). What is involved in surface perception? In J. Beck (Ed.), Organization and representation in perception. (pp. 151–157). Hillsdale, NJ Erlbaum.

Hochberg, J., & Hardy, D. (1960). Brightness and proximity factors in grouping. *Perceptual and Motor Skills, 10,* 22.

Hochberg, J., & Silverstein, A. (1956). A quantitative index of stimulus-similarity: Proximity versus differences in brightness. *American Journal of Psychology, 69,* 456–458.

Izumi, A. (2002). Auditory stream segregation in Japanese monkeys. *Cognition, 82,* B113–B122.

Kant, I. (1996). *Critique of pure reason* (W. S. Pluhar, Trans.). Indianapolis: Hackett. (Original work published 1787)

Kirk, G. S., & Raven, J. E. (1962). *The presocratic philosophers: A critical history with a selection of texts.* Cambridge, UK: Cambridge University Press.

Krantz, D. H., Luce, R. D., Suppes, P., & Tversky, A. (1971). *Foundations of measurement* (vol. I: *Additive and polynomial representations*). New York: Academic Press.

Kubovy, M. (1981). Concurrent pitch segregation and the theory of indispensable attributes. In M. Kubovy and J. R. Pomerantz (Eds.), *Perceptual organization* (pp. 55–98). Hillsdale, NJ: Lawrence Erlbaum.

Kubovy, M. (1994). The perceptual organization of dot lattices. *Psychonomic Bulletin & Review, 1,* 182–190.

Kubovy, M., Cohen, D. J., & Hollier, J. (1999). Feature integration that routinely occurs without focal attention. *Psychonomic Bulletin & Review, 6,* 183–203.

Kubovy, M., Cutting, J. E., & McGuire, R. M. (1974). Hearing with the third ear: Dichotic perception of a melody without monaural familiarity cues. *Science, 186,* 272–274.

Kubovy, M., & Daniel, J. E. (1983). Pitch segregation by interaural phase, by momentary amplitude disparity and by monaural phase. *Journal of the Audio Engineering Society, 31*, 630–635.

Kubovy, M., & Gepshtein, S. (2000). Gestalt: From phenomena to laws. In K. Boyer and S. Sarkar (Eds.), *Perceptual organization for artificial vision systems* (pp. 41–72). Dordrecht, The Netherlands: Kluwer Academic Publishers.

Kubovy, M., Holcombe, A. O., & Wagemans, J. (1998). On the lawfulness of grouping by proximity. *Cognitive Psychology, 35*, 71–98.

Kubovy, M., & Jordan, R. (1979). Tone-segregation by phase: On the phase sensitivity of the single ear. *Journal of the Acoustical Society of America, 66*, 100–106.

Kubovy, M., & Van Valkenburg, D. (2001). Auditory and visual objects. *Cognition, 80*, 97–126.

Kubovy, M., & Wagemans, J. (1995). Grouping by proximity and multistability in dot lattices: A quantitative gestalt theory. *Psychological Science, 6*, 225–234.

Luce, R. D. (1959). *Individual choice behavior.* New York: Wiley.

Mayo, B. (1961). Objects, events, and complementarity. *Mind, 70*, 340–361.

Mollon, J. (1995). Seeing colour. In *Colour: An & science* (pp. 127–150). Cambridge, UK: Cambridge University Press.

Monge, G. (1789). Memoire sure quelques phénomènes de la vision. *Annales de Chimie, 3*, 131–147.

Newton, I. (1999). *Mathematical principle of natural philosophy* (I. B. Cohen & A. Whitman, Trans.). Berkeley, CA: University of California Press. (Original work published 1726)

Object. (1993). In *Oxford English Dictionary* (2nd ed.). http://etext.lib.virginia.edu/etcbin/oedbin/oed2www?specfile=/web/data/oed/oed.o2w&act=text&offset=287948343&textreg=0&query=object [Retrieved October 1, 1999].

Parasuraman, R., & Davies, D. R. (Eds.). (1997). *Varieties of attention.* New York: Academic Press.

Peterson, M. A., & Gibson, B. S. (1994). Must figure–ground organziation precede object recognition? An assumption in peril. *Psychological Science, 5*, 253–259.

Savardi, U., & Bianchi, I. (Eds.). (1999). *Gli errori dello stimolo* [The stimulus errors]. Verona, Italy: Cierre.

Scholl, B. J. (2001). Objects and attention: The state of the art. *Cognition, 80*, 1–46.

Scholl, B. J., & Pylyshyn, Z. W. (1999). Tracking multiple items through occlusion: Clues to visual object-hood. *Cognitive Psychology, 38*, 259–290.

Spence, C., & Driver, J. (1997). Audiovisual links in exogenous overt spatial orienting. *Perception & Psychophysics, 59*, 1–22.

Spence, C., & Driver, J. (1998). Auditory and audiovisual inhibition of return. *Perception & Psychophysics, 60*, 125–139.

Spence, C., & Driver, J. (1999). Cross-modal attention. In G. W. Humphreys and A. Treisman (Eds.), *Attention, space, and action* (pp. 130–149). New York: Oxford University Press.

Stein, B. E., & Meredith, M. A. (1993). *The merging of the senses.* Cambridge, MA: MIT Press.

Suppes, P., Krantz, D. H., Luce, R. D., & Tversky, A. (1989). *Foundations of measurement* (Vol. II: Geometrical, threshold, and probabilistic representations). New York: Academic Press.

Treisman, A. M. (1993). The perception of features and objects. In A. Baddeley and L. Weiskrantz (Eds.), *Attention: Selection, awareness, and control: A tribute to Donald Broadbent* (pp. 5–32). Oxford, UK: Clarendon Press.

van Noorden, L. P. A. S. (1975). *Temporal coherence in the perception of tone sequences.* Unpublished doctoral dissertation, Institute for Perceptual Research, Eindhoven, The Netherlands.

Van Valkenburg, D., & Kubovy, M. (2003). In defense of indispensable attributes. *Cognition, 87*, 225–233.

Watkins, A. J. (1991). Central, auditory mechanisms of perceptual compensation for spectral-envelope distortion. *Journal of the Acoustical Society of America, 90*, 2942–2955.

Watkins, A. J. (1998). The precedence effect and perceptual compensation for spectral envelope distortion. In A. Palmer, A. Rees, A. Q. Summerfield, and R. Meddis (Eds.), *Psychophysical and physiological advances in hearing* (pp. 336–343). London: Whurr.

Watkins, A. J. (1999). The influence of early reflections on the identification and lateralization of vowels. *Journal of the Acoustical Society of America, 106*, 2933–2944.

Watkins, A. J., & Makin, S. J. (1996). Effects of spectral contrast on perceptual compensation for spectral-envelope distortion. *Journal of the Acoustical Society of America*, *99*, 3749–3757.

Wertheimer, M. (1938). Laws of organization in perceptual forms. In W. Ellis (Ed.), *A source book of Gestalt psychology* (pp. 71–88). London: Routledge & Kegan Paul. (Original work published in *Psychologische Forschung*, 1923, *4*, 301–350.)

Wightman, F. L., & Jenison, R. (1995). Auditory spatial layout. In W. Epstein and S. J. Rogers (Eds.), *Perception of space and motion* (2nd ed., pp. 365–400). San Diego, CA: Academic Press.

Woods, D. L., Alain, C., Diaz, R., Rhodes, D., & Ogawa, K. H. (2001). Location and frequency cues in auditory selective attention. *Journal of Experimental Psychology: Human Perception & Performance*, *27*, 65–74.

6

ECOLOGICAL PSYCHOACOUSTICS AND AUDITORY DISPLAYS

HEARING, GROUPING, AND MEANING MAKING

BRUCE N. WALKER AND GREGORY KRAMER

Auditory display is the use of nonspeech sound to communicate information to a listener. The field of auditory display encompasses everything from alarms to complex sonifications. Although there are many differences in the design of fire alarms and auditory graphs, the entire auditory display endeavor can benefit from and contribute to the study of ecological psychoacoustics.

A body of relevant knowledge about auditory perception and cognition is important to the successful design of auditory displays. We basically need to know enough about how people hear and think. Auditory display designers must then apply that knowledge, which is largely an issue of disseminating the information and training the designers to use it. The key question for this volume is whether traditional psychoacoustics research has provided the knowledge necessary to build useful and usable auditory displays. The short answer is that this research has provided a good starting point. Nevertheless, while a great deal of useful knowledge is available for basic perception of simple sounds, there remain many unaddressed scientific and practical questions that relate to the often complex sounds used in real-world auditory displays, the effects of typical listening environments, and the influence of the knowledge, experience, and expectations of the listener. A second, and perhaps equally important, question is how and what the field of auditory display research can contribute to psychoacoustics. We would contend that there is much to be shared in this direction as well.

One approach to this topic is to focus on the task of interacting with an auditory display to extract the meaning the designer intended. In this task-oriented approach, we can consider three general types of subtasks, each of which depends on the psychoacoustics research community for design recommendations. First, there is the "simple" perception of the sounds in the listening environment. If you cannot hear it or discern how it is changing, you cannot extract meaning from it. Many of the other chapters in this volume address particular aspects of this topic (e.g., Schmuckler; Schlauch). Second, there is the subtask of parsing the auditory scene into sound sources, or streams (i.e., segregating and grouping, Bregman, 1990, and see Van Valkenburg & Kubovy, this volume), and distinct variables such as pitch, loudness, and a host of timbral variable such as brightness or woodiness. Finally, there is the subtask of associative and cognitive processing that results in deriving meaning from the sounds in line with what the sound designer intended. All of these stages are required for successful communication of information via an auditory display.

The knowledge about each stage that has been contributed by the traditional psychophysical research community has been of considerable benefit to auditory displays that rely more on the first stage (perception) and has been somewhat less useful for the displays that place greater demands on the second and third stages (grouping and meaning making). Our contention is that the more recent ecological form of psychoacoustics has much to offer all types of auditory display designs, especially those that attempt to convey more information or are employed in acoustically complex environments. In fact, there is an increasingly direct and synergistic relationship between the ecological research community and the auditory display community: as more is known about complex sound perception, auditory stream analysis, and the cognitive processing of sound in real-world situations, better and more sophisticated displays can be created; and as those more advanced displays are used, much can be learned about the auditory perception and cognition that are taking place.

In this chapter we present a brief history of auditory displays and establish a basic vocabulary for discussing the field. We then outline the three subtasks of basic perception, discerning streams and variables, and meaning making. Next, we examine the contributions of traditional psychoacoustic research to auditory display and where this research has fallen short of the needs of the field. We then examine where recent research into higher level perceptual phenomena fills some of the gaps left by traditional research. We close with a short discussion of these research opportunities and how they stand to influence future auditory display design and, conversely, how new complex auditory displays may contribute to the emerging field of ecological psychoacoustics.

BRIEF HISTORY AND TERMINOLOGY

Auditory display is a broad term referring to the use of any type of sound to present information to a listener. This may include, but is certainly not limited to, warnings, alarms, status indicators, and data sonification. Nonspeech sounds have been used for a very long time to convey information. We provide only a brief introduction here, sufficient as a foundation for our subsequent discussion. See Kramer *et al.* (1999) for an excellent summary of the types of auditory displays and their development. Also, the amount of information that is intended to be conveyed by an auditory display is important to the topic of ecological psychoacoustics research. There is a wide range in the level of complexity of the intended message,[1] but it has tended to increase over the years.

The simplest (not to mention earliest and still most common) auditory displays are basic *alerts and notifications* (Sanders & McCormick, 1993; Sorkin, 1987). The sounds indicate that something has happened or is about to happen or that the listener's attention is required in some task. One example is the long beep indicating the cooking time on a microwave oven has expired. There is generally little information about the details of the event—the microwave beep does not indicate whether the food is cooked or not. Another commonly heard alert is the telephone ring—the basic ring tone does not indicate who is calling or why. *Cautions* and *warnings* are alert sounds that specifically indicate one of a limited class of adverse events. In this case, the sounds communicate more about the nature of the event, by virtue of the unique association. Through experience and learning the listener comes to equate a certain wailing sound with a fire alarm. Again, the information about the events that the alarm conveys is usually limited to binary threshold crossings. That is, the fire alarm signals that there is or is not a fire; not where or how hot it is. As technology and interfaces have advanced, there has been an increased need to provide more details about the events a sound is announcing. There have been two basic approaches to addressing this challenge: auditory icons and earcons.

Auditory icons are the auditory equivalent of visual icons, which are graphical symbols used to represent objects or processes. In the era of personal computing, icons have come to depict "functions of computer systems, the system objects, various types of system status, and [they] represent commands, cursors, menu items, windows, screen selection buttons, utilities, processes, programs and the like" (Uzilevsky & Andreev, 1993, p. 115). The ability of icons to simplify information display is largely due to their capacity to present a great deal of information in a concise and easily recognized format (Blattner, Sumikawa, & Greenberg, 1989; Gittins, 1986), and this may be due to the visual system's ability to process several dimensions (shape, color, etc.) in parallel. In addition, icons are more easily located and processed than words (Hemenway, 1982; Shneiderman,

---

[1] Note that the focus here is on *intentional* sounds, namely those that are put into a system by a designer to convey specific information. *Incidental* sounds, such as the clicking and whirring of a hard drive, do provide status and activity information to a user, even though these sounds were certainly not engineered into the system. It is interesting and instructive to note that in many cases designers are now intentionally mimicking incidental sounds, in recognition of their utility. One example is the artificially introduced clicks that one often hears when "pressing" the software buttons on a touch screen interface.

1998) and can help transcend linguistic and cultural barriers (Kolers, 1969; Ossner, 1990; Uzilevsky & Andreev, 1993).

Auditory icons, then, are brief sounds that have been introduced into the computer interface to represent objects, functions, and actions to the user via the auditory modality. Gaver suggests that, "Objects in the computer world should be represented by the objects involved in sound-producing events; actions by the interactions that cause sound; and attributes of the system environment . . . by attributes of the sonic environment" (Gaver, 1989, pp. 75–76). As an example, an auditory icon for a printer might be a brief sound of a line printer or typewriter. The directness or auditory similarity between the icon and the actual object can vary considerably. However, any sound that is intended to evoke the sound of an object or action is still generally classified as an auditory icon.

Modern interfaces involve many objects and actions for which there is no natural or even iconic sound, thereby precluding auditory icons. *Earcons* are sounds in an interface that represent a full range of "messages and functions, as well as states and labels" (Blattner *et al.*, 1989). Earcons often employ a simple, hierarchical language of sounds and are often musical in nature. The relationship between the earcon and the action is, at most, *metaphorical*. An example is a three-note pattern representing a file, in which a decrease in loudness and pitch represents "file deletion"—the diminishing loudness and pitch of the sound is a metaphor for the destruction of the file. Most earcons have purely *symbolic* mappings between the sounds and the information they represent. They are arbitrary and basically must be learned by the user. An example would be a plain "beep" to represent "file deletion," with no acoustic properties associated, even metaphorically, with the represented action. The iconic—metaphorical—symbolic distinction is not categorical so much as it represents a continuum of representational types (see Kramer, 1994b, for more on this topic).

Whereas auditory icons and earcons use sound to represent an event more or less metaphorically, a different and much more direct approach to conveying information with sound is simply to listen to the event or listen to data generated by the event. *Audification* is the direct translation of a data waveform into sound (Kramer, 1994a). This often requires that the data wave be frequency shifted into the audible range for humans or time shifted (slowed down or sped up) to allow appropriate inspection by the listener. A common example of audification is the playback of seismic data. Because of their complexity, visual seismograms are difficult to understand and categorize. By speeding up the playback of the recorded signal so that it falls into the human audible range, listeners have been able to classify seismic records as either atomic bomb blasts or earthquakes with accuracies greater than 90% (Speeth, 1961). More recent work has applied audification to oil exploration and further earthquake sonifications (Dombois, 2001, 2002; Hayward, 1994). Scarf (1979) used audification to explore data from the Voyager-2 space probe crossing the rings of Saturn. Visual data contained far too much noise for clear information to be extracted. However, certain types of wave structures had audio signatures that could easily be detected aurally despite the background noise. Audification results demonstrate that some data are better dealt with by modalities other than the traditional visual mode.

Many extant auditory displays, other than caution and warning tones, have been used as dynamic *process monitors*, capitalizing on "the listener's ability to detect small changes in auditory events or the user's need to have their eyes free for other tasks" (Kramer *et al.*, 1999, p. 3). Auditory displays have been developed for monitoring models of a cola bottling factory (Gaver, Smith, & O'Shea, 1991) and a crystal factory (B. N. Walker & Kramer, 1996b), among others, and for monitoring multiple streams of patients' data in an anesthesiologist's workstation (Fitch & Kramer, 1994).

The more recent, and in general most sophisticated, auditory displays utilize several of the approaches mentioned to this point in order to allow a listener to extract meaning from the sound. *Sonification* is the use of nonspeech audio to convey information such as that used in the interpretation of scientific results. Specifically, data sonification is "the transformation of data relations into perceived relations in an acoustic signal for the purposes of facilitating communication or interpretation" (Kramer *et al.*, 1999, p. 3). That is, scientific data of any sort is used to change the parameters of a synthesized tone, usually in a largely metaphorical or symbolic manner (e.g., changing pitch represents changing rainfall or temperature, Flowers & Grafel, 2002). A well-known early example is the Geiger counter—radiation density is represented by the rate of clicks.

It is often helpful to think of recent sonification efforts as the process of creating sophisticated "auditory graphs," analogous to the visualizations produced by modern graphing applications. Perhaps the first formal analysis of how to represent data using sound was Sara Bly's (1982) doctoral thesis from the University of California, Davis. Bly looked at how best to display multivariate, logarithmic, and time-varying data, using only sound. Part of sonification's growing appeal is that it can be used to display highly complex and multidimensional data. Participants in Fitch and Kramer's (1994) auditory anesthesiologist's workstation monitored eight simultaneously changing patient variables and performed significantly better with the auditory version than the visual display. Kramer has also described the sonification of five-dimensional financial data (Kramer, 1993) and nine-dimensional chaotic data (Kramer & Ellison, 1991).

Recent studies have pointed out that successful interpretation of the sonified data requires more than just the sonified data—context is also necessary. This includes the auditory equivalents of axes, tick marks, trend lines, labels, and so on (Smith & Walker, 2002; B. N. Walker, 2000, 2002). The implementation of the context elements basically involves all of the auditory display concepts discussed to this point (notifications, warnings, etc.) as well as some that are particular to the auditory data interpretation task.

Research has used sonification to detect tumors in a medical application (Martins & Rangayyan, 1997), make discoveries in physics (Pereverzev, Loshak, Backhaus, Davis, & Packard, 1997), and analyze structural data from concrete highway bridges (Valenzuela, Sansalone, Krumhansl, & Streett, 1997). Another important area of application is in virtual environments, where denoting objects, validating user interactions, providing environmental context, and enhancing veridicality are all aided by the careful use of sound. It is quickly becoming clear that we are only scratching the surface of the possibilities for using sound to display and help interpret complex scientific data. The key to continued utility is sorting out the more complex task elements that set modern sonification-style auditory displays apart from the somewhat more understood cautions and warnings.

By its very nature, sonification is interdisciplinary, integrating concepts from human perception, acoustics, design, the arts, and engineering. Thus, development of effective auditory representations of data requires interdisciplinary collaborations using the combined knowledge and efforts of psychologists, computer scientists, engineers, physicists, composers, and musicians, along with the expertise of specialists in the application areas being addressed. The potential contribution of ecological psychoacoustics is large and important to the continued evolution of auditory displays.

WHAT DESIGNERS NEED TO KNOW: AUDITORY DISPLAY SUBTASKS

Auditory display can be understood as a form of applied auditory perception. Designers need to take into account a lot of acoustic, environmental, and human factors when creating an auditory display. As discussed at the outset, it is helpful to consider the various subtasks involved in the use of auditory displays. This approach highlights the needs of the auditory display design community and frames our discussion of the successes and limits of traditional psychoacoustics research.

PERCEPTION

For all auditory displays the task of understanding the message is dominated by the perception subtask. That is, the most important aspects in their design relate to whether the listener can hear the sound and particular changes of particular parameters. This is especially true for more iconic displays such as notifications and warnings. It is crucial that the designer be able to predict if, when, and how well their sounds will be heard. Perception depends on a complex and dynamic interplay between the sound attributes, the environment, and the listener. For a design to be successful, issues of absolute detection thresholds, discrimination sensitivities, and masking top the list of issues an auditory display designer needs to consider. In order to have the optimal utility for designers, these factors need to be investigated using auditory display–like sounds that are presented in environments that are acoustically and cognitively realistic.

STREAM ANALYSIS

There are two main situations in which streaming issues are particularly relevant to auditory display. The first is when streaming is related to detecting the correct auditory signal. For example, many auditory displays will be heard in an environment with multiple competing sound sources. Following the task-relevant source can be crucial. Sometimes the environment will be predictably "sourcy," such as in a cockpit where there are multiple concurrent speech and nonspeech auditory streams. In other circumstances, the designer will not know the exact number of competing sources and will have to design for the worst-case scenario. The realm of computer interface notifications is a current example of where the designer must ensure distinction in the sound for the listener to determine where the sound originated (e.g., to know if it was the computer that was beeping, as opposed to the PDA that is also sitting on the desktop).

The second main type of stream dependence in auditory displays arises when a designer intentionally maps informational distinctions onto different streams. One example is the spatial segregation of different data streams. The monthly sales figures from a company's Los Angeles office could be presented in the front-left auditory space, while at the same time the sales figures from the New York office could be presented in the front-right auditory space. This spatial separation should allow the user to separate the two data sets mentally. Further, the LA:west:left versus NY:east:right mapping is spatially compatible (see Proctor & Reeve, 1990; B. N. Walker & Ehrenstein, 2000), which should help the listener remember which stream is which. Within a stream (say, the LA data), the sales data could be represented by the pitch of a continuously varying tone, while a series of intermittent clicks marks the passage of the days of the month. This would effectively result in two "substreams," one for data and one for context.

Thus, in order to make perceptible displays in a sourcy environment or make effective use of streams in a sonification, it is important to know what acoustic characteristics allow successful inter- and intrastream segregation as well as grouping. It is also important to know how well listeners will be able to listen analytically to one stream (or substream) at some times and listen holistically (integrating across streams) at another time. Again, this information needs to be available for ecologically valid sounds, environments, and listeners.

CONCEPTION AND MEANING MAKING

Once the auditory display is heard and streamed into sources, the listener needs to understand the meaning that the sounds convey. The simplest type of meaning making is identification of one of a set of sounds. The acoustic attributes of a sound that make it distinct and memorable need to be applied to the design of alerts and warnings to make sure that there is no ambiguity as to what the sound signifies. For example, the International Space Station caution and warning tones need to communicate unambiguously whether there is a fire, depressurization, or toxic environment condition, as all require immediate but different actions. It is important to know just how the manipulation of acoustic attributes such as the frequency or repetition rate affects a listener's categorization of the sound. For example, will a high-pitched alarm be perceived as more indicative of a fire or a depressurization?

A refinement of this is the study of the attributes that can allow a sound to be distinct and at the same time still belong within a family of sounds. This is important for the creation of metaphorical languages of sounds, as in the case of earcons. The computer object-related sounds (e.g., files, directories) need to be similar as a group but different from the action-related sounds (e.g., edit, delete). Of course, the semantic rules used to create the earcons play a large role in this meaning making. The extent to which listeners are able to learn the "language" is also highly relevant.

Another type of cognitive interpretation is the representation of a class of information (i.e., data dimension) by a varying sound parameter (i.e., display dimension). A sonification example would be representing changing temperature by varying a sound's frequency. As Walker has summarized (2000; 2002), it is important for a display designer to know (1) the optimal mapping: what sound parameter is best suited to represent a given type of data; (2) the optimal polarity: whether an increase in the sound parameter should indicate an increase or decrease in the data dimension; and (3) the optimal scaling function: how much change in a sound will represent a given change in the corresponding data dimension. Again, this information needs to be available for the kinds of sounds, environments, and listeners that will interact with a given auditory display.

WHAT HAS TRADITIONAL PSYCHOACOUSTICS CONTRIBUTED TO AUDITORY DISPLAY?

A rich history of research has provided valuable insight into the physiological, perceptual, and cognitive aspects of auditory perception for relatively simple auditory events, such as pure tones and noise bursts. Much of this work has contributed to a functional knowledge base of various auditory thresholds, psychophysical scales, and models of auditory perception. Following on from the previous section, this can be organized by the perceptual dimensions that are important in auditory display, starting with those that contribute most to our understanding of the perception of sounds, then moving through what we know about streaming, and on to the research that indicates how a listener in a given context will interpret an auditory display. Other chapters in this volume cover many of the following areas much more thoroughly. To avoid redundancy, where possible we will refer the reader to those chapters for the details, restricting our coverage to the relevance to auditory displays.

A FRAMEWORK: VOCABULARY, METHODS, AND LIMITS

We should start by making it clear that the field of psychoacoustics has provided a foundation for the methodical evaluation of auditory displays and thus a link to existing scientific literature. Auditory display is, in large measure, an "engineering art." As a solutions-driven endeavor, it requires guidelines and dependable results and a language with which to communicate. The vocabulary of limits, just noticeable differences (JNDs), octave bands, fundamentals and harmonics, and auditory streams are all foundations for auditory display designers, as are descriptions of the listening environment, such as characteristics of background noise. In addition, the ways of defining sounds, in terms of frequency, decibels, and so on, has had a large benefit for auditory display. (The musical vocabulary has also contributed enormously to the field of auditory display, but that is a separate topic, somewhat out of the scope of the present discussion.)

RIGOROUS EXPERIMENTAL METHODS

The field of psychoacoustics has made available to the auditory display community a whole set of experimental and analysis approaches. These range from magnitude estimation procedures (e.g., Stevens, 1975) to assess perception of sound dimensions to multidimensional scaling (e.g., Schiffman, Reynolds, & Young, 1981) used to assess the interaction of sound dimensions. More recently, more rigorous assessment of performance and effectiveness of auditory displays has involved experimental methods and statistical analysis techniques that, although not necessarily developed by psychoacoustics researchers, are characteristic of the methodical and quantitative heritage of psychoacoustics. The magnitude estimation literature (e.g., Stevens, 1975) has provided functions linking actual physical characteristics of the sound (amplitude, frequency, spectrum) with perceptions of those characteristics (e.g., loudness, pitch, timbre). This allows auditory displays to employ equal steps in the perceptual dimension, as opposed to the physical dimension, which is crucial for effective auditory displays.

LOUDNESS

The most common attribute of sound used to convey information to a listener is its presence or absence. Warnings, status messages, and alerts are usually silent until a message needs to be communicated. It is crucial to know that the listener can detect the sound when required. Thus, the psychoacoustic research on minimum thresholds is important (e.g., see Hartmann, 1997; Licklider, 1951). Beyond the absolute detection of sounds, psychoacoustics has determined a power function that describes the way listeners perceive changes in sound intensity. This can allow a designer to create linear steps in loudness (i.e., perceived intensity), which may be more suited to representing certain types of data. At the upper end of the loudness scale, psychoacoustics has established guidelines for maximum exposure, for both single-event and continuous sounds (OSHA, 1981;

Salvendy, 1997). This information allows a designer to create an effective and nondamaging auditory display, be it an alert, a fire alarm, or a cockpit sonification. See Schlauch, this volume, for a more thorough treatment of loudness.

MASKING

The absolute limits of detecting a sound in ideal conditions (typical thresholds approach 20 micropascals SPL) are less important to the auditory display designer than determining whether a particular sound will be heard in a given situation. The concept of masking and the experiments that have determined the intensity, frequency, and temporal characteristics of masking have been helpful (for an overview, see Moore, 1989). Now designers can predict in advance whether the sounds they design will be heard. There are effective masking models that take into account the properties of human hearing and allow accurate assessment of competing sounds in a display or the interplay of the display and background noise sources (e.g., Zwicker & Scharf, 1965). Patterson's (1982) work to study the masking of cockpit warning sounds was an example of the interplay of psychoacoustics research and auditory display design. Those research findings, and the guidelines that resulted, are now part of the auditory display vernacular.

PITCH

Pitch is the most commonly used auditory display dimension. This is because it is easy to manipulate and, generally speaking, changes in pitch are easily perceived. The fact that pitch is less influenced by the listening environment than is loudness makes it a more robust display dimension. The limits of frequency perception, often quoted as 20–20,000 Hz for young healthy listeners, are well known in the auditory display field. Widespread study of these limits provides a general context for auditory displays, so the designer knows to avoid frequencies much below 80 Hz or above 10,000 Hz. However, perhaps even more important and useful is the experimental finding that sensitivity to pitch change varies with frequency (Robinson & Dadson, 1956), with peak sensitivity in the 3000-Hz range. Auditory display designers use this to center their displays in the most effectively perceived frequency region, typically 200–5000 Hz. This also happens to correspond to the central range of typical musical instruments, which facilitates the use of musical instrument digital interface (MIDI) and other music-based auditory display tools. Like masking concepts, research in the perception of harmonics can be used by auditory display designers to know in advance what pitches will be perceived, even if there are multiple frequencies in the display. The missing fundamental (Licklider, 1956; Schouten, 1940) is an example where psychoacoustic research helps auditory display developers to predict the perceptual experience of listeners in the pitch domain. Another area where the study of pitch perception has influenced auditory display is in the perception of slightly different frequencies. The beats that are heard when two sounds are detuned slightly can be used as a diagnostic tool in an auditory display, indicating that two parts are not aligned or a process parameter is just off target (Wenzel, 1994). See Schmuckler, this volume, for a more thorough discussion of pitch perception in general.

INTERACTING DIMENSIONS

Some perceptual dimensions are separable and some interact (e.g., Garner, 1974). The knowledge that pitch and loudness are interacting dimensions is important for auditory displays. The availability of equal-loudness contours (ISO, 1987), based on more recent efforts to refine the original work of Fletcher and Munson (1933) and Robinson and Dadson (1956), means that auditory displays can account for the nonlinearities in human auditory perception. This makes auditory displays that rely on detection of a sound (e.g., warnings) more effective and those that rely on the level of pitch or loudness more accurate. For example, a designer can use the equal-loudness contours, now described by a family of functions (ISO, 1987), to account for the effects of frequency on loudness. That is, an auditory display that uses frequency to represent temperature can be corrected so that all of the sounds have equal-sounding loudness, thereby isolating the information to the frequency dimension (for an example of this technique in use see B. N. Walker, 2000, 2002). See, also, Neuhoff's chapter on sound interaction, this volume, for more on this topic.

TEMPO AND RHYTHM

Tempo has been used in auditory displays for some time, especially to indicate the rate of a process or the frequency of an event (e.g., Geiger counter). From the psychoacoustics literature, two basic features of auditory perception have been discovered that indicate that sound can be effective for representing data in a variety of settings. First, auditory perception is particularly sensitive to temporal characteristics, or changes in sounds over time. Human auditory perception is well designed to discriminate between periodic and aperiodic events and can detect small changes in the temporal frequency of continuous signals (Fletcher, 1940; Resnick & Feth, 1975). This points to a distinct advantage of auditory over visual displays. Fast-changing or transient data that might be blurred or completely missed by visual displays may be easily detectable in even a primitive but well-designed auditory display (Kramer, 1994b). Thus, sonification is likely to be useful for comprehending or monitoring complex temporal data or data that are embedded in other, more static, signals. Jones, this volume, presents more on timing and temporal attention.

TIMBRE

Timbre is a catchall term in both psychoacoustics and auditory display, often used to mean all those sound attributes that are not loudness, pitch, or tempo. The ability to distinguish sounds of different timbres has been important in mapping data to sounds. This is largely because timbre plays a large role in stream grouping and segregation. This allows, for example, one data stream played with a flute-like sound to be distinguished from a second data stream played with a clarinet-like sound. On the other side of the same coin, research on timbre has shown how sounds in displays can be similar (Ballas, 1993; Bonebright, 2001), facilitating the creation of sound families and hierarchies.

Also, the psychoacoustics (and plain acoustical physics) involved in sorting out what makes a particular instrument or other acoustical event, such as impact or scraping, sound the way it does has been important in synthesizing sounds. Auditory icons rely on the timbral (and other) attributes of interface sounds to be representative of actual event-related sounds.

It should not be forgotten that aesthetics and acceptability play a major role in the success of an auditory display. Timbre and overall spectral attributes are crucial in getting a display to sound correct and sound good.

PAIN AND FATIGUE

Generally, designers avoid painful displays (!). However, without the psychophysical testing literature on both frequency and loudness (and their interaction), the limits of auditory pain would not be readily available to the auditory display designer. We can now simply ensure that sound levels and frequencies fall well within appropriate guideline limits (OSHA, 1981) (Salvendy, 1997). Much as with pain, the limits of using a system can be predicted quite well based not only on psychoacoustic experimentation designed to test fatigue and attention but also on extensive serendipitous knowledge gained by conducting all sorts of listening experiments. Psychoacoustic researchers have found that listeners simply do not provide the same level of attention after half an hour of testing. These factors can be used by auditory display designers to maximize the effectiveness and acceptability of their systems by avoiding the thresholds of auditory pain and fatigue.

SPATIAL LOCATION

Psychoacoustic research on spatial hearing has been widely employed by auditory display developers. The extensive research on first understanding spatial perception of sound and then developing methods for creating artificially spatialized sound (Wenzel, 1994) has opened the door for more sophisticated and effective auditory displays. As discussed earlier, using the spatial location of a sound as a display dimension can provide information in itself (location of a target) and can improve the number of channels or sources of data that can be displayed, especially in multitalker radio environments (Brungart, Ericson, & Simpson, 2002). The location of the sound can be used to separate (or group) different streams. Location can also analogously represent a change in a data variable. Psychoacoustics research has determined the angular resolution of our auditory system with both real and virtual sounds approximately 1–2° of azimuth in the front and 5–6° to the side (McKinley & Ericson, 1992; Mills, 1958), which is crucial if we want to know how well our display users will be able to estimate the data being represented (see also Carlile, Leong, & Hyams, 1997; Middlebrooks & Green, 1991).

Another useful aspect of spatial location that has been highlighted by psychoacoustic research is the fact that, unlike vision, perception of sound does not require the listener to be oriented in a particular direction. Auditory displays can therefore be used in situations where the eyes are already busy with another task. These characteristics make sound highly suitable for monitoring and alarm applications, particularly when these alarms may arise from many possible locations or when visual attention may be diverted from the alarm location.

STREAMING

Much is known about what general sound attributes will encourage or discourage grouping (see Bregman, 1990, for a thorough treatment). Perceptual research about streaming is very useful in an auditory display, where it can be used to cause different data representations to hang together or remain distinct. Several examples have already been presented here. To examine one of the examples in a bit more detail, consider the use of streaming in providing context in an auditory graph (e.g., Smith & Walker, 2002). A steadily beeping sound can represent the maximum value in a data set, thus providing context, much like a grid line drawn on a visual graph. Making sure that the tempo of the "max" sound was quicker than that of the sound representing the data resulted in two separate but coexistent auditory streams. For the most part, it was simply the *concept* of streams that was most useful to auditory display. The idea that there were ways to have multiple "auditory elements" in a display opened the door to high-dimensionality in auditory displays (e.g., up to 10 dimensions in Kramer, 1993). This possibility for auditory displays will continue to be one of its best-selling features. Unfortunately, until recently, psychoacoustics research has not been able to provide much more than sets of guidelines that recommend ways to encourage segregation or grouping; there were certainly no hard and fast rules. However, see Van Valkenburg and Kubovy, this volume, for the latest developments that shed new light on the auditory scene.

OTHER ASPECTS OF PERCEPTION

Other findings in the area of auditory perception bear on the promise of sound as a medium for data display and have helped to illuminate the optimal means of mapping data to specific dimensions of sound. These aspects include some studies on parallel listening (ability to monitor and process multiple auditory data sets, Astheimer, 1993); rapid detection, especially in high-stress environments

(Mowbry & Gebhard, 1961); affective responses, such as ease of learning and high engagement qualities of different sounds; and auditory gestalt formation and the discerning of relationships or trends in data streams (Kramer, 1994a; Kramer *et al.*, 1999). McAdams and Bigand (1993) also present a collection of papers discussing various aspects of auditory cognition. All of these findings address somewhat more complex listening phenomena and build on previous psycho-acoustic knowledge in a seeming evolution toward studies of more dynamic and higher level perception. All of these results can be used in the creation of more effective auditory displays, especially the results that provide more insight into the cognitive and meaning extraction process in auditory display use.

TRAINING AND PRACTICE EFFECTS

One more research focus germane to the present discussion is the role of learn-ing in auditory display efficacy. There are applications for which training is nec-essary to provide highly efficient performance. Blind users of assistive technology typically attain high skill levels, but only after extended practice (Earl & Leven-thal, 1999). The special abilities of skilled sonar operators is another example that shows how learning can significantly enhance the efficiency with which audi-tory patterns can be discerned (Howard & Ballas, 1982). Because learning results in basic perception and higher level cognitive processes becoming streamlined, a great amount of the cognitive psychology literature can also be useful for audi-tory display designers.

WHAT HAVE BEEN THE LIMITATIONS OF TRADITIONAL PSYCHOACOUSTICS (IN TERMS OF AUDITORY DISPLAYS)?

SOUND ATTRIBUTES

The most common limitation in the application of traditional psychoacoustics to auditory display research is the issue of *external validity*, that is, whether the experimental findings apply directly to real-world situations. First of all, the nature of the sounds in psychoacoustics research is typically unlike that of the sounds in real applications. The test sounds used in traditional research are usually simpler (often sine waves), cleaner, clearer, and presented at a higher signal-to-noise ratio than is typically available for auditory displays. When sound parameters are changed in the course of an experiment, it is generally only one or sometimes two parameters that are changed, while the rest are held constant. Further, within a trial or listening episode the sounds are usually static, unlike many auditory display sounds that vary continuously and often rapidly, in terms of pitch, tempo, timbre, or volume as data values change. That is, in a psychoacoustic experiment, pitch might be different from stimulus to stimulus, or trial to trial, but in an auditory display the sounds are often changing continuously. Walker and Ehrenstein (2000) showed that these *changes* in pitch, and not only the pitch value itself, can affect perception and performance with auditory displays.

In addition to the dynamics of sounds, the spectral characteristics (timbre) of laboratory sounds are often unlike those in real applications. Auditory display sounds that need to be realistic, or even just iconically related to real sounds, will have rich, complex spectra. The detection, perception, and comprehension of these sounds may very well be different from those of the simple tones typical of psychoacoustics experiments. This may be especially relevant in situations where the complex sounds coincide with other complex sounds, where issues of masking, beats, hidden frequencies, and so on may play out differently. It should be noted that it is not certain that major differences would be apparent—it is just that the results are not generally available, so the auditory display designer at present has no choice but to extrapolate from what is known about the perception and interpretation of simpler and more static sounds.

LISTENING ENVIRONMENT

Typical psychoacoustics research is regularly conducted in some form of "sound-attenuated" listening environment, often involving an isolated booth or even an anechoic chamber. This leads to a high signal-to-noise ratio and removes virtually all competing sounds (not to mention most or all echoes). However, this is not at all typical of real auditory display listening situations, especially in military or industrial applications such as in-vehicle communication, assembly line warnings, and so on. Even a regular office can have 40–60 dB of background noise from sources that include computers and equipment, other workers, telephones ringing, and so on. This limits the direct applicability of psychoacoustic findings about perception of sounds. The two main problems with this are (1) the masking issues that arise in the real listening environment and (2) issues related to attention and meaning making. Any competing sounds that are present in a psychoacoustics listening study are usually introduced by the experimenter, and are often very unlike real competing sounds. Noise of various specific types (e.g., white, pink, brown) is generally used to simulate external noises. In some cases, real–world distracters (such as airplane engine roar) can be successfully simulated by filtered artificial noise; however, most competing sounds are not so predictable.

The other issue here is how competing sounds affect comprehension. It is well known that divided attention can seriously affect perception (e.g., Egan, Carterette, & Thwing, 1954; Treisman, 1964, and see Jones, this volume), but an additional and more cognitive problem arises when there are different and incompatible sonifications competing. The designer of an auditory graphing application for sales data might represent increasing dollar values with increasing pitch. However, another auditory display application in the operating system (or elsewhere in the environment) might also use increasing pitch to represent the progress in a large file transfer. The designers probably never anticipated that their systems would compete with another system for the attentional resources of the listener (not to mention the sound output capabilities of the computer's sound card). Thus, the environment can influence both simple perception and more cognitive elements of the task, and researchers need to investigate this in the context of auditory displays.

HOW PARAMETERS INTERACT WITHIN A SOUND

Pollack and Ficks (1954) found that displays using multiple parameters of sound generally outperformed unidimensional displays measured elsewhere. Their research also indicated that the subdivision of display dimensions into finer levels does not improve information transmission as much as increasing the number of display dimensions. Kramer (1996) has suggested multiple mappings of data, whereby one series of data is used to change two or more parameters of the sound. For example, temperature might drive pitch, tempo, and brightness. How the resulting auditory display is perceived, and the meaning that would be communicated, remains to be tested rigorously. We should point out the work of Hellier, Edworthy, and their colleagues, in which the perceived urgency of an alarm was varied by adjusting the sound attributes (e.g., Edworthy, Loxley, & Dennis, 1991; see also Guillaume, Drake, Rivenez, Pellieux, & Chastres, 2002; Hellier, Edworthy, & Dennis, 1993). Adjusting more than one sound attribute (e.g., frequency and amplitude envelope) had a greater effect than achieved by adjusting just one attribute. All this leads to clear (and still unanswered) questions about which sound dimensions to involve in a display and how to use them alone or in combination to evoke specific perceptual or conceptual responses.

LIMITATIONS IN TASKS AND COGNITIVE DEMANDS

The tasks participants are asked to do in traditional psychoacoustical research are usually highly contrived and have limited external validity. There are often very few cognitive requirements in the task. For example, detecting a signal sound amid a background masker is instructive for listening researchers but is of narrow utility to auditory display research. A real-world detection task would probably involve several other cognitive elements, often including interpreting the meaning in the sounds and then deciding on an appropriate course of action as a result. Cognitive load and distraction are typically achieved through added sounds or secondary tasks such as remembering a number or counting backward, which have little to do with the complex perception and cognition tasks involved in auditory display perception. Simple alerts and warnings might be less affected by task demand increases, but, as pointed out by Smith and Walker (2002, p. 365), even the "basic" task of determining the price of a stock at a given time of day can involve the following perceptual and cognitive subtasks: "When given the opening [stock] price and asked to report the price at a given time (noon, for example), the subject must listen to the entire graph, recall the pitch he or she perceived at approximately half the duration (noon time), compare it to the pitch perceived at the very onset of the graph (the opening of trading), estimate the change in price represented by the difference between the noon-time pitch relative to the opening pitch, and add or subtract that change in price to the opening price of the stock." The cognitive demands of traditional psychoacoustics experiments do not even approach this level of complexity.

METAPHORS AND CONCEPTUAL MAPPINGS

The relationships between underlying data and their acoustical representations need not be arbitrary. At the metaphorical and symbolic end of the auditory display spectrum, data are represented by sounds that often have little or no apparent relation to the sound. For example, pitch may be used to represent the volume of product sales; this is an arbitrary and purely analogic mapping. It is possible, though, that particular sound attributes are simply better suited to display particular data types (Barrass, 1997; B. N. Walker, 2000, 2002). A *categorical* sound dimension such as timbre (i.e., distinct musical instruments) might be well suited to convey a categorical data distinction, such as different product lines (e.g., the Los Angeles office's hardware sales being played by a piano and the software sales being played by a trumpet). That same dimension of timbre (or instrument) would be less suited to convey the variations in a continuous variable, such as sales volume. That is, we could have a sonification using the mappings {product: instrument, dollars: pitch}, but not {product: pitch, dollars: instrument}. Second, there may be a preferred polarity to the mapping. The intended listening population may agree (or, at least, there may be a majority) that increasing frequency should be used to represent increasing sales volume. The issues surrounding such mapping choices have been discussed to some extent in the design literature, notably by Bertin (see also Barrass, 1997; 1981); however, this has not been a topic where the traditional psychoacoustics community has ventured (but see more on this topic subsequently). Mapping is crucial, though, for auditory display designers in a practical setting where decisions must be made, so it is encouraging that new approaches have been made (Edworthy *et al.*, 1991; B. N. Walker, 2000, 2002).

RIGID EXPERIMENTAL METHODS AND LANGUAGE

The psychoacoustics research field has provided many useful approaches and experimentation techniques. This and the means to communicate the results of such experiments have been listed here already as beneficial contributions. However, it is a double-edged sword: The methodological rigor and experimental "purity" generally required in a psychophysical experiment may not be required, or even possible, in some auditory display research. It may be impossible, for example, to isolate rigorously a single independent variable in a sonification experiment involving multidimensional data represented by a highly multivariate sound. In some cases, such as assessing the effectiveness of a particular alarm, more qualitative methods, which can still be based on deep scientific foundations, may be appropriate. It is simply important for auditory display designers and researchers to cast their net wide in the search for useful and appropriate ways to evaluate their designs. Language presents further problems. It is sometimes limiting to feel compelled to describe sounds in the somewhat sterile terms of frequency and envelope rather than with more descriptive terms such as warmth, raspiness, or buzziness, especially if the participants in a study use those terms. It seems somehow less scientific to write "more boingy," even if that captures the phenomenological experience. This tension between science and, well, art is not unique to auditory displays. Not infrequently, visual display designers struggle between the scientific world of terms such as visual angle, information density, and contrast sensitivity functions and more vernacular terms such as busy and cluttered. Auditory display designers need to be conversant in both forms of communication and need to feel comfortable using both traditional and nontraditional methods of testing and evaluation. It may be less traditional, but it need not be less scientific.

WHAT HAS RECENT RESEARCH INTO HIGHER LEVEL PHENOMENA OFFERED TO AUDITORY DISPLAY?

GIBSONIAN THINKING IN GENERAL

The first key contribution to auditory display from recent ecological approaches to perception and acoustics has been the general acceptance of the need to explore complex acoustic and perceptual phenomena and find new and appropriate means to do so. The possibilities have grown for conducting studies that do not hold all but one variable strictly constant, that are not necessarily performed in acoustically pure listening environments, and that involve more cognitive and even ill-defined tasks. This makes it feasible to study auditory display design and usage in realistic conditions, raising the validity and utility of the findings.

COMPLEX, DYNAMIC (ECOLOGICAL) SOUNDS

Studies have begun to look at sounds that change dynamically within a trial. Walker and Kramer (1996b) took a fairly classic approach, employing reaction time and accuracy measures to study a fictional crystal factory sonification. However, the sounds were very dynamic, with one of several possible sound parameters varying continuously on each trial. Further, the experiment involved a fairly complex monitoring task, where the listener had to interpret the problem with the factory and make a corrective action. Thus, the participants were listening for "pressure" or "temperature" changes and not "pitch" or "loudness." This type of conceptual listening, and the inclusion of dynamic sounds, is not representative of traditional psychoacoustics studies but it certainly is relevant for auditory display tasks.

Walker and Ehrenstein (2000) also examined reaction times, accuracy, and stimulus–response (S-R) compatibility effects involving dynamic sounds that changed in pitch during a trial. The findings that pitch *change* can be considered a dimension (in addition to pitch itself), and that S-R compatibility effects can arise from it, pointed out the need for designers of auditory displays to consider not only the perceptual issues resulting from their sounds but also the response requirements.

Neuhoff and McBeath (1996) have also examined perception of dynamic sounds, notably those that change in pitch and loudness as if they are moving toward or away from the listener. The implications for train warning horns are clear; but the results more generally point out the over- and underestimation of pitch and loudness that occur in these kinds of multidimensional sounds. For proper calibration and maximum comprehension, auditory display designers need to consider these findings with dynamic sounds.

More realistic sounds are being used in otherwise "traditional" studies, as well. For example, Bonebright (2001) used multidimensional scaling techniques to study perception and categorization of environmental sounds. The results can help auditory display designers anticipate the conceptual groupings that will happen when such sounds are used in the interface, as with earcons, or auditory icons. Ballas (1994) and Gaver (1994) have also investigated the use of "real-world" sounds. These studies allow a better understanding of the recognition of, memory for, and meanings attributed to, common environmental sounds when used in an auditory display. In some cases, studying these reality-based sounds can also allow the designer to extract the salient features and thereby use parameter-based synthesis models to create auditory icons that can have more in common (acoustically) with the objects they represent. Thus, the study of realistic sounds in some cases allows auditory designers to use those with a better level of understanding and in some cases allows designers to create artificial sounds that are more efficient but equally compelling and useful.

ACOUSTIC ECOLOGIES FOR OVERALL DESIGN

As the use of sound in human–machine interfaces increases, it is even more important to know how individual sounds will blend in or stand out from the growing acoustic crowd. However, it is also important to take into consideration the whole sound environment and design a total auditory display environment that supports the tasks as well as the persons in that environment. These design issues have been considered, although perhaps still less rigorously than they might, by the auditory perception community. For example, Walker and Kramer (1996a) point out that the nature of the human–system interaction ("concert" versus "conversation" modes) can inform the auditory display needs. They recommend that auditory (and visual) displays be designed to be adaptive to the interaction style. Some auditory display designers are now considering these issues in their designs, under the aegis of "contextual computing" (e.g., Nagel, Kidd, O'Connell, Dey, & Abowd, 2001), and are developing displays that adapt to the location, activities, and preferences of the intended listener.

METAPHORS AND CONCEPTUAL MAPPINGS

Traditional psychoacoustics has long been concerned with the issue of how listeners' perceptions of a sound (e.g., pitch) compare with the sound's physical parameter (e.g., frequency). Psychophysical scaling functions have been determined for all kinds of sound dimensions (e.g., Stevens, 1975). As auditory displays fill out more of the conceptual and symbolic end of the spectrum, it is crucial to know how listeners are interpreting the sounds, not just how they perceive them. Walker has been using magnitude estimation to determine psychophysical scaling functions between sound dimensions (frequency, tempo, brightness) and *conceptual* data dimensions, such as pressure, temperature, and number of dollars (B. N. Walker, 2000, 2002). It turns out that the best mappings depend not only on what the sound is but also what the data dimension is. For example, if frequency is used to represent temperature, the preferred polarity is positive. That is, increasing frequency represents increasing temperature. However, increasing frequency best represents decreasing size (B. N. Walker, 2000, 2002). In addition to the findings regarding polarity, this research shows that the slope of the magnitude estimation graph can be different for each data dimension. For example, a given change in frequency may best indicate a certain percentage change in temperature but a different change in pressure or number of dollars. Both the polarity preferences and scaling factors are now being used to create auditory displays that conform better to population expectancies (Smith & Walker, 2002; B. N. Walker, 2002).

One additional contribution from this line of research has been the finding that different listener populations can interpret auditory displays differently. Most notably, Walker and Lane (2001) found that visually impaired listeners and sighted listeners used different mental models to interpret the sounds they heard. For example, sighted undergraduates preferred the positive polarity mapping for frequency: number of dollars. That is, a higher frequency meant a greater number of dollars. For the blind listeners, increasing frequency unanimously meant *fewer* dollars. The study points out that different listening experience can affect how we interpret the sounds we hear. These results have practical utility for auditory display designers in that the designers can use different mappings for blind listeners. However, the research is probably just as important for its "philosophical" contribution, pointing out that designers really do need to "know their users" at a more cognitive level than had been addressed in traditional studies that generally diminished the importance of learning and experience for interpretation of sounds.

ALTERNATIVE EXPERIMENTAL METHODS

The general trend has been for researchers interested in auditory displays to use somewhat traditional methods (psychophysical scaling, magnitude estimation, multidimensional scaling) but employ more dynamic sounds, nontraditional listening environments, or more cognitive tasks. However, there have been some new experimental approaches, such as the "ventriloquism effect" for multimodal displays (A. Walker & Brewster, 2001), "audio descriptive analysis" for spatial sound displays (Zacharov & Koivuniemi, 2001), and the use of auditory displays as part of the experimental task (e.g., a crystal factory, B. N. Walker & Kramer, 1996b). Traditional experimental approaches would not have been very well suited to uncovering mental models, and previous applications might not have even cared much about that. Auditory displays require a new game plan.

WHERE ARE WE NOW AND WHERE DO WE NEED TO GO VIS-À-VIS AUDITORY DISPLAY?

Research in auditory perception has progressed from the study of individual auditory dimensions, such as pitch, tempo, loudness, and localization, to the study of more complex phenomena, such as auditory streaming, dynamic sound perception, auditory attention, and multimodal displays. The main research areas that will continue to drive sonification research forward include (1) understanding dynamic sound perception; (2) investigating auditory streaming; (3) cognitive issues in the relationship between conceptual (data) and auditory (display) features; (4) determining how meaning is attributed to sounds, based on the sounds, the listener, and the task requirements; and (5) understanding the design and use of multimodal sonification.

Other pertinent research includes investigation of the normal variation in perceptual and cognitive abilities and strategies in the human population; differences in cognitive representations of auditory displays for selected populations, such as sighted and blind individuals or different cultural groups; and the role of learning and familiarity in display efficacy. Study of these issues is necessary for the formulation of design guidelines for constructing efficient multivariate data displays using sounds.

Substantial questions remain in the area of multimodal perception. It is clear from existing research that our senses differ in their underlying abilities, but further research is necessary to identify what data features are perceptually most salient to each sense and to determine how to use this knowledge in designing effective displays. Multimodal interactions (e.g., between visual and auditory displays) are poorly understood, yet they critically affect most sonification applications. When does redundant presentation (that is, presenting information in more than one modality) improve the ability to extract data (i.e., cross-modal synergy)? When does information presented in one modality interfere with the perception of information in another modality (i.e., cross-modal interference)? How can the total amount of information perceived across all modalities be maximized?

SYNERGIES BETWEEN AUDITORY DISPLAY AND ECOLOGICAL PSYCHOACOUSTICS RESEARCH

Many of the questions presented here regarding ecological psychoacoustics, and other questions as yet unformulated, may be best approached via the field of auditory display. That is, abstract questions regarding auditory perception such as "How well can a person discriminate these three auditory variables?" may be more effectively approached by practical questions such as "Can users of this three-variable display perform a task which involves discerning the relative values of each of the three data dimensions being represented?" That is, the perceptual questions are addressed via a sonification task, thereby ensuring that the results will be clearly relevant to auditory displays. At the same time, the perceptual questions will yield findings that also have broad theoretical relevance.

It also seems likely that auditory display research will present new questions and perspectives to ecological psychoacoustics researchers. Display designs may present novel cognitive tasks, such as cross-modal pattern detection or discerning trends in highly multivariate displays. Fortunately, the displays presenting these perceptual quandaries will often also provide the experimental tools for their exploration. Thus, a synergy is created wherein auditory display research pushes the boundaries of ecological psychoacoustics, and ecological psychoacoustics informs and validates auditory display research. Both fields are thus broadened, refined, and brought to greater practical application.

REFERENCES

Astheimer, P. (1993). Realtime sonification to enhance the human–computer interaction in virtual worlds. *Proceedings of the Fourth Eurographics Workshop on Visualization in Scientific Computing*, Abingdon, England.

Ballas, J. A. (1993). Common factors in the identification of an assortment of brief everyday sounds. *Journal of Experimental Psychology, 19*, 250–267.

Ballas, J. A. (1994). Delivery of information through sound. In G. Kramer (Ed.), *Auditory display: Sonification, audification, and auditory interfaces* (pp. 79–94). Reading, MA: Addison-Wesley.

Barrass, S. (1997). *Auditory information design*. Unpublished dissertation, Australian National University.

Bertin, J. (1981). *Graphics and graphic information processing*. Berlin: Walter de Gruyter.

Blattner, M. M., Sumikawa, D. A., & Greenberg, R. M. (1989). Earcons and icons: Their structure and common design principles. *Human-Computer Interaction, 4*, 11–44.

Bly, S. (1982). *Sound and computer information presentation.* Unpublished Ph.D. dissertation, University of California, Davis.

Bonebright, T. (2001). Perceptual structure of everyday sounds: A multidimensional scaling approach. *Proceedings of the 7th International Conference on Auditory Display* (pp. 73–78), Espoo, Finland.

Bregman, A. S. (1990). *Auditory scene analysis: The perceptual organization of sound.* Cambridge, MA: MIT Press.

Brungart, D. S., Ericson, M. A., & Simpson, B. D. (2002). Design considerations for improving the effectiveness of multitalker speech displays. *Proceedings of the 8th International Conference on Auditory Display* (pp. 424–430), Kyoto, Japan.

Carlile, S., Leong, P., & Hyams, S. (1997). The nature and distribution of errors in sound localization by human listeners. *Hearing Research, 114,* 79–196.

Dombois, F. (2001). Using audification in planetary seismology. *Proceedings of the 7th International Conference on Auditory Display* (pp. 227–230), Espoo, Finland.

Dombois, F. (2002). Auditory seismology—On free oscillations, focal mechanisms, explosions, and synthetic seismograms. *Proceedings of the 8th International Conference on Auditory Display* (pp. 27–30), Kyoto, Japan.

Earl, C., & Leventhal, J. A. (1999). Survey of Windows screen reader users: Recent improvements in accessibility. *Journal of Visual Impairment and Blindness, 93*(3), 174–177.

Edworthy, J., Loxley, S., & Dennis, I. (1991). Improving auditory warning design: Relationship between warning sound parameters and perceived urgency. *Human Factors, 33,* 205–232.

Egan, J., Carterette, E., & Thwing, E. (1954). Some factors affecting multichannel listening. *Journal of the Acoustical Society of America, 26,* 774–782.

Fitch, W. T., & Kramer, G. (1994). Sonifying the body electric: Superiority of an auditory over a visual display in a complex, multi-variate system. In G. Kramer (Ed.), *Auditory display: Sonification, audification, and auditory interfaces* (pp. 307–326). Reading, MA: Addison-Wesley.

Fletcher, H. (1940). Auditory patterns. *Reviews of Modern Physics, 12,* 47–65.

Fletcher, H., & Munson, W. A. (1933). Loudness: Its definition, measurement, and calculation. *Journal of the Acoustical Society of America, 5,* 82–88.

Flowers, J. H., & Grafel, D. C. (2002). Perception of sonified daily weather records. *Proceedings of the Annual Meeting of the Human Factors and Ergonomics Society,* Baltimore, Maryland.

Garner, W. R. (1974). *Processing of information and structure.* Hillsdale, NJ: Erlbaum.

Gaver, W. W. (1989). The SonicFinder: An interface that uses auditory icons. *Human–Computer Interaction, 4*(1), 67–94.

Gaver, W. W. (1994). Using and creating auditory icons. In G. Kramer (Ed.), *Auditory display: Sonification, audification, and auditory interfaces* (pp. 417–446). Reading, MA: Addison-Wesley.

Gaver, W. W., Smith, R. B., & O'Shea, T. (1991). Effective sounds in complex systems: The ARKola simulation. *Proceedings of the CHI'91,* New York.

Gittins, D. (1986). Icon-based human-computer interaction. *International Journal of Man-Machine Studies, 24,* 519–543.

Guillaume, A., Drake, C., Rivenez, M., Pellieux, L., & Chastres, V. (2002). Perception of urgency and alarm design. *Proceedings of the 8th International Conference on Auditory Display* (pp. 357–361), Kyoto, Japan.

Hartmann, W. M. (1997). *Sounds, signals, and sensation: Modern acoustics and signal processing.* New York: Springer Verlag.

Hayward, C. (1994). Listening to the earth sing. In G. Kramer (Ed.), *Auditory display: Sonification, audification, and auditory interfaces* (pp. 369–404). Reading, MA: Addison-Wesley.

Hellier, E. J., Edworthy, J., & Dennis, I. (1993). Improving auditory warning design: Quantifying and predicting the effects of different warning parameters on perceived urgency. *Human Factors, 35,* 693–706.

Hemenway, K. (1982). Psychological issues in the use of icons in command menus. *Proceedings of the CHI'82 Conference on Human Factors in Computer Systems* (pp. 21–24), New York.

Howard, J. H., & Ballas, J. A. (1982). Acquisition of acoustic pattern categories by exemplar observation. *Organizational Behavior and Human Decision Processes, 30*, 157–173.

ISO (1987). *Acoustics—Normal equal-loudness level contours* (No. ISO 226:1987). Geneva: International Organization for Standardization.

Kolers, P. (1969). Some formal characteristics of pictograms. *American Scientist, 57*, 348–363.

Kramer, G. (1993). Sonification of Financial Data: An Overview of Spreadsheet and Database Sonification. *Proceedings of the Virtual Reality Systems '93*, New York.

Kramer, G. (1994a). An introduction to auditory display. In G. Kramer (Ed.), *Auditory display: Sonification, audification, and auditory interfaces* (pp. 1–78). Reading, MA: Addison Wesley.

Kramer, G. (1994b). Some organizing principles for representing data with sound. In G. Kramer (Ed.), *Auditory display: Sonification, audification, and auditory interfaces* (pp. 185–222). Reading, MA: Addison Wesley.

Kramer, G. (1996). *Mapping a single data stream to multiple auditory variables: A subjective approach to creating a compelling design.* Paper presented at the International Conference on Auditory Display, Palo Alto, CA.

Kramer, G., & Ellison, S. (1991). Audification: The use of sound to display multivariate data. *Proceedings of the International Computer Music Conference* (pp. 214–221), San Francisco.

Kramer, G., Walker, B. N., Bonebright, T., Cook, P., Flowers, J., Miner, N., et al. (1999). *The Sonification Report: Status of the Field and Research Agenda. Report prepared for the National Science Foundation by members of the International Community for Auditory Display.* Santa Fe, NM: International Community for Auditory Display (ICAD).

Licklider, J. C. R. (1951). Basic correlates of the auditory stimulus. In S. S. Stevens (Ed.), *Handbook of experimental psychology* (pp. 985–1039). New York: Wiley.

Licklider, J. C. R. (1956). Auditory frequency analysis. In C. Cherry (Ed.), *Information theory* (pp. 253–268). New York: Academic Press.

Martins, A. C. G., & Rangayyan, R. M. (1997). Experimental evaluation of auditory display and sonification of textured images. *Proceedings of the Fourth International Conference on Auditory Display (ICAD97)* (pp. 129–134), Palo Alto, CA.

McAdams, S., & Bigand, E. (Eds.). (1993). *Thinking in sound: The cognitive psychology of human audition.* New York: Clarendon Press.

McKinley, R. L., & Ericson, M. A. (1992). Minimum audible angles for synthesized localization cues presented over headphones. *Journal of the Acoustical Society of America, 92*, 2297.

Middlebrooks, J. C., & Green, D. M. (1991). Sound localization by human listeners. *Annual Review of Psychology, 42*, 135–159.

Mills, A. W. (1958). On the minimum audible angle. *Journal of the Acoustical Society of America, 30*, 237–246.

Moore, B. C. J. (1989). *An introduction to the psychology of hearing.* London: Academic Press.

Mowbry, G. H., & Gebhard, J. W. (1961). Man's senses as informational channels. In H. W. Sinaiko (Ed.), *Human factors in the design and use of control systems* (pp. 115–149). New York: Dover.

Nagel, K., Kidd, C. C., O'Connell, T., Dey, A., & Abowd, G. D. (2001). The family intercom: Developing a context-aware audio communication system. *Proceedings of the Ubicomp 2001* (pp. 176–183), Atlanta GA.

Neuhoff, J., & McBeath, M. K. (1996). The Doppler illusion: The influence of dynamic intensity change on perceived pitch. *Journal of Experimental Psychology: Human Perception and Performance, 22*, 970–985.

OSHA (1981). *OSHA Standard 1910.95: Occupational noise exposure*: Occupational Safety and Health Administration.

Ossner, J. (1990). Transnational Symbols: The rule of pictograms and models in the learning process. In J. Nielsen (Ed.), *Designing user interfaces for international use* (pp. 11–38). Amsterdam: Elsevier.

Patterson, R. D. (1982). *Guidelines for auditory warning systems on civil aircraft.* London: Civil Aviation Authority.

Pereverzev, S. V., Loshak, A., Backhaus, S., Davis, J. C., & Packard, R. E. (1997). Quantum oscillations between two weakly coupled reservoirs of superfluid 3He. *Nature, 388*, 449–451.

Pollack, I., & Ficks, L. (1954). Information of elementary multidimensional auditory displays. *Journal of the Acoustical Society of America, 26*, 155–158.

Proctor, R. W., & Reeve, T. G. (Eds.). (1990). *Stimulus-response compatibility: An integrated perspective*. Amsterdam: North Holland.

Resnick, S. B., & Feth, L. L. (1975). Discriminability of time-reversed click pairs: Intensity effects. *Journal of the Acoustical Society of America, 57*, 1493–1499.

Robinson, D. W., & Dadson, R. S. (1956). A re-determination of the equal-loudness relations for pure tones. *British Journal of Applied Physics, 7*, 166–181.

Salvendy, G. (1997). *Handbook of human factors and ergonomics* (2nd ed.). New York: Wiley.

Sanders, M. S., & McCormick, E. J. (1993). *Human factors in engineering and design* (7th ed.). New York: McGraw-Hill.

Scarf, F. L. (1979). Possible traversals of Jupiter's distant magnetic tail by Voyager and by Saturn. *Journal of Geophysical Research, 84*, 4422.

Schiffman, H. R., Reynolds, M. L., & Young, F. L. (1981). *Introduction to multidimensional scaling*. New York: Academic Press.

Schouten, J. F. (1940). The residue and the mechanism of hearing. *Proceedings of the Koninklijke Nederlandse Akademie Van Wetenschappen, 43*, 991–999.

Shneiderman, B. (1998). *Designing the user interface: Strategies for effective human–computer-interaction* (3rd ed.). Reading, MA: Addison Wesley Longman.

Smith, D. R., & Walker, B. N. (2002, 2–5 July). Tick-marks, axes, and labels: The effects of adding context to auditory graphs. *Proceedings of the 8th International Conference on Auditory Display* (pp. 362–367), Kyoto, Japan.

Sorkin, R. D. (1987). Design of auditory and tactile displays. In G. Salvendy (Ed.), *Handbook of human factors* (pp. 549–576). New York: Wiley.

Speeth, S. D. (1961). Seismometer sounds. *Journal of the Acoustical Society of America, 33*, 909–916.

Stevens, S. S. (1975). *Psychophysics: Introduction to its perceptual, neural, and social prospects*. New York: Wiley.

Treisman, A. (1964). The effects of irrelevant material on the efficiency of selective listening. *American Journal of Psychology, 77*, 533–546.

Uzilevsky, G., & Andreev, V. (1993). Iconic signs and languages in user interface development. In L. J. Bass, J. Gomostaev, and C. Unger (Eds.), *Human-computer interaction. Selected papers from Third International Conference, EWHCI'93* (pp. 115–124). Heidelberg: Springer-Verlag.

Valenzuela, M. L., Sansalone, M. J., Krumhansl, C. L., & Streett, W. B. (1997). Use of sound for the interpretation of impact-echo signals. *Proceedings of the Fourth International Conference on Auditory Display (ICAD97)* (pp. 47–56), Palo Alto, CA.

Walker, A., & Brewster, S. (2001). "Sitting too close to the screen can be bad for your ears": A study of audio-visual location discrepancy detection under different visual projections. *Proceedings of the 7th International Conference on Auditory Display* (pp. 86–89), Espoo, Finland.

Walker, B. N. (2000). *Magnitude estimation of conceptual data dimensions for use in sonification*. Unpublished Ph.D. dissertation, Rice University, Houston, TX.

Walker, B. N. (2002). Magnitude estimation of conceptual data dimensions for use in sonification. *Journal of Experimental Psychology: Applied, 8*, 211–221.

Walker, B. N., & Ehrenstein, A. (2000). Pitch and pitch change interact in auditory displays. *Journal of Experimental Psychology: Applied, 6*, 15–30.

Walker, B. N., & Kramer, G. (1996a). Human factors and the acoustic ecology: Considerations for multimedia audio design. *Proceedings of the Audio Engineering Society 101st Convention*, Los Angeles.

Walker, B. N., & Kramer, G. (1996b). Mappings and metaphors in auditory displays: An experimental assessment. *Proceedings of the 3rd International Conference on Auditory Display (ICAD96)* (pp. 71–74), Palo Alto, CA.

Walker, B. N., & Lane, D. M. (2001). Psychophysical scaling of sonification mappings: A comparison of visually impaired and sighted listeners. *Proceedings of the 7th International Conference on Auditory Display* (pp. 90–94), Espoo, Finland.

Wenzel, E. M. (1994). Spatial sound and sonification. In G. Kramer (Ed.), *Auditory display: Sonification, audification, and auditory interfaces* (pp. 127–150). Reading, MA: Addison-Wesley.

Zacharov, N., & Koivuniemi, K. (2001). Audio descriptive analysis and mapping of spatial sound displays. *Proceedings of the 7th International Conference on Auditory Display* (pp. 95–104), Espoo, Finland.

Zwicker, E., & Scharf, B. (1965). A model of loudness summation. *Psychological Review, 72,* 3–26.

7

ENVIRONMENTAL ACOUSTICS:

PSYCHOLOGICAL ASSESSMENT OF NOISE

SEIICHIRO NAMBA AND SONOKO KUWANO

From the viewpoint of environmental psychology, especially environmental acoustics, noise is one of the important social problems. Noise is defined as "unwanted sounds" and brings us various adverse effects. When we are exposed to very intensive noise for some period, our hearing will be damaged. Perhaps needless to say, exposure to such intensive noise should be avoided. On the other hand, even if the noise is not so intensive, it may cause serious effects such as speech interference, sleep disturbance, effect on mental tasks, and annoyance. The noise problems occur on the basis of our perception of the sound. It is important to find a method for controlling the sounds in order to reduce the effect of noise. There are two aspects in the subjective assessment of noise.

The first is to find the physical metrics that show good correspondence with subjective impressions. Here, psychophysical measurement can be used as a basic method to find the law between physical values and subjective judgments. It is important to examine the validity of the law found in experiments in order to determine the applicability of the results to practical situations. A robust law is desirable.

The second is to measure the degree of disturbance effect of noise and determine the permissible level of noise and/or noise criteria. A rating scale or category scale is often used in order to measure annoyance. It must be carefully considered that the frame of reference has a great effect on the judgment using a category scale. In the case of annoyance judgment, the frame of reference includes both stimulus context and social background.

In this chapter, the effect of the social and psychological frame of reference as well as the physical stimulus context on the assessment of environmental noise is discussed on the basis of the results from our laboratory experiments and cross-cultural studies.

PSYCHOPHYSICAL METHODS AND PHYSICAL METRICS FOR THE EVALUATION OF NOISE

Various metrics for evaluating the effect of noise have been proposed (Architectural Institute of Japan, 1981). Because the metrics are used for the assessment of and/or finding countermeasures to noise, they are required to show good correspondence with subjective impressions. Several kinds of psychophysical methods are often used to find good metrics for noise.

The authors have conducted a series of experiments using artificial and actual noises and found that L_{Aeq} (equivalent continuous A-weighted sound pressure level, i.e., A-weighted mean energy level) shows a good correspondence with subjective impressions. Examples are shown in Figs. 1–4. The results of 11 experiments are plotted together in Fig. 1 (Namba, Kuwano, & Kato, 1978). Each of the experiments was conducted independently with each sound source. The method of adjustment and magnitude estimation were used in these experiments. It was found that loudness shows good correspondence with the mean energy level.

In the experiment shown in Fig. 2 (Namba & Kuwano, 1984), various sounds, such as aircraft noise, train noise, and road traffic noise, were included in a stimulus context and presented in random order. Their loudness was judged using magnitude estimation. Points of subjective equality (PSE) were calculated using a power function of road traffic noise as a reference. It can be seen that L_{Aeq} is a good measure of the loudness of various sounds as the first approximation.

The Environmental Quality Standard of Noise was revised in Japan in September 1998 and issued in April 1999, adopting the mean energy level (equivalent continuous A-weighted sound pressure level; L_{Aeq}) as the index of noise criteria.

The median of level fluctuation (L_{50}) was used in the former Environmental Quality Standard in Japan. In order to examine the applicability of L_{50}, the loudness of artificial level-fluctuating sounds was obtained using the method of adjustment (Namba, Nakamura, & Kuwano, 1972). The result is shown in Fig. 3. It was found that the loudness increases according to the mean energy level although the value of the median (L_{50}) was kept constant. It was confirmed that the mean energy level is a good measure of loudness. On the other hand, it is clear that loudness does not correspond with L_{50}.

Similar results were found when subjective impression was judged using the method of adjustment and category scale (Namba & Kuwano, 1991) as shown in Figs. 4 and 5. There is a good correspondence between the logarithmic scale of

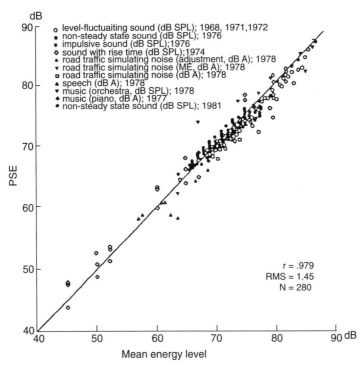

FIGURE 1 Relation between loudness and mean energy level. All 280 data points of our 11 experiments are plotted together. A high correlation can be seen between them. (From Namba *et al.*, 1978; Namba & Kuwano, 1984, Fig. 1, p. 136.)

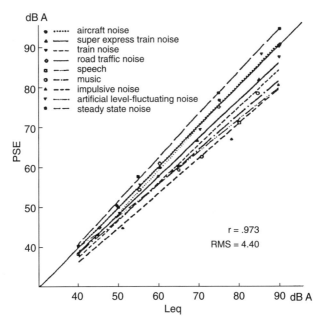

FIGURE 2 Relation between L_{Aeq} and loudness for nine kinds of sound sources judged in the same context. PSEs were calculated from magnitude estimation. (From Namba & Kuwano, 1984, Fig. 4, p. 141.)

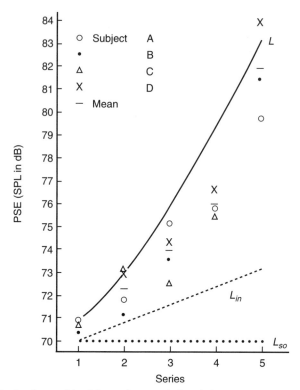

FIGURE 3 Loudness of level-fluctuating sounds in relation to L_{50} and mean energy level. Although the value of L_{50} was kept constant, loudness increased as the mean energy level increased. (From Namba *et al.*, 1972, Fig. 1, p. 253.)

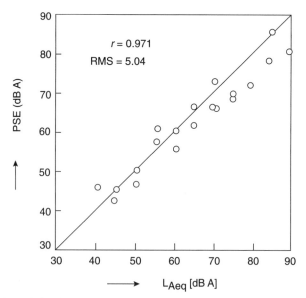

FIGURE 4 Relation between L_{Aeq} and loudness. PSEs were obtained using the method of adjustment. The results were similar to those in Fig. 2. (From Namba & Kuwano, 1991.)

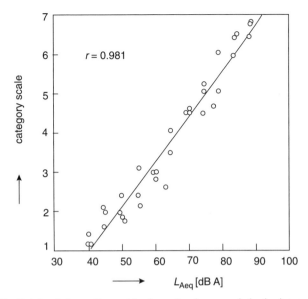

FIGURE 5   Relation between L_{Aeq} and loudness. Loudness was judged using a category scale. (From Namba & Kuwano, 1991.)

magnitude estimation and the linear scale of category scale as shown in Fig. 6. The fact that the same results were found with different methods suggests that the results of the measurements are valid.

The law of mean energy level is very robust and is applicable to various kinds of level-fluctuating sounds, except for impulsive sounds. In the case of impulsive sounds with duration shorter than about 1 second, the total energy of the sound, sound exposure level, L_{AE}, is a good measure of loudness (Kuwano, Namba, & Kato, 1978; Kuwano, Namba, Miura, & Tachibana, 1987).

STUDIES OF NOISE CRITERIA

CATEGORY SCALE

When the permissible level of noise is determined, the responses are usually obtained using category judgments and the dose–response relation between the percentages of highly annoyed people and L_{Aeq} is often used (e.g., Schultz, 1978). However, it is well known that there is a context effect in the judgments using the category scale as shown in Fig. 7. It is not clear whether the context effect is really a perceptual phenomenon or a kind of artifact by assignment of categories. The fact that a context effect was found even when reaction time (Namba, Yoshikawa, & Kuwano, 1968) and evoked potentials (Kuwano, Shimokochi, &

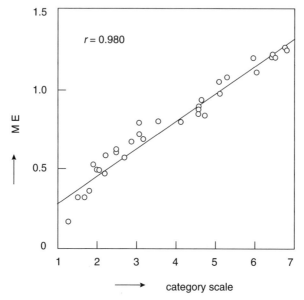

FIGURE 6 Relation between loudness obtained from magnitude estimation (ME) and a category scale. (From Namba & Kuwano, 1991.)

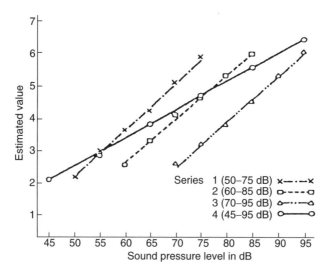

FIGURE 7 Context effect found in the judgment of the noisiness of train noise. (From Namba *et al.*, 1968, Fig. 1, p. 194.)

Yamaguchi, 1969) were used suggests that the context effect may exist reflecting the perceptual phenomenon. On the other hand, it cannot be denied that subjects may possibly assign the given categories to the whole stimulus range, as the "range-frequency model" proposed by Parducci (1963; 1974) predicted. When such an assignment is made, the judgment does not reflect the perception but may be a kind of ordering. This must be avoided, especially when the permissible level of noise is considered.

CATEGORY SCALE (ONE JUDGMENT BY ONE SUBJECT)

If subjects do not know the stimulus context, the context effect does not appear (Stevens & Poulton, 1956). In our experiment, in which the permissible level of air-conditioner noise was examined (Kuwano & Namba, 1985a), subjects judged the noisiness of air-conditioner noise after an exposure for 90 minutes during which they were devoted to mental tasks. Each subject judged the air-conditioner noise only once. Sometimes they reported that they did not notice the sound. It was suggested from this experiment that the permissible level of air-conditioner noise was about 45 dBA. The context effect can be avoided by this procedure, but because there are individual differences in the judgment, many subjects are needed.

CATEGORY SPLITTING PROCEDURE

Heller (1985) proposed the category splitting procedure. The sound is presented twice. When the sound is presented first, subjects are asked to judge the sound in five categories: "very soft," "soft," "medium," "loud," "very loud." When the sound is presented the second time, they judge it by subdividing the category they selected into 10 steps for finer grading. This means that the judgment is divided into 50 categories finally. It is reported that an absolute judgment of loudness can be obtained by this procedure. It seems that by splitting the judgments into two steps it would be difficult to assign the sounds and absolute judgment can be obtained compared with conventional category judgment. This method is used especially for hearing aid fitting, which requires absolute loudness judgment with high accuracy. Standardizing this method for audiological purposes is now being discussed in an International Organization for Standardization (ISO) working group (ISO TC43/WG 7).

FREQUENCY OF THE RESPONSE

Many social surveys of noise problems have been conducted in various places in the world. They are usually conducted independently, and their results cannot be compared with each other. If they could be compared with each other, more valuable information would be obtained. A committee of the Acoustical Society of Japan (Namba et al., 1996) has proposed the fundamental items that should be included in the social surveys on noise problems so that the social surveys can be compared. Category scale is often used in social surveys. After a great deal of discussion in the committee about whether the category scale should be used, it was decided not to use the category scale. This is partly because the word that indicates the degree—e.g., very, fairly, a little—is vague. Instead of the category scale, a filter question about whether a given sound is audible or not and a question about whether the sound is annoying or not were adopted. This type of question is fairly free from the problems involved in the category scale, and it was found that the percentage of annoyed people can be used as an index for dose–response relations as shown in Fig. 8 (Kuwano, Namba, & Florentine, 1997). This figure shows a good correspondence between the frequency of the responses and L_{Aeq} as usually found in category judgment (Fig. 9). At present, the fundamental items for social surveys are being discussed again by the Committee of the Acoustical Society of Japan. The idea of having common items that should be used in social surveys on noise problems has also been discussed internationally in the ISO (ISO/TS 15666:2003), and the International Commission on Biological Effects of Noise (ICBEN).

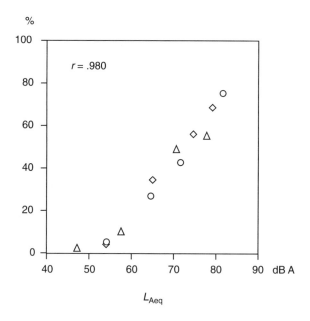

sleep distubance

O; aircraft noise,   ◇; train noise,   △; road traffic noise

FIGURE 8   Relation between L_{Aeq} and the percentages of the respondents who were disturbed by the noise. (From Kuwano et al., 1997, Fig. 2, p. 770.)

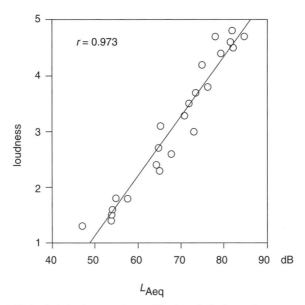

FIGURE 9   Relation between L_{Aeq} and loudness judged on a five-category scale.

CONTINUOUS JUDGMENTS BY CATEGORY

When a vehicle is approaching, we feel that the sound is becoming louder and louder. When it is leaving, we feel that the sound is becoming softer and softer. It is impossible to obtain this kind of continuous judgment by conventional psychological methods. Namba and Kuwano *et al.* (e.g., Kuwano & Namba, 1985b; Namba & Kuwano, 1980) have developed a method called the "method of continuous judgment by category" in order to obtain instantaneous judgment continuously. Valuable information can be obtained by relating instantaneous judgments and instantaneous physical properties of the sounds and by relating instantaneous judgments and the overall impression of a whole range of the sounds. In an experiment using the method of continuous judgment by category, subjects are asked to judge the instantaneous impression of the sound using seven categories and to press a key on a computer keyboard corresponding to their impression at that time. Subjects need not respond if their impression does not change. When they press a key, it is presented on a monitor and the impression registered on the monitor is considered to remain. When their impression changes, they are required to press the corresponding key. This method is free from assignment of numbers to the sounds because subjects are not compelled to respond all the time.

Using the method of continuous judgment by category, many experiments have been conducted (e.g., Kuwano, 1996). Some experiments were conducted outdoors in which subjects were asked to judge the loudness of the sounds that were audible in the surroundings (Kaku, Kato, Kuwano, & Namba, 1997, 1999;

Kuwano, Kaku, Kato, & Namba, 1998). There were some varieties in the range of the sounds. The results for eight locations are plotted together in Fig. 10. The lowest stimulus range was from 49 to 57 dB (L7 in Fig. 10) and the highest was from 55 to 74 dB (L5 in Fig. 10). Although there is a slight difference in judgment according to the stimulus range, it is much smaller than that found in Fig. 7.

In an experiment using the method of continuous judgment by category, assignment can be avoided and there is little end effect. This may be because subjects are not required to respond to all the stimuli. Subjects have to respond only when their impression of the sound changes. Even if the stimulus changes physically, subjects do not always have to respond to the change. This causes little range effect.

In addition to having little range effect, the method of continuous judgment by category has other merits as follows: (1) it is easy for subjects to judge the stimulus, (2) judgments can be made in a situation similar to that of daily life, (3) subjects judge the sound in a stream and do not pay special attention to any specific stimulus, (4) the method can be applied for a long sound, and (5) various analyses can be done using the data stored in a computer.

Simple dose–response relationships can be measured with any psychophysical methods and scaling methods. However, in the decision about a permissible level, it is necessary to find the absolute degree of the effect of noise, such as that noise is intolerable, serious, endurable, not annoying at all, and so on (Schick, 1979, 1981). For this purpose the category scale is often used. An attempt should

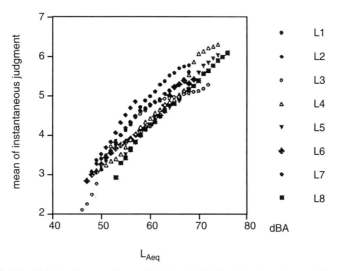

FIGURE 10 Relation between L_{Aeq} and loudness judged at eight locations outside. Although there is a slight difference in the judgment according to the stimulus range, it is much smaller than the context effect shown in Fig. 7. (From Kuwano et al., 1998.)

be made to avoid the biases that accompany the category judgment when the absolute effect of noise is examined. The method of continuous judgment by category is proposed as one of such trials.

THE EFFECT OF CULTURAL AND SOCIAL FACTORS AS A FRAME OF REFERENCE

Noise is defined psychologically as "unwanted sound." The subjective meaning of sounds has significant effects on the judgment of actual sounds. If the sound is accepted as being pleasant, such as music, it is judged as being softer than, for example, aircraft noise, which is usually accepted as being unpleasant. This may be a psychological frame of reference. Also, cultural and social factors compose the frame of reference. This kind of the frame of reference should be taken into account in the evaluation of noise (Kuwano & Namba, 2000).

THE EFFECT OF THE SUBJECTIVE MEANING OF SOUND SOURCES

L_{Aeq} showed good correlation with loudness of various sounds as shown in Fig. 2. Strictly speaking, however, there were slight but significant difference in the loudness among different sound sources when the sound level was high. Aircraft noise was judged louder than train noise, for example, when their L_{Aeq} values were equal. In addition to the experiment, a questionnaire survey was conducted and the result suggests that the subjective meaning of the sounds has an important effect even on loudness judgment. This result suggests that L_{Aeq} can be used as a basic metric that can be applied to various level-fluctuating sounds with the same cognitive meaning. But the effects of noise are strongly affected by non-physical factors, such as the utility of noise sources and the degree of acceptance of noise sources in society. It is necessary to take these factors into account to determine the noise criteria. To avoid the effect of these nonphysical factors, it may be important to determine the permissible level of each sound source independently.

When synthesized sounds were judged that simulate the sound level patterns of actual sounds used in the former experiments with pink noise as the carrier, there was no difference among sound sources except for impulsive sounds (Kuwano, Namba, & Fastl, 1988). An example of the results is shown in Fig. 11. When the sound sources cannot be identified, the loudness is determined mainly by L_{Aeq}.

THE EFFECT OF CULTURAL DIFFERENCE

In the evaluation of noise, cultural and social factors should be taken into account. In order to examine these factors, cross-cultural study is effective.

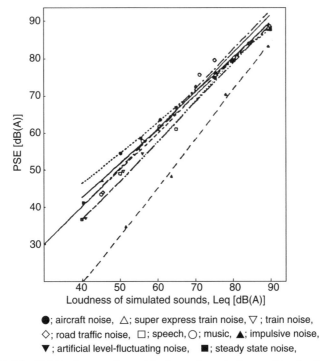

●; aircraft noise, △; super express train noise, ▽ ; train noise,
◇; road traffic noise, □; speech, ○; music, ▲; impulsive noise,
▼ ; artificial level-fluctuating noise, ■; steady state noise,

FIGURE 11 Relation between L_{Aeq} and loudness of sounds, the sound level patterns of which were simulations of actual sounds. When the sound sources were not identified, the loudness shows a good correlation with L_{Aeq} except for impulsive sounds. (From Kuwano *et al.*, 1988, Fig. 4, p. 460.)

It was found in our cross-cultural study (Namba, Kuwano, & Schick, 1986; Namba *et al.*, 1991) that there is a cross-cultural difference in the impression of sounds and attitude toward noise. The impression of various sounds was judged using a semantic differential in Japan, Germany, the United States, and China in our study (Kuwano *et al.*, 1999). The sounds used were aircraft noise, train noise, road traffic noise, speech, music, and construction noise. The relation of loudness judgments between German and Japanese subjects is shown in Fig. 12. German subjects tend to consider construction noise louder than Japanese subjects, while they considered music and speech softer. There was little difference between Japan, the United States, and China in loudness judgments.

It is desirable to have an international standard for audio signals that tell people when something dangerous happens. In our study of danger signals (Kuwano, Namba, Fastl, & Schick, 1997), the impression of synthesized signals was judged using a semantic differential in Germany and Japan. It was suggested that frequency-modulated sounds are appropriate for danger signals because both German and Japanese subjects judged them as being dangerous. On the other hand, a cross-cultural difference was found in the impression of a sound such as a bell. An example is shown in Fig. 13. This signal was perceived as being

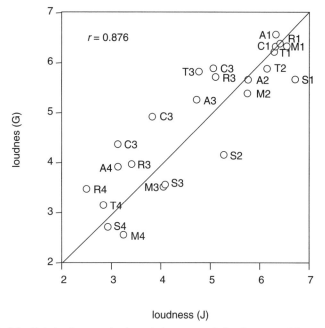

FIGURE 12 Relation between loudness judgments made by German and Japanese subjects. (From Kuwano *et al.*, 1999.)

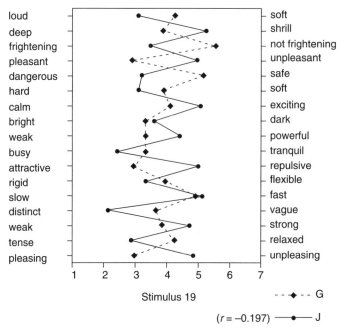

FIGURE 13 Semantic profiles for the sound of a bell judged by German and Japanese subjects. (From Kuwano *et al.*, 1997, Fig. 4, p. 126.)

dangerous by Japanese subjects but as being safe by German subjects. German subjects associated the sound with a church bell, but Japanese subjects associated it with a fire engine. The impression of sounds may be affected by cognitive differences.

CONCLUSION

There are two aspects in the subjective assessment of noise. The first is to find physical metrics that show a good correspondence with subjective impressions in order to predict the effect of noise. Psychophysical methods of measurement such as magnitude estimation are good methods for this purpose. It was found that there is a good correlation between the mean energy level (L_{Aeq}) and the loudness of level-fluctuating sounds. Moreover, the validity of the law of mean energy level has been confirmed using various methods of measurement. It was also found that the law can be applied to various kinds of environmental noises.

The second is to measure the degree of the disturbance effect of noise and determine noise criteria. A category scale is often used for this purpose. However, biases are included in category judgment in which the given categories may be assigned to the whole stimulus range as in the range-frequency model of Parducci. This is a law of judgment, not of sensation. Various approaches to reduce the effect of range have been introduced. The method of continuous judgment is one of the examples in which subjects do not always have to respond to changes in the sounds. Finally, cultural and social factors as well as physical properties of the sounds have an effect on noise evaluation, and cross-cultural studies are effective in examining the effects of cultural and social factors.

REFERENCES

Architectural Institute of Japan (Ed.). (1981). *Methods for evaluating the effect of noise.* Tokyo: Shokokusha.

Heller, O. (1985). Hrfeldaudiometrie mit dem Verfahren der Kategorienuntereiling (KU). *Psychologische Beitraege, 27,* 478–493.

Kaku, J., Kato, T., Kuwano, S., & Namba, S. (1997). A field experiment on the evaluation of environmental noise: An approach of the method of continuous judgment by category. *Proceedings of the Spring Meeting of the Acoustical Society of Japan* (pp. 767–768), Tokyo.

Kaku, J., Kato, T., Kuwano, S., & Namba, S. (1999). Predicting overall reaction to multiple noise source. EAA/ASA Joint Meeting, Berlin.

Kuwano, S. (1996). Continuous judgment of temporally fluctuating sounds. In H. Fastl, S. Kuwano, and A. Schick (Eds.). (1996). *Recent trends in hearing research* (pp. 193–214). Oldenburg: BIS.

Kuwano, S., & Namba, S. (1985a). Permissible level of air-conditioner noise. *Journal of the ergonomic Society of Japan, 21,* 144–145.

Kuwano, S., & Namba, S. (1985b). Continuous judgment of level-fluctuating sounds and the relationship between overall loudness and instantaneous loudness. *Psychological Research, 47,* 27–37.

Kuwano, S., & Namba, S. (2000). Psychological evaluation of temporally varying sounds with LAeq and noise criteria in Japan. *Journal of the Acoustical Society of Japan. (E), 21*(6), 319–322.

Kuwano, S., Kaku, J., Kato, T., & Namba, S. (1998). Psychological evaluation of sound environment with mixed sources. *Proceedings of the International Congress on Acoustics* (pp. 1131–1132). Seattle, WA.

Kuwano, S., Namba, S., & Fastl, H. (1988). On the judgment of loudness, noisiness, and annoyance with actual and artificial noises. *Journal of Sound and Vibration, 127,* 457–465.

Kuwano, S., Namba, S., Fastl, H., & Schick, A. (1997). Evaluation of the impression of danger signals—comparison between Japanese and German subjects. In A. Schick and M. Klatte (Eds.), *Contribution to psychological acoustics* (pp. 115–128). Oldenburg: BIS.

Kuwano, S., Namba, S., Fastl, H., Florentine, M., Schick, A., Zheng, D. R., Hoege, H., & Weber, R. (1999). *A cross-cultural study of the factors of sound quality of environmental noise.* Presented at the EAA/ASA Joint Meeting, Berlin.

Kuwano, S., Namba, S., & Florentine, M. (1997). Style of questionnaires in social survey on noise problems. *Proceedings of the Spring Meeting of the Acoustical Society of Japan* (pp. 769–770), Tokyo.

Kuwano, S., Namba, S., & Kato, T. (1978). Loudness of impulsive sounds. *Journal of the Acoustical Society of Japan, 34,* 316–317.

Kuwano, S., Namba, S., Miura, H., & Tachibana, H. (1987). Evaluation of the loudness of impulsive sounds using sound exposure level based on the results of a round robin test in Japan. *Journal of the Acoustical Society of Japan (E), 8,* 241–247.

Kuwano, S., Shimokochi, M., & Yamaguchi, Y. (1969). Context effect on loudness judgment and V-potential. *Japanese Journal of Physiology, 31,* 119.

Namba, S., & Kuwano, S. (1980). The relation between overall noisiness and instantaneous judgment of noise and the effect of background noise level on noisiness. *Journal of the Acoustical Society of Japan (E), 1,* 99–106.

Namba, S., & Kuwano, S. (1984). Psychological study on L_{eq} as a measure of loudness of various kinds of noises. *Journal of the Acoustical Society of Japan (E), 5,* 135–148.

Namba, S., & Kuwano, S. (1991). The loudness of non–steady state sounds—Is a ratio scale applicable? In S. J. Bolanowski, Jr. and G. A. Gescheider (Eds.), *Ratio scaling of psychological magnitude* (pp. 229–245). Hillsdale, NJ: Lawrence Erlbaum Associates.

Namba, S., Igarashi, J., Kuwano, S., Kuno, K., Sasaki, M., Tachibana, H., Tamura, A., & Mishina, Y. (1996). Report of the Committee on the Social Survey on Noise Problems. *Journal of the Acoustical Society of Japan (E), 17,* 109–113.

Namba, S., Kuwano, S., Hashimoto, T., Berglund, B., Zheng, D. R., Schick, A., Hoege, H., & Florentine, M. (1991). Verbal expression of emotional impression of sound: A cross-cultural study. *Journal of the Acoustical Society of Japan (E), 12,* 19–29.

Namba, S., Kuwano, S., & Kato, T. (1978). On the investigation of L_{eq}, L_{10} and L_{50} in relation to loudness. *Journal of the Acoustical Society of America, 64,* S58.

Namba, S., Kuwano, S., & Schick, A. (1986). A cross-cultural study on noise problems. *Journal of the Acoustical Society of Japan (E), 7,* 279–289.

Namba, S., Nakamura, T., & Kuwano, S. (1972). The relation between the loudness and the mean of energy of level-fluctuating noises. *Japanese Journal of Psychology, 43,* 251–260.

Namba, S., Yoshikawa, T., & Kuwano, S. (1968). Context effects in loudness judgment. *Japanese Journal of Psychology, 39,* 191–199.

Parducci, A. (1963). A range-frequency compromise in judgment. *Psychological Monographs, 77*(2, whole no. 565), 1–50.

Parducci, A. (1974). Context effects: A range-frequency analysis. In E. C. Carterette and M. P. Friedman (Eds.), *Handbook of perception* (vol. II), *Psychophysical judgment and measurement* (pp. 127–142). New York: Academic Press.

Schick, A. (1979). *Schallwirkung aus psychologischer Sicht.* Stuttgart: Klett-Cotta.

Schick, A. (1981). *Akustik zwischen Physik und Psychologie*. Stuttgart: Klett-Cotta.

Schultz, T. J. (1978). Synthesis of social surveys on noise annoyance. *Journal of the Acoustical Society of America, 64*, 377–405.

Stevens, S. S., & Poulton, E. C. (1954). The estimation of loudness by unpracticed observers. *Journal of Experimental Psychology, 51*, 71–78.

8

ECOLOGICAL

DEVELOPMENTAL

PSYCHOACOUSTICS

LYNNE A. WERNER AND LORI J. LEIBOLD

Ecological theories of perception hold that perception involves detecting affordances, the fit between an organism's capabilities and the environmental opportunities to exercise those capabilities. Further, the ecological view is that the environment provides patterns of optic, acoustic, and other information that designate the nature of the affordances of objects and events (Gibson, 1986). Whereas psychophysics is the study of the relationship between characteristics of stimuli and sensation, ecological psychophysics studies the relationship between characteristics of stimuli as they occur in the real world and perception of real-world objects and events. Ecological psychoacoustics has dual goals. First, it identifies the available acoustic information specifying objects and events. Second, it seeks to determine what of the available information is used by listeners and the relationship between variations in that information and the objects or events perceived.

Several of the chapters in this book lament the lack of information regarding auditory perception in real environments and try to understand the factors that have led to the paucity of research in this area. In the case of perceptual development, however, there is a long-standing interest in infants' or children's perception of ecologically relevant objects and events because it has long been understood that these perceptions are what drive many aspects of development. Anyone who has watched an infant "playing" will quickly come to the conclusion that the infant is learning about affordances of objects and events. Thus, although not all perceptual development research could be classified as "ecological," the approach is not foreign to anyone in the field and different aspects of the ecological approach appear in many papers on perceptual development (e.g., Cooper, 1997; Gogate, Bahrick, & Watson, 2000; Walker-Andrews, 1997).

Moreover, there is extensive literature explicitly addressing the ecological approach to perceptual development, clearly summarized by Gibson and Pick (2000).

What is lacking in the perceptual development literature is information on perceptual development in the auditory domain. The purpose of this chapter is to attempt to apply the ecological approach to an account of auditory development. The chapter has two parts. First, we consider how the development of psychoacoustic abilities would be expected to influence the information available to infants and children about auditory objects or events. Second, we consider the development of auditory perception within the framework of ecological psychology, asking whether ecological theory provides a reasonable account of age-related changes in complex auditory perception.

DEVELOPMENTAL PSYCHOACOUSTICS AND THE PICKUP OF ACOUSTIC INFORMATION

To identify an auditory object, a listener must analyze the complex sound reaching the ear in terms of its component frequencies, their amplitude, and temporal variations in the spectrum. Once this analysis is completed, the components of sound emanating from a given auditory object must be identified and usually coordinated with information received through other sensory modalities. These processes typically occur under conditions of uncertainty: the listener does not know exactly when an event will occur and does not know *a priori* what event will occur. Each of these components of object identification develops during infancy and childhood. The question is how development in these realms influences what infants and children hear.

DEVELOPMENT OF FREQUENCY, INTENSITY, AND TEMPORAL RESOLUTION

Frequency resolution is a fundamental characteristic of the auditory system. Individual components of sounds must be selectively analyzed before more complex processing takes place. Not surprisingly, frequency resolution abilities have been well examined during development. Although it is immature during early infancy, the findings of several studies suggest that frequency resolution is mature by 6 months postnatal age (Hall & Grose, 1991; Olsho, 1984; Spetner & Olsho, 1990).

Several paradigms have been used to examine frequency resolution during development. In psychophysical tuning curve methods, the level of a narrowband masker needed to just mask a pure tone signal is estimated. Because the masker affects only the audibility of signals passing through the same auditory filter, plotting the level of the masker required to mask the signal, as a function of masker frequency, provides an estimate of the auditory filter.

Olsho (1984) reported psychophysical tuning curves for 6-month-old infants using signal frequencies ranging from 500 to 4000 Hz. Average infant and adult tuning curve shape and width were similar at each of the signal frequencies tested. Subsequent studies by Schneider, Morrongiello, and Trehub (1990) and Spetner and Olsho (1990) produced results consistent with those of Olsho (1984). Spetner and Olsho (1990) also measured psychophysical turning curves for 3-month-old infants using signal frequencies of 500, 1000, and 4000 Hz. Although mature tuning was observed at 500 and 1000 Hz, immature tuning curves were measured at 4000 Hz. Taken together, these studies indicate that auditory filter width is immature at high frequencies among 3-month-olds but is mature across frequency by 6 months of age. Because similarly immature high-frequency resolution has been observed in the auditory brainstem response, but not in cochlear responses (e.g., Abdala & Folsom, 1995; Abdala & Sininger, 1996; Folsom & Wynne, 1987), it is believed that early age-related deficits in frequency resolution are neural in origin.

The auditory filter width paradigm has been used to examine the frequency resolution abilities of older children. As with the psychophysical tuning curve paradigm, the task is to detect a pure tone signal in the presence of a masker. However, the masker contains a spectral notch with no acoustic energy falling in the frequency region surrounding the signal frequency. The width of this notch is systematically varied, altering the amount of masker energy that is allowed to pass through the auditory filter containing the signal. Signal threshold is then measured at different notch widths, and the shape of the function describing notch width and threshold provides an estimate of auditory filter width. Using this method, mature auditory filter widths have been measured in 4- and 6-year-old children (Hall & Grose, 1991)

Infant performance on measures of intensity processing appears to take longer to reach mature levels than on measures of frequency resolution (reviewed by Werner, 1996). Infant high-frequency detection thresholds in quiet improve by approximately 40 dB to near adult-like levels between birth and early childhood. Low-frequency detection thresholds in quiet, although initially more mature, take longer to develop, reaching mature levels by about age 10 (Allen & Wightman, 1994; Olsho, Koch, Carter, Halpin, & Spetner, 1988; Schneider, Trehub, Morrongiello, & Thorpe, 1986; Werner & Gillenwater, 1990).

Intensity discrimination and detection thresholds in noise follow a time course of development similar to that of detection thresholds observed in quiet, although they do not show the same "high-frequency-first" frequency gradient. Moreover, mature levels are typically reached for both measures at the end of the preschool years (Allen & Wightman, 1994; Bargones, Werner, & Marean, 1995; Jensen & Neff, 1993; Schneider, Trehub, Morrongiello, & Thorpe, 1989; Sinnott & Aslin, 1985).

It appears that the differences between infants and adults in intensity processing result from several different factors. In particular, the development of the middle ear has been shown to play a significant role in the apparent age differences in absolute sensitivity observed during infancy and childhood (Keefe, Bulen, Arehart, & Burns, 1993; Keefe, Burns, Bulen, & Campbell, 1994; Keefe & Levi, 1996). Contributions are also thought to come from neural immaturity, inattentiveness, and listening strategy (discussed later; Allen & Wightman, 1994; Bargones et al., 1995; Werner & Boike, 2001; Werner, Folsom, & Mancl, 1994).

Temporal resolution refers to the ability to follow rapid changes in the envelope of a sound. Most investigations of infants and young children have estimated temporal resolution using gap detection methods. In brief, gap detection paradigms measure the shortest silent gap in a sound that is detected by the listener. Using this paradigm, temporal resolution abilities in infants and young children appear to be quite poor. For example, Irwin, Ball, Kay, Stillman, and Rosser (1985) reported that children's performance did not reach adult levels until age 10 using low-frequency noise bands. However, only slight improvements in performance were observed between age 6 and adulthood using high-frequency noise bands. In a later study, Wightman, Allen, Dolan, Kistler, and Jamieson (1989) reported immature gap thresholds for noise bands centered at 400 and 2000 Hz in preschoolers. Their results suggest that 3- and 4-year-olds have immature temporal resolution abilities, although performance was adult-like by age 5. No difference in performance across noise-band frequencies was observed. Similarly, Werner, Marean, Halpin, Spetner, and Gillenwater (1992) reported no frequency gradient in the gap detection thresholds of 3-, 6-, and 12-month-old infants. Infants at all three ages tested performed poorly.

Performance on other measures of temporal processing, including duration discrimination and temporal integration, does not appear to mature until at least age 6 (reviewed by Werner & Marean, 1995). In particular, studies of duration discrimination in 4- to 10-year-olds follow the age-related changes in performance observed in the gap detection studies (Elfenbein, Small, & Davis, 1993; Jensen & Neff, 1993; Morrongiello & Trehub, 1987).

Several investigators have suggested that temporal resolution is, in fact, much better than performance on gap detection tasks would indicate and that the poorer performance observed during infancy and childhood results from immaturities in other areas of processing (reviewed by Werner, 1996). In particular, intensity coding may affect infant performance on measures of temporal processing. Several studies report more mature temporal resolution estimates using a temporal modulation transfer function (TMTF) method that separates the effects of temporal and intensity processing (Hall & Grose, 1994; Levi & Werner, 1996). TMTF methods estimate temporal resolution by determining the depth of amplitude modulation that is required for modulation detection as a function of modulation frequency.

Thus, frequency resolution appears to be mature by 6 months of age and temporal resolution may well be mature by 6 months of age, but intensity resolution follows a more prolonged developmental course extending into the preschool years. There is a growing consensus that intensity processing immaturity among preschoolers results from processing inefficiency (e.g., Hartley, Wright, Hogan,

& Moore, 2000). Thus, by 6 months of age humans have a fairly precise, if noisy, neural representation of sounds.

DEVELOPMENT OF SOUND LOCALIZATION

Of all auditory capacities, sound localization is most clearly expected to undergo development during infancy and childhood because the head grows. Growth of the head leads to a progressive change in all of the acoustic cues to sound source location, including interaural intensity differences, interaural time (or phase) differences, and the shape imposed upon the spectra of sounds by the direction-dependent resonance characteristics of the external ear. Not only the magnitude of the cues but also the frequency ranges within which they are useful will change as the head grows. Blauert (1983) discusses the acoustic cues to sound location and the psychophysics of sound localization in detail.

Despite the acoustic limitations on sound localization during infancy, even newborn infants have been shown to localize sound at least crudely. For example, Field *et al.* (1980) demonstrated that newborn infants would, if properly supported, turn their head toward the hemifield in which a sound is presented. This response, however, depends on the characteristics of the sound presented; temporally varying broadband sounds, including speech, are effective stimuli (Clarkson & Clifton, 1991; Clarkson, Clifton, Swain, & Perris, 1989; Tarquinio, Zelazo, & Weiss, 1990). That newborns can localize sounds to some extent within hemifields is indicated by the fact that the magnitude of the head turn they make, although always undershooting the actual position of the sound source, increases progressively as the position of the sound source is shifted in azimuth (Morrongiello, Fenwick, Hillier, & Chance, 1994).

The head turn is limited as a measure of sound localization ability, however, because it depends on both sensory and motor development. Indeed, the sort of head turn made by newborns toward a sound source occurs less frequently among 2-month-olds than among younger infants (Clifton, Morrongiello, & Dowd, 1984; Field, Muir, Pilon, Sinclair, & Dodwell, 1980) and is only truly robust among infants older than 5.5 months of age (Moore, Thompson, & Thompson, 1975). This change is generally thought to result from a sensorimotor reorganization rather than a regression of sound localization ability (e.g., Clifton, 1992).

The minimum audible angle (MAA), the threshold for a shift in sound source angular position, can be estimated without relying on robust directional head turns, however. Morrongiello and her colleagues (1994) used an observer-based procedure (Werner, 1995) to estimate the MAA in the horizontal plane for newborn infants. Basically, they determined how big a shift from midline to one side in the horizontal plane was needed for an observer to determine reliably that a shift had occurred on the basis of the infant's response to the sound shift. The MAA estimated was about 30° in azimuth. Morrongiello, Fenwick, and Chance (1990) followed the development of the MAA between 8 and 28 weeks of age, reporting a progressive decline from about 26 to about 14° in azimuth over that age range. A number of studies have estimated the MAA in infants and children older than 6 months of age. Their results are summarized by Clifton (1992). The MAA appears to decrease progressively from about 14° at 6 months to about 5° at 18 months to near-adult levels at 5 years of age[1] (Ashmead, Clifton, & Perris, 1987; Litovsky, 1997; Morrongiello & Rocca, 1990).

Morrongiello's group has also examined the development of the MAA in the vertical plane (Morrongiello, 1988; Morrongiello & Rocca, 1987). MAAs were measurable for infants only for the highest frequency stimulus used, an 8- to 12-kHz noise band. Again, the MAA was found to decrease with age between 6 and 18 months of age from about 14° to less than 4°, similar to that estimated for adults for broadband stimuli.

Finally, some work has been done on the development of distance perception among infants (Clifton, Perris, & Bullinger, 1991; Perris & Clifton, 1988). These studies have made observations of infants' reaching for objects in the dark. Infants are familiarized with a visible sounding object. Then the lights are turned out and the infant's responses to the now invisible sounding object are recorded when the object is within the infant's reach and when the object is beyond the infant's reach. The results showed that 6-month-olds reached for within-reach objects but not for beyond-reach objects. Moreover, when the position of the object was held beyond reach but the intensity of sound produced by the object was increased to simulate a near object, infants did not reach for the object (Litovsky & Clifton, 1992). This result was particularly interesting because adults asked to estimate the position of the object tended to depend solely on sound intensity to judge distance. Thus, in this case infants appeared to use more cues to estimate distance than adults did.

An important question is the source of immaturities in sound localization during infancy. Certainly, the acoustic information available to infants for sound localization is limited, but is that the entire explanation? Ashmead, Davis, Whalen, and Odom (1991) approached this question by comparing the time course of maturation of interaural time difference (ITD) discrimination with that of the MAA. Although the MAA improved between 16 and 28 weeks, ITD discrimination did not. Moreover, the ITD discrimination thresholds obtained would predict an MAA much better than that observed. Although this experiment does not eliminate acoustic factors as contributors to poor sound localization, it does suggest that other factors are at work. It is often suggested that the development of sound localization largely depends on the development of a map of auditory space. This idea is supported by observations that normal experience with sound is necessary for the development of sound localization (e.g., Knudsen, 1988), that humans with abnormal binaural experience can discriminate interaural differ-

---

[1] This is not to say that sound localization is entirely mature at 5 years. Litovsky (1993) has demonstrated that 5-year-olds do not integrate information about reflected sound into their perceptions of sound location as adults do.

ences but still not localize sound accurately (Wilmington, Gray, & Jahrsdorfer, 1994), and that measured auditory spatial maps become increasingly organized with age in at least one nonhuman species (Gray, 1992).

DEVELOPMENT OF SOUND
SOURCE SEGREGATION

Sound source segregation refers to the process by which acoustic components are identified as coming from one or more sound sources. The problem of sound source segregation, as noted in several of the previous chapters, is very complex. Not only does each sound source produce waveforms consisting of many individual frequencies, but also these spectral patterns change over time. In addition, many sound sources can be active at once and the listener must determine which frequency components arose both sequentially and simultaneously from the same source. An important question during auditory development is whether infants are born with mature sound source segregation abilities or whether experience and/or sensory development is required to realize these skills fully.

Streaming methods are often used to assess sound source segregation in adults. These methods take advantage of the fact that a single sound sequence is often perceived as more than one distinct sound source, provided that certain acoustic characteristics are sufficiently different across alternating sound elements. For example, a listener might perceive a single sound stream when a sequence consists of elements that are similar in frequency, intensity, and/or spatial location. However, frequencies, intensities, and/or spatial locations located far apart usually come from different sound sources. Thus, two distinct streams might be perceived if individual elements alternate between two remote values in any of these characteristics.

The literature describing the development of sound source segregation abilities is sparse. In part, this lack of information reflects how difficult it is for infants and young children to perform the conventional tasks. In contrast to the case of adults and older children, verbal instructions cannot be used to direct the attention of infants or young children, nor can infants directly indicate whether they perceive a sound sequence as a single stream or multiple streams. Nonetheless, infants are obviously able to segregate sound sources to some degree. Otherwise, they would not be able to identify their mother's voice in the presence of other sounds. However, it is unclear which cues infants use to segregate incoming sound sources and whether there are cues that infants cannot use because of limitations in their sensory processing abilities. In addition, it is unclear whether infants are as proficient as adults at using these cues.

The results of several investigations suggest that infants organize auditory streams at least qualitatively as adults do. These studies were interested in determining which streaming cues infants use on auditory streaming tasks using simple musical sequences that adults are known to organize into two different streams

(Demany, 1982; Fassbender, 1993; McAdams & Bertoncini, 1997). Because infants cannot verbalize their judgments, discrimination paradigms were used to assess indirectly streaming abilities in infants. Two types of tonal sequences were the stimuli. Adults were easily able to tell that the order of tones in one type of sequence had changed when the sequence was heard as two auditory streams. It was impossible for a listener to tell that the order of tones in the other type of sequence had changed when the sequence was heard as one auditory stream. The logic is that if infants detect a change in order for the first type of sequence but not the second, they had heard the sequences as two auditory streams. The infants were presented with a particular sequence of tones. The sequence was repeated until infants' response habituated. Recovery of response to the changed sequence was taken as evidence of discrimination. Using these procedures, Demany (1982) examined the performance of 7- to 15-week-old infants using sequences that adults organized into two streams on the basis of frequency proximity. Infants' discriminination of changes in tone order mirrored that of adults.

A second study examined the ability of 2- to 5-month-old infants to discriminate tone sequences using frequency range, intensity, or timbre (Fassbender, 1993). Again, the findings suggest that infants organize the streams in a similar way to adults. Finally, McAdams and Bertoncini (1997) examined musical streaming in 3- to 4-day-old infants using both timbre and spatial position as cues for streaming. Infants and adults discriminated the sequences in a similar way, although the infants were not able to discriminate the sequences when a fast tempo/small interval configuration was used. The authors suggested that neonates possess the ability to segregate musical streams, although there are limits in their temporal or frequency resolution abilities. Taken together, these three studies suggest that sound source segregation abilities are present in some form very early during infancy and that infants can use the same types of information that adults use to segregate sound sources. However, the limits of infants' sound source segregation abilities have not been tested. Further, the existing studies used very simple stimuli consisting of tones that never overlapped in time. In contrast, most everyday sounds are more complex, overlapping in both frequency and time.

There is evidence that 7.5-month-old infants can separate two overlapping streams of speech produced by two different talkers provided that a signal-to-noise ratio (SNR) of 5–10 dB exists between the two sources (Newman & Jusczyk, 1996). Of interest, both voices were presented over the same loudspeaker, suggesting that the infants do not require spatial cues in order to segregate the sources. The authors suggest that infants may be able to perform this task at a lower SNR with increased spatial separation.

Following sound source segregation, listeners must selectively choose a source to attend to. Thus, a complete discussion of the development of sound source segregation cannot be completed without considering how auditory selective attention develops. Although the results from Newman and Jusczyk (1996) strongly suggest that 7.5-month-olds can selectively attend to a single sound source presented with a competing source, selective attention in the auditory system has not been well studied during infancy. Several dichotic listening studies have been conducted with children. In these studies, listeners are presented with dichotic speech stimuli and asked to attend selectively and repeat back the information heard in one ear. On these tasks, older children perform better and produce fewer errors than younger children (e.g., Doyle, 1973), suggesting that the ability to attend selectively to sound sources continues to improve into childhood. However, alternative explanations have not been eliminated, including developmental improvements in short-term memory, planning, or sustained attention. Investigations using stimuli that are known to be easily segregated by infants are necessary to study auditory selective attention during development.

DEVELOPMENT OF LISTENING UNDER UNCERTAIN CONDITIONS

Everyday sounds are broadband and dynamic, containing both relevant and irrelevant signals. Listeners often do not know when a relevant signal will occur or what information will be contained in the signal. Understanding how infants and young children learn to identify the important signals from a background that is unpredictable is a critical step toward understanding development in the auditory system.

Many studies have examined the effects of stimulus uncertainty on detection and discrimination in trained adults (e.g., Kidd, Mason, Deliwala, Woods, & Colburn, 1994; Neff & Dethlefs, 1995; Neff & Green, 1987; Oh & Lutfi, 1999; Watson, Wroton, Kelly, & Benbassat, 1975). Stimulus uncertainty can be created by variations in either the relevant target (the signal) or the irrelevant background (the masker). In adults, the influence of signal uncertainty on detection threshold is typically small (3–6 dB). Although signal frequency has usually been varied (e.g., Green, 1961), similar findings have been reported for signal duration (Dai & Wright, 1995). In contrast, substantial detection threshold elevations have been observed under conditions in which masker uncertainty is high. In particular, large threshold elevations are observed when the frequency content of the masker is varied from presentation to presentation (e.g., Neff & Green, 1987; Watson et al. 1975). Although most investigations have used noise or tonal stimuli, similar findings have been reported using everyday sounds (Oh & Lutfi, 1999). This increase in masking is observed in the absence of overlapping patterns of excitation on the basilar membrane, indicating that it cannot be explained by conventional "energetic" masking principles that involve peripheral limitations of the auditory system (e.g., Fletcher, 1940) That is, masking is observed even though the signal and masker are well resolved by the peripheral auditory system.

Masking that cannot be explained by peripheral limitations has been referred to as "informational" masking (Pollack, 1975).

The literature regarding performance under conditions of stimulus uncertainty during development is sparse. In particular, performance under conditions of uncertainty has not been directly investigated during infancy. However, at least two studies have examined the listening strategies of young children under conditions of uncertainty. The findings suggest that children have more difficulty than adults in detecting a tone in an uncertain background. First, Allen and Wightman (1995) measured detection thresholds for a 1000-Hz pure tone in the presence of broadband noise and a single, random-frequency pure tone. Although large individual variability was observed for both groups, children generally performed worse than adults. Of the 17 preschoolers tested, only 7 had thresholds less than 90 dB SPL. However, in the 7 children who produced measurable thresholds, performance was often adult-like. Second, Oh, Wightman, and Lutfi (2001) examined informational masking in preschoolers and adults by measuring detection threshold for a 1000-Hz pure tone in the presence of a simultaneous multitone masker complex. The frequencies and amplitudes of the masker components varied independently and randomly on each presentation. The number of components in the masker ranged from 2 to 906 across experimental conditions. Again, large individual differences were evident for both groups, although the average child's performance was worse than the average adult's performance. Further, the observed age differences were well modeled as an increase in the number of auditory filters over which children integrate information compared with adults.

In addition to the substantial threshold elevations exhibited by adults under conditions of uncertainty, large individual differences in performance are observed. It is interesting that elevated thresholds and large individual variability are hallmark characteristics of infants' and children's psychoacoustic performance (Werner, 1996). Thus, the performance of infants and children in conventional psychoacoustic tasks appears similar to adults' performance in studies of stimulus uncertainty. In other words, infants and children behave as if they are uncertain even when the stimulus is not. Although the data are few, they are generally consistent with this viewpoint. For example, Bargones and Werner (1994) demonstrated that infants do not listen for an expected signal during a detection task. Listeners were presented with an "expected" 1000-Hz signal on 75% of the signal trials. In the remaining 25% of signal trials, two "unexpected" probe frequencies were presented. Consistent with previous studies, adults detected the expected 1000-Hz signal at a higher rate than the unexpected probes. In sharp contrast, infants detected expected and unexpected frequencies equally well. These results indicate that adults listen selectively in the frequency domain but that infants do not.

Subsequent research describing the psychometric function for detection is consistent with the idea that infants and adults listen differently (e.g., Bargones *et al.*, 1995; Werner & Boike, 2001; Werner & Marean, 1995). Specifically, infants appear to monitor many auditory filters at the same time. That is, they use a "broadband" listening strategy. As a result, infants exhibit masking when neither energetic nor informational masking would occur in adults. Werner and Bargones (1991) have described such "distraction effects" in 6-month-old infants. Infant and adult detection thresholds for a 1000-Hz tone were measured in quiet. Thresholds for the same 1000-Hz tone were also determined in the presence of a gated, bandpass noise (4000–10,000 Hz) presented at either 40 or 50 dB SPL in separate conditions. Finally, thresholds for the same tone were estimated in the presence of a continuous bandpass noise masker (4000–10,000 Hz), presented at 40 dB SPL. Threshold elevations of approximately 10 dB were observed for the infants in the presence of the noise band. These elevations were observed whether the noise was continuous or gated with the target on each trial. Because the frequency of the noise was far removed from the critical band of the 1000-Hz signal, the findings suggest that the cause of the threshold elevation was not at the level of the auditory periphery. In contrast, adult thresholds in quiet and in noise were not significantly different.

In summary, several studies of young children suggest that they have particular difficultly when masker uncertainty is high (Allen & Wightman, 1995; Oh *et al.*, 2001). Moreover, both infants and children appear to integrate information across auditory filters differently than adults. Although no studies have directly investigated infants' performance when masker uncertainty is high, the characteristics of infant listening are consistent with the idea that listeners become more selective in the way they extract information from complex sounds as they mature.

DEVELOPMENT OF INTERSENSORY PERCEPTION

How coordination of information acquired through different sensory modalities arises in development has long provided a battleground for the empiricist–nativist war. Whereas empiricists argue that information from different sensory modalities must become associated, or integrated, based on observations of co-occurrence in the environment, nativists hold that the sensory modalities are initially integrated, that the organism naturally perceives events as unified across modalities. Piaget (e.g., 1954) is frequently cited as a proponent in the empiricist tradition, and James and Eleanor Gibson (e.g., Gibson, 1986, 2000) are often cited in more recent papers as rooted in the nativist tradition. It is clear on several grounds that neither of these extreme positions can actually explain the development of intersensory perception. For example, although it is known that the brain has evolved to handle intersensory events, with circuitry designed to represent an event equivalently whether it is sensed through the visual, auditory, or somatosensory system (Stein & Meredith, 1993), it is also known that the development of the circuitry depends on experience with events sensed simultaneously through multiple sensory systems (e.g., Knudsen, 1988; Withington-Wray, Binns, & Keating, 1990). Further, not all intersensory information is redundant (or "amodal" in the Gibsonian terminology). For example, whereas the sight, the sound, and the feel of a rattle shaking all indicate the rhythm of the rattle's motion, the sight, the sound, and the feel of a car idling in the driveway do not provide equivalent information about the vehicle. Some intersensory perception, then, involves relatively arbitrary associations of information from different sensory modalities that must be learned through experience with events in the environment. Although perception of such events is no less holistic in the mature perceiver, it must involve integration of information across sensory modalities rather than a simple coordination (e.g., Massaro, 1998; McGurk & MacDonald, 1976).

Another important observation in this regard is that intersensory perception appears to undergo age-related change during the first year of postnatal life in humans. It has been demonstrated that 1-month-olds discriminate a change in temporal synchrony between auditory and visual events (Lewkowicz, 1996) although their "window" for simultaneity or colocation may be considerably wider than that of an adult (Lewkowicz, 1999). In addition, newborns notice when previously colocated sound and sight move to separate locations (Morrongiello, Fenwick, & Chance, 1998). Thus, it appears that infants notice correspondences between auditory and visual events from birth.

In contrast, attempts to demonstrate that infants perceive events coordinated in the auditory and visual domains as unitary events are typically successful only with infants older than about 4 months of age. Infants older than about 4 months of age have been reported to perceive all manner of unitary auditory–visual unit events. For example, Kuhl and Meltzoff (1982) showed that 4-month-olds looked longer at the talking head articulating the temporally synchronized vowel in the accompanying soundtrack. Further, infants did not demonstrate a similar preference when the soundtrack was a temporally synchronized pure tone (Kuhl, Williams, & Meltzoff, 1991). Five-month-olds looked longer at a film of a car driving away than of a car driving toward them when the sound of the motor on the accompanying soundtrack was decreasing in intensity and vice versa (Walker-Andrews & Lennon, 1985). However, Lewkowicz (1999) reported that 6-month-olds, but not 3-month-olds, look longer at a display when the durations of auditory and visual events are equal than they do when the durations are mismatched. Bahrick (1987) showed 3- and 6-month-olds films of one of two transparent cylinders moving back and forth. One of the cylinders contained one large marble; the other contained several smaller marbles. The 6-month-olds, but not the 3-month-olds, looked longer at the film that matched the synchronized soundtrack of the appropriate object(s) hitting the ends of the cylinder. Lewkowicz (1992) has argued that the unitary perception of events on the basis of rate or rhythm does not develop until some time after 8 months of age. Finally, Lewkowicz (1996; 2000) has reported that 8-month-olds may not even discriminate a change in the voice and content in the soundtrack of a talking head when the auditory stimulus is continuous speech spoken as if addressing an adult. Infants older than 6 months, however, may notice a change in continuous speech if the manner of speaking is switched from adult-directed to infant-directed (see later) along with the gender of the speaker.

In the current context, an important question is whether these age-related changes in intersensory perception result from maturation within the individual sensory systems as opposed to maturation of the mechanisms involved in intersensory coordination. For example, do infants have difficulty perceiving the unitary nature of an event specified in terms of rate because temporal resolution is poor in the auditory or visual system or because the mechanisms coordinating rate in the two systems are immature? In the case of coordination on the basis of rate, it is likely that the source of the immaturity is in the intersensory coordination system: At the rates employed in the studies cited (8 Hz or lower) even the immature auditory or visual systems should have little difficulty following (Kellman & Arterberry, 1998; Werner, 1996). Similarly, the temporal and spatial windows for coordinating sight and sound seem far wider than would be predicted on the basis of unimodal judgments of simultaneity or location (e.g., Clifton, 1992; Jusczyk, Rosner, Reed, & Kennedy, 1989; Kellman & Arterberry, 1998). In other cases, it is difficult to draw a conclusion in this regard because it is difficult to describe the stimulus quantitatively. For example, how "big" is the change from one sort of continuous female speech to another? Are there differences in fundamental frequency, speaking rate, intensity? Without knowing what the stimulus is in greater detail, it is impossible to determine whether the discrimination is within the capacity of an infant of a given age.

THE DEVELOPMENT OF ACOUSTIC INFORMATION PICKUP: CONCLUSIONS

The development of acoustic information pickup may be roughly described in three stages. Between birth and about 6 months of age, the ability of the primary auditory system to encode the spectral and temporal characteristics of sound is still maturing. Thus, information pickup in this period is limited by the quality of auditory information available. In later infancy and the preschool period, the developmental process involves improvement in processing efficiency—learning when, where, and how to use the information provided by the sensory system. Beyond the preschool period, information pickup continues to be refined as children develop more sophisticated and flexible approaches to information pickup. This final developmental phase is discussed in more detail in subsequent sections.

AUDITORY PERCEPTUAL LEARNING AND DEVELOPMENT

According to the ecological view of perception, perceptual development occurs because infants and children learn to use the appropriate information to identify objects and events (Gibson, 2000; Gibson & Pick, 2000). Perceptual learning has several characteristics that are important to understanding how development occurs. First, it is active learning. That is, the infant or child actively seeks out information, in many cases creating information by acting on the environment. Second, perceptual learning entails increasing specificity and economy in the information used in perception. Third, perception becomes more flexible with development, allowing perceivers to adjust information pickup to the environmental context. Finally, perceptual learning involves discovering order in the stimulus stream. In this section, the extent to which each of these characteristics can be applied to auditory development is assessed. Because most of the research on complex auditory perceptual development has dealt with the development of speech perception, the material reviewed is largely limited to that topic.

ACTIVE AUDITORY LEARNING

That infants explore the world around them is obvious to anyone who spends any time with a baby. The nature of infants' exploration of the world may change with age, however. Even young infants are highly attentive to a speaking face, but infants do not become truly involved in object manipulation until they are 4 or 5 months old (Eppler, 1995). Beginning at 4 months, infants reach for objects and explore them in all modalities: looking, touching, mouthing, and, of interest here, producing sounds by manipulating sound-producing objects (e.g., a rattle) or knocking objects against any available surface (e.g., a spoon on the high-chair tray). Thus, the infant at this age not only is attentive to sound but also is often engaged in creating sounds using objects.

Another active learning opportunity is vocalization. A 2-month-old infant produces open vocal tract sounds, called cooing. By 4 months infants begin producing a variety of vocal sounds, including squeals and raspberries, described as vocal play. Beginning at around 6 months, infants begin to articulate consonant-like sounds, producing streams of consonant–vowel syllables, or babbling (Stark, 1986). It is important to recognize that infants' early vocalizations frequently occur whenever the infant is awake and alert and do not depend on the presence of a conversation partner. Infant vocalizations, then, represent another form of exploring sound and in particular the sound-producing properties of the infants' own vocal apparatus.

Of course, infants frequently vocalize in a social context, and they are highly responsive to speech directed at them by parents, siblings, and others. So-called infant-directed speech is a style of speech distinguished from that directed to adults by several acoustic characteristics. Infant-directed speech contains exaggerated fundamental frequency and amplitude contours, and syllable duration is longer (Fernald et al., 1989; Grieser & Kuhl, 1988). Many preference-type studies have demonstrated that infants will choose to listen to infant-directed over adult-directed speech (e.g., Fernald, 1985), although the characteristics of infant-directed speech leading to the preference may change as the infant becomes older (Cooper & Aslin, 1994). There is some indication that infants are actually more sensitive to sounds of this type (Colombo, Frick, Ryther, Coldren, & Mitchell,

1995), consistent with the idea that adults are compensating for immature sound source segregation. Furthermore, studies show that adults tend to exaggerate the acoustic features of phonetic units when they are speaking to infants; for example, formant-frequency differences between vowels are greater in infant- than in adult-directed speech (Burnham, Kitamura, & Vollmer-Conna, 2002; Kuhl et al., 1997). Adults also imitate the sounds produced by an infant, and infants learn to take turns in a conversation at an early age. Although it is possible that mere exposure to speech is sufficient to allow infants to learn the acoustic characteristics of their native spoken language (e.g., Cheour et al., 2002; Saffran, 2001), it is also important that infants frequently hear speech in a social exchange. Infants not only vocalize in response to infant-directed speech (Kuhl & Meltzoff, 1996; Niwano & Sugai, 2002; Siegel, Cooper, Morgan, & Brenneise-Sarshad, 1990) but also show clear positive emotional responses (Werker & McLeod, 1989). These infant behaviors tend to elicit speech from adults and to prolong the interaction (Elias & Broerse, 1995). Thus, infants elicit speech that appears to be designed to allow them to pick up relevant phonetic distinctions.

INCREASING SPECIFICITY AND ECONOMY OF AUDITORY PERCEPTION

Speech perception becomes more specific during development in two ways. First, as infants grow older they become better able to make fine-grained distinctions between speech sounds. Bertoncini and her colleagues (1993, 1988, 1981) have shown that infants' discrimination of speech improves during the first several months of life. For example, newborns notice when a new syllable is added to a series of consonant–vowel syllables they had previously heard but only if both the consonant and the vowel are new. Two-month-olds noticed the new syllable even when only one phonetic unit was new. Bertoncini et al. (1988) suggest that at birth, speech perception is more global than it is at older ages. It is interesting to note that exposing newborns to a series of syllables varying in only one phonetic unit improves their ability to make discriminations between such stimuli; 2-month-olds were able to make the finer discrimination regardless of the degree of variability present in the initial syllable series (Jusczyk, Bertoncini, Bijeljac-Babic, Kennedy, & Mehler, 1990). However, it is clear that sensitivity to the acoustic information in speech is not adult-like by 2 months of age because 2-month-olds have difficulty making fine-grained discriminations if the stimuli are bisyllables rather than monosyllables (Jusczyk, Jusczyk, Kennedy, Schomberg, & Koenig, 1995) or if there is a delay between the initial exposure to the syllable series and the addition of the changed syllable. Eimas (1999), in fact, reported little evidence that 3- to 4-month-olds came to recognize a common initial or final consonant in a series of mono- or bisyllabic stimuli.

Although most discussion of the development of speech perception concentrates on the abilities of infants, the process of phonetic identification appears to continue well into childhood, possibly even into adolescence. As Hazan and Barrett (2000) point out, nearly all studies of infant speech discrimination and many studies of speech discrimination by older children present listeners with only clear exemplars of phonemes. Studies that have examined the discrimination of ambiguous stimuli frequently report developmental effects. For example, the steepness of the categorical identification gradient has been found to increase with age, at least for some contrasts (Nittrouer & Miller, 1997; Walley & Flege, 1999) (but see Sussman & Carney, 1989). Further, the location of category boundaries may shift as children grow older, even as late as 17 years of age (Flege & Eefting, 1986). Hazan and Barrett, for example, examined the categorization of four phonemic contrasts among 6- to 12-year-old children. The contrasts included /g/-/k/ and /d/-/g/, which occur in most languages, as well as two fricative contrasts, /s/-/z/ and /s/-/ʃ/, which occur in less than 20% of languages (Maddieson, 1984). The results showed significant increases in the category identification gradients with age for all contrasts. Even the 12-year-olds had significantly shallower gradients than the adults. This result suggests that adults are more consistent than children in the way that they categorize ambiguous exemplars of a phoneme, although the phonemic boundary did not vary with age for these contrasts. Further, variability between subjects was much higher for children than for adults. In all age groups there were some children who were as consistent as adults in their identification of phonemes. It was interesting, moreover, that children's performance was qualitatively like that of adults in that the steepness of the identification gradient changed with contrast in the same way for all age groups. Thus, while school-age children are in some respects adult-like in their identification of speech, they appear to be less efficient in the way that they use acoustic information (see also the later section on flexibility).

The second way in which speech perception becomes more "economical" with experience is that it becomes increasingly specific to the native spoken language during the first year of life. Newborn infants are capable of discriminating between spoken languages on the basis of rhythmic differences (Nazzi, Bertoncini, & Mehler, 1998). Moreover, infants appear to be initially able to discriminate between phonetic units in nonnative languages that their parents are unable to discriminate (Werker & Tees, 1983). The change from language-general to language-specific discrimination ability appears between 6 and 12 months of age (Werker & Lalonde, 1988; Werker & Tees, 1984), although differences in the perception of native and nonnative vowels can be demonstrated as early as 6 months of age (Kuhl, Williams, Lacerda, Stevens, & Lindblom, 1992). In other words, a 12-month-old may be unable to discriminate between two nonnative speech sounds that could be discriminated well at 6 months. Further, between 6 and 9 months of age, infants become sensitive to the distributional properties of phonetic patterns characteristic of their native language (Jusczyk & Luce, 1994). They show evidence of recognizing their native spoken language stress pattern between 6 and 9 months of age (Jusczyk, Cutler, & Redanz, 1993).

THE DISCOVERY OF ORDER IN THE STREAM OF
ACOUSTIC INFORMATION

One of the traditional arguments for an innate "language acquisition device" is the difficulty in formulating rules for segmenting continuous speech into individual words (Liberman & Whalen, 2000). In other words, how can an infant impose any order on the speech stream when there are no universal cues to indicate where one word ends and the next begins? The information that infants use to segment the speech stream into words has become a popular research topic. In these studies, habituation techniques are commonly used to determine whether infants are sensitive to a particular type of acoustic information: One sound is repeatedly presented to the infant until the infant's response habituates; then a different sound is presented to see if the infant's response recovers, indicating discrimination. Preference techniques, on the other hand, give infants the ability to choose between stimuli by fixating a pattern or sucking on a blind nipple. Preference techniques are used in two ways. First, infants may be given a choice between two types of speech without prior laboratory exposure. If the infant prefers one type of speech over another, it is concluded that the infant recognizes the preferred type of speech in some way. In the second sort of study, infants might be exposed to a stream of speech without any requirement of a response. Subsequently, the infant is given a choice between two types of speech, perhaps a list of words that were embedded in the original exposure stream versus a list of words that had not been in that stream. If the infant shows a preference in the test, it is concluded that the infant recognized the speech from the earlier exposure.

Jusczyk and Luce (2002) cite several sources of information that provide some information about where one word ends and the next begins. The first of these is the "position specificity" of phonemes. That is, the acoustic characteristics of a phoneme depend on whether it occurs in syllable-initial or syllable-final position. Although this cue is believed to play a minor role in identifying word boundaries in adults, Hohne and Juczyk (1994) showed that infants as young as 2 months of age could discriminate between allophonic variants of a consonant. However, infants did not appear to use this cue to find word boundaries until they were 10.5 months old (Jusczyk, Hohne, & Bauman, 1999).

A second cue to word boundaries is based on the rhythmic characteristics of speech. In English, for example, most words begin with a stressed, or strong, syllable. Thus, a stressed syllable typically indicates the beginning of a word. Jusczyk *et al.* (1993) showed that at 6 months of age, English-learning infants listening to a list of bisyllabic words showed no preference for a strong/weak stress pattern over a weak/strong stress pattern. By 9 months, however, English-learning infants preferred to listen to the word list with the strong/weak stress pattern, the predominant pattern in English words. Further, Jusczyk, Houston, and Newsome (1999) showed that infants as young as 7.5 months of age would segment words with a strong/weak stress pattern from running speech. Interestingly at this age, infants would missegment weak/strong pattern words at the beginning of the strong syllable. If stress pattern cues conflicted with other cues to word boundaries, moreover, infants tended to segment on the basis of the stress pattern (Johnson & Jusczyk, 2001; Mattys, Jusczyk, Luce, & Morgan, 1999). It was not until 10.5 months of age that infants were able to segment weak/strong stress pattern words from running speech, suggesting that this ability depends on infants learning some other cues to word boundaries.

Language-specific phonotactic patterns provide another source of information about word boundaries. By phonotactic pattern is meant the permissible sounds and sound sequences in a language. For example, the sequence /tl/ may end a word in English or occur in the middle of a word but never begins a word. Infants appear to be sensitive to this information by 9 months of age. Jusczyk *et al.* (1993) showed that English-learning 9-month-olds preferred to listen to English word lists over Dutch word lists, whereas Dutch-learning infants preferred to listen to Dutch over English word lists. Because the predominant stress pattern is very similar in English and Dutch, this finding suggests that infants were sensitive to the phonotactic pattern of their native language. In addition, Mattys & Juczyk (2001) demonstrated that 9-month-olds were more likely to segment words from running speech for which phonotactic patterns suggested a word boundary.

A related source of information about word boundaries is based on the fact that a word represents a recurring pattern of sounds. If the same sequence of sounds is frequently repeated, there is a good chance that the sequence is a word. Even 4.5-month-olds listen preferentially to fluent speech containing their own name, suggesting that even younger infants are able to segment out a sound sequence with which they are highly familiar (Jusczyk & Luce, 2002). Jusczyk and Aslin (1995) found that 7.5-month-old infants exposed to single monosyllabic words listened preferentially to fluent speech containing those words on subsequent tests, suggesting that the infants segmented the familiar words from the speech stream. Further, infants appear to be sensitive to the distributional statistics of the speech stream by 8 months of age. Saffran, Aslin, and Newport (1996) presented 8-month-old infants with a 150-second-long string of consonant-vowel (CV) syllables. The probability that some syllables occurred in sequence was 1, whereas for others the probability was low. In a subsequent posttest, infants preferred to listen to sequences of syllables that had occurred together in the original string over sequences that had occurred together only by chance. Of course, once some words are known, identifying the known word in the speech stream provides information about where the next word begins and the process of segmentation of speech may be considerably more complex in older infants, children, and adults (e.g. Hollich, Jusczyk, & Luce, 2000; Johnson, Jusczyk, Cutler, & Norris, 2000).

In summary, studies of infants' ability to segment the speech stream into words suggest a couple of conclusions, each of which raises additional questions. The first conclusion is that infants tend to have the discriminative skills required to process cues to word segmentation before they actually can use these cues to identify word boundaries. The question is why infants cannot use the cues at an earlier age. What are the limitations on infants' ability to use the information provided by their auditory system? The second conclusion is that there is a regular progression in the cues that infants use to identify word boundaries as they grow older. Younger infants tend to rely on the stress patterns of words, whereas older infants are able to use phonotactic patterns and distributional properties to identify potential words. It is not clear why this particular progression occurs, nor is it known when infants begin to integrate these cues in their identification of word boundaries. What is clear is that from a very young age infants begin to use the information they obtain from their auditory system to discover order in the stream of sound to which they are frequently exposed.

INCREASING FLEXIBILITY OF AUDITORY PERCEPTION

Perhaps the best example of developmental changes in the flexibility of auditory perception is the predictable change in the cues that infants and children use to identify speech units, the eventual ability to integrate these cues, and finally the ability to change the weight given to each cue depending on the context. The cues that infants use to identify word boundaries in fluent speech are one example, discussed in the previous section. However, even the process of phoneme identification becomes more flexible with age throughout the preschool years.

Nittrouer and her colleagues have conducted a series of experiments examining cue use and integration in the discrimination of fricative consonants by children between the ages of 4 and 7 years. In these experiments, listeners are asked to identify each phoneme as either /s/ or /ʃ/. These stimuli are typically discriminated by adults on the basis of two major cues, the onset frequency of the F2 transition and the spectrum of the frication noise. The onset frequency of the F3 transition changes along with that of F2, but F3 is a more informative cue in some vowel contexts that in others. In Nittrouer's experiments, the frequency of the frication noise is systematically changed, and as the frequency changes, the listener's identification of the consonant shifts from /s/ to /ʃ/, but with a relatively sharp drop in /s/ identifications at a frequency of 3000 Hz. If the F2 transition onset frequency is fixed at a value appropriate for the phoneme /s/, the boundary between /s/ and /ʃ/ shifts toward lower frication noise frequencies, whereas if the transition appropriate to /ʃ/ is appended to all the stimuli in the series, the boundary shifts toward the higher frication noise frequencies. Thus, it is clear that adults integrate information about the two cues in their identification. Nittrouer and her colleagues (1997, 1987), however, showed that the F2 transition onset frequency had a much stronger effect on 4-year-olds' identification of these fricatives than did the frication noise, relative to adults'. Nittrouer concluded that children weight the available cues differently from adults and, in particular, that they weight dynamic cues, such as frequency transitions, more heavily than they weight static cues such as the frequency of the frication noise.

Nittrouer and Miller (1997) hypothesized that, in addition, young children would not change the weights that they assigned to different cues in fricative identification in different vowel environments. They showed that adults' identification of fricatives was more affected by the elimination of F3 variation when the following vowel was /ɑ/ than when it was /u/. Among 4-year-olds, eliminating F3 variation affected identification in the two vowel contexts equivalently. Conversely, when F3 transition onset frequency was varied consistently with that of F2, adults' identification showed an increased effect of transition onset frequency in the /u/ over the /ɑ/ context, and identification by 3- and 5-year-olds was similarly affected in both vowel contexts. Thus, preschoolers appear to maintain a fixed strategy in consonant identification, regardless of the context in these experiments. Nittrouer believes that they have not yet learned that the information provided by a given cue varies with the context.

Walley and Flege (1999) have also documented differences between the vowel categories formed by 5-year-olds and adults but showed that 5-year-olds can be flexible in their category definitions with changes in context. It is likely, then, that children's ability to switch between identification strategies varies with the categories and cues involved.

By 7 years of age, children in Nittrouer's experiments showed context effects that were similar to those shown by adults. Similarly, Hazan and Barrett (2000) showed that by 6 years, children integrate cues as adults do and that when they are restricted to a single cue, their categorization is affected as it is in adults. However, Nittrouer and Boothroyd (1990) showed that when higher level context is involved, children might still be less able to modify their identification strategies. They found that 4- to 7-year-olds' use of word context in identifying phonemes was similar to that of adults but that their use of sentence context was reduced compared with that of adults.

AUDITORY PERCEPTUAL LEARNING AND
DEVELOPMENT: CONCLUSIONS

Clearly, all of the hallmarks of ecological perceptual development can be identified in the development of speech perception: The process is active; it involves increases in specificity, economy, and flexibility; and a major focus is the discovery of order in the stream of continuous speech. Whether there are exceptions to these tendencies, however, has not been thoroughly explored (see Cheour *et al.*, 2002; Saffran, 2001; Werker & Desjardins, 2001). An additional unaddressed issue is whether or not these tendencies characterize the perception of complex nonspeech sounds.

GENERAL CONCLUSIONS

The course of auditory perceptual development is quite prolonged, especially when one considers ecologically relevant stimuli such as speech. The Gibsonian approach to development holds that infants come into the world able to extract information from the environment about the affordances of objects but that perceptual learning is required to become efficient and proficient users of that information. What does this review suggest about the ecological approach to perceptual development?

It is clear that the assumption that the sensory system is capable of representing acoustic information at birth as it does in adults does not hold. Human infants go through a period when the spectral and temporal characteristics of sound are a little fuzzy and the precise location of the sound source is uncertain. This is reflected in infants' tendency to notice only rather gross changes in speech in the first months of life. Thus, infants may be picking up acoustic information, but for the young infant that information is not equivalent to that available to the adult. Moreover, that infants are capable of discriminating between events on the basis of certain acoustic cues does not necessarily mean that they use those cues in perceiving events in their normal environment.

It is similarly clear that infants do not come equipped with a preformed intersensory, or amodal, processing structure. The sensory systems clearly communicate even at birth; infants certainly notice intersensory correspondence within an event. However, they do not apparently expect that correspondence to be present. The realization that some properties of visual and auditory stimulation generally coincide takes some time to develop. The relative contributions of sensory and intersensory maturation to this aspect of perceptual development remain to be elucidated.

Finally, there are suggestions in the literature on the development of speech perception that perceptual development may not be readily described in terms of universal tendencies. For example, whereas infants appear to take a broad, rather unselective initial approach to sounds, older children may actually be too selective in the information that they use to identify speech sounds. In other words, the ability to integrate multiple cues and to change the way that cues are weighted depending on the context indicates increasing flexibility in perception, but it also implies that children ignore relevant information before they achieve that flexibility. Development is probably not unidimensional or even unidirectional.

REFERENCES

Abdala, C., & Folsom, R. C. (1995). The development of frequency resolution in humans as revealed by the auditory brain-stem response recorded with notched-noise masking. *Journal of the Acoustical Society of America, 98*, 921–930.

Abdala, C., & Sininger, Y. S. (1996). The development of cochlear frequency resolution in the human auditory system. *Ear and Hearing, 17*, 374–385.

Allen, P., & Wightman, F. (1994). Psychometric functions for children's detection of tones in noise. *Journal of Speech and Hearing Research, 37*, 205–215.

Allen, P., & Wightman, F. (1995). Effects of signal and masker uncertainty on children's detection. *Journal of Speech and Hearing Research, 38*, 503–511.

Ashmead, D., Davis, D., Whalen, T., & Odom, R. (1991). Sound localization and sensitivity to interaural time differences in human infants. *Child Development, 62*, 1211–1226.

Ashmead, D. H., Clifton, R. K., & Perris, E. E. (1987). Precision of auditory localization in human infants. *Developmental Psychology, 23*, 641–647.

Bahrick, L. E. (1987). Infants' intermodal perception of two levels of temporal structure in natural events. *Infant Behavior and Development, 10*, 387–416.

Bargones, J. Y., & Werner, L. A. (1994). Adults listen selectively; infants do not. *Psychological Science, 5*, 170–174.

Bargones, J. Y., Werner, L. A., & Marean, G. C. (1995). Infant psychometric functions for detection: Mechanisms of immature sensitivity. *Journal of the Acoustical Society of America, 98*, 99–111.

Bertoncini, J. (1993). Infants' perception of speech units: Primary representation capacities. In B. de Boysson-Bardies, S. de Schonen, P. Jusczyk, P. McNeilage, and J. Morton (Eds.), *Developmental neurocognition: Speech and face processing in the first year of life* (pp. 249–257). Dordrecht: Kluwer.

Bertoncini, J., Bijeljac-Babic, R., Jusczyk, P. W., Kennedy, L. J., & Mehler, J. (1988). An investigation of young infants' perceptual representations of speech sounds. *Journal of Experimental Psychology: General, 117*, 21–33.

Bertoncini, J., & Mehler, J. (1981). Syllables as units of infant speech perception. *Infant Behavior and Development, 4*, 247–260.

Blauert, J. (1983). *Spatial hearing: The psychophysics of human sound localization* (J. S. Allen, Trans., rev. ed.). Cambridge, MA: MIT Press.

Burnham, D., Kitamura, C., & Vollmer-Conna, U. (2002). What's new, pussycat? On talking to babies and animals. *Science, 296*, 1435–1435.

Cheour, M., Martynova, O., Naatanen, R., Erkkola, R., Sillanpaa, M., Kero, P., et al. (2002). Speech sounds learned by sleeping newborns. *Nature, 415*, 599–600.

Clarkson, M. G., & Clifton, R. K. (1991). Acoustic determinants of newborn orienting. In M. J. S. Weiss and P. R. Zelazo (Eds.), *Newborn attention: Biological constraints and the influence of experience* (pp. 99–119). Norwood, NJ: Ablex Publishing.

Clarkson, M. G., Clifton, R. K., Swain, I. U., & Perris, E. E. (1989). Stimulus duration and repetition rate influences newborns' head orientation toward sound. *Developmental Psychology, 22*, 683–705.

Clifton, R. K. (1992). The development of spatial hearing in human infants. In L. A. Werner and E. W. Rubel (Eds.), *Developmental psychoacoustics* (pp. 135–157). Washington, DC: American Psychological Association.

Clifton, R. K., Morrongiello, B. A., & Dowd, J. M. (1984). A developmental look at an auditory illusion: The precedence effect. *Developmental Psychobiology, 17*, 519–536.

Clifton, R. K., Perris, E. E., & Bullinger, A. (1991). Infants' perception of auditory space. *Developmental Psychology, 27*, 187–197.

Colombo, J., Frick, J. E., Ryther, J. S., Coldren, J. T., & Mitchell, D. W. (1995). Infants' detection of analogs of "motherese" in noise. *Merrill-Palmer Quarterly, 41*, 104–113.

Cooper, R. P. (1997). An ecological approach to infants' perception of intonation contours as meaningful aspects of speech. In C. Dent-Read and P. Zukow-Goldring (Eds.), *Evolving explanations of development: Ecological approaches to organism-environment systems* (pp. 55–85). Washington, DC: American Psychological Association.

Cooper, R. P., & Aslin, R. N. (1994). Developmental differences in infant attention to the spectral properties of infant-directed speech. *Child Development, 65*, 1663–1677.

Dai, H., & Wright, B. A. (1995). Detecting signals of unexpected or uncertain durations. *Journal of the Acoustical Society of America, 98*, 798–806.

Demany, L. (1982). Auditory stream segregation in infancy. *Infant Behavior and Development, 5*, 261–276.

Doyle, A. B. (1973). Listening to distraction: A developmental study of selective attention. *Journal of Experimental Child Psychology, 15*, 100–115.

Eimas, P. D. (1999). Segmental and syllabic representations in the perception of speech by young infants. *Journal of the Acoustical Society of America, 105*, 1901–1911.

Elfenbein, J. L., Small, A. M., & Davis, M. (1993). Developmental patterns of duration discrimination. *Journal of Speech and Hearing Research, 36*, 842–849.

Elias, G., & Broerse, J. (1995). Temporal patterning of vocal behaviour in mother-infant engagements: Infant-initiated "encounters" as units of analysis. *Australian Journal of Psychology, 47*, 47–53.

Eppler, M. A. (1995). Development of manipulatory skills and the deployment of attention. *Infant Behavior and Development, 18*, 391–405.

Fassbender, C. (1993). *Auditory grouping and segregation processes in infancy.* Norderstedt, Germany: Kaste Verlag.

Fernald, A. (1985). Four-month-old infants prefer to listen to motherese. *Infant Behavior and Development, 8*, 181–195.

Fernald, A., Taeschner, T., Dunn, J., Papousek, M., de Boysson-Bardies, B., & Fukui, I. (1989). A cross-language study of prosodic modifications in mothers' and fathers' speech to preverbal infants. *Journal of Child Language, 16*, 477–501.

Field, T. J., Muir, D., Pilon, R., Sinclair, M., & Dodwell, P. (1980). Infants' orientation to lateral sounds from birth to three months. *Child Development, 51*, 295–298.

Flege, J. E., & Eefting, W. (1986). Linguistic and develeopmental effects on the production and perception of stop consonants. *Phonetica, 43*, 155–171.

Fletcher, H. (1940). Auditory patterns. *Reviews of Modern Physics, 12*, 47–65.

Folsom, R. C., & Wynne, M. K. (1987). Auditory brain stem responses from human adults and infants: Wave V tuning curves. *Journal of the Acoustical Society of America, 81*, 412–417.

Gibson, E. J. (2000). Perceptual learning in development: Some basic concepts. *Ecological Psychology, 12*, 295–302.

Gibson, E. J., & Pick, A. D. (2000). *An ecological approach to perceptual learning and development.* London, England: Oxford University Press.

Gibson, J. J. (1986). *The ecological approach to visual perception.* Hillsdale, NJ: Erlbaum.

Gogate, L. J., Bahrick, L. E., & Watson, J. J. (2000). A study of multimodal motherese: The role of temporal synchrony between verbal labels and gestures. *Child Development, 71*, 878–894.

Gray, L. (1992). Interactions between sensory and nonsensory factors in the responses of newborn birds to sound. In L. A. Werner and E. W. Rubel (Eds.), *Developmental psychoacoustics* (pp. 89–112). Washington, DC: American Psychological Association.

Grieser, D. L., & Kuhl, P. K. (1988). Maternal speech to infants in a tonal language: Support for universal prosodic features in motherese. *Developmental Psychology, 24*, 14–20.

Hall, J. W., III and Grose, J. H. (1991). Notched-noise measures of frequency selectivity in adults and children using fixed-masker-level and fixed-signal-level presentation. *Journal of Speech and Hearing Research, 34*, 651–660.

Hall, J. W., III and Grose, J. H. (1994). Development of temporal resolution in children as measured by the temporal modulation transfer function. *Journal of the Acoustical Society of America, 96*, 150–154.

Hartley, D. E. H., Wright, B. A., Hogan, S. C., & Moore, D. R. (2000). Age-related improvements in auditory backward and simultaneous masking in 6- to 10-year-old children. *Journal of Speech Language and Hearing Research, 43*, 1402–1415.

Hazan, V., & Barrett, S. (2000). The development of phonemic categorization in children aged 6–12. *Journal of Phonetics, 28*, 377–396.

Hohne, E. A., & Jusczyk, P. W. (1994). Two-month-olds' sensitivity to allophonic variants. *Perception and Psychophysics, 56*, 613–623.

Hollich, G., Jusczyk, P. W., & Luce, P. A. (2000). Infant sensitivity to lexical neighborhoods during word learning. *Journal of the Acoustical Society of America, 108*, 2481.

Irwin, R. J., Ball, A. K. R., Kay, N., Stillman, J. A., & Rosser, J. (1985). The development of auditory temporal acuity in children. *Child Development, 56*, 614–620.

Jensen, J. K., & Neff, D. L. (1993). Development of basic auditory discrimination in preschool children. *Psychological Science, 4,* 104–107.

Johnson, E. K., & Jusczyk, P. W. (2001). Word segmentation by 8-month-olds: When speech cues count more than statistics. *Journal of Memory and Language, 44,* 548–567.

Johnson, E. K., Jusczyk, P. W., Cutler, A., & Norris, D. (2000). 12-month-olds show evidence of possible word constraint. *Journal of the Acoustical Society of America, 108,* 2481.

Jusczyk, P. W., & Aslin, R. N. (1995). Infants' detection of the sound patterns of words in fluent speech. *Cognitive Psychology, 29,* 1–23.

Jusczyk, P. W., Bertoncini, J., Bijeljac-Babic, R., Kennedy, L. J., & Mehler, J. (1990). The role of attention in speech perception by young infants. *Cognitive Development, 5,* 265–286.

Jusczyk, P. W., Cutler, A., & Redanz, N. J. (1993). Infants' preference for the predominant stress patterns of English words. *Child Development, 64,* 675–687.

Jusczyk, P. W., Friederici, A. D., Wessels, J. M. I., Svenkerud, V. Y., & Jusczyk, A. M. (1993). Infants' sensitivity to the sound patterns of native language words. *Journal of Memory and Language, 32,* 402–420.

Jusczyk, P. W., Hohne, E. A., & Bauman, A. (1999). Infants' sensitivty to allophonic cues for word segmentation. *Perception and Psychophysics, 61,* 1465–1476.

Jusczyk, P. W., Houston, D., & Newsome, M. (1999). The beginnings of word segmentation in English-learning infants. *Cognitive Psychology, 39,* 159–207.

Jusczyk, P. W., Jusczyk, A. M., Kennedy, L. J., Schomberg, T., & Koenig, N. (1995). Young infants retention of information about bisyllabic utterances. *Journal of Experimental Psychology: Human Perception and Performance, 21,* 822–836.

Jusczyk, P. W., & Luce, P. A. (1994). Infants sensitivity to phonotactic patterns in the native language. *Journal of Memory and Language, 33,* 630–645.

Jusczyk, P. W., & Luce, P. A. (2002). Speech perception and spoken word recognition: Past and present. *Ear and Hearing, 23,* 2–40.

Jusczyk, P. W., Rosner, B. S., Reed, M. A., & Kennedy, L. J. (1989). Could temporal order differences underlie 2-month-olds' discrimination of English voicing contrasts? *Journal of the Acoustical Society of America, 85,* 1741–1749.

Keefe, D. H., Bulen, J. C., Arehart, K. H., & Burns, E. M. (1993). Ear-canal impedance and reflection coefficient in human infants and adults. *Journal of the Acoustical Society of America, 94,* 2617–2638.

Keefe, D. H., Burns, E. M., Bulen, J. C., & Campbell, S. L. (1994). Pressure transfer function from the diffuse field to the human infant ear canal. *Journal of the Acoustical Society of America, 95,* 355–371.

Keefe, D. H., & Levi, E. C. (1996). Maturation of the middle and external ears: Acoustic power-based responses and reflectance typmanometry. *Ear and Hearing, 17,* 1–13.

Kellman, P. J., & Arterberry, M. E. (1998). *The cradle of knowledge: Development of perception in infancy.* Cambridge, MA: MIT Press.

Kidd, G., Mason, C. R., Deliwala, P. S., Woods, W. S., & Colburn, H. S. (1994). Reducing informational masking by sound segregation. *Journal of the Acoustical Society of America, 95,* 3475–3480.

Knudsen, E. I. (1988). Experience shapes sound localization and auditory unit properties during development in the barn owl. In G. M. Edelman, W. E. Gall, and W. M. Cowan (Eds.), *Auditory function: Neurobiological bases of hearing* (pp. 137–149). New York: John Wiley & Sons.

Kuhl, P. K., Andruski, J. E., Chistovich, I. A., Chistovich, L. A., Kozhevnikova, E. V., Ryskina, V. L., *et al.* (1997). Cross-language analysis of phonetic units in language addressed to infants. *Science, 277,* 684–686.

Kuhl, P. K., & Meltzoff, A. N. (1982). The bimodal perception of speech in infancy. *Science, 218,* 1138–1140.

Kuhl, P. K., & Meltzoff, A. N. (1996). Infant vocalizations in response to speech: Vocal imitation and developmental change. *Journal of the Acoustical Society of America, 100,* 2425–2438.

Kuhl, P. K., Williams, K., & Meltzoff, A. (1991). Cross-modal speech perception in adults and infants using nonspeech auditory stimuli. *Journal of Experimental Psychology, 17,* 829–840.

Kuhl, P. K., Williams, K. A., Lacerda, F., Stevens, K. N., & Lindblom, B. (1992). Linguistic experience alters phonetic perception in infants by 6 months of age. *Science, 255,* 606–608.

Levi, E. C., & Werner, L. A. (1996). Amplitude modulation detection in infancy: Update on 3-month-olds. *Abstracts of the Association for Research in Otolaryngology, 19,* 142.

Lewkowicz, D. J. (1992). Infants' response to temporally based intersensory equivalence: The effect of synchronous sounds on visual preferences for moving stimuli. *Infant Behavior and Development, 15,* 297–304.

Lewkowicz, D. J. (1996). Perception of auditory-visual temporal synchrony in human infants. *Journal of Experimental Psychology: Human Perception and Performance, 22,* 1094–1106.

Lewkowicz, D. J. (1999). The development of temporal and spatial intermodal perception. In G. Aschersleben, & T. Bachmann (Eds.), *Cognitive contributions to the perception of spatial and temporal events. Advances in psychology, 129* (pp. 395–420). Amsterdam: North-Holland/ Elsevier Science Publishers.

Lewkowicz, D. J. (2000). Infants' perception of the audible, visible, and bimodal attributes of multimodal syllables. *Child Development, 71,* 1241–1257.

Liberman, A. M., & Whalen, D. H. (2000). On the relation of speech to language. *Trends in Cognitive Sciences, 4,* 187–196.

Litovsky, R. Y. (1997). Developmental changes in the precedence effect: Estimates of minimum audible angle. *Journal of the Acoustical Society of America, 102,* 1739–1745.

Litovsky, R. Y., & Clifton, R. K. (1992). Use of sound-pressure level in auditory distance discrimination by 6-month-old infants and adults. *Journal of the Acoustical Society of America, 92,* 794–802.

Maddieson, I. (1984). *Patterns of sounds.* New York: Cambridge University Press.

Massaro, D. W. (1998). *Perceiving talking faces: From speech perception to a behavioral principle.* Cambridge, MA, MIT Press.

Mattys, S. L., & Jusczyk, P. W. (2001). Do infants segment words or recurring patterns? *Journal of Experimental Psychology: Human Perception and Performance, 27,* 644–655.

Mattys, S. L., Jusczyk, P. W., Luce, P. A., & Morgan, J. L. (1999). Word segmentation in infants: How phonotactics and prosody combine. *Cognitive Psychology, 38,* 465–494.

McAdams, S., & Bertoncini, J. (1997). Organization and discrimination of repeating sound sequences by newborn infants. *Journal of the Acoustical Society of America, 102,* 2945–2953.

McGurk, H., & MacDonald, J. (1976). Hearing lips and seeing voices. *Nature, 264,* 746–748.

Moore, J. M., Thompson, G., & Thompson, M. (1975). Auditory localization of infants as a function of reinforcement conditions. *Journal of Speech and Hearing Disorders, 40,* 29–34.

Morrongiello, B. A. (1988). Infants' localization of sounds along two spatial dimensions: Horizontal and vertical axes. *Infant Behavior and Development, 11,* 127–143.

Morrongiello, B. A., Fenwick, K., & Chance, G. (1990). Sound localization acuity in very young infants: An observer-based testing procedure. *Developmental Psychology, 26,* 75–84.

Morrongiello, B. A., Fenwick, K. D., & Chance, G. (1998). Crossmodal learning in newborn infants: Inferences about properties of auditory-visual events. *Infant Behavior and Development, 21,* 543–554.

Morrongiello, B. A., Fenwick, K. D., Hillier, L., & Chance, G. (1994). Sound localization in newborn human infants. *Developmental Psychobiology, 27,* 519–538.

Morrongiello, B. A., & Rocca, P. T. (1987). Infants' localization of sounds in the median sagittal plane: Effects of signal frequency. *Journal of the Acoustical Society of America, 82,* 900–905.

Morrongiello, B. A., & Rocca, P. T. (1990). Infants' localization of sounds within hemifields: Estimates of minimum audible angle. *Child Development, 61,* 1258–1270.

Morrongiello, B. A., & Trehub, S. E. (1987). Age-related changes in auditory temporal perception. *Journal of Experimental Child Psychology, 44,* 413–426.

Nazzi, T., Bertoncini, J., & Mehler, J. (1998). Language discrimination by newborns: Toward an understanding of the role of rhythm. *Journal of Experimental Psychology: Human Perception and Performance, 24*, 756–766.

Neff, D. L., & Dethlefs, T. M. (1995). Individual differences in simultaneous masking with random-frequency, multicomponent maskers. *Journal of the Acoustical Society of America, 98*, 125–134.

Neff, D. L., & Green, D. M. (1987). Masking produced by spectral uncertainty with multicomponent maskers. *Perception and Psychophysics, 41*, 409–415.

Newman, R. S., & Jusczyk, P. W. (1996). The cocktail effect in infants. *Perception and Psychophysics, 58*, 1145–1156.

Nittrouer, S., & Boothroyd, A. (1990). Context effects in phoneme and word recognition by young children and older adults. *Journal of the Acoustical Society of America, 87*, 2705–2715.

Nittrouer, S., & Miller, M. E. (1997). Predicting developmental shifts in perceptual weighting schemes. *Journal of the Acoustical Society of America, 101*, 3353–3366.

Nittrouer, S., & Studdert-Kennedy, M. (1987). The role of coarticulatory effects in the perception of fricatives by children and adults. *Journal of Speech and Hearing Research, 30*, 319–329.

Niwano, K., & Sugai, K. (2002). Acoustic determinants eliciting Japanese infants' vocal response to maternal speech. *Psychological Reports, 90*, 83–90.

Oh, E. L., & Lutfi, R. A. (1999). Informational masking by everyday sounds. *Journal of the Acoustical Society of America, 106*, 3521–3528.

Oh, E. L., Wightman, F., & Lutfi, R. A. (2001). Children's detection of pure-tone signals with random multitone maskers. *Journal of the Acoustical Society of America, 109*, 2888–2895.

Olsho, L. W. (1984). Infant frequency discrimination. *Infant Behavior and Development, 7*, 27–35.

Olsho, L. W., Koch, E. G., Carter, E. A., Halpin, C. F., & Spetner, N. B. (1988). Pure-tone sensitivity of human infants. *Journal of the Acoustical Society of America, 84*, 1316–1324.

Perris, E. E., & Clifton, R. K. (1988). Reaching in the dark toward sound as a measure of auditory localization in infants. *Infant Behavior and Development, 11*, 473–491.

Piaget, J. (1954). *The construction of reality in the child.* New York: Basic Books.

Pollack, I. (1975). Auditory informational masking. *Acoustical Society of America, Suppl. 1*, 57.

Saffran, J. R. (2001). Words in a sea of sounds: The output of infant statistical learning. *Cognition, 81*, 149–169.

Saffran, J. R., Aslin, R. N., & Newport, E. L. (1996). Statistical learning by 8-month-old infants. *Science, 274*, 1926–1928.

Schneider, B. A., Morrongiello, B. A., & Trehub, S. E. (1990). The size of the critical band in infants, children, and adults. *Journal of Experimental Psychology: Human Perception and Performance, 16*, 642–652.

Schneider, B. A., Trehub, S. E., Morrongiello, B. A., & Thorpe, L. A. (1986). Auditory sensitivity in preschool children. *Journal of the Acoustical Society of America, 79*, 447–452.

Schneider, R. A., Trehub, S. E., Morrongiello, B. A., & Thorpe, L. A. (1989). Developmental changes in masked thresholds. *Journal of the Acoustical Society of America, 86*, 1733–1742.

Siegel, G. M., Cooper, M., Morgan, J. L., & Brenneise-Sarshad, R. (1990). Imitation of intonation by infants. *Journal of Speech and Hearing Research, 33*, 9–15.

Sinnott, J. M., & Aslin, R. N. (1985). Frequency and intensity discrimination in human infants and adults. *Journal of the Acoustical Society of America, 78*, 1986–1992.

Spetner, N. B., & Olsho, L. W. (1990). Auditory frequency resolution in human infancy. *Child Development, 61*, 632–652.

Stark, R. E. (1986). Prespeech segmental feature development. In P. Fletcher and M. Garman (Eds.), *Language acquisition* (2nd ed., pp. 149–173). New York: Cambridge University Press.

Stein, B. E., & Meredith, M. A. (1993). *The merging of the senses.* Cambridge, MA: MIT Press.

Sussman, J. E., & Carney, A. E. (1989). Effects of transition length on the perception of stop consonants by children and adults. *Journal of Speech and Hearing Research, 32*, 151–160.

Tarquinio, N., Zelazo, P. R., & Weiss, M. J. (1990). Recovery of neonatal head turning to decreased sound pressure level. *Developmental Psychology, 26*, 752–758.

Walker-Andrews, A. S. (1997). Infants' perception of expressive behaviors: Differentiation of multimodal information. *Psychological Bulletin, 121*, 437–456.

Walker-Andrews, A. S., & Lennon, E. M. (1985). Auditory-visual perception of changing distance by human infants. *Child Development, 56*, 544–548.

Walley, A. C., & Flege, J. E. (1999). Effect of lexical status on children's and adults' perception of native and non-native vowels. *Journal of Phonetics, 27*, 307–332.

Watson, C. S., Wroton, H. W., Kelly, W. J., & Benbassat, C. A. (1975). Factors in the discrimination of tonal patterns. I. Component frequency, temporal position, and silent intervals. *Journal of the Acoustical Society of America, 57*, 1175–1185.

Werker, J. F., & Desjardins, R. N. (2001). Listening to speech in the 1st year of life. In M. Tomasello and E. Bates (Eds.), *Language development: The essential readings* (pp. 26–33). Blackwell Publishers: Oxford.

Werker, J. F., & Lalonde, C. E. (1988). Cross-language speech perception: Initial capabilities and developmental change. *Developmental Psychology, 24*, 672–683.

Werker, J. F., & McLeod, P. J. (1989). Infant preference for both male and female infant-directed talk: A developmental study of attentional and affective responsiveness. *Canadian Journal of Psychology, 43*, 230–246.

Werker, J. F., & Tees, R. C. (1983). Developmental changes across childhood in the perception of non-native speech sounds. *Canadian Journal of Psychology, 37*, 278–286.

Werker, J. F., & Tees, R. C. (1984). Cross-language speech perception: Evidence for perceptual reorganization during the first year of life. *Infant Behavior and Development, 7*, 49–63.

Werner, L. A. (1995). Observer-based approaches to human infant psychoacoustics. In G. M. Klump, R. J. Dooling, R. R. Fay, and W. C. Stebbins (Eds.), *Methods in comparative psychoacoustics* (pp. 135–146). Boston: Birkhauser Verlag.

Werner, L. A. (1996). The development of auditory behavior (or what the anatomists and physiologists have to explain). *Ear and Hearing, 17*, 438–446.

Werner, L. A., & Bargones, J. Y. (1991). Sources of auditory masking in infants: Distraction effects. *Perception and Psychophysics, 50*, 405–412.

Werner, L. A., & Boike, K. (2001). Infants' sensitivity to broadband noise. *Journal of the Acoustical Society of America, 109*, 2101–2111.

Werner, L. A., Folsom, R. C., & Mancl, L. R. (1994). The relationship between auditory brainstem response latencies and behavioral thresholds in normal hearing infants and adults. *Hearing Research, 77*, 88–98.

Werner, L. A., & Gillenwater, J. M. (1990). Pure-tone sensitivity of 2- to 5-week-old infants. *Infant Behavior and Development, 13*, 355–375.

Werner, L. A., & Marean, G. C. (1995). *Human auditory development.* Boulder, CO: Westview Press.

Werner, L. A., Marean, G. C., Halpin, C. F., Spetner, N. B., & Gillenwater, J. M. (1992). Infant auditory temporal acuity: Gap detection. *Child Development, 63*, 260–272.

Wightman, F., Allen, P., Dolan, T., Kistler, D., & Jamieson, D. (1989). Temporal resolution in children. *Child Development, 60*, 611–624.

Wilmington, D., Gray, L., & Jahrsdorfer, R. (1994). Binaural processing after corrected congenital unilateral conductive hearing loss. *Hearing Research, 74*, 99–114.

Withington-Wray, D. J., Binns, K. E., & Keating, M. J. (1990). A four-day period of bimodality auditory and visual experience is sufficient to permit normal emergence of the map of auditory space in the guinea pig superior colliculus. *Neuroscience Letters, 116*, 280–286.

9

PERCEIVING

ARTICULATORY EVENTS:

LESSONS FOR AN ECOLOGICAL

PSYCHOACOUSTICS

LAWRENCE D. ROSENBLUM

Of all areas of auditory *perception*, speech arguably provides the most conceptually developed research topic. This fact positions speech as a prototypic research area for an ecological psychoacoustics. In this chapter, it will be argued that it behooves auditory perceptionists to heed a number of lessons from speech research. These lessons include understanding the importance of assumed perceptual primitives; the necessity of thorough event-informed informational descriptions; and consideration of hearing in its multimodal context. It will be argued that over 50 years of research suggests a speech function whose perceptual primitives are distal event properties (gestures); whose information takes a higher-order, time-varying form; and for which modality is, in an important way, invisible. Moreover, research indicates that these properties are not specific to speech, suggesting analogous characteristics for all of auditory perception.

The time is ripe for a science of auditory *perception*. A majority of the research on human audition has concentrated on how the ear works rather than on what the ear hears. Emphasis has been placed on understanding sensitivity to sounds rather than on the recognition of sound-specified events. Put simply, sensation has been emphasized over perception. Certainly, the two levels of analysis are coconstraining and one of the central goals of this book is to examine just this relationship. Still, with the shortage of research on auditory perception, the necessary constraints on models of sensation might also be lacking. One hopes that a new science of hearing—an ecological psychoacoustics—can be developed that considers what, as well as how, we hear (Gaver, 1993a, 1993b).

In developing an ecological psychoacoustic approach to auditory perception, important questions will need to be addressed. For example, what should be considered the objects or perceptual primitives of auditory perception? Put another way, does auditory perception conform more to properties of the surface dimensions of the acoustic signal or to properties of distal, sound-structuring events? Relatedly, where should we expect to find the most salient information in the acoustic signal: in the short-term, surface acoustics or in acoustic dimensions that are time varying and higher order? Finally, how should we consider audition's place in multimodal animals? For example, to what degree will audition exhibit perceptual properties continuous with those of the other senses? Although these three interrelated questions constitute a list far from complete, they establish positions that will strongly shape the course of auditory perception research.

Fortunately, these questions have been addressed extensively in the literature on speech perception. Of all areas of auditory science, speech is arguably the most conceptually mature. This is probably a consequence of the obvious ecological relevance of speech as well as the fact that speech perception necessarily involves recovery of *meaningful* events, whether gesturally or linguistically defined. Speech research has examined the entire perceptual function from the sound-producing event (intended and/or realized gestures) through thorough descriptions of information (both acoustic and multimodal) to careful evaluation of perceptual experience (whether consistent with acoustic or gestural properties). The thoroughness with which speech research has addressed its function stands in stark contrast to extant descriptions of nonspeech audition, much of which has concentrated on sensory processes. In fact, this disparity in our understanding of speech versus general audition has led, in part, to one influential perspective that speech is perceived in a functionally different way from nonspeech sounds (Liberman & Mattingly, 1985; Liberman & Whalen, 2000). Nevertheless, over a half-century of speech perception research has provided important perspective on conceptual issues that audition must now face. In this sense, lessons could be extracted from the speech literature to help develop a thorough science of auditory perception.

The goal of this chapter is to review issues in the speech perception literature that have particular relevance to the development of an ecological psychoacoustics. The speech literature is discussed in three sections pertaining to issues of perceptual primitives, informational descriptions, and multimodal perception. Throughout, relevant research on nonspeech auditory perception is addressed. This nonspeech research, although scant, could provide good exemplars for future ecological psychoacoustics research.

LESSON 1: WE HEAR EVENTS, NOT SOUNDS

If a tree falls in the forest and no one is there, why is its ability to make a *sound* in question? Why isn't the tree's ability to reflect light disputable? It seems that our conception of sound involves a subjective component not intrinsic to light. Moreover, there often seems to be an implicit assumption that we hear *sounds*, but we see *things*. Thus, while the job of vision is to decipher visible cues to see the *world*, the job of hearing is to decipher acoustic cues to hear *sounds* (see also, Fowler, 1996). It is as if we see properties of the world, but we hear the properties of the world only as coded in sound (e.g., Ohala, 1996). Although on the surface this dichotomy might seem largely semantic, it has had far-reaching effects on perceptual theory and methodology (see Fowler, 1986). Modern research on vision emphasizes recovery of distal event properties (shapes, distances, movement), whereas research on audition emphasizes recovery of sensory dimensions (pitch, timbre), which presumably codes distal properties. This dichotomy is readily apparent in contemporary perception textbooks (e.g., Goldstein, 2003), which typically have chapters on visual perception of distance, objects, and movement (distal properties) and auditory chapters devoted to perception of pitch, loudness, and timbre (sensory properties).[1]

More important, the dichotomy appears in descriptions of *information* with the informational primitives for audition often described in terms of acoustic properties and the primitives for vision described as distal object properties. For example, we recognize a person from hearing the timbre and pitch of the person's voice or by seeing the features and configuration of the person's face. We recognize a musical instrument by hearing its timbre, pitch range, and onset envelope or by seeing its shape, size, and material. Finally, and most relevant to the current chapter, we recognize speech from hearing formants, noise bursts, and silent intervals or seeing (lipreading) mouth shape, tongue position, and teeth visibility. In each of these examples, the perceptual primitives for audition are sounds and the primitives for vision are distal object properties.

The conceptual dichotomy of seeing things versus hearing sounds is probably based on a number of factors including the philosophical history of primary versus secondary experiential properties (Locke, 1689/1975; Newton, 1730), the fact that humans can (physiologically) *make* sound but not light, as well as the fact that humans are presumed to be visually dominated animals ("seeing is believing"). Also, the notion of sound as code might be related to our intensive experience with sound as conveying language—the ultimate human code. Nevertheless, the influence of this dichotomy is rampant in the perception literature and could be to blame for the overwhelming sensory emphasis of classic psychoacoustics relative to vision science. Arguably, then, the development of an ecological psychoacoustics should involve an evaluation of whether the perceptual primitives for hearing are better considered sounds or sound-structuring objects and events.

---

[1] Certainly there are exceptions to this dichotomy in both the research and pedagogical literatures (e.g., color and brightness for vision, speech and music for audition). However, in surveying informational descriptions, as well as empirical questions, the emphasis for vision research seems to be on recovering (distal) object and event properties, whereas the emphasis for audition research is on recovering properties of sound (proximal or energy dimensions).

HEARING SPEECH EVENTS

Fortunately, the issue of perceptual primitives has been examined extensively in the literature on speech perception. One of the most addressed conceptual questions in speech is whether the perceptual primitives correspond to articulatory gestures or to surface acoustic dimensions. Although this question is not settled (e.g., Diehl & Kluender, 1989; Ohala, 1996), from this author's perspective, there is compelling evidence that speech perception corresponds more closely to gestural primitives. This evidence has been thoroughly discussed in numerous chapters and papers (e.g., Fowler, 1996; Fowler & Rosenblum, 1991; Liberman & Mattingly, 1985; Liberman & Whalen, 2000). However, it is useful to present some of the most well known findings here in considering implications for general audition.

Early on, speech research revealed a clear incongruity between phonetic perception and simple acoustic cues (Liberman, Cooper, Shankweiler, & Studdert-Kennedy, 1967). Work in speech synthesis revealed that the distinguishing cue for a specific consonant takes a form that is exceedingly dependent on vowel context. In one well-known example, the distinguishing acoustic cue for a /d/ is thought to be the form of the transition contained in the second formant. In the syllable /di/, a rising second formant transition can distinguish /di/ from /bi/ and /gi/. However, this consonantal distinction is signaled by a different acoustic component when in the context of a /u/ vowel. Thus, /du/ is distinguished from /bu/ and /gu/ by a *descending* second formant transition. It would seem that the cue for /d/ depends on whether it is heard in an /i/ or /u/ context.

This simple example highlights at least three facts about speech. Most obviously, speech cues are crucially dependent on the context of adjacent segments. This dependence is based on the fact that segments are rarely produced in isolation but instead are coproduced—or *coarticulated*—with adjacent segments. At any one time, articulation is simultaneously influenced by as many as three different segment productions. This coarticulation necessarily induces contextual influences on the production of phonetic segments as well as on the acoustic consequences of this production.

The second fact highlighted by the /di-du/ example is the lack of correspondence between surface properties of the acoustic signal and perceived speech segments. In /di-du/, coarticulation causes the same perceived phonetic segment to correspond to two different critical features (a rising vs. descending second formant transition). This apparent ambiguity in surface speech cues is ubiquitous and is considered one of the major reasons for the difficulty in designing speech recognition systems (Liberman & Mattingly, 1985). A third characteristic of speech highlighted by the /di-du/ example is that although perceptual correspondences to the surface acoustics might be absent, there is close correspondence to properties of articulation. Perceiving /d/ whether in an /i/ or /u/ context corresponds to a "d" articulatory event, that is, vocal tract constriction formed by the tongue blade against the alveolar ridge. Although the acoustic cues for this event might change, perception seems to correspond uniformly to this articulatory primitive.

These characteristics of speech appear in numerous other findings in the literature. Perhaps the most striking evidence for the opacity of acoustic cues to speech perception is from a set of findings known as *trading relations*. A number of studies have shown that two different acoustic cues for a phonetic segment can be heard as equivalent, at least to the degree that they can offset one another (e.g., Fitch, Halwes, Erikson, & Liberman, 1980). This produces the unusual finding that two speech signals that are different from each other in two separate ways are less distinguishable than two signals different in only one of these ways. For example, the words "slit" and "split" can be distinguished by two acoustic dimensions: by the length of the silent interval between the /s/ and /l/ or by the presence or absence of formant transitions associated with /p/. Research with synthetic speech has shown that whereas manipulating just one of these dimensions (e.g., shortening the silent interval) can change the perceived word from "split" to "slit," simultaneously changing both dimensions in opposite directions (shortening the silent interval while adding formant transitions associated with /p/) does not change the perceived word. Moreover, when asked to discriminate pairs of these words, listeners find it substantially easier to discriminate pairs that are different along one dimension (e.g., silent interval) than pairs different on both dimensions (Fitch *et al.*, 1980). These findings have been interpreted as evidence that the two types of cues (silent interval; formant transitions) are functionally equivalent (and can be functionally *traded*) in specifying the same articulatory gesture.

Turning to evidence for gestural speech primitives, it seems that the perception of even a sensory dimension of speech—loudness—is based on articulatory properties. As mentioned in the introductory chapter of this volume (Neuhoff, 2004), judgments of speech loudness correspond more closely to articulatory effort than acoustic intensity or any other simple acoustic dimension or combination thereof (frequency; spectral composition) (Ladefoged & McKinney, 1963; Lehiste & Peterson, 1959; but see Glave & Reitveld, 1975; and see Rosenblum & Fowler, 1991, for a review). For example, Ladefoged and McKinney (1963) were able to predict loudness judgments of syllables more accurately with a vocal work metric than with the acoustic intensity of those syllables. Their metric of vocal work was defined as the product of subglottal pressure and air velocity across the glottis, both of which were measured for their speakers. It may be that the correspondence of speech loudness to articulatory effort is related to the ability to perceive contrastive syllabic stress (e.g., CONvict vs. conVICT), despite little consistency in intensity differences for this purpose. It seems that even when asked to perceive sensory aspects of speech, listeners refer to primitives of the speech production mechanism.

Other striking evidence for gestural speech primitives comes from multimodal influences on heard speech. This research is discussed in detail in a subsequent section, but the general finding is relevant to the current topic. It seems that

listeners cannot help but integrate speech from any reliable source whether conveyed auditorily or otherwise. In the McGurk effect (McGurk & MacDonald,
1976), seeing the articulating mouth of a speaker can have a substantial influence
on what observers report hearing. For example, when a visual syllable /va/ is syn-
chronously dubbed onto a /ba/ audio syllable, listeners report *hearing* a /va/ syllable. Other examples induce perceived segments that are compromised between
the audio and visual signals (e.g., visual /ga/ + audio /ba/ = heard /da/; visual /ba/
+ audio /ga/ = heard /bga/). These types of effects seem to work on all observers
regardless of awareness of the stimulus manipulation, native language background (e.g., Massaro, Cohen, Gesi, Heredia, & Tsuzaki, 1993; Sekiyama and
Tohkura, 1991, 1993), and age (e.g., Rosenblum, Schmuckler, & Johnson, 1997).
The ubiquity and automaticity of visual influences on heard speech have been
taken as evidence that perceptual primitives of speech are not acoustic but are
gestural. It is argued that the speech system integrates multimodal signals so
readily because its job is to recover gestural events regardless of the energy
medium through which the events are conveyed. This interpretation is bolstered
by the findings that visual speech can induce changes in auditory cortex activity
similar to those induced by auditory speech (Calvert *et al.*, 1997; MacSweeney,
Amaro, Calvert, & Campbell, 2000; but see Bernstein *et al.*, 2002). More details
and implications of these findings are discussed subsequently.

HEARING NONSPEECH EVENTS

To summarize, by this author's interpretation of the speech literature, perceptual primitives are better construed as gestural than auditory in nature. Although
this interpretation is not without controversy (e.g., see Diehl & Kluender, 1989;
and Ohala, 1996 for reviews), it would behoove ecological psychoacoustics to
examine the possibility that nonspeech auditory perception is based on distal
event primitives. In fact, a literature is emerging which shows that listeners can
be impressively sensitive to nonspeech event primitives. This research can be
classified into two categories: research showing abilities to judge event properties explicitly by virtue of sound and research showing that auditory judgments
correspond more closely to event than acoustic primitives.

There is now strong evidence that listeners are impressive at judging properties
of sound-structuring events and objects. Certainly, anecdotal examples abound,
including auditory-based diagnosis of automotive and medical problems as well
as musicians' uncanny sensitivity to instrument quality. What has emerged more
recently is an empirical literature showing that even untrained listeners can
recover subtle properties of both familiar and novel events. These properties
include event identity and cause, as well as the size, shape, and material of objects
involved in the events. Much of this research is reviewed in a chapter by Carello,
Wagman, and Turvey in press.

Early on, Vanderveer (1979) asked listeners to describe a series of 30 everyday sounds including shaking keys, tearing paper, hammering, and footsteps.

Three interesting findings were reported. First, listeners were impressively accurate at identifying most of these events. Second, identification mistakes were often made along sensible lines, so that events confused with one another were often similar in physical attributes (e.g., hammering was confused with walking but not with paper tearing). Finally, even though subjects were simply asked to describe what they heard, they most often responded by identifying the sound-producing objects and events rather than labeling the sound itself (e.g., "shaking keys" was a much more common response than "jingling sound"). In fact, only when subjects were unable to identify the sounding event did they resort to sensory descriptions. Although none of these results are particularly surprising, they do provide descriptive evidence for sensitivity to event primitives for non-speech stimuli.

More recent research has revealed an impressive ability of listeners to identify very specific characteristics of events and objects. These characteristics include the width of struck bars (Lakatos, McAdams, & Canssé, 1997), the length of dropped rods (Carello, Anderson, & Peck, 1998), the hardness of struck mallets (Freed, 1990), the size, material, and even shape of struck plates (Kunkler-Peck & Turvey, 2000), as well as whether a vessel is being filled, emptied, or maintained with different levels of fluid (Cabe & Pittenger, 2000). There is also evidence that listeners can hear characteristics of individuals and their behavior from events other than speech. By listening to footsteps, listeners can recover actor gender and whether actors are ascending or descending a staircase (Gaver, 1988; Li, Logan, & Pastore, 1991). Also, listeners can easily recognize the style and configuration of clapping hands (Repp, 1987). Finally, as reviewed in Chap. 4 of this volume (Neuhoff, 2004), a literature exists demonstrating listener accuracy in anticipating the trajectory of approaching sound sources (e.g., Lufti & Wang, 1999; Rosenblum, Wuestefeld, & Saldaña, 1993; Schiff & Oldak, 1990). Although most of the events discussed here are familiar to listeners, it is unlikely that subjects in these experiments had practice in making explicit judgments of the sounds.

Not only do listeners show impressive sensitivity in judging sounding event primitives, they often seem to base sensory judgments on those primitives. As stated, speech research has shown many examples in which observers cannot help but base perception on articulatory primitives. This fact seems true even when listeners are asked to judge more sensory properties of the speech signal (i.e., loudness) (e.g., Ladefoged & McKinney, 1963; Lehiste & Peterson, 1959). There is also some evidence that nonspeech auditory sensory judgments are constrained by distal event primitives. Elsewhere in this volume (Chaps. 1 and 10), there is extensive discussion of how judgments of tone pitch can be influenced by changes in intensity (and vice versa) in ways predicted by the physical properties of the Doppler shift (and, by implication, the moving sound sources that structure the shift). Moreover, there is evidence that listeners judge the change in loudness as greater for increasing intensities than for equivalent decreasing intensity (Neuhoff, 1998). This finding has been interpreted as reflecting the relative ecological salience of approaching versus receding sound sources: overestimating the intensity increase of an approaching source could provide a margin of safety for collision avoidance. Thus, both the intensity–frequency interactions and heightened sensitivity to increasing intensity could constitute evidence that listeners are sensitive to distal event properties (of approaching or receding sound sources) when making sensory judgments.

More generally, there is a theory of psychophysics which argues that *all* sensory judgments are based on environmental or physical primitives. From the perspective of Richard Warren's (1981) physical correlate theory, the unnaturalness of sensory judgment tasks forces observers to rely on tacit knowledge of environmental properties, including physical laws. Warren argues that even the most basic sensory judgments of light brightness and tone loudness reflect implicit estimates of the distance of visible and audible objects, along with tacit knowledge of how intensity changes with distance. As support, he shows that the psychophysical functions for brightness and loudness follow the inverse-square law of energy's change with source distance. He applies similar strategies to explaining the psychoacoustic scales for perceived lightness of grays and for lifted weight. Thus, from the perspective of the physical correlate theory, listeners cannot help but rely on environmental object or event primitives when making sensory judgments. (A similar physically grounded approach to musical universals has been proposed by David Schwartz and his colleagues: Schwartz, Howe, & Purves, 2003).

Finally, hints that observers base nonspeech auditory perception on distal event properties can be found in the multimodal perception literature. There is a rich literature on cross-modal influences on auditory judgments that is discussed in detail in the following. Suffice it to say at this point that, like the McGurk effect in speech, visual and tactile stimuli can influence nonspeech auditory responses even when observers are asked to base judgments solely on what they hear (e.g., Bermant & Welch, 1976; Radeau & Bertelson, 1974; Rosenblum & Fowler, 1991; Saldaña & Rosenblum, 1993). Also noteworthy is the fact that these cross-modal effects can occur on judgments of *sensory* dimensions such as loudness (e.g., Rosenblum & Fowler, 1991). To the degree that cross-modal influences on audition can be interpreted as evidence for distal event primitives (e.g., Fowler & Rosenblum, 1991; Liberman & Mattingly, 1985), nonspeech events share this characteristic with speech.

In summary, although it is certainly not a settled issue (Diehl & Kluender, 1989; Ohala, 1996), there is a history of compelling evidence supporting gestural objects of speech perception. The implications of distal event speech primitives have been far reaching and have provided the groundwork for one of the most influential theories of speech perception, namely the motor theoretic perspective (Liberman & Mattingly, 1985). The details of the motor theory are discussed in numerous chapters (Liberman & Mattingly, 1985; Liberman & Whalen, 2000). One of its most notable claims is that the speech function is unique in working with distal primitives and that the function's operations are specialized to speech input. However, as argued throughout this chapter, it is this author's perspective that speech is not unique in either its primitives or operations. Rather, all of auditory perception corresponds to distal event primitives, and this is one reason why speech research has much to inform an ecological psychoacoustics.

One implication of distal primitives for both speech and nonspeech perception is the challenge to find how these primitives are specified in acoustic structure. Because of evidence for the equivocal relationship between speech perception and surface acoustic properties, speech researchers have looked to more abstract, higher order descriptions of acoustic information. Potentially, this tack could also work for nonspeech auditory perception. These issues are addressed in the next section.

LESSON 2: TO UNDERSTAND INFORMATION, UNDERSTAND EVENTS

As discussed, there is a long history of research showing an incongruity between speech as perceived (and produced) and any obvious acoustic cues. This fact is thought responsible for such phenomena as perceptual context effects and cue trading, as well as for difficulties in designing effective speech recognition systems. Many theories of speech perception have taken this apparent opacity of cues to posit cognitive mechanisms that compensate for the lack of information (Diehl & Kluender, 1989; Liberman & Mattingly, 1985; Massaro, 1987; McClelland & Elman, 1986; Stevens, 1989). However, other approaches propose that with the appropriate description of the acoustic signal, auditory structure for speech can be shown to be fully informative (Browman & Goldstein, 1986; Fowler, 1986; Fowler & Rosenblum, 1991; Summerfield, 1987). These approaches proffer that appropriate descriptions of the acoustics depend on thorough analysis of the articulatory events themselves. Potentially, these are lessons applicable to an ecological psychoacoustics.

INFORMATION FOR ARTICULATORY EVENTS

Thorough descriptions of articulatory events have proved to be critical to much speech perception research. Certainly, this fact is related to arguments for gestural perceptual primitives. However, the importance of understanding speech production is also based on the assumed destructive nature of articulation with regard to intended phonetic gestures. As mentioned, it is thought that the fact that segments are coarticulated is at least partially responsible for the opacity of the acoustic cues. Traditionally, intended gestures are considered something akin to phonetic segments. While a speaker intends to produce /d/'s, /a/'s, and /f/'s, these are never actualized in production: coarticulation as well as physiological and dynamic constraints cause production distortions, undershoots, and general assimilations. In this sense, the gestures as intended are never realized in the vocal tract intact. This has led some theorists to argue that the true perceptual primitives of speech are more precisely *intended*, than actualized, gestures (e.g., Liberman & Mattingly, 1985).

However, not all theories consider speech production a destructive process relative to intended gestures. According to *gestural phonology*, speech production actually involves a layering of two concurrent production streams that sometimes share specific articulators (Browman & Goldstein, 1986). The layering of gestural streams can be thought of as akin to dual influences on a human arm—swinging; forward movement—on the *overall* movement of the arm during walking (Fowler & Rosenblum, 1991). Regarding speech production, the streams correspond roughly to vowel and consonant productions. In gestural phonology, the linguistic primitives are these dual streams *themselves* (not abstract phonemes), which are realized intact in the vocal tract and are perceived as such. Thus, perceivers recover the distal primitives qua gestures, which are intended, realized, and, potentially, specified acoustically.

The details of gestural phonology go beyond the current chapter and are discussed elsewhere (Browman & Goldstein, 1986; Fowler & Rosenblum, 1991; Goldstein, 2002). However, the take-home message is that a reevaluation of articulatory events supports a description of the perceptual objects not just as mental constructs but as realized events. Moreover, this revised description motivates a very different conception of the acoustic information for speech. In this sense, gestural phonology can potentially take the onus off the speech perceiver to reconstruct distorted primitives informed by ambiguous information. Instead, the responsibility is placed on the speech scientist to discover how realized articulatory primitives are specified in unambiguous information.

One upshot of reconsidering speech primitives as overlapping production streams is that it points to a description of auditory information emphasizing the time-varying aspects of the signal. Traditional descriptions of speech acoustics have emphasized relatively short-term and unchanging components of the signal. Classic cues of speech include steady-state formant properties such as bandwidth and onset spectral composition (e.g., noise bursts) (e.g., Liberman & Studdert-Kennedy, 1978). However, over 20 years of research has shown that these short-term properties are unnecessary as long as the more time-varying, temporally extended dimensions of the signal are present. This fact has been demonstrated with sine wave speech stimuli that delete all short-term spectral dimensions of the speech signal and retain time-varying dimensions via the simultaneous changes of three simple sine waves (Remez, Rubin, Pisoni, & Carrell, 1981). These sine waves are synthesized to track an utterance's first three center formant frequencies and amplitudes. Sine wave speech can convey syllables, words, and sentences and can induce some of the classic speech effects discussed earlier. In that sine wave speech does not retain any of the shorter term cues of the speech signal (noise bursts), it demonstrates that the more time-varying changes contained in the isolated sine waves can be sufficient for speech perception.

Not only are the time-varying dimensions of the speech signal informative, but also there is evidence that in some contexts they are more salient than shorter term dimensions. Research has shown that the most salient information for perceiving a vowel in the context of two surrounding consonants (a consonant-vowel-consonant (CVC) syllable such as "bob" or "pad") is contained in the most dynamic parts of the signal. Thus, contrary to intuition as well as "target" theories of vowel perception (e.g., Lieberman, Crelin, & Klatt, 1972), the best information for the vowel in CVC context is not contained in the most centered, "pure" portion of the vowel signal. Instead, the richest information for the vowel is in the portions surrounding the vowel center—the portions most heavily coarticulated with the consonants. In fact, up to 60% of a vowel's center can be deleted from a CVC (and replaced with silence) without hindering identification accuracy of the vowel. Moreover, these "silent-center" syllables support better vowel identification than the less coarticulated, pure vowel portion extracted from these syllables (Strange, Jenkins, & Johnson, 1983). Analogous results have also been observed for consonant perception (Blumstein, Isaacs, & Mertus, 1982; Walley & Carrell, 1983) in vowel-consonant-vowel (VCV) contexts. This evidence suggests that the articulatory transitions into and out of a segment provide better acoustic information than the more steady-state, pure segment portions of the signal. Possibly, then, listeners are most sensitive to gestural overlaying as hypothesized by the gestural phonology theory (Browman & Goldstein, 1986).

Thus, many researchers now consider speech information as predominantly instantiated in the time-varying dimensions of the signal. This emphasis on time-varying information has helped motivate a general switch to searching for speech information in the more abstract, higher order aspects of the signal. Evidence discussed in the previous section shows the inadequacy of the surface-level, unidimensional acoustic signal properties to act as speech information. Instead, true speech information could lie with the higher order relation between unidimensional acoustic parameters or parameters that are revealed only in the time-varying changes of these dimensions.

Consider the case of how fundamental frequency, F0, can play a role in speech information (Fowler & Rosenblum, 1991). Although the F0 of a speech utterance is a single acoustically identifiable dimension, it has multiple, simultaneous perceptual correlates. Most obviously, F0 corresponds to the perceived "pitch" or intonational contour of an utterance, whether rising for a question or lowering for a declarative statement. However, F0 also corresponds to the "height" of a produced vowel, allowing distinctions such as that between /i/ and /æ/. In addition, F0 will change along with the general declination of an utterance as the speaker expels air, thereby decreasing subglottal pressure.

The fact that F0 corresponds to—and can help inform about—these three linguistic events is surprising when considering that F0 itself depends *solely* on the rate of vocal fold vibration. Somehow listeners are able to parse perceptually the three separate articulatory influences of intonation, vowel height, and declination on vocal fold vibration, along with the different linguistic intents behind these influences.

In fact, upon considering exactly how these articulatory dimensions influence vocal fold vibration, it becomes clear that distinctive, and potentially informative, physiological consequences correspond to each. For example, changes in vocal fold vibration from declination are based on changes in subglottal pressure—a production parameter also known to affect amplitude (e.g., Gelfer, 1987). In contrast, changes in vocal fold vibration due to vowel height are induced by the position of the hyoid bone, a production parameter that also changes the signal's spectral structure (via tongue position). Finally, the changes in vocal fold vibration induced by intonational contour seem to be produced by specific contractions of the glottal muscles, which, for the most part, have only an acoustic consequence specific to F0.

The fact that there are three different sets of physiological influences on vocal fold vibration is fortunate for the listener. Whereas changes in F0 on their own might not be specific to, or fully informative about, the articulatory changes that modulate them, there are specific consequences of each linguistic intent present in the *relation over time* between F0, amplitude, and spectral composition. In this sense, the information for declination, intonation, and vowel height is not contained simply in F0 but in the higher order relation between F0 and these other acoustic dimensions. Potentially, then, a listener would be able to determine which production influence is occurring by attending to these higher order relations. In fact, there is evidence that listeners do attend to these relations during speech perception (e.g., Silverman, 1986, 1987).

Two points can be taken from this example. First, it is only when examining the higher order relations existent across simple acoustic dimensions that parameters specific to the event, as well as to perception, become apparent. If only the dimension of F0 is considered, the perception function is faced with multiple interpretations. But from this perspective, F0, although certainly an acoustic parameter related to production, does not constitute true speech information. The true information is contained in the higher order relation between F0 and other acoustic dimensions. The second point is that the discovery of specificational speech information has been informed by a thorough understanding of the production mechanism, in this case the multiple physiological influences on F0. This understanding of production suggested the possible relation between unidimensional acoustic changes that were specific to these different articulatory events. A similar approach has been taken toward understanding the salient information for perceiving syllabic stress (see Smith, 1984 for a review).

To summarize the lessons from this section, speech research has demonstrated that when considering perceptual information, it pays to look carefully at the details of production events and to establish effective descriptions of these events. As corollary lessons, the emphasis on production has revealed two important aspects of speech information: (1) speech information often takes a form that is time varying, and (2) information also takes a higher order form instantiated as specific relations between lower level acoustic dimensions. Potentially, all of these lessons could be applied to an ecological psychoacoustics.

INFORMATION FOR NONSPEECH EVENTS

In fact, there is some research in the audition literature demonstrating these principles. For example, work on determining the information for sound source identification has turned to source mechanics for clues. Analyses of source mechanics are not new to acoustics and have been used to improve electronic synthesis of musical instruments (e.g., Borin, De Poli, & Sarti, 1993). More recent are analyses of source mechanics for purposes of understanding auditory perception itself. One of the first formal efforts along these lines was provided by William Gaver (1993a, 1993b) in two seminal papers. In these papers Gaver argues that only through examination of sound source mechanics is a complete understanding of true acoustic information possible. As an early pass at this approach, he derived models of event classes including impacts, scrapes, and drips. These models were derived from event mechanics with emphasis on the mechanical components most likely to have audible consequences. For example, the physical differences in the vibratory behavior of struck wooden versus metal bars involve different damping functions, which, in turn, have different acoustic outcomes. The decay of a wooden bar's signal is overall faster, with the lower frequency components lasting longer than the higher frequency components. In contrast, the decay of a metal bar's signal involves longer lasting higher frequency components relative to the lower frequency components. Potentially, listeners sensitive to these differences would be able to distinguish which of these two materials had been struck.

Along these lines, Wildes and Richards (1988) proposed that the ability to hear differences in object elasticity might be related to an internal friction component that differentially structures decay rate as well as harmonic bandwidth structure. These authors support their proposition by using these mechanical parameters to control acoustic synthesis with perceptually convincing results.

Carello and her colleagues (Anderson, Carello, & Kunkler-Peck, 1996; Carello, Andersen, & Kunkler-Peck, 1998), examined the parameters that could account for the heard length of dropped wooden rods. These authors found that they could best predict length judgments from the rods' mechanical properties rather than the acoustic amplitude, frequency, or duration of the resultant sounds. Specifically, they found that the most consistent predictive parameter was a combination of each rod's elasticity and the inertial tensor. Together, these parameters accounted for 91% of heard length judgments regardless of rod diameter. Potentially, then, when judging rod length, listeners attend to some higher order combination of acoustic dimensions that specify these mechanical parameters. In a similar vein, Kunkler-Peck and Turvey (2000) showed how auditory perception of the size, material, and shape of struck plates can be accurately predicted from mechanical parameters of the impact events. These authors found that a two-dimensional wave equation of the event mechanics could account for 87% of size judgment variance. Thus, as for speech, mechanically informed descriptions of acoustic information can provide successful predictors of perceptual judgments.

There is also evidence that, as for speech, there is salient information for nonspeech events in the time-varying components of the signal. Warren and Verbrugge (1983) found that recognition of a bouncing versus breaking jar is based largely on the pattern of acoustic change over time. The most obvious acoustic differences between a bouncing and breaking jar would seem to lie in the initial crash noise associated with glass shattering. However, Warren and Verbrugge found that when the initial portions of the sounds were removed from the signal, the events were still largely recognizable. Moreover, when the spectral structure from one event was applied to the temporal patterning of the other event, it was the temporal patterning that mostly determined event identification. Other nonspeech experiments that have shown greater relative salience of time-varying properties involve the distinguishing of male and female hand clapping (with slower hand claps judged as produced by males) (Repp, 1987) and judgments of ramp incline based on the sound of a ball rolling down the ramp (Fowler, 1990).

The salience of time-varying acoustic information is also evident in the literature on sound localization. The time-varying structure induced by listener movement has been shown to facilitate judgments of both sound source horizontal location (Pollack & Rose, 1967; Thurlow & Runge, 1967) and distance (Ashmead, Davis, & Northington, 1995; Speigle & Loomis, 1993). Listener movement can also facilitate human echolocation judgments of a reflecting surface's distance (Rosenblum, Gordon, & Jarquin, 2000). This class of results is continuous with findings in the *visual* perception literature (e.g., Cutting, 1986; Rogers & Collett, 1989) and shows how time-varying information can be facilitative when the transformations are induced by listeners themselves.

The final lesson from speech research discussed here concerns the salience of higher order acoustic information. With regard to nonspeech, it should be noted that most of the acoustic information described in the preceding paragraphs takes a higher order form. Motivating informational descriptions from source mechanics as well as emphasizing time-varying parameters will compel the descriptions to be higher order. This is clearly true in the aforementioned examples of recognizing wooden versus metal bars and the length of dropped rods. Recall that in the latter example, none of the single dimensions of amplitude, frequency, or duration could predict length judgments. The best predictor was the dual consideration of a rod's elasticity and inertial tensor, properties no doubt specified in some higher order combination of acoustic dimensions.

Speculations on the importance of higher order information have also appeared in the literature on auditory time to arrival (Shaw, McGowan, & Turvey, 1991), auditory distance perception (Rosenblum, Wuestefeld, & Anderson, 1996), and human echolocation (Rosenblum, Gordon, & Jarquin, 2000; Stoffregen & Pittenger, 1995) to name a few functions. More generally, a number of the nonspeech examples discussed in the previous section (i.e., events are perceived, not sounds) are consistent with the salience of higher order structure. Recall that the previous section introduced examples of Neuhoff (Neuhoff, 1998; Neuhoff & McBeath, 1996) in which unidimensional acoustics (changes in intensity, frequency) could not predict even sensory judgments (loudness, pitch). Instead, sensory judgments were necessarily influenced by more than one acoustic dimension. This would suggest that the salient information (e.g., for approach) in these examples involved some critical combination of lower order dimensions.

The assumption that the informational form for audible events is based on higher order, time-varying, production-based parameters certainly has implications for acoustic analyses and experimental methodology. Moreover, the assumption is consistent with an emphasis on uncovering information that is specific to, and fully informative about, relevant auditory events. This emphasis on information over mental process is, to at least this author's interpretation, central to an ecological psychoacoustics. The final section examines the possibility that the information for speech and nonspeech events takes a form even more abstract than that discussed so far. Evidence is presented supporting that the true information for events takes a form that is neutral with regard to modality.

LESSON 3: AUDITION SERVES A MULTIMODAL BRAIN

MULTIMODAL SPEECH PERCEPTION

Arguably one of the most important discoveries in speech research over the last 25 years is that speech perception is primarily a multimodal function. Although speech can certainly be recognized from auditory information alone, it is now clear that most of us do extract speech from visual means (lip-reading) on a daily basis and even have the potential for extracting speech through touch (e.g., Fowler & Dekle, 1991). Normal hearing individuals commonly use visual speech when faced with a noisy environment (MacLeod & Summerfield, 1990; Sumby & Pollack, 1954), a complicated message (Arnold & Hill, 2001; Reisberg, McLean, & Goldfield, 1987), or heavily accented speech (Reisberg et al., 1987). Visual speech seems to play an important role in normal speech development (for a review, see Mills, 1987), not to mention as an aid to individuals with various levels of hearing loss. It has been argued that visual speech had an important influence on the evolution of spoken language (e.g., Corballis, 2002; Mac-Neilage, 1998), and languages themselves may have developed to take advantage of visual as well as auditory sensitivities (Rosenblum, in press).

The most phenomenologically compelling demonstration of multimodal speech salience is the aforementioned McGurk effect. The effect involves the automatic integration of discrepant but synchronized auditory and visual syllables (auditory /ba/ + visual /ga/ = perceived /da/). The effect is compelling to the degree that observers report "hearing" the integrated syllable and do so regardless of whether they are aware (1) of the dubbing procedure, (2) that the auditory and visual stimuli are derived from different speakers, or even (3) that they are looking at a face. As mentioned, the effect works with listeners from all native language backgrounds and works with prelinguistic infants.

Moreover, there is evidence from both behavioral and neurophysiological research that multimodal integration occurs at a very early stage of the speech function. Behaviorally, visual speech information has been shown to influence auditory speech at the stage of feature extraction (Green, 1998; Summerfield, 1987). Visual influences can induce changes in auditory perception of voice onset time and coarticulatory influences (e.g., Green & Gerdeman, 1995; Green & Norrix, 2001) in ways analogous to influences induced unimodally. Early cross-modal speech influences are also evident in the neuropsychological literature. Imaging techniques have shown evidence for visual speech induction of auditory cortex (Calvert et al., 1999; MacSweeney et al., 2000; but see Bernstein et al., 2002). For example, using functional magnetic resonance imaging (fMRI) technique, Calvert and her colleagues (Calvert et al., 1999; MacSweeney et al., 2000) have shown that silent lipreading can induce activity in primary auditory cortex similar to that induced by analogous auditory speech. Similar findings have been observed using other imaging techniques as well as in the context of audiovisual speech integration (Callan et al., 2001; Mottonen Krause, Tiippana, & Sams, 2002; Sams et al., 1991).

To summarize, there is mounting evidence that speech perception is truly a multimodal function. Elsewhere, I have argued that this evidence suggests a *primacy of multimodal speech* (Rosenblum, In press), in the sense of an automaticity and neurophysiologic priority of cross-modal integration. I have also argued that a more radical suggestion follows from this perspective. It could be that in an important way, the speech function is insensitive to modality and might be attuned to a form of external information (in light and sound) that is essentially modality neutral. If speech primitives take the form of articulatory gestures rather than acoustic dimensions, salient information can exist in a way that is independent of any specific energy medium. Furthermore, if these gestures structure media as higher order time-varying patterns, then in principle, these patterns could be structured in multiple media. This renders the job of the auditory or visual system to extract this common structure as it is instantiated in the modality to which it is sensitive. This is not to imply that every articulatory gesture is equally available auditorily and visually, nor does it deny that languages have developed to often take advantage of auditory sensitivities (e.g., Diehl & Kluender, 1989; Ohala, 1984, 1996). Rather, the perspective argues that the informational form which the speech function extracts is modality neutral.

Moreover, if the salient aspects of the informational structure exist at an abstract, modality-neutral—and sensory-neutral—level, the concept of modality integration becomes very different. From this perspective, integration becomes a function of the information itself, not something that occurs after separate extraction of modality-specific features.

The thesis of modality-neutral information is not completely new. It is continuous with theoretical positions in both speech (e.g., Summerfield, 1987) and nonspeech (e.g., Gibson, 1966, 1979; Stoffregen & Bardy, 2001) domains. What is novel here is how the evidence from both behavioral and neuropsychological research supports the thesis. Some of this research has already been discussed, and some will be discussed in the following. At this juncture it is important to distinguish the notions of modality-neutral information espoused in this chapter and the modality-neutral theory of perceptual objecthood discussed in Chap. 5. In their chapter (and elsewhere, e.g., Kubovy & Van Valkenburg, 2001), Van Valkenburg and Kubovy build toward a unified theory of the senses by establishing connections between indispensable informational attributes defined for each modality. These indispensable attributes are informational dimensions that are modality specific (e.g., spatial separation for vision; frequency separation for audition) and might be connected via methodological and mathematical analogy. In contrast, the notion of modality-neutral information proposed here and elsewhere (e.g., Gibson, 1966; 1979; Rosenblum, In press; Stoffregen & Bardy, 2001; Summerfield, 1987), assumes that the salient informational dimensions are *themselves* modality neutral in being defined as higher order relations between energy characteristics. As will be shown later, this relational aspect of information allows information to be established in multiple energy media and picked up by multiple perceptual systems. Thus, although both the modality-neutral information thesis and modality-neutral theory of perceptual objecthood strive toward a unifying principle for the senses, the former is more radical in proposing that there is no relevant way in which perceptual information is modality specific (Rosenblum, In press).

What might constitute examples of modality-neutral speech information? Thus far, the examples have taken both specific and general forms. Regarding specific examples, Summerfield (1987) has argued that aspects of the acoustic and optic signals could be seen as similar in form as they correspond to articulatory rate, quantal changes in position, and changes in articulatory direction. During an utterance, a reversal of lip direction (e.g., from opened to closed) can structure a "reversal" in acoustic intensity and spectra as well as a "reversal" in optical structure. In this sense, kinematic *reversal* could be considered a modality-neutral property of structured energy, whether optically or acoustically instantiated. Perceptual systems sensitive to this more abstract property of energy would be working with the modality-neutral dimensions of the information. Summerfield has made similar conjectures for articulatory rate and quantal changes in position.

Vatikiotis-Bateson and his colleagues (Munhall & Vatikiotis-Bateson, 1998; Yehia, Rubin, & Vatikiotis-Bateson, 1998) have provided more concrete examples of specific cross-modal informational correspondence. Using sophisticated extra- and intraoral kinematic tracking along with acoustical analyses, these researchers observed impressively close correspondence between visible and audible consequences of articulation (e.g., root mean square amplitude [RMS], spectral composition). Some interesting findings include a closer correspondence between the acoustics and the *visible* (extraoral) articulation than the less visible, intraoral movements. Moreover, these researchers show that an intelligible acoustic signal can be synthesized using parameters from the visible kinematics. They explain their results by proposing that both the visible kinematics and acoustic signal can reflect the time course and amplitude of vocal tract opening and closing. Following Summerfield (1987), these authors speculate that because these are gestural properties that are instantiated in both modalities, their informational outcome is modality neutral.

The evidence for modality-neutral information also takes the form of a more general similitude across energy media. This "informational similitude" (Rosenblum, In press) reveals that idiosyncratic dimensions of speech information seem to exist across modalities. At present, informational similitude has been identified along two dimensions: a bimodal salience of (1) time-varying and (2) indexical properties. As stated previously, research on auditory speech has shown a clear salience of time-varying, dynamic acoustic dimensions. This has been evidenced in the salience of sine wave speech, for which only the time-varying characteristics of the signal are retained (Remez et al., 1981). In addition, findings using silent-center syllables show that at least in some contexts, the more dynamic (coarticulated) portions of the speech signal are the most informative (e.g., Strange et al., 1983).

Research in our laboratory and others has shown similar characteristics for *visual* speech. For example, we have used a point-light technique to show that isolated dynamic information for an articulating face can be used to recognize speech (for a review see Rosenblum & Saldaña, 1998). Our point-light technique involves placing fluorescent dots on various positions of a speaker's face including lips, teeth, and tongue and then videotaping the speaker in the dark. The resultant images show only motion of the points against a black background: all other facial information (mouth shape, skin) is deleted from these images. Point-light speech can convey phonetic information in enhancing auditory speech in noise (Rosenblum, Johnson, & Saldaña, 1996) and is treated like real visual speech to the degree that it integrates with auditory speech in a McGurk effect context (Rosenblum & Saldaña, 1996). We have argued that point-light speech is the visual analogue of sine wave speech in isolating the time-varying dynamic information present in a speech signal. The fact that isolated dynamic speech information is usable across modalities could constitute an informational similitude.

Moreover, similarly to auditory speech, visual speech displays a greater relative salience of time-varying properties for vowels in CVC contexts (Yakel, 2000). Using a methodology analogous to that of the auditory speech research (Strange et al., 1983), we extracted out the middle portion of videotaped CVC syllables so that most of the vowel articulations were unseen. These blank-center syllables replaced the vowel articulation with black video frames while retaining the surrounding consonantal productions. As found for the auditory silent-center syllables, the vowels of these blank-center syllables were recognized as well as their intact counterparts and better than the extracted vowel centers themselves. This advantage for the blank-center syllables was maintained even after the extracted vowel center stimuli were extended to have the same number of video frames as the blank-center tokens. Thus, as for auditory speech, the most salient information for a visible vowel might well be in the more dynamic, coarticulated portions of the signal.

Another example of cross-modal informational similitude exists in the relationship between phonetic and indexical properties of speech. The last 10 years of auditory speech research has revealed that contrary to previous theories (e.g., Halle, 1985; Liberman & Mattingly, 1985), the speaker-specific properties of an utterance bear on phonetic perception (for a review, see Nygaard & Pisoni, 1998). Research has shown that listeners recover speech more easily from familiar talkers (e.g., Nygaard, Sommers, & Pisoni, 1994; Nygaard & Pisoni, 1998), and that speaker information is retained along with memory for spoken words (Bradlow, Nygaard, & Pisoni, 1999; Palmeri, Goldinger, & Pisoni, 1993). Moreover, it could be that the observed contingencies of phonetic perception on speaker-specific information are based on a common sensitivity to phonetic information for both functions (where phonetic refers to the specific segments produced during speech, including the aspects of production that retain idiolectic speaking style) (Remez, Fellowes, & Rubin, 1997). Using a sine wave speech resynthesis technique, Remez and his colleagues (Remez *et al.*, 1997) have shown that the speaker-specific phonetic properties isolated in these signals are sufficient to support speaker identification. Sine wave speech resynthesis deletes all spectral detail of the speech signal, much of which (F0, timbre, breathiness) would normally be considered essential for speaker recognition. The fact that speaker recognition is still possible with these severely reduced signals could mean that the speaker-specific phonetic (idiolectic) properties maintained in the signals could be used for both speech and speaker identification.

Within the last 5 years, analogous speech–speaker contingencies have been observed for *visual* speech perception. There is evidence that visual speaker familiarity can facilitate lipreading and that long-term memory for lip-read words can be effected by visible speaker properties (Sheffert & Fowler, 1995; Schweinberger & Soukup, 1998; Yakel, Rosenblum, & Fortier, 2000). There is also evidence that isolated visual phonetic information can be used for speaker identification in a way analogous to auditory speech. Using the point-light paradigm to extract out pictorial face information (skin tone, hairline, feature and face shape), we have found that speakers can be recognized from their isolated articulations in both matching and identification contexts (Rosenblum, Yakel, Baseer, Panchal, Nordarse, & Niehus, 2002; Rosenblum, Smith, & Niehus, in preparation). We interpret these findings as evidence that as with sine wave auditory speech, observers are able to identify speakers by virtue of the idiolectic information available in point-light speech. It could also be that, as for auditory speech, the contingencies observed between visual speech and speaker recognition might be partially based on the common use of visible phonetic information. Regardless, the fact that speaker-informing phonetic information can be conveyed both auditorily and visually could mean that the information is best construed as modality neutral.

Before leaving this discussion, an interesting prediction can be addressed. If speaker-informing phonetic information takes a modality-neutral form, this information should support cross-modal speaker matching: essentially, observers should be able to "hear a face." In fact, there is some evidence that subjects can perform cross-modal speaker matching using both fully illuminated and point-light faces (Lachs, 1999; Rosenblum, Smith, Nichols, Lee, & Hale, under review). In our laboratory we have established that observers can match heard voices to point-light speaking faces with better than chance accuracy and that these matches are based on the dynamic properties of the speaking face (and not any spurious static features available in the point-light stimuli). We are currently testing whether speaker matching can be performed across sine wave and point-light speech, which should constitute the most stringent test of isolated phonetic information for cross-modal matching.

To summarize, there is evidence for a general informational similitude across auditory and visual speech in the salience of both dynamic and indexical properties of the signals. These findings dovetail with the more specific examples of informational similitude for audiovisual speech described by Summerfield (1987) and Vatikiotis-Bateson et al. (Munhall & Vatikiotis-Bateson, 1998; Yehia, Rubin, & Vatikiotis-Bateson, 1998). Evidence for informational similitude is supportive of a modality-neutral perspective and its implication that, to an important degree, modality is invisible to the speech function. Additional support for this idea is provided by neuropsychological evidence that the auditory cortex is reactive to visible speech information (Calvert et al., 1997; MacSweeney et al., 2000) as well as behavioral and neurophysiological findings for very early integration of multimodal speech (Callan et al., 2001; Green, 1998; Mottenen et al., 2002; Sams et al., 1991; Summerfield, 1987). All of these concepts are consistent with the notion of a multimodal primacy for speech perception and that audition should be thought of as serving this primacy.

MULTIMODAL NONSPEECH PERCEPTION

The question arises whether these concepts are also relevant to nonspeech perception. In other words, does multimodal primacy apply to all of perception, and might modality-neutral descriptions of all perceptual information be the most appropriate? In fact, for some theorists, multimodal primacy has been evident in the nonspeech literature for some time (for reviews, see Shimojo & Shams, 2001; Stein & Meredith, 1993; Stoffregen & Bardy, 2001). Research has shown a predominance of early, cross-modal influences unexpected from the perspective of classic unimodal theories of perception. Vision has been shown to have a strong, early influence on auditory judgments of event location and identity and can induce auditory aftereffects (Bermant & Welch, 1976; Kitagawa & Ichihara, 2002; Radeau & Bertelson, 1974; Saldaña & Rosenblum, 1993). Vision can also influence kinesthetic, haptic, and vestibular judgments (e.g., Clark & Graybiel, 1966; Mergner & Rosemeier, 1998; Kinney & Luria, 1970; Lee, 1976). Audition, on the other hand, has been shown to influence visual judgments of location, duration, and number of events (Bertelson & Radeau, 1981; O'Leary & Rhodes, 1984; Shams et al., 2001; Walker & Scott, 1981), while kinesthetic information can influence auditory and visual judgments (Henn, 1986; Roll et al., 1991). Interestingly, a number of these nonspeech cross-modal effects were discovered by attempts to replicate speech integration (McGurk-type) phenomena. For example, using a McGurk effect methodology, research in our laboratory (Saldaña & Rosenblum, 1993) has revealed small but significant influences of visible pluck and bow events on auditory judgments of pluck–bow sounds. Also, taking their cues from McGurk-type effects, Shams and her colleagues (Shams et al., 2001) were able to visually induce qualitative changes in judgments of unambiguous auditory stimuli. Although cross-modal influences on their own do not prove multimodal primacy, the automaticity, impenetrability, and ubiquity with which most of the effects occur certainly are supportive of the concept.

Turning to neurophysiology, there is growing evidence that the nonspeech perceptual brain is organized around multimodal input (e.g., Shimojo & Shams, 2001). Research continually reveals a predominance of brain regions that are specifically tuned to multimodal input (Stein & Meredith, 1993), including areas once thought to be sensitive to unimodal input (Eimer, 2001; Ladavas, Pavani, & Farne, 2001; Laurienti et al., 2002; Pavani, Meneghello, & Ladavas, 2001; Shams, Kamitani, & Shimojo, 2001; Zangaladze et al., 1999). Further evidence for multimodal primacy is found in research on neuroplasticity in animals and humans (Buechel et al., 1998; Cohen et al., 1997; Rauschecker & Korte 1993; Rebillard, Carlier, Rebillard, & Pujol, 1977; and Sadato et al., 1996) including evidence that developing neural sites for seemingly unimodal perceptual skills often require tuning from other modalities (e.g., Knudsen, 2002; Knudsen & Knudsen, 1983; Neville, 1990; Rebillard, Rebillard & Pujol, 1980). In sum, much of the emerging neurophysiological data on perception is supportive of multimodal primacy (but see Bernstein, Auer, & Moore, In press; Mesulam, 1998).

Behavioral and neurophysiological evidence for multimodal primacy raises the question of whether all of the perceptual functions are most sensitive to a form of information that is modality neutral. Less empirical work has been designed to test the issue. One research program that has addressed modality-neutral information consists of the aforementioned tests on hearing the length of dropped rods (Carello et al., 1998; Fitzpatrick, Carello, & Turvey, 1994). Recall that this research showed that the best predictor of length judgments was the combination of each rod's elasticity and the inertial tensor. Notably, the authors of this work point out that these dimensions also proved to be the strongest predictors of length judgments when similar rods were *wielded by hand* rather than heard. Thus, whether rod length is judged haptically or auditorily, the most salient information might be a rod's inertial tensor–elasticity: a modality-neutral metric that can be instantiated kinesthetically and acoustically. Similar conjectures have been made with regard to hearing metal plates (see earlier Kunkler-Peck & Turvey, 2000). Certainly, before a true modality-neutral account of these phenomena can be tenable, determination and evaluation of the acoustic forms of these mechanical dimensions must be provided.

There exists one other nonspeech domain where multimodal instantiation of a modality-neutral parameter has been discussed and most recently addressed empirically. The perception of approach, or *time to arrival*, has been examined in both visual and auditory domains. In these experiments, an object (e.g., vehicle) is seen or heard approaching an observer and then vanishes at some position (varied between trials) before it reaches him or her. The job of the observers is to signal when the object would have reached them if it had continued approaching with the same velocity. Although the visual work on this issue is far more extensive, auditory work has shown that time-to-arrival perception in both modalities displays similar properties and possibly uses similar information. For example, whether judging an approaching object visually or auditorily, observers generally underestimate the time to arrival with a magnitude proportional to the amount of time between the vanishing position and the ostensive time of arrival. With regard to informational support, the equation often used to describe time-to-arrival information is not specific to any energy medium (e.g., light or sound). Instead, the informational equation is based on the inverse rate of change of some energy dimension over time. This changing energy dimension has been defined as a dilating optical angle for the case of visual time to arrival (Lee, 1976; 1980), a dilating acoustic reflectance angle for the case of bat echolocation (Lee *et al.*, 1992), and an intensity change for perceiving sound source approach (Shaw, McGowan, & Turvey, 1991). Moreover, there is some evidence that the inverse rate of change information is salient for time-to-arrival perception in each of these contexts (and modalities) (e.g., Erwin, 1995; Lee, 1990; Lee *et al.*, 1992). This could mean that for perceiving the approach of an object, the information might take a modality-neutral form.

We have tested this proposal in our laboratory (Gordon, 2002; Gordon & Rosenblum, In press). We reasoned that if the perceptual function for approach perception is most sensitive to modality-neutral information (and modality is relatively invisible to the function), switches of stimulus modality within an approach event should have relatively little effect on judgment accuracy. For our tests, time-to-arrival events were videotaped and binaurally recorded involving a car approaching and passing an observation point at different speeds. The events were digitized and edited so that different vanishing positions could be established and the modality of presentation could be changed for the entirety or parts of the approach events. Conditions were designed so that the events were presented as visual only, audio only, audiovisual intact, or audiovisual alternating. The last condition, audiovisual alternating, was the most direct test of modal invisibility and involved a stimulus composed of alternating visual and audio channels. During these trials, the visual and audio channels alternated every 500 ms, producing a stimulus with discontinuous media but continuous event information. Results revealed that observers were as accurate in their time-to-arrival judgments with these audiovisually alternating trials as with the audiovisual intact condition. Other conditions revealed that whereas the modalities could be alternated without a detriment in performance as long as a single, coherent event was conveyed, any stimulus that failed to convey a single continuous event depressed accuracy. We interpret these results as initial evidence that if a coherent event is conveyed, the perceptual function for time-to-arrival perception is relatively unaffected by changes in modality. This finding is consistent with the modality-neutral information thesis.

As far as we know, this time-to-arrival research constitutes one of the only nonspeech projects to test explicitly the modality-neutral information thesis. Certainly, more research needs to be conducted to determine whether the notion fits general perception as well as it is starting to fit speech (but see Bernstein *et al.*, in press).

CONCLUSIONS

This chapter has argued that the speech perception literature offers a number of lessons for a burgeoning ecological psychoacoustics. Speech perception is perhaps the most conceptually mature area of auditory research. Consequently, the speech field has grappled with many of the important theoretical issues now facing ecological psychoacoustics. So what have we learned from speech? From this author's perspective, the following main and subordinate lessons can be taken from the more than 50 years of speech research:

1. We hear events, not sounds. Perception corresponds more closely to event primitives than properties of the surface acoustics.
2. To understand information, understand events. The most fruitful descriptions of acoustic information are informed by a thorough understanding of the event mechanics that structure the acoustics. Event-informed informational descriptions reveal a salience of time-varying, higher order acoustic properties.
3. Audition serves a multimodal brain. Multimodal perception is primary, and, in an important way, perception might not care from which modality the information comes. This interpretation implies that the most accurate descriptions of perceptual information are modality neutral.

A developing ecological psychoacoustics will need to directly address these issues both conceptually and empirically. However, the early evidence suggests that general auditory perception shares these properties with speech. Although still sparse, research on auditory *perception* has shown that judgments often do correspond well to event properties, even when listeners are asked to judge sensory dimensions. Furthermore, event-informed descriptions of auditory information have proved to be impressively useful and have revealed a salience of time-varying, higher order acoustic dimensions. Finally, neurophysiological and behavioral research supports a primacy of multimodal perception both in and out of the speech domain. Relatedly, some conceptual and early empirical work adds credibility to the modality-neutral information notion.

When a tree falls in the forest, it *does* structure sound as well as light regardless of the presence of an observer. If there happens to be someone nearby, that person hears and/or sees the tree falling, *as such*. The person does not *perceive* the sight or sound of the event. Although these claims might seem obvious or simply semantic, they are neither in their implications for auditory perception. There has been an overemphasis in auditory research on the hearing of sounds rather than events. It behooves ecological psychoacoustics to contemplate the lessons from speech science and motivate empirical questions as well as informational descriptions from the simple assumption that we hear things, not sounds.

REFERENCES

Anderson, K., Carello, C., & Kunkler-Peck, A. J. (May, 1996). *Rotational inertia constrains perception of object length by sound.* Poster presented at the North American Society for Ecological Psychology, Hartford, CT.

Arnold, P., & Hill, F. (2001). Bisensory augmentation: A speechreading advantage when speech is clearly audible and intact. *British Journal of Psychology, 92*, 339–355.

Ashmead, D. H., Davis, D. L., & Northington, A. (1995). Contribution of listeners' approaching motion to auditory distance perception. *Journal of Experimental Psychology: Human Perception and Performance, 21*, 239–256.

Bermant, R. I., & Welch, R. B. (1976). The effect of degree of visual-auditory stimulus separation and eye position upon the spatial interaction of vision and audition. *Perception and Motor Skills, 43*, 487–493.

Bernstein, L. E., Auer, E. T. Jr., & Moore, J. K. (In press). Audiovisual speech binding: convergence or association? In G. Calvert, and C. Spence, and B. E., (Eds.), *Handbook of Multisensory Processes.* Cambridge: MIT Press.

Bernstein, L. E., Auer, E. T., Moore, J. K., Ponton, C., Don, M., & Singh, M. (2002). Visual speech perception without primary auditory cortex activation. *NeuroReport, 13*, 311–315.

Blumstein, S., Isaacs, E., & Mertus, J. (1982). The role of gross spectral shape as a perceptual cue to place of articulation in initial stop consonants. *Journal of the Acoustical Society of America, 72*, 43–50.

Borin, G., De Poli, G., & Sarti, A. (1993). Algorithms and structures for synthesis using physical models. *Computer Music Journal, 16*, 30–42.

Bradlow, A. R., Nygaard, L. C., & Pisoni, D. B. (1999). Effects of talker, rate, and amplitude variation on recognition memory for spoken words. *Perception and Psychophysics, 61*, 206–219.

Browman, C. P., & Goldstein, L. M. (1986). Towards an articulatory phonology. *Phonology Yearbook, 3*, 219–252.

Buechel, C., Price, C., & Friston, K. (1998). A multimodal language region in the ventral visual pathway. *Nature, 394,* 274–277.

Cabe, P., & Pittenger, J. B. (2000). Human sensitivity to acoustic information from vessel filling. *Journal of Experimental Psychology: Human Perception and Performance, 26,* 313–324.

Callan, D. E., Callan, A. M., Kroos, C., & Vatikiotis-Bateson, E. (2001). Multimodal contribution to speech perception revealed by independent component analysis: A single-sweep EEG case study. *Cognitive Brain Research, 10,* 349–353.

Calvert, G. A. Brammer, M. J., Bullmore, E. T., Campbell, R., Iversen, S. D., & David, A. S. (1999). Response amplification in sensory-specific cortices during crossmodal binding. *Neuroreport, 10,* 2619–2623.

Calvert, G. A., Bullmore, E., Brammer, M. J., Campbell, R., Iversen, S. D., Woodruff, P., McGuire, P., Williams, S., & David, A. S. (1997). Silent lipreading activates the auditory cortex. *Science, 276,* 593–596.

Carello, C., Anderson, K. L., & Kunkler-Peck, A. J. (1998). Perception of object length by sound. *Psychological Science, 9,* 211–214.

Carello, C., Anderson, K. L., & Peck, A. (1998). Perception of object length by sound. *Psychological Science, 9,* 211–214.

Carello, C., Wagman, J. B., & Turvey, M. T. (In press). Acoustic specification of object properties. In J. Anderson and B. Anderson (Eds.), *Moving image theory: Ecological considerations.* Carbondale, IL: Southern Illinois Press.

Cohen, L. G., Celnik, P., Pascual-Leone, A., Faiz, L., Corwell, B., Honda, M., Sadato, H., Gerloff, C., & Catala, M. D., & Hallett, M. (1997). Functional relevance of crossmodal plasticity in the blind. *Nature, 389,* 180–182.

Corballis, M. C. (2002). *From hand to mouth: The origins of language.* Princeton: Princeton University Press.

Clark, B., & Graybiel, A. (1966). Influence of Contact Cues on the Perception of the Oculogravic Illusion. *U. S. Navy Aerospace Medical Institute and National Aeronautics and Space Administration Joint Report,* 976.

Cutting, J. E. (1986). *Perception with an eye for motion.* Cambridge, MA: MIT Press.

Diehl, R. L., & Kluender, K. R. (1989). On the objects of speech perception. *Ecological Psychology, 1,* 121–144.

Eimer, M. (2001). Crossmodal links in spatial attention between vision, audition, and touch: Evidence from event-related brain potentials. *Neuropsychologia, 39,* 1292–1303.

Erwin, T. (1995). Prospective acoustic information for object pass by. In B. G. Bardy, R. J. Bootsma, and Y. Guiard (Eds.), *Studies in perception and action III* (pp. 325–328). Mahwah, NJ: Erlbaum.

Fitch, H. L., Halwes, T., Erickson, D. M., & Liberman, A. M. (1980). Perceptual equivalence of two acoustic cues for stop consonant manner. *Perception and Psychophysics, 27,* 343–350.

Fitzpatrick, P., Carello, C., & Turvey, M. T. (1994). Eigenvalues of the inertia tensor and exteroception by the "muscular sense." *Neuroscience, 60,* 551–568.

Fowler, C. A. (1986). An event approach to the study of speech perception from a direct-realist perspective. *Journal of Phonetics, 14,* 3–28.

Fowler, C. A. (1990). Sound-producing sources as object of perception: Rate normalization and nonspeech perception. *Journal of the Acoustical Society of America, 88,* 1236–1249.

Fowler, C. A. (1996). Listeners do hear sounds, not tongues. *Journal of the Acoustical Society of America, 99,* 1730–1741.

Fowler, C. A., & Dekle, D. J. (1991). Listening with eye and hand: Cross-modal contributions to speech production. *Journal of Experimental Psychology: Human Perception and Performance, 17,* 816–828.

Fowler, C. A., & Rosenblum, L. D. (1991). Perception of the phonetic gesture. In I. G. Mattingly and M. Studdert-Kennedy (Eds.), *Modularity and the motor theory* (33–59). Hillsdale, NJ: Lawrence Erlbaum.

Freed, D. J. (1990). Auditory correlates of perceived mallet hardness for a set of recorded percussive events. *Journal of the Acoustical Society of America, 87,* 311–322.

Gaver, W. W. (1988). *Everyday listening and auditory icons.* Unpublished doctoral dissertation, University of California, San Diego.

Gaver, W. W. (1993a). What in the world do we hear? An ecological approach to auditory event perception. *Ecological Psychology, 5,* 1–29.

Gaver, W. W. (1993b). How do we hear in the world? Explorations in ecological acoustics. *Ecological Psychology, 5,* 285–313.

Gelfer, M. P. (1987). An AER study of stop-consonant discrimination. *Perception and Psychophysic, 42,* 318–327.

Gibson, J. J. (1979). *The ecological approach to visual perception.* Boston: Houghton-Mifflin.

Gibson, J. J. (1966). *The senses considered as perceptual systems.* Boston: Houghton Mifflin.

Glave, R. D., & Reitveld, A. C. M. (1975). Is the effort dependence of speech loudness explicable on the basis of acoustical cues? *Journal of Speech and Hearing Research, 10,* 133–140.

Goldstein, E. B. (2002). *Sensation and perception* (6th edition). Pacific Grove, CA: Wadsworth Thomson.

Gordon, M. S. (2002). *Audiovisual time-to-arrival judgments: Testing the primacy of multimodal integration.* Ph.D. dissertation, University of California, Riverside.

Gordon, M. S., & Rosenblum, L. D. (In press). Effects of intra-stimulus modality change on audiovisual time-to-arrival judgments. *Perception and Psychophysics.*

Green, K. P. (1998). The use of auditory and visual information during phonetic processing: Implications for theories of speech perception. In R. Campbell and B. Dodd (Eds.), *Hearing by eye II: Advances in the psychology of speechreading and auditory-visual speech* (pp. 3–25). London, England: Lawrence Erlbaum.

Green, K. P., & Gerdman, A. (1995). Cross-modal discrepancies in coarticulation and the integration of speech information: The McGurk effect with mismatched vowels. *Journal of Experimental Psychology: Human Perception and Performance, 21,* 1409–1426.

Green, K. P., & Norrix, L. (2001). The perception of /r/ and /l/ in a stop cluster: Evidence of cross-modal context effects. *Journal of Experimental Psychology: Human Perception and Performance, 27,* 166–177.

Halle, M. (1985). Speculations about the representation of words in memory. In V. A. Fromkin (Ed.), *Phonetic linguistics* (pp. 101–104). New York: Academic Press.

Kinney, J. A., & Luria, S. M. (1970). Conflicting visual and tactual-kinesthetic stimulation. *Perception and Psychophysics, 8,* 189–192.

Kitagawa, N., & Ichihara, S. (2002). Hearing visual motion in depth. *Nature, 416,* 172–174.

Knudsen, E. I. (2002). Instructed learning in the auditory localization pathway of the barn owl. *Nature, 417,* 322–328.

Knudsen, E. I., & Knudsen, P. F. (1983). Space-mapped auditory projections from the inferior colliculus to the optic tectum in the barn owl (*Tyto alba*). *Journal of Comparative Neurology, 218,* 187–196.

Kubovy, M., & Van Valkenburg, D. (2001). Auditory and visual objects. *Cognition, 80,* 97–126.

Kunkler-Peck, A., & Turvey, M. T. (2000). Hearing shape. *Journal of Experimental Psychology: Human Perception and Performance, 1,* 279–294.

Lachs, L. In *Research on spoken language processing* 241–258 (Indiana University, Speech Research Laboratory, Department of Psychology, Bloomington, Indiana, 1999).

Ladavas, E., Pavani, F., & Farne, A. (2001). Auditory peripersonal space in humans: A case of auditory-tactile extinction. *Neurocase, 7,* 97–103.

Ladefoged, P., & McKinney, N. P. (1963). Loudness, sound pressure, and subglottal pressure in speech. *Journal of the Acoustical Society of America, 35,* 454–460.

Lakatos, S., McAdams, S., & Caussé, R. (1997). The representation of auditory source characteristics: Simple geometric form. *Perception and Psychophysics, 59,* 1180–1190.

Laurienti, P. J., Burdette, J. H., Wallace, M. T., Yen, Y. F., Field, A. S., & Stein, B. E. (2002). Deactivation of sensory-specific cortex by cross-modal stimuli. *Journal of Cognitive Neuroscience, 14,* 420–429.

Lee, D. N. (1990). Getting around with light or sound. In R. Warren and A. Wertheim (Eds.), *Perception and control of self-motion* (pp. 487–505). Hillsdale, NJ: Erlbaum.

Lee, D., van der Weel, F. R., Hitchcock, T., Matejowssky, E., & Pettigrew, J. (1992). Common principle of guidance by echolocation and vision. *Journal of Comparative Physiology A, 171,* 563–571.

Lee, D. N. (1976). A theory of visual control of braking based on information about time-to-collision. *Perception, 5,* 437–459.

Lehiste, I., & Peterson, G. E. (1959). Vowel amplitude and phonemic stress in American English. *Journal of the Acoustical Society of America, 31,* 428–435.

Li, X., Logan, R. J., & Pastore, R. E. (1991). Perception of acoustic source characteristics: Walking sounds. *Journal of the Acoustical Society of America, 90,* 3036–3049.

Liberman, A. M., & Mattingly, I. G. (1985). The motor theory of speech perception revised. *Cognition, 21,* 1–36.

Liberman, A., & Studdert-Kennedy, M. (1978). Phonetic perception. In R. Held, H. Leibowitz, and H. L. Teuber (Eds.), *Handbook for sensory physiology, Vol. VIII: Perception.* New York: Springer-Verlag.

Liberman, A. M., & Whalen, D. H. (2000). On the relation of speech to language. *Trends in Cognitive Sciences, 4,* 187–196.

Liberman, A. M., Cooper, F. S., Shankweiler, D. P., & Studdert-Kennedy, M. (1967). Perception of the speech code. *Psychological Review, 74,* 431–461.

Lieberman, P., Crelin, E. S., & Klatt, D. H. (1972). Phonetic ability and related anatomy of the newborn and adult human, Neanderthal man, and the chimpanzee. *American Anthropologist, 74,* 287–307.

Locke, J. (1689). *An essay concerning human understanding.* 1974. New York: Anchor Books.

Lufti, R. A., & Wang, W. (1999). Correlational analysis of acoustic cues for the discrimination of auditory motion, *Journal of the Acoustical Society of America, 106,* 919–928.

MacLeod, A., & Summerfield, Q. (1990). A procedure for measuring auditory and audio-visual speech reception thresholds for sentences in noise: Rationale, evaluation, and recommendations for use. *British Journal of Audiology, 24,* 29–43.

MacNeilage, P. F. (1998). The frame/content theory of evolution of speech production. *Behavioral and Brain Sciences, 21,* 499–546.

MacSweeney, M., Amaro, E., Calvert, G. A., & Campbell, R. (2000). Silent speechreading in the absence of scanner noise: An event-related fMRI study. *Neuroreport: For Rapid Communication of Neuroscience Research, 11,* 1729–1733.

Massaro, D. W. (1987). Speech perception by ear and eye. In B. Dodd and R. Campbell (Eds.), *Hearing by eye: The psychology of lip-reading* (pp. 53–83). London: Lawrence Erlbaum.

Massaro, D. W., Cohen, M. M., Gesi, A., Heredia, R., & Tsuzaki, M. (1993). Bimodal speech perception: An examination across languages. *Journal of Phonetics, 21,* 445–478.

McClelland, J. L., & Elman, J. L. (1986). The TRACE model of speech perception. *Cognitive Psychology, 18,* 1–86.

McGurk, H., & MacDonald, J. W. (1976). Hearing lips and seeing voices. *Nature, 264,* 746–748.

Mergner, T., & Rosemeier, T. (1998). Interaction of vestibular, somatosensory and visual signals for postural control and motion perception under terrestrial and microgravity conditions—a conceptual model. *Brain Research Reviews, 28,* 118–135.

Mesulam, M. M. (1998). From sensation to cognition. *Brain, 121,* 1013–1052.

Mills, A. E. (1987). The development of phonology in the blind child. In B. Dodd and R. Campbell (Eds.), *Hearing by eye: The psychology of lip-reading.* Hillsdale, NJ: Lawrence Erlbaum Associates.

Mottonen, R., Krause, C. M., Tiippana, K., & Sams, M. (2002). Processing of changes in visual speech in the human auditory cortex. *Cognitive Brain Research, 13,* 417–425.

Munhall, K. G., & Vatikiotis-Bateson, E. (1998). The moving face during speech communication. In R. Campbell, B. Dodd, and D. Burnham (Eds.), *Hearing by Eye: Part 2, The Psychology of Speechreading and Audiovisual Speech* (pp. 123–139). Hillsdale, NJ: Lawrence Erlbaum.

Neuhoff, J. G. (1998). Perceptual bias for rising tones. *Nature, 395*, 123–124.

Neuhoff, J. G. (2004). Localization and motion. In J. Neuhoff (Ed.), *Ecological psychoacoustics*. Burlington, Mass.: Elsevier.

Neuhoff, J. G., & McBeath, M. K. (1996). The Doppler illusion: The influence of dynamic intensity change on perceived pitch. *Journal of Experimental Psychology: Human Perception and Performance, 22*, 970–985.

Neville, H. J. (1990). Intermodal competition and compensation in development. Evidence from studies of the visual system in congenitally deaf adults. *Annals of the New York Academy of Sciences, 608*, 71–91.

Newton, I. (1730) *Opticks, or, A treatise of the reflections, refractions, inflections and colours of light* (4th ed.). London: Printed for W. Innys.

Nygaard, L. C., & Pisoni, D. B. (1998). Talker-specific learning in speech perception. *Perception and Psychophysics, 60*, 355–376.

Nygaard, L. C., Sommers, M. S., & Pisoni, D. B. (1994). Speech perception as a talker-contingent process. *Psychological Science, 5*, 42–46.

Ohala, J. J. (1984). An ethological perspective on common cross-language utilization of F0 of voice. *Phonetica, 41*, 1–16.

Ohala, J. J. (1996). Speech perception is hearing sounds, not tongues. *Journal of the Acoustical Society of America, 99*, 1718–1725.

Palmeri, T. J., Goldinger, S. D., & Pisoni, D. B. (1993). Episodic encoding of voice attributes and recognition memory for spoken words. *Journal of Experimental Psychology: Learning, Memory, and Cognition, 19*, 309–328.

Pavani, F., Meneghello, F., & Ladavas, E. (2001). Deficit of auditory space perception in patients with visuospatial neglect. *Neuropsychologia, 39*, 1401–1409.

Pollack, I., & Rose, M. (1967). Effect of head movement on localization of sounds in the equatorial plane. *Perception and Psychophysics, 2*, 591–596.

Radeau, M., & Bertelson, P. (1974). The after-effects of ventriloquism. *Quarterly Journal of Experimental Psychology, 26*, 63–71.

Rauschecker, J. P., & Korte, M. (1993). Auditory compensation for early blindness in cat cerebral cortex. *Journal of Neuroscience, 13*, 4538–4548.

Rebillard, G., Carlier, E., Rebillard, M., & Pujol, R. (1977). Enhancement of visual responses on the primary auditory cortex of the cat after an early destruction of cochlear receptors. *Brain Research, 129*, 162–164.

Rebillard, G., Rebillard, M., & Pujol, R. (1980). Factors affecting the recording of visual-evoked potentials from the deaf cat primary auditory cortex (AI). *Brain Research, 188*, 252–254.

Reisberg, D., McLean, J., & Goldfield, A. (1987). Easy to hear but hard to understand: A lip-reading advantage with intact auditory stimuli. In B. Dodd and R. Campbell (Eds.), *Hearing by eye: The psychology of lip reading*. Hillsdale, NJ: Lawrence Erlbaum.

Remez, R. E., Fellowes, J. M., & Rubin, P. E. (1997). Talker identification based on phonetic information. *Journal of Experimental Psychology: Human Perception and Performance 23*, 651–666.

Remez, R., Rubin, P., Pisoni, D., & Carrell, T. (1981). Speech perception without traditional speech cues. *Science, 212*, 947–950.

Repp, B. H. (1987). The sound of two hands clapping: An exploratory study. *Journal of the Acoustical Society of America, 81*, 1100–1110.

Rogers, B. J., & Collett, T. S. (1989). The appearance of surfaces specified by motion parallax and binocular disparity. *Quarterly Journal of Experimental Psychology: Human Experimental Psychology, 41*, 697–717.

Rosenblum, L. D. (In press). The primacy of multimodal speech perception. In D. Pisoni and R. Remez (Eds.), *Handbook of Speech Perception*. Blackwell: Malden, MA.

Rosenblum, L. D., & Fowler, C. A. (1991). Audiovisual investigation of the loudness-effort effect for speech and nonspeech events. *Journal of Experimental Psychology: Human Perception and Performance*, *17*, 976–985.

Rosenblum, L. D., & Saldaña, H. (1996). An audiovisual test of kinematic primitives for visual speech perception. *Journal of Experimental Psychology: Human Perception and Performance*, *22*, 318–331.

Rosenblum, L. D., & Saldaña, H. (1998). Time-varying information for visual speech perception. In R. Campell, B. Dodd, and D. Burnham (Eds.), *Hearing by eye II: Advances in the psychology of speech reading and auditory-visual speech* (pp. 61–81). Hillsdale, NJ: Lawrence Erlbaum.

Rosenblum, L. D., Johnson, J. A., & Saldaña, H. M. (1996). Visual kinematic information for embellishing speech in noise. *Journal of Speech and Hearing Research 39*, 1159–1170.

Rosenblum, L. D., Schmuckler, M. A., & Johnson, J. A. (1997). The McGurk effect in infants. *Perception and Psychophysics*, *59*, 347–357.

Rosenblum, L. D., Gordon, M. S., & Jarquin, L. (2000). Echolocation by moving and stationary listeners. *Ecological Psychology*, *12*, 181–206.

Rosenblum, L. D., Smith, N. M., Nichols, S. Lee, J., & Hale, S. (Under review). Hearing a face: Cross-modal speaker matching using isolated visible speech. *Perception and Psychophysics*.

Rosenblum, L. D., Wuestefeld, A., & Anderson, K. (1996). Auditory reachability: An affordance approach to the perception of distance. *Ecological Psychology*, *8*, 1–24.

Rosenblum, L. D., Wuestefeld, A., & Saldaña, H. (1993). Auditory looming perception: influences on anticipator judgments. *Perception*, *22*, 1467–1482.

Rosenblum, L. D., Yakel, D. A., Baseer, N., Panchal, A., Nordarse, B. C., & Niehus, R. P. (2002). Visual speech information for face recognition. *Perception and Psychophysics*, *64*(2), 220–229.

Sadato, N., Pascual-Leone, A., Grafman, J., Ibanez, V., Deiber, M. P., Dold, G., & Hallett M. (1996). Activation of the primary visual cortex by Braille reading in blind subjects. *Nature*, *380*, 526–528.

Saldaña, H. M., & Rosenblum, L. D. (1993). Visual influences on auditory pluck and bow judgments. *Perception and Psychophysics*, *54*, 406–416.

Sams, M., Aulanko, R., Hamalainen, M., Hari, R., Lounasmaa, O. V., Lu, S.-T., & Simola, J. (1991). Seeing speech: Visual information from lip movements modifies activity in the human auditory cortex. *Neuroscience Letters*, *127*, 141–145.

Schiff, W., & Oldak, R. (1990). Accuracy of judging time to arrival: Effects of modality, trajectory, and gender. *Journal of Experimental Psychology: Human Perception and Performance*, *16*, 303–316.

Schwartz, D. A., Howe, C., & Purves, D. (2003). The statistical structure of human speech sounds predicts musical universals. *Journal of Neuroscience*, *23*, 7160–7168.

Schweinberger, S. R., & Soukup, G. R. (1998). Asymmetric relationships among perceptions of facial identity, emotion, and facial speech. *Journal of Experimental Psychology: Human Perception and Performance*, *24*, 1748–1765.

Sekiyama, K., & Tokhura, Y. (1991). McGurk effect in non-English listeners: Few visual effects for Japanese subjects hearing Japanese syllables of high auditory intelligibility. *Journal of the Acoustical Society of America*, *90*, 1797–1805.

Sekiyama, K., & Tokhura, Y. (1993). Inter-language differences in the influence of visual cues in speech perception. *Journal of Phonetics*, *21*, 427–444.

Shams, L., Kamitani, Y., Thompson, S., & Shimojo, S. (2001). Sound alters visual evoked potentials in humans. *Neuroreport: For Rapid Communication of Neuroscience Research*, *12*, 3849–3852.

Shaw, B. K., McGowan, R., & Turvey, M. T. (1991). An acoustic variable specifying time to contact. *Ecological Psychology*, *3*, 253–261.

Sheffert, S. M., & Fowler, C. A. (1995). The effects of voice and visible speaker change on memory for spoken words. *Journal of Memory & Language*, *34*, 665–685.

Shimojo, S., & Shams, L. (2001). Sensory modalities are not separate modalities: Plasticity and interactions. *Current Opinion in Neurobiology*, *11*, 505–509.

Silverman, K. (1986). Fo segmental cues depend on intonation: The case of the rise after voiced stops. *Phonetica*, *43*, 76.

Silverman, K. (1987). *The structure and processing of fundamental frequency contours*. Unpublished doctoral dissertation. Cambridge: Cambridge University.

Smith, M. R. (1984). Temporal aspects of word stress. *Dissertation Abstracts International*. *44*(10-A), 3052–3053.

Speigle, J. M., & Loomis, J. M. (1993). Auditory distance perception by translating observers. In *Proceedings of IEEE 1993 Symposium on Research Frontiers in Virtual Reality* (pp. 92–99). San Jose, CA: Institute of Electrical and Electronics Engineers Computer Society.

Stein, B. E., & Meredith, M. A. (1993). *The merging of the senses*. Cambridge, MA: MIT Press.

Stevens, K. N. (1989). On the quantal nature of speech. *Journal of Phonetics*, *17*, 3–45.

Stoffregen, T. A., & Bardy, B. G. (2001). On specification and the senses. *Behavioral and Brain Sciences*, *24*, 195–261.

Stoffregen, T. A., & Pittenger, J. B. (1995). Human echolocation as a basic form of perception and action. *Ecological Psychology*, *7*, 181–216.

Strange, W., Jenkins, J. J., & Johnson, T. L. (1983). Dynamic specification of coarticulated vowels. *Journal of the Acoustical Society of America*, *74*, 695–705.

Sumby, W. H., & Pollack, I. (1954). Visual contribution to speech intelligibility in noise. *Journal of the Acoustical Society of America*, *26*, 212–215.

Summerfield, Q. (1987). Some preliminaries to a comprehensive account of audio-visual speech perception. In B. Dodd and R. Campbell (Eds.), *Hearing by eye: The psychology of lip-reading* (pp. 53–83). London: Lawrence Erlbaum.

Thurlow, W. R., & Runge, P. S. (1967). Effect of induced head movements on localization of direction of sounds. *Journal of the Acoustical Society of America*, *42*, 480–488.

Vanderveer, N. J. (1979). Ecological acoustics: Human perception of environmental sounds. *Dissertation Abstracts International*, *40/09B*, 4543 (University Microfilms No. 8004002).

Walley, A., & Carrell, T. (1983). Onset spectra and formant transitions in the adult's and child's perception of place of articulation in stop consonants. *Journal of the Acoustical Society of America*, *73*, 1011–1022.

Warren, R. M. (1981). Measurement of sensory intensity. *Behavioral and Brain Sciences*, *4*, 175–223.

Warren, W. H., & Verbrugge, R. R. (1983). Auditory perception of breaking and bouncing events: A case study in ecological acoustics. *Journal of Experimental Psychology: Human Perception and Performance*, *10*, 704–712.

Wildes, R., & Richards, W. (1988). Recovering material properties from sound. In W. Richards (Ed.), *Natural computation* (pp. 356–363). Cambridge, MA: MIT Press.

Yakel, D. A. (2000) *Effects of time-varying information on vowel identification accuracy in visual speech perception*. Doctoral dissertation, University of California, Riverside.

Yakel, D. A., Rosenblum, L. D., & Fortier, M. A. (2000). Effects of talker variability on speechreading. *Perception and Psychophysics*, *62*, 1405–1412.

Yakel, D. A., Rosenblum, L. D., Smith, N., & Burns, D. (In preparation). Salience of time varying information for visual speech perception.

Yehia, H. C., Rubin, P. E., & Vatikiotis-Bateson, E. (1998) Quantitative association of vocal-tract and facial behavior. *Speech Communication*, *26*, 23–43.

Zangaladze, A., Epstein, C. M., Grafton, S. T., & Sathian, K. (1999). Involvement of visual cortex in tactile discrimination of orientation. *Nature*, *401*, 587–590.

10

INTERACTING PERCEPTUAL DIMENSIONS

JOHN G. NEUHOFF

In many psychoacoustic experiments, the objective is to investigate some aspect of a particular perceptual dimension. Some of the most commonly examined perceptual dimensions include pitch, loudness, perceived spatial location, timing, and timbre. Often, the experimental design dictates that the acoustic characteristics of all but the dimension of interest be held constant and changes in the dimension under investigation occur only from trial to trial. For example, in an experiment on loudness scaling, listeners might assign a particular constant-intensity tone a number that denotes its loudness. On subsequent trials the listener is presented with different intensity tones and is asked to assign a number to the loudness that represents the relationship to the first tone heard. Aside from intensity, all other characteristics of the stimuli (e.g., frequency and spectrum) are held constant. Even in experiments that use dynamic stimuli it is typical to only vary one parameter of the sound at a time. The advantages of this paradigm are clear. It allows greater experimental control and increases the internal validity of the experiment by ruling out the confounding influences of parametric changes in other acoustic dimensions.

However, in the real world things are seldom so tidy. In natural listening environments, sounds continuously undergo simultaneous dynamic changes in multiple perceptual dimensions. It is all too common for sound sources to produce sounds that vary in frequency, intensity, and spectral characteristics all at once. Furthermore, in the rare cases in which sounds *are* produced with constant frequency, intensity, and spectral content, they are rarely perceived as such. Relative motion between the source and the listener or disturbances in the medium can create dynamic change in the acoustic characteristics of the signal. A car horn, for example, produces a signal that is relatively stable in frequency, intensity, and spectrum. However, as the source draws closer to the listener, the observed intensity grows in accordance with the inverse square law, the fundamental frequency shifts due to the Doppler effect, and the spectrum changes because the damping effect of the atmosphere on high-frequency components is diminished at closer range. Even if there is no relative motion between a static sound source and the listener, a breeze can cause dynamic changes in intensity and spectrum, and other sounds in the environment can create intermittent masking effects. Moreover, the attention and physiological state of the listener can influence any number of perceptual characteristics. Finally, other perceptual modalities (particularly vision) can influence how we hear the world. Sensory systems have evolved together. As such, they provide complementary advantages to organisms in that the weaknesses of one system are often compensated by strengths in another.

In this chapter, we examine both the perceptual interaction of auditory dimensions (such as the effect of change in pitch on loudness) and the interaction of perceptual modalities (namely vision and hearing). Both of these areas have real-world significance in that they constantly occur in natural settings. Both have also been studied very little compared with more traditional areas of psychoacoustic research, such as pitch and loudness.

THE INTERACTION OF
AUDITORY DIMENSIONS

The interaction of perceptual dimensions has been of great interest to cognitive psychologists. At issue is whether an object (either auditory or visual) is perceived analytically or holistically. Analytical perception implies that the components or "parts" that make up an object are separately analyzed and then perceptually "glued together" to form the whole. Holistic perception implies that objects are not broken into their component parts but simply perceived as wholes. This debate stems from early perspectives in experimental psychology. The structuralist (analytic) perspective suggests that objects are assembled from their parts. In contrast, the Gestalt approach suggests that objects are perceived holistically and that the relationships between components can be as important as the components themselves. The most recent evidence suggests that the nature of object perception, whether analytic or holistic, depends on the type of object or stimulus characteristics being perceived as well as the conditions that can increase or decrease the salience of dimensional structures (Potts, Melara, & Marks, 1998).

DIMENSIONAL INTERACTION

Garner (1974) proposed a set of converging operations (speeded sorting, restricted classification, and dissimilarity scaling) that have been used to determine whether a set of perceptual dimensions (e.g., pitch and loudness) interact. Typically, only two perceptual dimensions are examined at a time, and observers are instructed to attend to one and ignore the other. Generally speaking, if static orthogonal trial-to-trial variation of an unattended dimension influences performance in the dimension of interest, the two dimensions are said to be "integral." If performance on the dimension of interest is unaffected, the dimensions are said to be "separable." According to this traditional view, stimuli consisting of integral dimensions are initially perceived as dimensionless, unanalyzable, holistic "blobs" (Garner, 1974; Lockhead, 1972, 1979). The psychological distance between stimuli can best be described by a Euclidean metric, and stimuli themselves are processed in a holistic, "unitary" manner (Shepard, 1964). In other words, the perceiver does not have primary access to the dimensions in question and cannot selectively attend to one dimension.

Alternatively, Melara and his colleagues (Melara & Marks, 1990a, 1990b; Melara, Marks, & Potts, 1993a, 1993b) have advanced a model of dimensional interaction that proposes a mandatory and immediate access to interacting dimensions. This access to primary dimensional axes is called attribute-level processing because participants extract individual attributes from the dimensions of interest. With interacting dimensions, the extraction of a dimensional attribute creates a context in which attributes of the other dimension are perceived. This influence of context is called stimulus-level processing. In the case of interacting dimensions, then, the perception of an attribute on one dimension is influenced by the context created by an attribute in the other dimension. For example, a loud tone is perceived differently in the context created by high pitch than in the context created by low pitch (it should be noted that this work employs strict controls to ensure equal loudness of stimuli as a function of frequency).

However, both the traditional and the more recent theories of multidimensional perception have employed only static stimuli methodologies in studying multidimensional perception, thus limiting the generalizability of the findings to stimuli that seldom occur in a natural environment.

Experiments using static stimuli have shown that that trial-to-trial variation in pitch influences loudness judgments and that loudness variation similarly influences pitch (e.g., Melara & Marks, 1990a). It should be noted that this influence is different from the "equal loudness countours" and "equal pitch contours" discovered by Stevens because all of the stimuli are equated for these contours depending on whether pitch or loudness is being judged. Rather, the phenomenon here appears to be a cognitive influence of the trial-to-trial variation in the unattended dimentsion. For example, if the listener is asked to judge on successive trials whether a pitch is "high" or "low," trial-to-trial variation in the loudness ("loud" or "soft") will affect reaction time to judge the pitch. However, the specific nature of this influence has been an issue of considerable dispute. The debate centers on exactly what characteristics or attributes of a multidimensional stimulus are available or can be accessed by a perceiver. Melara, Marks, and their colleagues have argued that the perception of pitch and loudness is an analytic process (Marks, 1989; Melara & Marks, 1990a, 1990b; Melara et al., 1993a, 1993b). Listeners are said to have "primary" access to each of the respective dimensions. In their view, the interaction of pitch and loudness occurs because the context created by the unattended dimension (e.g., pitch) influences judgments about the attended dimension (e.g., loudness). A high-pitched tone is perceived differently in the context of high loudness than it is in the context of low loudness.

Alternatively, the traditional model of multidimensional interaction suggests that interacting dimensions are perceived holistically (Garner, 1974; Kemler, 1983; Kemler Nelson, 1993; Smith & Kemler, 1978). The stimulus dimensions themselves are not directly perceived without great effort. Instead, integral stimulus dimensions are perceived initially as dimensionless, unitary "blobs" (Lockhead, 1972, 1979; Shepard, 1964). Because perceivers do not have primary access to the stimulus dimensions, they cannot selectively attend to one stimulus dimension. The perceptual experience of such a multidimensional stimulus then is the vector sum of the weighted values on each dimension.

Interacting dimensions have typically been defined by performance on speeded sorting, dissimilarity scaling, and categorization tasks using static stimuli. Some more recent work shows that using more ecologically valid dynamic stimuli, the principles of dimensional interaction still hold (Neuhoff & McBeath, 1996; Neuhoff, McBeath, & Wanzie, 1999; Neuhoff, Wayand, & Kramer, 2002; Walker & Ehrenstein, 2000). However, both Garner's and Melara and Marks' models of perceptual interaction would predict such results. If, according the traditional model, pitch and loudness are processed holistically, listeners would not be able to attend selectively to changes in only one dimension. So when tracking dynamic intensity change, a listener will be influenced not only by changes in intensity but also by changes in frequency. Depending on the degree to which the participant can selectively access frequency and the relative amount of change in each dimension, the holistic analysis may give way to an experience of changing loudness that is quite at odds with the change in acoustic intensity. On the other hand, applying the case of dynamic stimuli to the more recent model of Melara and Marks, we need only assume that a greater degree of dimensional change creates a more influential context in which the dimension of interest is perceived. Then perceivers who extract the stimulus attribute constant loudness in the context of the attribute rising pitch may be so influenced by the context of this rising pitch that they report rising loudness.

To provide a test of these two models under more ecological conditions of dynamic pitch and loudness change, Neuhoff, McBeath, & Wanzie (1999) used a dichotic listening task in which changes in the intensity of broadband noise were presented to one ear and changes in frequency of a complex tone were presented to the other ear. The task of the listener was to judge the amount of loudness change that occurred in the noise while ignoring the pitch change of the tone in the opposite ear. The results showed that when frequency and intensity in opposite ears changed in the same direction, the perceived change in loudness of the noise was greater than when the stimulus attributes changed in opposite directions. Because frequency change in one ear influenced loudness change in the contralateral ear, the findings suggest that the dynamic interaction of pitch and loudness occurs centrally in the auditory system and is an analytic rather than holistic process. Moreover, the authors suggested that the interaction of pitch and loudness perception has evolved to take advantage of a ubiquitous covariation of frequency and intensity change in natural environments (McBeath & Neuhoff, 2002). At the very least, the findings reflect a shortcoming of traditional static models of loudness perception in a more dynamic setting. The findings also provide support for Melara et al.'s analytic and contextually dependent model of the processing of pitch and loudness. It is unlikely that participants perceived the dichotic sounds as one dimensionless blob (Lockhead, 1972, 1979). Thus, it seems reasonable to conclude that the context created by changing frequency in one ear influenced loudness change in the other. The interaction of pitch and loudness under dynamic conditions has also been implicated in the "Doppler illusion" (McBeath & Neuhoff, 2002; Neuhoff & McBeath, 1996; Ryffert, Czajkowska, Jorasz, & Markarewicz, 1979), a finding demonstrating that listeners tend to hear a rise in pitch as a sound source approaches despite the drop in frequency that occurs because of the Doppler shift. The rise in pitch is thought to occur because of the influence of the dramatically rising intensity that occurs as the sound source draws closer to the listener.

   The perceptual interaction of pitch and loudness has been proposed as an efficient processing strategy because in nature there is a reliable correlation between changes in intensity and frequency. When sound sources increase in intensity, they tend to increase in frequency and vice versa. This effect is perhaps most apparent in one of the most commonly occurring sources that humans are exposed to, human speech (Alain, 1993; Brenner, Doherty, & Shipp, 1994; Cutler & Butterfield, 1991; Fisher & Tokura, 1995). Other organisms also produce and attend more closely to calls in which frequency and intensity are positively correlated (Gaioni & Evans, 1986, 1989). Finally, music perception research has shown that there is an expectation that melody lines that rise in frequency will also rise in intensity (Repp, 1995). Scharine (2002) showed that listeners exhibit a lower threshold for tones presented in noise when their change in frequency is positively correlated with their change in intensity, supporting the hypothesis that perceptual interaction is an element that may aid listeners in segregating sound objects.

   Walker and Ehrenstein (2000) showed that similar perceptual interaction effects can occur between the dimensions of "relative pitch" (high versus low) and the direction of dynamic pitch change (up versus down), essentially "pitch" and "pitch change." They presented listeners with 250-ms pitch glides that either rose in frequency of fell in frequency and were either initially "high" or "low" in pitch. "Congruent" stimuli were either high-frequency stimuli that became higher or low-stimuli frequency that became lower. "Incongruent" stimuli were those that started at a high pitch and became lower or those that started at a high pitch and became higher. They found that reaction time to identify either relative pitch or direction of pitch change was faster when the stimuli were congruent than when the stimuli were incongruent. Their results demonstrate that auditory perceptual dimensions do not necessarily map neatly onto acoustic dimensions because in both cases in their experiment the relevant physical dimension of frequency creates the perceptual dimensions of both relative pitch and pitch change.

The auditory dimensions of pitch and timbre have also been shown to interact (Demany & Semal, 1993; Krumhansl & Iverson, 1992; Warrier & Zatorre, 2002). For example, Krumhansl and Iverson (1992) manipulated pitch and timbre in a speeded classification task and showed interference from uncorrelated variation in the unattended dimension and facilitation from correlated variation. However, they also showed that when the variations of pitch and timbre are embedded in longer, more meaningful musical passages, the effect is reduced considerably. Similarly, Warrier and Zatorre (2002) found that providing an increasingly meaningful tonal context in the form of either tone sequences or short melodies reduced the perceptual interaction of pitch and timbre.

Pitt (1994) examined the interaction of pitch and timbre in subjects who were either musicians or nonmusicians. This work confirmed that variation in timber can influence judgments about pitch and vice versa. Interestingly, however, musicians showed less influence than nonmusicians. In addition, nonmusicians showed an asymmetry in their responses such that variation in timbre influenced pitch judgments more than variation in pitch influenced timbre. The musicians showed an influence of one dimension upon the other but no such asymmetry. Other work has shown that the perceptual interaction of pitch and timbre in musicians can influence both perception and performance (Greer, 1969; Worthy, 2000). When wind instrumentalists are asked to play a note that matches a presented stimulus, they play slightly higher in pitch (sharp) when matching bright timbre tones and slightly lower in pitch when matching dark timbre tones (Worthy, 2000). These findings should also be viewed in light of some work that draws a distinction between "perceptual interaction" and "decisional interaction" (Ashby & Townsend, 1986; Maddox, 2001; Maddox & Bogdanov, 2000).

Finally, other dimensions beside pitch, loudness, and timbre have been shown to interact perceptually, including spatial location, tempo, and rhythmic structure (Boltz, 1998; Patel & Balaban, 2000; Phillips & Hall, 2001). For example, the duration of tones can interact with intensity and pitch, particularly in sequences of tones (Tekman, 1997; Thompson & Sinclair, 1993). Higher order dimensions such as the perception of musical accents also interact with intensity (Tekman, 1998). Moreover, if listeners are asked to detect either timing or intensity variations in a sequence of tones, variation in the unattended dimension can influence judgments in the dimension of interest (Tekman, 2002). When the timing and intensity are uncorrelated, variation in the unattended dimension interferes with the detection of variation in the relevant dimension. When variation in the two dimensions is positively correlated, the detection of variation in the dimension of interest is better than it is with the absence of variation in the irrelevant dimension only for listeners who attended to timing. In the case of a negative correlation, the effect is the opposite.

DIMENSIONAL INTERACTION SUMMARY

The notion that distinct changes in acoustic characteristics of a stimulus such as frequency, intensity, and spectrum are perceptually distinct events is intuitively appealing. However, there is growing evidence that suggests that changes in a specific dimension affect not only the overall percept of the stimulus but also specific perceptual characteristics of other perceptual dimensions. In other words, changes in one dimension can affect perceived changes in the others. Some emerging paradigms and methodologies are beginning to elucidate specific neural mechanisms that may be involved in processing these perceptual effects (Dyson & Quinlan, 2002; Melara, Rao, & Tong, 2002; Patching & Quinlan, 2002; Zatorre, Mondor, & Evans, 1999). Given that the auditory system has evolved in an environment where stimuli constantly undergo simultaneous dynamic change of multiple acoustic parameters, perhaps this should come as no surprise.

MULTISENSORY INTERACTION

The perception of space is crucial to behaviors as diverse as traversing terrain, landing aircraft, or catching prey. These navigational abilities are informed by both vision and audition. The relatively distinct channels of modality specific research that are conducted suggest two independent sensory systems. Yet, perceptual modalities clearly interact. Thus, an organism must have some means of combining these distinct sources of information to form a unified representation of external space. If one accepts the position that perceptual abilities evolve because they provide an organism with selective advantages, it should come as no surprise that vision and audition provide complementary capabilities. The localization strengths of one modality compensate for weaknesses in the other. For example, the accuracy of visual spatial localization surpasses that of audition in part because of the depictive representation of the environment that falls on the retinae. The obvious disadvantage of such an arrangement in vision is that no spatial information can be obtained for hidden objects that fail to project a retinal image. There is no similar depictive representation of space in the auditory system. Spatial localization is accomplished in part by computing differences between the characteristics of the acoustic stimulus at each ear. The advantage is that the auditory system can provide spatial information about sound sources that are occluded, out of the line of sight, or present in conditions such as darkness or fog that make viewing impossible.

Humans rely primarily on vision to guide navigation and to a lesser extent audition. It is not surprising, then, that considerably more perceptual research has been conducted on visually guided navigation than on navigation guided by audition. In addition, the overwhelming majority of research, whether visual or auditory, has focused on the navigational implications of a single modality studied in isolation. Yet, in a natural environment distinct sources of auditory and visual information are integrated seamlessly to form a unified representation of external space that guides navigation (Auerbach & Sperling, 1974; Welch & Warren, 1980). Evidence for this unified spatial representation comes from both behavioral and neurophysiological studies.

The history in perceptual research of greater research efforts toward vision and a concentration on a single modality has been mirrored to a certain extent in neuroscience. We have relatively detailed accounts of the function of structures in the visual pathways compared with those in audition. We know even less about the physiological interaction of the two systems. However, there are some clear examples of auditory and visual interaction at both the neurological and behavioral levels. Here, we first examine some of the perceptual and behavioral evidence of the interaction of visual and auditory information as it pertains to localization and navigation. Next, some physiological findings that begin to provide a neural basis for this interaction are presented.

A UNIFIED SPATIAL REPRESENTATION

It is generally accepted that one function of the auditory system is to orient visual attention and that this ability appears to be present at birth (Heffner & Heffner, 1992; Robinson & Kertzman, 1995; Spence & Driver, 1997). Clearly, though, the interaction of perceptual modalities in navigation is much more complex than simple orienting responses. In many cases, the interaction of vision and audition produces performance that exceeds what would be predicted by the performance of either modality alone (Perrott, Sadralodabai, Saberi, & Strybel, 1991; Stein, Meredith, Huneycutt, & McDade, 1989). In some instances, the combination of visual and auditory stimuli produces inhibitory effects that suppress inappropriate responses given the characteristics of the stimuli (Stein *et al.*, 1989).

When we move through an environment we use different sensory modalities to perceive the characteristics of the terrain, identify potential obstacles, and plan the appropriate motor functions that allow us to reach our destination. Thus, we have different sources of information that guide navigation. The visual system provides information about the layout of the environment and any visible obstacles. The auditory system provides information about both visible and hidden sound sources. The vestibular and kinesthetic senses provide us with information about body position relative to the environment. In some cases, these different sensory channels provide unique information. An obstacle in one's path that is silent can be detected by the visual system but not the auditory system. The locations of predators, machinery, or friends that are hidden from sight are determined through audition. However, in other cases more than one sensory system contributes information about the location of a single object. An ambulance that passes on the street is both seen and heard, so both vision and audition aid in its localization.

Despite the contribution of both unique and redundant information from distinct sensory systems, organisms have a unified representation of external space that typically transcends perceptual modality (Auerbach & Sperling, 1974). For example, within the localization limits of audition and vision, an object that is both seen and heard can be located in space and spatially referenced with an object that is only seen and another object that is only heard. Together with the characteristics of the terrain, other auditory and visual objects, and the body position of the organism relative to the environment, this array of objects is integrated into a unitary representation of external space.

On the rare occasions that optical and acoustic information are discrepant and the observer recognizes that the visual and auditory modalities are providing conflicting information about the location of an object, distinct modality-specific spatial percepts may become apparent. For example, an airplane flying overhead can give discrepant auditory and visual cues about its location because the speed of sound is much slower than the speed of light. The sound waves emitted by the airplane take more time to reach the observer than the reflected light and so specify a spatial position that is somewhat behind the spatial position specified by vision. When looking skyward to see the plane, observers often orient to the spatial position specified by the sound that the plane emitted seconds earlier, so the gaze is directed to a position behind the plane. When the plane is finally located visually, a strange discontinuity between visual and auditory space is sometimes perceived. More often, however, the unified representation of external space is preserved, and the perceptual system resolves the discrepancy by the "visual capture" of auditory information.

Visual capture of audition is a distortion of perceived auditory location when visual and auditory information specify discrepant spatial positions (Howard & Templeton, 1966; Mateeff, Hohnsbein, & Noack, 1985; Thurlow & Jack, 1973; Warren, Welch, & McCarthy, 1981). In a movie theater, for example, the actors on the screen move their lips, but the vocal sound is projected from a speaker at some distance from the image of the actor. Yet, moviegoers typically do not perceive the discrepancy. The correlation between the visual stimulus (the moving lips) and the auditory stimulus (the voice) is so strong that the perceptual system resolves the spatial discrepancy by shifting the perceived auditory location to match the position of the visual stimulus. The voices sound as though they come from the actors' mouths, and the unified spatial representation is preserved.

BEHAVIORAL EVIDENCE OF MULTI-SENSORY INTERACTION

Perhaps the most well known interaction of vision and audition occurs in the perception of speech (see Rosenblum, this volume, for an extended discussion of this topic). Discrepant auditory and visual speech cues can create auditory percepts that are modified by the visual stimuli. Observers who are presented with the acoustic stimulus /ba/ and simultaneously view a speaker producing /ga/ report hearing /da/ (McGurk & MacDonald, 1976). The "McGurk effect" clearly demonstrates an interaction of the two perceptual modalities when speech cues are discrepant and has even been shown to occur in prelinguistic infants (Rosenblum, Schmuckler, & Johnson, 1997). Speech has also been shown to be more intelligible if the listener can see the speaker (Massaro & Cohen, 1995; Rosenblum & Saldana, 1996; Sanders & Goodrich, 1971; Sumby & Pollack, 1954). The redundancy of consistent auditory and visual speech information typically affords better performance than information in either modality presented alone.

In a similar vein, the auditory and visual systems have been shown to work together in localization tasks. Some research has examined the relative contributions of vision and audition in localization. Although there are exceptions (e.g., Schiff & Oldak, 1990), the general findings that come from such experiments are that vision affords superior performance compared with audition and that if one can use both the eyes and ears, localization performance is better than with either modality alone. Bimodal spatial detection of a stimulus, for example, is better than detection by either the auditory or visual system alone (Auerbach & Sperling, 1974; Lakatos, 1995; Perrott et al., 1991). Superior performance in auditory localization tasks under favorable versus unfavorable visual conditions provides further evidence for a bimodal advantage in the perception of external space (Mastroianni, 1982; Platt & Warren, 1972; Warren, 1970). Some work has even shown that sighted listeners who are blindfolded can localize auditory stimuli better than blind listeners (Fisher, 1964). This finding suggests that not only do auditory and visual localization skills interact on a sensory level but also a mental (or neural) representation of external space that is based on both auditory and visual experience provides localization advantages even when only one modality is stimulated (but see Loomis, Klatzky, Golledge, Cicinelli, et al., 1993; Roeder et al., 1999). This finding is consistent with physiological studies showing the development of a neural map of auditory space is highly dependent upon visual experience (King, Hutchings, Moore, & Blakemore, 1988; Knudsen, 1983, 2002; Knudsen & Brainard, 1991; Knudsen & Knudsen, 1985).

In many instances, vision dominates other modalities when the information from the respective modalities is discrepant. Thus, the phrase "seeing is believing" may stem from actual experience, as vision can dominate even proprioceptive judgments. In a classic example of visual dominance, observers who moved their hands along a straight edge nevertheless reported the edge to be curved when they performed the task wearing prism glasses that made the edge appear curved (Gibson, 1933). Visual dominance is common, and there are various theories that attempt to explain it (Lee & Aronson, 1974; Posner, Nissen, & Klein, 1976; Rock, 1966). However, the robustness of this dominance has occasionally been brought into question (Wolters & Schiano, 1989), and under some conditions auditory stimuli can also influence vision (Radeau & Bertelson, 1976; Spence & Driver, 1997). For example, presenting a spatially coincident auditory cue can enhance orientation and attention to a visual stimulus. If the visual and auditory cues are spatially discrepant, performance falls below baseline (visual stimulus only). The increase in performance with spatially coincident stimuli is multiplicative and exceeds the bimodal performance predicted by performance in either modality alone, suggesting a true interaction of vision and audition in locomotor activities (Stein *et al.*, 1989). In addition, an auditory stimulus can increase both the detection of and the perceived brightness of a light regardless of whether the light and sound are spatially coincident or discrepant (Stein, London, Wilkinson, & Price, 1996; Watkins & Freeher, 1965). Auditory stimuli have also been shown to influence the perception of visual apparent motion (Gilbert, 1939; Hall, Earle, & Crookes, 1952; Staal & Donderi, 1983).

Invariant Environmental Cues

A crucial task in navigation is determining time to contact with another object. This information is important not only if an organism wishes to avoid obstacles, catch prey, or avoid capture but also in fundamental aspects of controlled navigation such as appropriate steering and braking (Lee, 1976; Lee, Simmons, & Saillant, 1995). There are environmental invariants in both vision and audition that can provide information that is potentially useful to an organism in navigating an environment. In vision, the rate of optical expansion (tau) can provide reliable information about time to contact with an approaching object (Lee, 1976; Lee & Reddish, 1981). Although there is some debate about whether the use of tau best describes how organisms anticipate the arrival of an approaching object (Guski, 1992; Neuhoff, 2001; Wann, 1996), it is generally accepted that the information is available in the stimulus. In theory, the visual system does not need to estimate the distance or velocity of an approaching object in order to specify time to contact. It need only register the relative rate of optical expansion produced by the approaching object.

In audition, a similar phenomenon has been identified regarding the rate of change in intensity (Lee, van der Weel, Hitchcock, Matejowsky, & Pettigrew, 1992; Rosenblum, 1986; Shaw, McGowan, & Turvey, 1991). A steady-state approaching sound source produces an observed pattern of intensity change specified by the inverse square law. For example, halving the distance between source and observer increases the observed intensity fourfold. Auditory attention to changing intensity then could plausibly specify time to contact. Studies of auditory looming suggest that listeners can indeed specify time to contact based on the intensity change that occurs as a sound source approaches (Lee *et al.*, 1992; Rosenblum, Carello, & Pastore, 1987; Rosenblum, Wuestefeld, & Saldana, 1993; Schiff & Oldak, 1990).

Thus, a visible approaching sound source provides invariant information about time to contact in both the visual and auditory domains. As a visible sound source approaches an observer, the image of the object grows larger optically in the visual field and its observed acoustic intensity increases. In both modalities the rate of change is dependent upon the velocity of the source and the distance between the source and the observer. Auditory or visual information alone could presumably provide information about time to contact. If the ability to detect time to contact is enhanced by the use of bimodal information in the same manner as detecting spatial position, the use of both optical and acoustic information might provide more accurate estimates. However, the problem has not been researched in sufficient detail with environmentally rich stimuli. One study that used film of approaching objects failed to find an advantage of audiovisual information over only visual information (Schiff & Oldak, 1990). Clearly, a bimodal advantage would exist if either the auditory or visual information provided by an approaching source were intermittent. In a natural environment, such intermittency surely occurs. Approaching objects may be temporarily occluded or only occasionally make noise. In this case the redundancy of the information carried by the unobstructed modality would presumably provide a performance advantage.

Yet, for there to be a bimodal advantage in specifying time to contact, an organism must first be able to unify the information from the auditory and visual inputs and make judgments of equivalence across perceptual modalities. Humans are relatively good at such cross-modal associations (Marks, 1978; Welch & Warren, 1986). An observer must also detect the correlation between the optical expansion and increasing observed intensity that occur as an object approaches. In humans the ability to make use of this information appears to be present at a very early age. Infants as young as 5 months can detect the correlated relationship between the rising intensity specified by an approaching sound source and its rate of optical expansion (Morrongiello, Hewitt, & Gotowiec, 1991; Pickens, 1994; Walker-Andrews & Lennon, 1985).

The behavioral characteristics of multisensory interactions are apparent and continue to be explored by perceptual researchers. Multisensory perception provides a redundancy of stimulus information that increases the likelihood of stimulus detection, discrimination, and localization. The findings of behavioral investigations of multisensory interaction often prompt neuroscientists to search for the physiological underpinnings of multisensory perceptual experience.

PHYSIOLOGICAL EVIDENCE OF MULTISENSORY INTERACTION

There is a growing cross-fertilization between perception researchers interested in the perceptual experience and behavioral characteristics of an organism and neuroscientists interested in the cellular behavior during perceptual processing. Behavioral research can be used to corroborate neurophysiological findings, examine phenomena that cannot yet be studied at the cellular level, and suggest new areas of inquiry for neuroscientists. Cellular recording can provide information about the structure and function that underlie perceptual experience and behavior. In many instances the response patterns of individual neurons are strikingly parallel to important sensory and perceptual activities that precede environmentally important behavioral responses. For example, cells have been identified that respond to a stimulus moving toward an organism regardless of the direction of approach. The cells respond to any stimulus motion provided that the trajectory of the stimulus is toward the organism's face (Colby, Duhamel, & Goldberg, 1993). Thus, identifying the function of individual neurons can clearly have significant implications for understanding perception and behavior.

Similarly, studies of perception that illustrate the behavioral interaction of the auditory and visual modalities suggest that there are analogous interactions at the cellular level in the central nervous system. Although multisensory interaction takes place at many sites, including the hippocampus (Tamura, Ono, Fukuda, & Nakamura, 1990, 1992) and various cortical areas (Wilkinson, Meredith, & Stein, 1996), the area of the brain that mediates multisensory interaction that is best understood is the superior colliculus (or optic tectum in nonmammalian species).

The superior colliculi are symmetrical structures at the top of the brainstem. The structures are composed of seven layers that are functionally divided into two sections. The superficial layers (1–3) are not thought to be involved in sensory integration. The deep layers (4–7) integrate sensory information and send efferent projections to motor areas in the brainstem and spinal cord (Stein & Meredith, 1994).

Traditionally, the superior colliculus has been identified as part of the visual system. However, certain cells in the deep layers respond best to multisensory (auditory, visual, and somatosensory) stimulation (Meredith & Stein, 1983, 1986). Of these cells, those that respond most weakly to a single modality, for example, a noise burst, respond most vigorously when a spot of light and somatosensory stimulation accompanies the noise burst. For spatial information from different modalities to be coordinated, the modality-specific information must converge at some point. The existence of cells that respond best to multimodal input is crucial, therefore, to the perception of a unified external space.

In addition to integrating input from the sense organs, the superior colliculus receives input from various cortex areas. Auditory, visual, and somatosensory cortices have all been show to converge on multisensory neurons in the superior colliculus. The same multisensory neurons have also been shown to mediate motor behaviors (Meredith & Stein, 1986; Wallace, Meredith, & Stein, 1993). This organization demonstrates cortical control over attentive and orienting behaviors.

In addition to multisensory neurons in the superior colliculus, multisensory neurons have been identified in various cortex areas, typically at the boundaries or transition areas of the modality-specific cortical regions (Stein & Meredith, 1994; Wallace, Meredith, & Stein, 1992). Surprisingly, these multisensory cortical neurons do not synapse with the multisensory neurons in the superior colliculus. Cortical input to the multisensory neurons in the superior colliculus comes from unimodal cortical cells (Wallace *et al.*, 1993). This suggests that distinct processes of sensory integration take place independently in the cortex and superior colliculus. However, input to multisensory neurons in the superior colliculus from the various modality-specific cortical cells is not sufficient for multisensory integration in the superior colliculus. The process is also dependent upon input from the association cortex. Deactivation of input to the superior colliculus from the association cortex eliminates multisensory integration in the superior colliculus, but the multisensory neurons still respond to unimodal cortical input (Wallace & Stein, 1994). Thus, multisensory integration in the superior colliculus is dependent upon input from the association cortex.

Multisensory neurons in the superior colliculus do not appear to be present at birth. Wallace and Stein (1997) tested developing kittens and found no evidence of multisensory neurons until the kittens were 12 days old. Furthermore, although these early multisensory neurons responded to multimodal input, their response characteristics were weak and erratic. In addition, they did not integrate sensory information in the multiplicative manner found in adult cats. The response pattern was much like that of fully developed multisensory neurons that had been cut off from input from the association cortex. Thus, it may be that projections from the association cortex to the superior colliculus are not fully developed at birth, thus preventing sensory integration in the superior colliculus (Wallace & Stein, 1997).

Auditory and Visual Spatial Maps

There is an emerging body of research that begins to demonstrate a coordinated neural representation of visual and auditory space. Neurons in the superior colliculus tuned to specific auditory localization cues provide a basis for a map of auditory space. Thus, auditory space is represented by the topographic organization of spatially tuned auditory neurons. Retinotopic organization is also preserved in the superior colliculus, with visual receptive fields providing a neuronal map of visual space. The auditory and visual maps are closely aligned, with visual receptive fields in close proximity to corresponding spatially tuned auditory neurons (Knudsen & Brainard, 1995). In addition, the deep layers of the superior colliculus contain neurons that respond best to auditory and visual input from a specific spatial location, providing a unified bimodal map of external space (Knudsen & Brainard, 1991; Meredith & Stein, 1986, 1996; Stein & Meredith, 1994).

The neural maps of auditory and visual space in the superior colliculus develop with perceptual experience, and the map of auditory space appears to align itself with the visual map (King et al., 1988). There is considerable plasticity in the development of the auditory map with visual experience playing a critical role. For example, barn owls raised with prism glasses that optically displace the visual field show a corresponding shift in auditory receptive fields that matches the amount of displacement produced by the prisms (Knudsen & Brainard, 1991). The auditory cueing of spatial position is highly dependent upon differences in the characteristics of the acoustic stimuli that arrive at the two ears. Nevertheless, visual experience is so crucial to the development of auditory spatial maps that animals raised with monaural occlusion still have properly aligned auditory maps provided they have normal visual experience (Knudsen, 1983; Knudsen & Knudsen, 1985). Monocularly occluded animals that are raised blind have disorganized auditory maps by comparison (Knudsen & Mogdans, 1992). There is also evidence of neural plasticity in the cortex. For example, if cortical development occurs in the absence of particular modality-specific stimulation, input from other modalities can overtake these cortical areas. Areas of visual cortex in cats that are raised blind can be taken over by auditory inputs. The result is sharper auditory spatial tuning and improved auditory localization performance (Palleroni & Hauser, 2003; Rauschecker, 1995a, 1995b; Weeks *et al.*, 2000).

For audition to orient visual attention accurately, the auditory and visual maps must be aligned. The correspondence between the spatial maps of the visual and auditory systems is probably a result of the naturally occurring correlation between perceived auditory, visual spatial locations of objects in the environment. Perception research shows that organisms use a unified spatial representation to navigate their environment. The dependence of the development of accurately aligned auditory spatial maps on visual experience suggests that the unified representation of external space may be rooted in the visual map (Welch, DuttonHurt, & Warren, 1986).

CONCLUSION

This discussion has focused primarily on the sensory and perceptual interaction of vision and audition, which clearly provides cues to localization and navigation beyond those of the individual modalities themselves. Distinct modality-specific information is integrated to form a unified representation of external space that is used to guide navigation. The various neural structures responsible for integrating multisensory input provide a substrate on which this unified perceptual experience is formed.

By no means, however, does the audiovisual interaction provide all of the information that organisms use to get around. In humans, vestibular and haptic cues have been shown to interact with both visual and auditory information (Clark & Graybiel, 1966; Clark & Graybiel, 1949; Demer, 1994; Graybiel & Hupp, 1946; Graybiel & Niven, 1951; Lackner, 1974a, 1974b; Paige & Tomko, 1991; Probst & Wist, 1990; Rosenblum & Saldana, 1996; Wade & Day, 1968). Male gypsy moths use the interaction of both visual information and the perception of pheromone concentration to guide flight in locating females (Willis & Carde, 1990; Willis, David, Murlis, & Carde, 1994). Some species use the interaction of olfaction with vision and audition to locate prey (Wells & Lehner, 1978). Echolocating horseshoe bats use both the acoustic characteristics of the reflected sound and the motoric characteristics of the vocalization to guide flight in catching prey (Metzner, 1993).

There are large bodies of work in both perception and neuroscience that have examined unimodal spatial perception. In some cases the complexity of the issues explored necessitates this unimodal approach. Yet, it is apparent that the integration of multisensory information can yield perception and performance that are not predicted by the functioning of any modality in isolation. Some researchers have already begun to examine the interaction of vision, audition, and other modalities in the formation of a unified spatial representation. As technology emerges to enable further the study of the form and function of the individual modalities, the next research frontier will be understanding more completely their interaction.

REFERENCES

Alain, C. (1993). The relation among fundamental frequency, intensity, and duration varies with accentuation. *Journal of the Acoustical Society of America, 94*, 2434–2436.

Ashby, F. G., & Townsend, J. T. (1986). Varieties of perceptual independence. *Psychological Review, 93*, 154–179.

Auerbach, C., & Sperling, P. (1974). A common auditory-visual space: Evidence for its reality. *Perception and Psychophysics, 16*, 129–135.

Boltz, M. G. (1998). Tempo discrimination of musical patterns: Effects due to pitch and rhythmic structure. *Perception and Psychophysics, 60*, 1357–1373.

Brenner, M., Doherty, E. T., & Shipp, T. (1994). Speech measures indicating workload demand. *Aviation, Space, and Environmental Medicine, 65*, 21–26.

Clark, B., & Graybiel, A. (1966). Contributing factors in the oculogravic illusion. *American Journal of Psychology, 79*, 377–388.

Clark, B., & Graybiel, A. (1949). The effect of angular acceleration on sound localization: The audiogyral illusion. *Journal of Psychology, 28*, 235–244.

Colby, C. L., Duhamel, J.-R., & Goldberg, M. E. (1993). Ventral intraparietal area of the macaque: Anatomic location and visual response properties. *Journal of Neurophysiology, 69*, 902–914.

Cutler, A., & Butterfield, S. (1991). Word boundary cues in clear speech: A supplementary report. *Speech Communication, 10*, 335–353.

Demany, L., & Semal, C. (1993). Pitch versus brightness of timbre—Detecting combined shifts in fundamental and formant frequency. *Music Perception, 11*, 1–14.

Demer, J. L. (1994). Effect of aging on vertical visual tracking and visual-vestibular interaction. Special issue: David A. Robinson: Four decades of seminal eye movement research. *Journal of Vestibular Research Equilibrium and Orientation, 4*, 355–370.

Dyson, B. J., & Quinlan, P. T. (2002). Within- and between-dimensional processing in the auditory modality. *Journal of Experimental Psychology: Human Perception and Performance, 28*, 1483–1498.

Fisher, C., & Tokura, H. (1995). The given-new contract in speech to infants. *Journal of Memory and Language, 34*, 287–310.

Fisher, G. H. (1964). Spatial localization by the blind. *American Journal of Psychology, 77*, 2–14.

Gaioni, S. J., & Evans, C. S. (1986). Perception of distress calls in mallard ducklings (*Anas platyrhynchos*). *Behaviour, 99*, 250–274.

Gaioni, S. J., & Evans, C. S. (1989). Perception of the frequency characteristics of distress calls by mallard ducklings (*Anas platyrhynchos*). *Behaviour, 111*, 13–33.

Garner, W. R. (1974). *The processing of information and structure.* New York: Wiley.

Gibson, J. J. (1933). Adaptation, after-effect and contrast in the perception of curved lines. *Journal of Experimental Psychology, 16*, 1–31.

Gilbert, G. M. (1939). Dynamic psychophysics and the phi phenomenon. *Archives of Psychology (Columbia University)* (237), 43.

Graybiel, A., & Hupp, D. I. (1946). The oculo-gyral illusion, a form of apparent motion which may be observed following stimulation of the semi-circular canals. *Journal of Aviation Medecine, 17*, 3–27.

Graybiel, A., & Niven, J. I. (1951). The effect of a change in direction of resultant force on sound localization. *Journal of Experimental Psychology* (42), 227–230.

Greer, R. (1969). *The effect of timbre on brass-wind intonation.* Unpublished Ph.D. dissertation, University of Michigan, Ann Arbor.

Guski, R. (1992). Acoustic tau: An easy analogue to visual tau? *Ecological Psychology, 4,* 189–197.

Hall, K. R. L., Earle, A. E., & Crookes, T. G. (1952). A pendulum phenomenon in the visual perception of apparent movement. *Quarterly Journal of Experimental Psychology, 4,* 109–120.

Heffner, R. S., & Heffner, H. E. (1992). Hearing in large mammals: Sound-localization acuity in cattle (*Bos taurus*) and goats (*Capra hircus*). *Journal of Comparative Psychology, 106,* 107–113.

Howard, I. P., & Templeton, W. B. (1966). *Human Spatial orientation.* London: Wiley.

Kemler, D. G. (1983). Exploring and reexploring issues of integrality, perceptual sensitivity, and dimensional salience. *Journal of Experimental Child Psychology, 36,* 365–379.

Kemler Nelson, D. G. (1993). Processing integral dimensions: The whole view. *Journal of Experimental Psychology: Human Perception and Performance, 19,* 1105–1113.

King, A. J., Hutchings, M. E., Moore, D. R., & Blakemore, C. (1988). Developmental plasticity in the visual and auditory representations in the mammalian superior colliculus. *Nature, 332,* 73–76.

Knudsen, E. I. (1983). Early auditory experience aligns the auditory map of space in the optic tectum of the barn owl. *Science, 222,* 939–942.

Knudsen, E. I. (2002). Instructed learning in the auditory localization pathway of the barn owl. *Nature, 417,* 322–328.

Knudsen, E. I., & Brainard, M. S. (1991). Visual instruction of the neural map of auditory space in the developing optic tectum. *Science, 253,* 85–87.

Knudsen, E. I., & Brainard, M. S. (1995). Creating a unified representation of visual and auditory space in the brain. *Annual Review of Neuroscience, 18,* 19–43.

Knudsen, E. I., & Knudsen, P. F. (1985). Vision guides the adjustment of auditory localization in young barn owls. *Science, 230,* 545–548.

Knudsen, E. I., & Mogdans, J. (1992). Vision-independent adjustment of unit tuning to sound localization cues in response to monaural occlusion in developing owl optic tectum. *Journal of Neuroscience, 12,* 3485–3493.

Krumhansl, C. L., & Iverson, P. (1992). Perceptual interactions between musical pitch and timbre. *Journal of Experimental Psychology: Human Perception and Performance, 18,* 739–751.

Lackner, J. R. (1974a). Changes in auditory localization during body tilt. *Acta Oto Laryngologica, 77,* 19–28.

Lackner, J. R. (1974b). The role of posture in sound localization. *Quarterly Journal of Experimental Psychology, 26,* 235–251.

Lakatos, S. (1995). The influence of visual cues on the localisation of circular auditory motion. *Perception, 24,* 457–465.

Lee, D. N. (1976). A theory of visual control of braking based on information about time-to-collision. *Perception, 5,* 437–459.

Lee, D. N., & Aronson, E. (1974). Visual proprioceptive control of standing in human infants. *Perception and Psychophysics, 15,* 529–532.

Lee, D. N., & Reddish, P. E. (1981). Plummeting gannets: A paradigm of ecological optics. *Nature, 293,* 293–294.

Lee, D. N., Simmons, J. A., & Saillant, P. A. (1995). Steering by echolocation: A paradigm of ecological acoustics. *Journal of Comparative Physiology A Sensory Neural and Behavioral Physiology, 176,* 246–254.

Lee, D. N., van der Weel, F. R., Hitchcock, T., Matejowsky, E., & Pettigrew, J. D. (1992). Common principle of guidance by echolocation and vision. *Journal of Comparative Physiology A Sensory Neural and Behavioral Physiology, 171,* 563–571.

Lockhead, G. R. (1972). Processing dimensional stimuli: A note. *Psychological Review, 79,* 410–419.

Lockhead, G. R. (1979). Holistic versus analytic process models: A reply. *Journal of Experimental Psychology: Human Perception and Performance, 5,* 746–755.

Loomis, J. M., Klatzky, R. L., Golledge, R. G., Cicinelli, J. G., *et al.* (1993). Nonvisual navigation by blind and sighted: Assessment of path integration ability. *Journal of Experimental Psychology: General, 122,* 73–91.

Maddox, W. T. (2001). Separating perceptual processes from decisional processes in identification and categorization. *Perception and Psychophysics, 63,* 1183–1200.

Maddox, W. T., & Bogdanov, S. V. (2000). On the relation between decision rules and perceptual representation in multidimensional perceptual categorization. *Perception and Psychophysics, 62,* 984–997.

Marks, L. E. (1978). *The unity of the senses: Interrelations among modalities.* New York: Academic Press.

Marks, L. E. (1989). On cross-modal similarity: The perceptual structure of pitch, loudness, and brightness. *Journal of Experimental Psychology: Human Perception and Performance, 15,* 586–602.

Massaro, D. W., & Cohen, M. M. (1995). Perceiving talking faces. *Current Directions in Psychological Science, 4,* 104–109.

Mastroianni, G. R. (1982). The influence of eye movements and illumination on auditory localization. *Perception and Psychophysics, 31,* 581–584.

Mateeff, S., Hohnsbein, J., & Noack, T. (1985). Dynamic visual capture: Apparent auditory motion induced by a moving visual target. *Perception, 14,* 721–727.

McBeath, M. K., & Neuhoff, J. G. (2002). The Doppler effect is not what you think it is: Dramatic pitch change due to dynamic intensity change. *Psychonomic Bulletin and Review, 9,* 306–313.

McGurk, H., & MacDonald, J. (1976). Hearing lips and seeing voices. *Nature, 264,* 746–748.

Melara, R. D., & Marks, L. E. (1990a). Interaction among auditory dimensions: Timbre, pitch, and loudness. *Perception and Psychophysics, 48,* 169–178.

Melara, R. D., & Marks, L. E. (1990b). Perceptual primacy of dimensions: Support for a model of dimensional interaction. *Journal of Experimental Psychology: Human Perception and Performance, 16,* 398–414.

Melara, R. D., Marks, L. E., & Potts, B. C. (1993a). Early-holistic processing or dimensional similarity? *Journal of Experimental Psychology: Human Perception and Performance, 19,* 1114–1120.

Melara, R. D., Marks, L. E., & Potts, B. C. (1993b). Primacy of dimensions in color perception. *Journal of Experimental Psychology: Human Perception and Performance, 19,* 1082–1104.

Melara, R. D., Rao, A., & Tong, Y. X. (2002). The duality of selection: Excitatory and inhibitory processes in auditory selective attention. *Journal of Experimental Psychology: Human Perception and Performance, 28,* 279–306.

Meredith, M. A., & Stein, B. E. (1983). Interactions among converging sensory inputs in the superior colliculus. *Science, 221,* 389–391.

Meredith, M. A., & Stein, B. E. (1986). Spatial factors determine the activity of multisensory neurons in cat superior colliculus. *Brain Research, 365,* 350–354.

Meredith, M. A., & Stein, B. E. (1996). Spatial determinants of multisensory integration in cat superior colliculus neurons. *Journal of Neurophysiology, 75,* 1843–1857.

Metzner, W. (1993). An audio-vocal interface in echolocating horseshoe bats. *Journal of Neuroscience Letters, 13,* 1899–1915.

Morrongiello, B. A., Hewitt, K. L., & Gotowiec, A. (1991). Infants' discrimination of relative distance in the auditory modality: Approaching versus receding sound sources. *Infant Behavior and Development, 14,* 187–208.

Neuhoff, J. G. (2001). An adaptive bias in the perception of looming auditory motion. *Ecological Psychology, 13,* 87–110.

Neuhoff, J. G., & McBeath, M. K. (1996). The Doppler illusion: The influence of dynamic intensity change on perceived pitch. *Journal of Experimental Psychology: Human Perception and Performance, 22,* 970–985.

Neuhoff, J. G., McBeath, M. K., & Wanzie, W. C. (1999). Dynamic frequency change influences loudness perception: A central, analytic process. *Journal of Experimental Psychology: Human Perception and Performance, 25,* 1050–1059.

Neuhoff, J. G., Wayand, J., & Kramer, G. (2002). Pitch and loudness interact in auditory displays: Can the data get lost in the map? *Journal of Experimental Psychology: Applied, 8,* 17–25.

Paige, G. D., & Tomko, D. L. (1991). Eye movement responses to linear head motion in the squirrel monkey: II. Visual-vestibular interactions and kinematic considerations. *Journal of Neurophysiology*, *65*, 1183–1196.

Palleroni, A., & Hauser, M. (2003). Experience-dependent plasticity for auditory processing in a raptor. *Science*, *299*, 1195.

Patching, G. R., & Quinlan, P. T. (2002). Garner and congruence effects in the speeded classification of bimodal signals. *Journal of Experimental Psychology: Human Perception and Performance*, *28*, 755–775.

Patel, A. D., & Balaban, E. (2000). Temporal patterns of human cortical activity reflect tone sequence structure. *Nature*, *404*, 80–84.

Perrott, D. R., Sadralodabai, T., Saberi, K., & Strybel, T. Z. (1991). Aurally aided visual search in the central visual field: Effects of visual load and visual enhancement of the target. *Human Factors*, *33*, 389–400.

Phillips, D. P., & Hall, S. E. (2001). Spatial and temporal factors in auditory saltation. *Journal of the Acoustical Society of America*, *110*, 1539–1547.

Pickens, J. (1994). Perception of auditory-visual distance relations by 5-month-old infants. *Developmental Psychology*, *30*, 537–544.

Pitt, M. A. (1994). Perception of pitch and timbre by musically trained and untrained listeners. *Journal of Experimental Psychology: Human Perception and Performance*, *20*, 976–986.

Platt, B. B., & Warren, D. H. (1972). Auditory localization: The importance of eye movements and a textured visual environment. *Perception and Psychophysics*, *12*, 241–244.

Posner, M. I., Nissen, M. J., & Klein, R. M. (1976). Visual dominance: An information-processing account of its origins and significance. *Psychological Review*, *83*, 157–171.

Potts, B. C., Melara, R. D., & Marks, L. E. (1998). Circle size and diameter tilt: A new look at integrality and separability. *Perception and Psychophysics*, *60*, 101–112.

Probst, T., & Wist, E. R. (1990). Impairment of auditory processing by simultaneous vestibular stimulation: Psychophysical and electrophysiological data. *Behavioural Brain Research*, *41*, 1–9.

Radeau, M., & Bertelson, P. (1976). The effect of a textured visual field on modality dominance in a ventriloquism situation. *Perception and Psychophysics*, *20*, 227–235.

Rauschecker, J. P. (1995a). Compensatory plasticity and sensory substitution in the cerebral cortex. *Trends in Neurosciences*, *18*, 36–43.

Rauschecker, J. P. (1995b). Developmental plasticity and memory. *Behavioural Brain Research*, *66*, 7–12.

Repp, B. H. (1995). Detectability of duration and intensity increments in melody tones: A partial connection between music perception and performance. *Perception and Psychophysics*, *57*, 1217–1232.

Robinson, D. L., & Kertzman, C. (1995). Covert orienting of attention in macaques: III. Contributions of the superior colliculus. *Journal of Neurophysiology*, *74*, 713–721.

Rock, I. (1966). *The nature of perceptual adaptation*. Oxford, England: Basic Books.

Roeder, B., Teder-Saelejaervi, W., Sterr, A., Roesler, F., Hillyard, S. A., & Neville, H. J. (1999). Improved auditory spatial tuning in blind humans. *Nature*, *400*, 162–166.

Rosenblum, L. D., Carello, C., & Pastore, R. E. (1987). Relative effectiveness of three stimulus variables for locating a moving sound source. *Perception*, *162*, 175–186.

Rosenblum, L. D., & Saldana, H. M. (1996). An audiovisual test of kinematic primitives for visual speech perception. *Journal of Experimental Psychology: Human Perception and Performance*, *22*, 318–331.

Rosenblum, L. D., Schmuckler, M. A., & Johnson, J. A. (1997). The McGurk effect in infants. *Perception and Psychophysics*, *59*, 347–357.

Rosenblum, L. D., Wuestefeld, A. P., & Saldana, H. M. (1993). Auditory looming perception: Influences on anticipatory judgments. *Perception*, *22*, 1467–1482.

Rosenblum, L. D. (1986). Acoustical information for controlled conditions. In A. Shick, H. Höge, & G. Lazarus-Mainka (Eds.), *Contributions to psychological acoustics: Results of the Fourth Old-*

enburg Symposium on Psychological Acoustics (p. 455). Oldenburg: Bibliotheks- und Informationssystem der Universität Oldenburg.

Ryffert, H., Czajkowska, A., Jorasz, U., & Markarewicz, R. (1979). Dynamic approach to sound pitch. *Archives of Acoustics, 4*, 3–10.

Sanders, D. A., & Goodrich, S. J. (1971). The relative contribution of visual and auditory components of speech to speech intelligibility as a function of three conditions of frequency distortion. *Journal of Speech and Hearing Research, 14*, 154–159.

Scharine, A. A. (2002). *Auditory scene analysis: The role of positive correlation of dynamic changes in intensity and frequency.* Ann Arbor, MI: University Microfilms International.

Schiff, W., & Oldak, R. (1990). Accuracy of judging time to arrival: Effects of modality, trajectory, and gender. *Journal of Experimental Psychology: Human Perception and Performance, 16*, 303–316.

Shaw, B. K., McGowan, R. S., & Turvey, M. T. (1991). An acoustic variable specifying time-to-contact. *Ecological Psychology, 3*, 253–261.

Shepard, R. N. (1964). Attention and the metric structure of the stimulus space. *Journal of Mathematical Psychology, 1*, 54–87.

Smith, L. B., & Kemler, D. G. (1978). Levels of experienced dimensionality in children and adults. *Cognitive Psychology, 10*, 502–532.

Spence, C., & Driver, J. (1997). Audiovisual links in exogenous covert spatial orienting. *Perception and Psychophysics, 59*, 1–22.

Staal, H. E., & Donderi, D. C. (1983). The effect of sound on visual apparent movement. *American Journal of Psychology, 96*, 95–105.

Stein, B. E., London, N., Wilkinson, L. K., & Price, D. D. (1996). Enhancement of perceived visual intensity by auditory stimuli: A psychophysical analysis. *Journal of Cognitive Neuroscience, 8*, 497–506.

Stein, B. E., & Meredith, M. A. (1994). *The merging of the senses.* Cambridge, MA: MIT Press.

Stein, B. E., Meredith, M. A., Huneycutt, W. S., & McDade, L. (1989). Behavioral indices of multisensory integration: Orientation to visual cues is affected by auditory stimuli. *Journal of Cognitive Neuroscience, 1*, 12–24.

Sumby, W. H., & Pollack, I. (1954). Visual contribution to speech intelligibility in noise. *Journal of the Acoustical Society of America, 26*, 212–215.

Tamura, R., Ono, T., Fukuda, M., & Nakamura, K. (1990). Recognition of egocentric and allocentric visual and auditory space by neurons in the hippocampus of monkeys. *Neuroscience Letters, 109*, 293–298.

Tamura, R., Ono, T., Fukuda, M., & Nakamura, K. (1992). Spatial responsiveness of monkey hippocampal neurons to various visual and auditory stimuli. *Hippocampus, 2*, 307–322.

Tekman, H. G. (1997). Interactions of perceived intensity, duration, and pitch in pure tone sequences. *Music Perception, 14*, 281–294.

Tekman, H. G. (1998). Effects of melodic accents on perception of intensity. *Music Perception, 15*, 391–401.

Tekman, H. G. (2002). Perceptual integration of timing and intensity variations in the perception of musical accents. *Journal of General Psychology, 129*, 181–191.

Thompson, W. F., & Sinclair, D. (1993). Pitch pattern, durational pattern, and timbre: A study of the perceptual integration of auditory qualities. *Psychomusicology, 12*, 3–21.

Thurlow, W. R., & Jack, C. E. (1973). Certain determinants of the "ventriloquism effect." *Perceptual and Motor Skills, 36*(3, Pt. 2), 1171–1184.

Wade, N. J., & Day, R. H. (1968). Apparent head position as a basis for visual aftereffect of prolonged head tilt. *Perception and Psychophysics, 3*, 324–326.

Walker, B. N., & Ehrenstein, A. (2000). Pitch and pitch change interact in auditory displays. *Journal of Experimental Psychology: Applied, 6*, 15–30.

Walker-Andrews, A. S., & Lennon, E. M. (1985). Auditory-visual perception of changing distance by human infants. *Child Development, 56*, 544–548.

Wallace, M. T., Meredith, M. A., & Stein, B. E. (1992). Integration of multiple sensory modalities in cat cortex. *Experimental Brain Research, 91*, 484–488.

Wallace, M. T., Meredith, M. A., & Stein, B. E. (1993). Converging influences from visual, auditory, and somatosensory cortices onto output neurons of the superior colliculus. *Journal of Neurophysiology, 69*, 1797–1809.

Wallace, M. T., & Stein, B. E. (1994). Cross modal synthesis in the midbrain depends on input from the cortex. *Journal of Neurophysiology, 71*, 429–432.

Wallace, M. T., & Stein, B. E. (1997). Development of multisensory neurons and multisensory integration in cat superior colliculus. *Journal of Neuroscience, 17*, 2429–2444.

Wann, J. P. (1996). Anticipating arrival: Is the tau margin a specious theory? *Journal of Experimental Psychology: Human Perception and Performance, 22*, 1031–1048.

Warren, D. H. (1970). Intermodality interactions in spatial localization. *Cognitive Psychology, 1*, 114–133.

Warren, D. H., Welch, R. B., & McCarthy, T. J. (1981). The role of visual-auditory "compellingness" in the ventriloquism effect: Implications for transitivity among the spatial senses. *Perception and Psychophysics, 30*, 557–564.

Warrier, C. M., & Zatorre, R. J. (2002). Influence of tonal context and timbral variation on perception of pitch. *Perception and Psychophysics, 64*, 198–207.

Watkins, W. H., & Freeher, C. E. (1965). Acoustic facilitation of visual detection. *Journal of Experimental Psychology, 70*, 332–333.

Weeks, R., Horwitz, B., Aziz-Sultan, A., Tian, B., Wessinger, C. M., Cohen, L. G., Hallett, M., & Rauschecker, J. P. (2000). A positron emission tomographic study of auditory localization in the congenitally blind. Journal of Neuroscience, *20*, 2664–2672.

Welch, R. B., DuttonHurt, L. D., & Warren, D. H. (1986). Contributions of audition and vision to temporal rate perception. *Perception and Psychophysics, 39*, 294–300.

Welch, R. B., & Warren, D. H. (1980). Immediate perceptual response to intersensory discrepancy. *Psychological Bulletin, 88*, 638–667.

Welch, R. B., & Warren, D. H. (1986). Intersensory interactions. In K. R. Boff, L. Kaufman, & J. P. Thomas (Eds.), *Handbook of perception and human performance* (pp. 25:21–25:36) New York: Wiley.

Wells, M. C., & Lehner, P. N. (1978). The relative importance of the distance senses in coyote predatory behaviour. *Animal Behaviour, 26*, 251–258.

Wilkinson, L. K., Meredith, M. A., & Stein, B. E. (1996). The role of anterior ectosylvian cortex in cross-modality orientation and approach behavior. *Experimental Brain Research, 112*, 1–10.

Willis, M. A., & Carde, R. T. (1990). Pheromone-modulated optomotor response in male gypsy moths, *Lymantria dispar* L.: Upwind flight in a pheromone plume in different wind velocities. *Journal of Comparative Physiology A Sensory Neural and Behavioral Physiology, 167*, 699.

Willis, M. A., David, C. T., Murlis, J., & Carde, R. (1994). Effects of pheromone plume structure and visual stimuli on the pheromone-modulated upwind flight of male gypsy moths (*Lymantria dispar*) in a forest (Lepidoptera: Lymantriidae). *Journal of Insect Behavior, 7*, 385–410.

Wolters, N. C., & Schiano, D. J. (1989). On listening where we look: The fragility of a phenomenon. *Perception and Psychophysics, 45*, 184–186.

Worthy, M. D. (2000). Effects of tone-quality conditions on perception and performance of pitch among selected wind instrumentalists. *Journal of Research in Music Education, 48*, 222–236.

Zatorre, R. J., Mondor, T. A., & Evans, A. C. (1999). Auditory attention to space and frequency activates similar cerebral systems. *Neuroimage, 10*, 544–554.

11

PITCH AND PITCH STRUCTURES

MARK A. SCHMUCKLER

INTRODUCTION

This chapter has two purposes. The first is straightforward and involves providing an introduction to the basics of pitch and pitch perception. The second goal, however, is more difficult and likely much more elusive. The aim in this case is to describe the perception of pitch from an ecological perspective. The obvious problem, of course, is that although the ecological approach has been developed as a general theoretical framework, the primary applications of this theory have been to vision (e.g., J. J. Gibson, 1950, 1979) and movement (e.g., Turvey, 1977, 1990; Turvey & Carello, 1986; Turvey, Carello, & Kim, 1990) and to issues in perceptual development and learning (e.g., E. J. Gibson, 1969, 1984; Gibson & Pick, 2000). Despite the fact that there have been some notable attempts to generalize these principles to audition, with some important successes (e.g., Balzano, 1986; Bregman, 1990; Fowler & Dekle, 1991; Fowler & Rosenblum, 1991; Jones & Hahn, 1986; McCabe, 1986; Warren & Verbrugge, 1984), it unfortunately remains unclear how the insights into perceptual processing delineated by this approach might be fruitfully employed when considering an auditory dimension such as pitch. To put it simply, it is not evident what an ecological perspective on pitch might look like.

As a starting point, it is instructive to consider some of the most basic innovations advanced by this framework. One such insight involves a concern with the most appropriate scale or level at which to analyze the perceptual process (J. J. Gibson, 1979). For the Gibsons, the history of perceptual research was one that focused too much on the microlevel and not on a level appropriate for describing the behavior of the animal within an environment. As an example, one serious limitation to research in vision was that such work was far too concerned with reducing the variables of visual perception to those of physics (J. J. Gibson, 1960, 1961; Michaels & Carello, 1981) and not concerned enough with the variables relevant to animals acting within a cluttered world. Accordingly, perceptual psychologists needed to focus on the "ecological level, with the habitat of animals and men" (J. J. Gibson, 1979, p. 9), looking at how perceptual processes function during goal-directed behavior in the environment (J. J. Gibson, 1979; Michaels & Carello, 1981; Turvey & Shaw, 1979; Wagman & Miller, 2003).

This basic tenet of the ecological perspective has at least two important consequences. First, there is a recurrent emphasis on studying perceptual processing within the most relevant context or environment. Although this issue sometimes reduces to an almost knee-jerk concern with the "ecological validity" of the experimental context, the inherent limitations in such an emphasis (see Schmuckler, 2001, for a discussion and historical review of problems with the concept of ecological validity) do not diminish the important lesson that the environmental (and often experimental) context in which perception occurs is a critical, and frequently neglected, part of the perceptual process.

Second, there is the issue of studying the perceptual process at the appropriate behavioral level. The aim, of course, is to avoid reducing the perceptual object so much that it becomes behaviorally meaningless. Accordingly, the relevant variables for vision are objects and surfaces having certain functional uses to perceivers with certain action capabilities, or the "affordances" of the environment (Adolph, Eppler, & Gibson, 1993; E. J. Gibson, 1982; J. J. Gibson, 1979).

Despite this theoretical background, however, the question remains of how to translate these ideas into the study of pitch. In an attempt to be concrete, the first consequent just described suggests that a principal guideline for understanding an ecological perspective on pitch might be a concern with the influence of (environmental) context on the perception of pitch. Although context could (and should) be construed in any number of ways, in the present discussion context refers to surrounding auditory events, specifically other tones. This idea is explored in the initial section of this chapter. Another guideline stems from the second consequent and involves attempting to identify the most appropriate level of analysis for pitch perception. On this basis, rather than studying pitch per se, one might focus on the apprehension of pitch objects; one interpretation of such pitch objects might be pitch structures. The notion of pitch structures is developed subsequently.

With these ideas in mind, it is possible to map out the course of this chapter. After a brief review of the basics of pitch, this chapter quickly discusses the perception of pitch, with an eye toward illuminating the critical role of context in pitch perception. Following this discussion, the importance of pitch structures in audition is explored, highlighting two complementary means of organizing pitch. This chapter then concludes with an attempt to bring the discussion back around to the implications of these ideas for an ecological approach.

At the start, there are two important caveats. First, given the themes of behavioral level and context, it is most relevant to focus on pitch perception as it operates in the apprehension of complicated auditory objects and events—namely, speech and music. Because, however, speech is the focus of another chapter (Chap. 9), the current discussion is limited primarily to understanding pitch within a musical context. Second, this chapter is not meant to provide a thorough review of research in music cognition generally or even pitch perception in music specifically. Within the past few decades, several excellent books, review chapters, and review articles have appeared on these topics (e.g., Deutsch, 1999; Dowling, 2001; Justus & Bharucha, 2002; Krumhansl, 1990, 1991, 2000a; McAdams & Bigand, 1993; McAdams & Drake, 2002). Thus, for more complete reviews of this area, one should consult any (or all) of these sources.

PERCEIVING SINGLE TONES

THE BASICS OF PITCH

Sounds are most frequently characterized in terms of the basic dimensions of pitch, loudness, duration, and timbre; of these dimensions, the most characteristic property of sound is pitch. What is pitch? Essentially, pitch is the subjective psychological attribute associated with the objective physical variable of the repetition rate or periodicity of the waveform (Moore, 2001b). For example, a periodic clicking sound produces pitch when the click is repeated about 100 times a second (Krumbholz, Patterson, & Pressnitzer, 2000; Pressnitzer, Patterson, & Krumbholz, 2001). More typically, for simple sounds, or sine waves, it is the *frequency* of the waveform, or the number of repetitions of the waveform per second, that is related to its pitch.

Sine waves are not the most common type of sounds, despite the fact that the history of psychophysical research in pitch might suggest otherwise. Most of the pitched sounds one encounters in daily life, such as speech and music, are periodic complex tones. Complex tones are frequently made up of a number of sine waves (called *harmonics* or *partials*), each having a frequency that is an integer multiple of the frequency of a common fundamental component. In others words, one can think of a complex tone as a conglomeration of simple tones (Moore, 2001a). This common fundamental component, called the *fundamental frequency*, is typically a frequency equivalent to the periodicity of the entire waveform as a whole.

Although the pitch of a complex tone is generally that associated with the pitch of the fundamental frequency, this pitch can also be influenced by the presence and relative strengths of the remaining harmonics. Interestingly, though, not all of these harmonics contribute equally to the pitch. Instead, evidence suggests the existence of a "dominance region" in pitch perception, in which the harmonics falling in the low regions are most influential in determining the pitch of the complex tone (e.g., Dai, 2000; Hartmann, 1996; Moore, 1993; Plomp, 1967; Ritsma, 1967).

Moreover, since the 1800s it has been known that one can perceive the pitch of a complex tone even though there may be no frequency present corresponding to that pitch (Seebeck, 1843, cited in Preisler, 1993). Sometimes called the "missing fundamental," this phenomenon similarly demonstrates that the percept of a complex tone can be determined by the harmonics of that tone (Preisler, 1993) and hence provides more evidence for the principle of dominance just described (e.g., Plomp, 1967; Ritsma, 1967).

BASIC PITCH PERCEPTION

Moving beyond this rather simplistic discussion of what pitch is leads naturally to the question of pitch perception. Although a thorough review of pitch perception is beyond the scope of this chapter (see Moore, 2001b), it is nevertheless instructive to consider briefly some of the basics. In fact, pitch perception has been remarkably well researched over the years, resulting in a wealth of knowledge about its fundamentals. Over the years, two different theories have been proposed to explain pitch perception. The first view, called the *place theory*, is based on the finding that different frequencies cause differential excitation along the basilar membrane and thus produce the sensation of pitch as a result of the firing of different neurons. An alternative view, called the *temporal theory*, assumes that the pitch of a sound is related to the temporal pattern of neural impulses in response to a frequency, with the neural impulses approximating integer multiples of the waveform (Moore, 2001b). Although often presented in opposition, many feel that both mechanisms are operative in pitch perception, with their relative roles varying with tone frequency and with specific task (Moore, 2001b).

As for the actual psychological bases of pitch perception, many of the basics devolve to fundamental psychophysical questions. Thus, one can ask about the shortest duration of an auditory event that gives rise to a sensation of pitch or the smallest differences in pitch that listeners can detect. Again, although a thorough review of the psychophysics of pitch lies outside of the purview of this work, such questions have been investigated by numerous researchers over the years. For example, it is known that about 8 to 10 cycles of a complex waveform are required for stable pitch perception (Patterson, Peters, & Milroy, 1983; Robinson & Patterson, 1995; Whitfield, 1979) and that only a single cycle of a waveform is needed to identify a vowel sound, which requires the perception of pitch (Suen & Beddoes, 1972). Similarly, work on frequency detection has discovered that, although the exact thresholds for detecting pitch differences vary as function of how these thresholds are measured, listeners can detect changes in the frequency of a tone on the order of about 0.5–1.0% (Krumhansl, 2000a; Olsho, Schoon, Sakai, Turpin, & Sperduto, 1982; Wier, Jesteadt, & Green, 1977).

Along with considering psychophysical questions related to pitch perception, one can look at the interaction between the perception of pitch and other auditory dimensions; put differently, how might a tone's loudness or its timbre influence its perceived pitch? Research on this question has uncovered some intriguing results. Some work has found that the loudness of a tone influences the perception of its pitch. The classic Fletcher and Munson curves (Fletcher & Munson, 1933), for example, clearly show that the ability to detect pitch varies as function of the frequency of the to-be-detected tone, with detection lowest in the range between 2 and 5 kHz. Considering this question from the standpoint of dimensional integrality and separability (this issue is discussed at length by Neuhoff, Chap. 10 of this volume), other work has similarly found an interactive relation between pitch and loudness. Grau and Kemler Nelson (1988), using various Garnerian tasks, observed unitary processing of pitch and loudness, a result suggestive of psychological interaction. Similarly, Melara and Marks (1990) found that the pitch and loudness dimensions of an auditory tone were perceptually interactive, with processing of one dimension influencing processing of the other dimension.

Comparable evidence has been found for the impact of timbre on the perception of pitch. For instance, using a variety of techniques, multiple authors have produced findings suggestive of a perceptual interaction between pitch and timbre (Krumhansl & Iverson, 1992; Pitt, 1994; Platt & Racine, 1985; Singh & Hirsch, 1992; Wapnick & Freeman, 1980; Warrier & Zatorre, 2002). And, of course, there is the missing fundamental (described earlier), in which the pitch of a tone depends upon the presence and relative strengths of its upper harmonics. Because these harmonics also (largely) determine the timbre of the tone, the missing fundamental is thus evidence for the influence of timbre on pitch perception.

An intriguing aspect of much of this research is that many of these basics vary when pitch perception occurs within a larger musical context. For example, a great deal of research indicates that pitch detection, as well as pitch memory, is dramatically influenced when such factors are tested within what is called a "tonal context" (e.g., Deutsch, 1972a, 1972b; Dewar, Cuddy, & Mewhort, 1977; Krumhansl, 1979; Ranvaud, Thompson, Silveira-Moriyama, & Balkwill, 2001; Warrier & Zatorre, 2002); tonal contexts, or tonality, are described in much more detail subsequently. To provide just one out of many possible examples here, Warrier and Zatorre (2002) observed that the ability to detect minor changes in the frequency of a tone varied depending on the context in which that tone was heard. In this study, listeners judged whether a specific tone was in tune or out of tune when the tone was heard either in isolation or in the context of other tones. The results showed that context significantly affected pitch change detection, with listeners able to hear frequency differences when the changes were embedded in a melody that they were literally unable to detect when the changes were heard in isolation.

Other research shows that pitch memory is similarly influenced by the context in which it occurs (e.g., Deutsch, 1972a, 1972b; Dewar et al., 1977; Krumhansl,

1979). A study by Dewar *et al.* (1977) provides a classic case in point. In this study, listeners heard sequences of tones, with their recognition memory for individual tones of this sequence tested under varying degrees of musical context. The results of multiple studies convincingly demonstrated that recognition memory for an individual tone was much more accurate when this tone was embedded in a musical context than when the tone was presented in isolation. Findings such as these, as well as many others, have led to the general conclusion that pitch representations, including the perception of and memory for pitch, are very much constrained by the relation of that pitch to other pitches within a musical context (e.g., Krumhansl, 1979).

Similarly, there is evidence that the dimensional interaction patterns just described also vary as a function of musical context. For example, Krumhansl and Iverson (1992) found that pitch and timbre interacted when the tones were presented in isolation (Experiment 1) but not when presented in musical sequences (Experiments 2 and 3). Similar findings have been observed by Platt and Racine (1985) as well as other researchers (Semal & Demany, 1991, 1993). Finally, Pitt (1994) found that musical expertise influences dimensional interaction, with nonmusicians showing more influence of timbre on pitch perception than the reverse, whereas musicians showed no asymmetry in pitch–timbre interactions. Taken together, the works on pitch detection, pitch memory, and dimensional interaction converge in the implication that even basic parameters of pitch perception vary depending upon whether or not these pitches are heard within a musical context.

PSYCHOLOGICAL SCALES OF PITCH

Unidimensional Models

Consideration of the basics of pitch perception leads naturally to the question of how to characterize the psychological organization of pitch. Although there are multiple ways to address this issue (some of which are broached subsequently), one concern might be with the psychological scaling of pitch.

Probably the simplest psychological pitch scale views this attribute one-dimensionally, ranging from low to high, isomorphically related to frequency. Actually though, even when viewed in this fashion, there are multiple possible characterizations of this scale (Rasch & Plomp, 1999). For example, pitch can be characterized along a *psychoacoustic scale,* related to continuous frequency. In this case, the perception of pitch is driven by the (fundamental) frequency of the waveform and occurs on a logarithmic basis (Rasch & Plomp, 1999).

One could also derive a *psychophysical scale* for pitch. The classic example of a psychophysical pitch scale is the mel scale (Siegel, 1965; Stevens & Volkmann, 1940; Stevens, Volkmann, & Newman, 1937), which maps listeners' percepts of subjective pitch to actual frequency. The mel scale was determined by assigning a standard 1000-Hz tone to a level of 1000 mels and then having listeners adjust another tone relative to this standard based on phrases such as "half as high" and "twice as high." Figure 1 shows the results of experiments of this sort, graphing the relation between subjective pitch in mels and frequency in hertz. What is most obvious from Fig. 1 is that frequency does not map directly onto subjective pitch, with changes in subjective pitch not as large as changes in frequency. For example, a ninefold increase in frequency (say from 1000 to 9000 Hz) produces only a threefold increase in perceived pitch (from 1000 to 3000 mels).

Although the mel scale is prominently discussed in introductory texts on the physics and psychology of sound (e.g., Handel, 1989; Pierce, 1983; Rossing, 1982; Shepard, 1999a, 1999c), many have questioned the usefulness of this scale, pointing out that it may be related to aspects other than pitch (e.g., perceived brightness, Pierce, 1983) or that it is unreliable (Rasch & Plomp, 1999) given its method of construction. Nevertheless, what Fig. 1 does demonstrate is that, in terms of psychological scaling, the relation between subjective pitch and frequency is much more complicated than might be initially supposed. At the same time, it is important to note that despite the lack of an isomorphic relation between pitch and frequency, this scale is still one-dimensional, with continuous changes in frequency producing continuous changes in pitch.

As with the work on basic pitch perception, the psychological scaling of pitch is also influenced by larger auditory context. In fact, one important drawback to both psychoacoustic and psychophysical scales is that neither provides a good

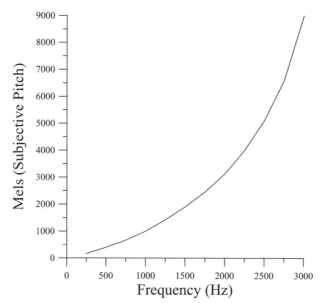

FIGURE 1 The mel scale, which graphs the relation between objective frequency (in hertz) and subjective pitch (in mels). (Adapted from Handel, 1989, p. 69.)

account of the psychological experience of pitch within a musical context. Musical context, it seems, induces other relations on pitch, ones that are not captured by these approaches.

Within a musical context, the most obvious refinement of the pitch scale is that the continuous frequency dimension is now divided into discrete steps. Why, of course, the continuous frequency dimension is discretized in this fashion is admittedly a puzzle, one that has been debated for decades (e.g., Helmholtz, 1885/1954, see Dowling & Harwood, 1986, for discussion). Nevertheless, it is the case that musical systems all over the world base their musical practice on a finite number of discrete pitches (Dowling, 2001). In Western music, the smallest frequency difference employed between two successive pitches is called a *semitone*, with the entire set of discrete tones employed in music called the *chromatic scale*.

Multidimensional Models

Just as with the psychoacoustic and psychophysical scales, the discrete chromatic scale is still unidimensional with respect to frequency. Musical context, however, induces an even more important change in the psychological scaling of pitch. Within a musical context, the unidimensional description of pitch now simply becomes inadequate for capturing the mental representation of pitch (e.g., Justus & Bharucha, 2002); instead, musical pitch is better described by a bidimensional model (Shepard, 1982b). This bidimensional model, sometimes called the "pitch helix" (Shepard, 1982a, 1982b), is shown in Fig. 2. The first dimen-

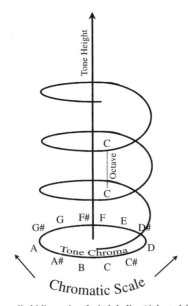

FIGURE 2   Shepard's bidimensional pitch helix. (Adapted from Shepard, 1982a.)

sion in this model, called *pitch* or *tone height*, corresponds to changes in logarithmic frequency as just described and is represented in Fig. 2 by movement along the vertical axis of the figure. The second dimension, called *pitch* or *tone chroma*, is a circular representation of the chromatic scale, in which movement from one pitch to its neighboring pitch (in either direction) eventually brings one back around to the original starting point; this dimension is represented in Fig. 2 by circular, horizontal movement. Pitch chroma has been proposed to capture a fundamentally important musical relation that exists between tones whose frequencies lie in a 2:1 ratio. Within musical parlance, such tones are called *octaves* and are assumed to be functionally equivalent. Such "octave equivalence" motivates the naming of pitches in Western music, with octave-related tones sharing the same name.

The bidimensional pitch model raises two important questions. First, is there evidence that this bidimensional model of pitch truly characterizes percepts of musical pitch? That is, do pitch height and pitch chroma have psychological reality? Second, are tones with frequencies in a 2:1 ratio truly equivalent? That is, does octave equivalence have psychological reality?

Research on the first question has produced robust evidence for the psychological reality of pitch height and chroma. In some classic work, Shepard (1964) created tones that independently varied pitch height and pitch chroma (see Krumhansl, 1991, or Shepard, 1964, for complete descriptions of these tones) such that these tones provided listeners with a well-defined sense of pitch chroma (e.g., placement along the chroma circle) but little sense of pitch height (e.g., no definite placement on the frequency dimension). In this research, Shepard (1964) found that when pairs of these tones were played to listeners, they heard successive tones as ascending if the shorter distance between the tones on the chroma circle produced increasing frequency (counterclockwise movement) but descending if the shorter distance produced decreasing frequency (clockwise movement). Intriguingly, if the tones were equidistant (halfway) on this circle, the perceived direction of pitch movement was ambiguous, with some listeners hearing ascending movement and other listeners hearing descending movement. Subsequent work has suggested that the actual direction of movement (i.e., ascending vs. descending) in this last situation is a stable individual difference phenomenon (Deutsch, 1986a, 1987; Deutsch, Kuyper, & Fisher, 1987), one related to speech and/or linguistic variables (Dawe, Platt, & Welsh, 1998; Deutsch, 1991, 1994, 1997; Deutsch, North, & Ray, 1990; Giangrande, 1998).

As for the psychological reality of octave equivalence, the results on this topic are much more mixed. Early research in this domain (Deutsch, 1973b) found that general interference effects that had been observed in pitch recognition studies (Deutsch, 1972a, 1973a) also occurred when the pitches of the interfering tones were shifted by an octave. In other words, tones separated by an octave produced comparable psychological interference, suggestive of octave equivalence. In contrast, Deutsch (1972c) also found that randomly choosing the octave for each note of a melody destroyed listeners' abilities to recognize that melody; hence, tones separated by an octave were not functioning comparably, suggestive of a failure of octave equivalence. Although these apparently contradictory results are compatible with Deutsch's (1969, 1982a, 1982b) two-channel model of pitch processing (which posits different processing channels for single and simultaneous tones versus successive tones), other evidence fails to support this model. For example, multiple researchers (Dowling & Hollombe, 1977; House, 1977; Idson & Massaro, 1978; Kallman & Massaro, 1979) have observed that octave-distorted melodies are (somewhat) recognizable if the octave displacements preserve the relative patterns of pitch increases and decreases between notes as occur in the original melody. Thus, these findings do demonstrate octave equivalence, while simultaneously arguing against Deustch's two-channel model. But, using a different paradigm, Kallman (1982) found that similarity ratings of pairs of tones and pairs of tone sequences showed no evidence of octave equivalence (e.g., high ratings for pairs tones or sequences separated by an octave). To make matters even more confusing, there is some evidence that animals are sensitive to octaves (Irwin & Terman, 1970; Ralston & Herman, 1995; Wright, Rivera, Hulse, Shyan, & Neiworth, 2000). Accordingly, the psychological status of octave equivalence remains unresolved, leading some researchers (Sergeant, 1982, 1983) to suggest that "octaveness" might be a concept more reliant on experience, and possibly musical training, than being of perceptual origin.

One drawback to the pitch helix is that although it captures the important octave relation, it fails to represent other theoretically important relations imposed by musical context. In response to this limitation, a number of higher dimensional pitch models have been proposed (Krumhansl, 1979, 1990; Krumhansl & Kessler, 1982; Shepard, 1982a, 1982b, 1999b) in an attempt to represent some of these relations. For example, Shepard (1982a, 1982b, 1999b), among others, has suggested that another critically important musical relation that should be incorporated is that between tones separated by seven semitones or, in musical terms, a perfect fifth. If the fifths are arranged in a circle, this *circle of fifths* can be combined with pitch height to produce a "double pitch helix" model of musical pitch (see Shepard, 1982a, 1982b, for graphical representations of this and other models). Extending this approach further, putting together different combinations of the pitch height, pitch chroma, and circle of fifth dimensions results in other multidimensional models. For instance, combining pitch chroma and the circle of fifths produces a four-dimensional model of pitch, and combining all three dimensions results in a five-dimensional model. Other authors (Krumhansl, 1979, 1990; Krumhansl & Kessler, 1982) have proposed related multidimensional models; one of these models (Krumhansl & Kessler, 1982) is described more fully in a subsequent section. The details of these models aside, the critical point here is that the addition of a larger musical context clearly induces a very complex, multidimensional set of perceived psychological relations between tones.

SUMMARY

Overall, it is clear that even the simple perception of pitch is highly constrained by the context in which the pitches occur. Although context can be construed in different ways, the focus here has been on the overarching musical framework. Examination of this area has convincingly demonstrated that the perception of pitch, and the corresponding psychological representation of a tone, changes dramatically when it is heard relative to other tones.

Of course, this discussion is limited by its devotion to considering only single tones. Probably the most fundamental problem with this focus is that when a listener hears an auditory stimulus the perceptual goal is *not* the apprehension of individual tones, but rather it is the organization of larger grouping of tones, or what might be considered auditory objects. Arguably, then, focusing on the perception of single tones represents an inappropriate level of analysis, one against which an ecological approach would argue vociferously.

In fact, highlighting the higher level of auditory objects is conceptually akin to the well-known ecological emphasis on event perception (Bruce & Green, 1985; Cutting & Proffitt, 1981; Gibson & Spelke, 1983; J. J. Gibson, 1975, 1979; Johansson, 1973, 1975; Lombardo, 1987). Just as with visual events, auditory events exist on multiple hierarchically nested levels. In speech and language, these events range from phonemes to words to phrases, sentences, conversations, and so on. In music, events range from individual notes and chords (simultaneous soundings of two or more notes) to phrases to melodies, sections, movements, pieces, and so on. As such, any discussion of pitch must not only explore the apprehension of individual tones but also examine how pitches are perceived when presented in collections, or in pitch structures. Exploring this level of pitch perception is the focus of the next part of this chapter.

PERCEIVING PITCH STRUCTURES

The previous section ended with the realization that, although a focus on the perception of single tones is instructive and easily illuminates the critical role of context in pitch perception, it paradoxically emphasizes what some might consider the wrong level of analysis. Accordingly, attention may be more profitably employed by adopting a more appropriate behavioral unit of analysis, one emphasizing the perception of pitch during the apprehension of auditory objects. Of course, the first issue that must be addressed following this realization is an answer to the question of what might be considered a viable auditory object. Although multiple candidates could be proposed for an auditory object (e.g., sound sources, meaningful linguistic units; see Chap. 5, Van Valkenburg & Kubovy, for a discussion of auditory objecthood), one possibility is to construe pitch organizations, or pitch structures, as auditory objects.

The idea of pitch structures as auditory objects raises some additional questions, however. One could ask, for example, about the constraints that influence the formation and subsequent processing of pitch structures. Or, one could ask about the types of pitch organizations that operate while listening to music. And if multiple pitch structures exist, what are the relations between these organizations?

In an attempt to answer such questions, it is helpful to make a distinction between pitch organization as it occurs in space (e.g., frequency) and pitch organization as it occurs in time. Of course, such a division is simply a pedagogical convenience, in that pitch structures in space implicitly have time built in, and pitch structures in time are intimately involved with frequency. Nevertheless, because most models of pitch organizations treat the frequency and temporal domains separately, it is worthwhile to explore each form of pitch structure on its own.

ORGANIZATION OF PITCH IN SPACE

Krumhansl (2000a) has reviewed some of the major approaches to pitch structure. Her analysis is not reiterated in detail here, but she delineates three different approaches to the organization of pitch. The first organization is a *rule-based* approach, stemming from the work of Simon and colleagues (Simon, 1972; Simon & Kotovsky, 1963; Simon & Sumner, 1968). In this approach, pitch structures are characterized by an alphabet of elements and a set of operators used to manipulate these elements such that the application (or improper application) of the operators leads to patterned (or unpatterned) sequences. This approach has been widely applied in music cognition, with success in predicting listeners' apprehensions of sequences (Deutsch, 1980, 1986b; Deutsch & Feroe, 1981; Jones, 1981; Jones, Maser, & Kidd, 1978).

The second approach is based on models of *linguistic analyses*, the most extensive example of which is by Lerdahl & Jackendoff (1983). In Lerdahl and Jackendoff's (1983) theory, a set of grouping rules are used to parse the musical surface, with the goal of segmenting and ultimately reducing the music into a nested hierarchical tree structure representing a theoretical (and presumably psychological) hierarchy of importance. As with the preceding approach, there exists a fair amount of evidence that this characterization of pitch organization has a certain degree of psychological reality. Palmer and Krumhansl (1987a, 1987b) and Dibben (1994), for example, have all provided evidence for the role of hierarchical reductions (as outlined by Lerdahl & Jackendoff, 1983) in listeners' judgments of musical passages. Similarly, Deliège (1987) has shown that the grouping rules posited by this theory are actually used by listeners in perceptually segmenting music.

The third approach described by Krumhansl (2000a) is *geometric* in nature and outlines the similarity and stability relations between musical elements such as tones, chords, and pairs of tones and chords within a musical context. There are a number of models that are examples of this approach; one such exemplar was described earlier in the discussion of multidimensional models of musical pitch (Shepard, 1982a, 1982b, 1999b).

Tonal Models

Of these three approaches, the organization most useful for the present purposes is the geometric model because it easily describes the most fundamental pitch structure of Western music—that of tonality or key. In musical parlance, tonality refers to the hierarchical organization of the notes of the chromatic scale around a single reference pitch. This reference pitch is called the *tonic* or *tonal center*, and the remaining tones are judged in relation to this tone.

Tonality also induces on the chromatic scale a hierarchical organization of importance (see Table 1). In this hierarchy the tonic is positioned at the top and is seen as the point of greatest stability. The second and third levels of the hierarchy contain tones of intermediate import. At the second level are the notes that are four and seven semitone steps above the tonic; along with the tonic tone, these levels constitute the *tonic triad*. The third level of this hierarchy contains the next most important tones. Combining this level with the two levels above it produces the *diatonic set*. Finally, at the lowest level of the hierarchy are the remaining six notes of the chromatic set. These tones, called the *nondiatonic tones*, are outside the tonality and are considered to be the least important, least stable tones of the entire set.

Two additional properties are important for an understanding of Western tonality. First, there are two distinct categories of tonality. The first is a *major tonality* and involves the structure just described. The second is a *minor tonality*. Its pattern of hierarchical relations is similar to that of the major tonality (e.g., the tonic and seventh semitone are at the top two levels), with some critical differences. For example, in a minor tonality the third as opposed to the fourth semitone is part of the tonic triad; the minor tonality hierarchy is also shown in Table 1.[1]

The second important property is that a tonality can be built using any one of the chromatic tones as the tonic, with the tonic tone, combined with the tonality's form (major or minor), giving the tonality its name. For example, a tonality with the note "F" as its tonic and containing the hierarchical structure for a major key would be "F major." Similarly, a minor tonality based on the tone "E" would be called "E minor." One critical implication of these properties is that combining the 12 notes of the chromatic scale with the two different forms for each tonality produces 24 possible tonalities in all (12 major and 12 minor). Western music

---

[1] The musically astute reader will no doubt recognize that Table 1 presents only one of three possible forms of a minor tonality. This type of minor set, called the "natural minor," is presented because it is the form of the minor that has been most often employed in psychological research. In fact, although theoretically distinct, very little research has actually examined any differences in the perceived psychological stability of the different forms of the minor sets.

TABLE 1   The theoretical hierarchy of importance for a major and minor tonality. Semitones are numbered 0–11

Hierarchy level	Major hierarchy					Minor hierarchy				
Tonic tone			0					0		
Tonic triad		4	7				3	7		
Diatonic set	2	5	9	11		2	5	8	10	
Nondiatonic set	1	3	6	8	10	1	4	6	9	11

makes use of all of these tonalities, albeit not typically within a single piece of music.

Thus far what has been described is a music-theoretic hierarchy of importance of the 12 chromatic tones within a particular tonal context; the existence of this theoretical hierarchy raises the question of whether or not listeners are sensitive to this organization. Krumhansl, in some classic tests of this question (Krumhansl & Shepard, 1979; Krumhansl & Kessler, 1982), provided evidence of the psychological reality of this pitch hierarchy and its importance in musical processing. To examine this question, Krumhansl and Shepard (1979) employed the "probe-tone" method (see Krumhansl & Shepard, 1979 or Krumhansl, 1990 for thorough descriptions of this procedure), in which listeners heard a musical context designed to instantiate a specific tonality, followed by a probe event. The listeners then rated how well this probe fit with the preceding context in a musical sense. Using this procedure, Krumhansl and colleagues (Krumhansl & Shepard, 1979; Krumhansl & Kessler, 1982) demonstrated that listeners' perceived hierarchy of stability matched the theoretic hierarchy described earlier. Figure 3 shows the averaged ratings for the chromatic notes relative to a major and a minor context; these ratings are called the "tonal hierarchy" (Krumhansl, 1990), with the tonic functioning as a psychological reference point (e.g., Rosch, 1975) by which the remaining tones of the chromatic set are judged.

Subsequent work on the tonal hierarchy extended these findings in different directions. Some research demonstrated that these ratings were robust across different musical tonalities (Krumhansl & Kessler, 1982) with, for example, the hierarchy for F# major a transposition of the C major hierarchy. Krumhansl and Kessler used these hierarchy ratings to derive a four-dimensional map of psychological musical key space; a two-dimensional representation of this map appears in Fig. 4. This map is intriguing in that it incorporates different important musical relations, such as fifths, and parallel and relative keys. Other work generalized this approach outside the realm of tonal music, looking at the hierarchies of stability in non-Western music such as traditional Indian music (Castellano, Bharucha, & Krumhansl, 1984) and Balinese gamelan music (Kessler, Hansen, & Shepard, 1984), or exploring extensions and alternatives to the Western tonal system (Krumhansl, Sandell, & Sargeant, 1987; Krumhansl &

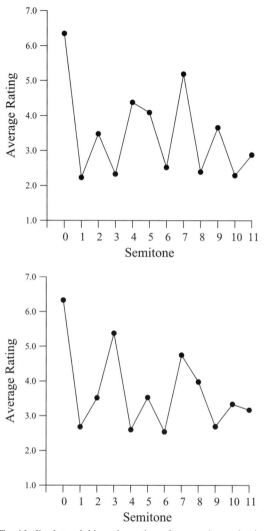

FIGURE 3   The idealized tonal hierarchy ratings for a major and minor context. (From Krumhansl and Kessler, 1982.)

Schmuckler, 1986b). Krumhansl and Schmuckler (1986b), for example, looked at the tonal organization of sections of Stravinsky's ballet *Petroushka*. This piece is notable in being a well-known example of polytonality, or the simultaneous sounding of multiple tonalities. Using both selective and divided attention tasks, Krumhansl and Schmuckler (1986b) demonstrated that the two tonalities juxtaposed in this piece did not exist as separate psychological entities. Instead, listeners' psychological organization of the pitch material from this piece was

ECOLOGICAL PSYCHOACOUSTICS

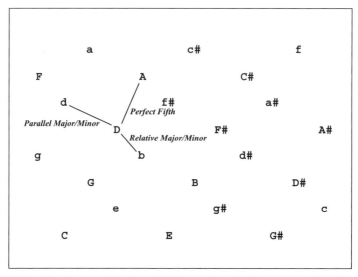

FIGURE 4 Krumhansl and Kessler's (1982) map of musical key space, with major tonalities indicated by capital letters and minor tonalities by lowercase letters. Because this figure represents a four-dimensional torus, the top and bottom edges, and the left and right edges, designate the same place in key space. Note that this map incorporates a variety of important musical relations, with neighboring keys on the circle of fifths close to one another, as well as parallel major/minor (major and minor keys sharing the same tonic) and relative major/minor (major and minor keys sharing the same diatonic set but different tonics) near one another.

best explained with reference to an alternative hierarchy of priorities proposed by Van den Toorn (1983).

Musical Correlates of Tonality

Clearly, the pitch structure imposed by tonal instantiation represents a formidable constraint for perceiving musical structure. Given its fundamental role, a critical question arises as to how listeners perceive tonality. What information exists to specify a tonality, and how sensitive are listeners to this information?

The first of these questions has been thoroughly addressed by Krumhansl (1990, Chap. 3) in a series of extensive analyses of the frequency of occurrence and/or total duration of the 12 chromatic tones within tonal contexts. The results of these analyses convincingly demonstrate that the tonal hierarchy is strongly reflected in how long and how often the various chromatic tones occur. Thus, within a given tonality, the tones that are theoretically and perceptually stable are also the tones that are heard most often; in contrast, perceptually and theoretically unstable tones occur much more rarely. Accordingly, musical contexts provide robust information for the apprehension of tonal structure.

Questions still remain, however, concerning listeners' sensitivity to tonal information. Although in a gross sense listeners clearly pick up such regularities (they do, after all, perceive musical keys), it is still reasonable to wonder how much information is needed for apprehending tonality. And relatedly, what happens in musical contexts when the tonal material changes over time? Such change, called *modulation*, is a typical, indeed expected, component of Western tonal music. Are listeners sensitive to such tonal modulations and, if so, how quickly is the tonal sense reoriented? Finally, is it possible to model listeners' developing percepts of tonality, and of tonal modulation, based on the musical surface information available? These questions have been explored in a variety of experimental contexts.

Sensitivity to Pitch Distributional Information

The issue of how much information is necessary for listeners to apprehend a sense of musical key has been explored by Smith and Schmuckler (2000, 2004) in their studies of pitch-distributional influences on perceived tonality. Specifically, this work examined the impact of varying pitch durations on the perception of tonality by manipulating the absolute durations of the chromatic pitches within a musical sequence while at the same time maintaining the relative durational pattern across time. Thus, tones of longer duration (relative to shorter duration) remained long, despite variation in their actual absolute duration. This manipulation, which produces equivalent duration profiles (in a correlational sense), is called "tonal magnitude," appears schematically in Fig. 5, and is produced by raising the Krumhansl and Kessler (1982) profiles to exponents ranging from 0 (producing a flat profile) through 1 (reproducing the original profile) to 4.5 (producing an exaggerated profile). Smith and Schmuckler also varied the hierarchical organization of the pitches by presented them either in the typical hierarchical arrangement (as represented by the tonal hierarchy) or in a nonhierarchical arrangement produced by randomizing the assignment of durations to individual pitches; examples of randomized profiles are also seen in Fig. 5.

In a series of experiments, Smith and Schmuckler created random melodies in which note durations were based on the various profiles shown in Fig. 5. Using the probe tone procedure, listeners' percepts of tonality in response to these melodies were assessed by correlating stability ratings with Krumhansl and Kessler's idealized tonal hierarchy values. A sample set of results from these series appears in Fig. 6 and demonstrates that increasing tonal magnitude led to increasingly stronger percepts of tonality, but only when pitches were organized hierarchically. Later studies revealed that varying frequency of occurrence while holding duration constant failed to instantiate tonality (a result also found by Lantz, 2002; Lantz & Cuddy, 1998; Oram & Cuddy, 1995) and that the cooccurrence of duration and frequency of occurrence led to the most robust tonal percepts. Interestingly, tonality was not heard until the note duration pattern exceeded what would occur based on a direct translation of Krumhansl and Kessler's (1982) ratings. These studies revealed that listeners are not uniformly sensitive to relative differences in note duration but instead require a divergent

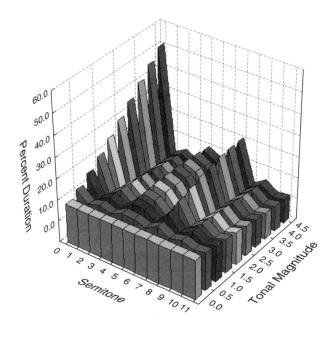

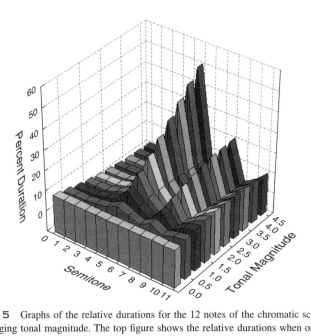

FIGURE 5   Graphs of the relative durations for the 12 notes of the chromatic scale as a function of changing tonal magnitude. The top figure shows the relative durations when organized hierarchically, based on Krumhansl and Kessler (1982); the bottom figure shows a nonhierarchical (randomized) organization.

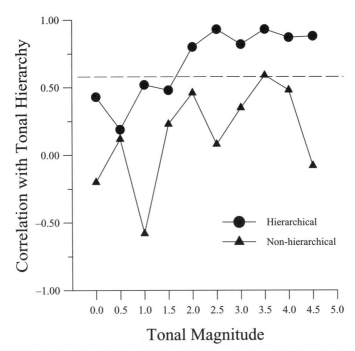

Tonal Magnitude

FIGURE 6   Findings from Smith and Schmuckler's investigations of the impact of tonal magnitude and hierarchical organization manipulations on perceived tonality. The .05 significance level for the correlation with the tonal hierarchy is notated.

degree of duration differences (combined with hierarchical organization) to induce tonality in random note sequences.

Musical Key-Finding Models

The question of how to model the apprehension of musical key, as well as the ability to shift one's sense of tonality while listening to music, has been addressed in work on musical key finding, or what has been rechristened "tonality induction" (Cohen, 2000; Krumhansl, 2000b; Krumhansl & Toiviainen, 2001; Vos, 2000; Vos & Leman, 2000). Such research has as its goal the modeling of the processes by which listeners determine a sense of musical key. Although key-finding models have a relatively long history in music-theoretic and psychological work (see Krumhansl, 2000a; Schmuckler & Tomovski, 2002a; Vos, 2000, for reviews), the most currently successful models of this process have been proposed by Butler and colleagues (Brown, 1988; Brown & Butler, 1981; Brown, Butler, & Jones, 1994; Browne, 1981; Butler, 1989, 1990; Butler & Brown, 1994; Van Egmond & Butler, 1997) and Krumhansl and Schmuckler (Krumhansl & Schmuckler, 1986b; Krumhansl, 1990; Schmuckler & Tomovski, 2002a, 2002b).

Butler's approach to key finding emphasizes the importance of temporal order information, and sequential interval information, in inducing a sense of tonality.

This model, called the intervallic rivalry model (Brown, 1988; Brown & Butler, 1981; Brown et al., 1994; Browne, 1981; Butler, 1989, 1990; Butler & Brown, 1984, 1994), proposes that listeners determine a musical key by recognizing the presence of rare intervals that unambiguously delineate a tonality. Results from studies based on this approach (Brown, 1988; Brown & Butler, 1981) have demonstrated that listeners can, in fact, use rare interval information (when combined with a third, disambiguating tone) to determine tonality when such information is presented both in isolation and in short melodic passages.

In contrast, the Krumhansl–Schmuckler key-finding algorithm (Krumhansl, 1990; Krumhansl & Schmuckler, 1986a) focuses on the pitch content of a musical passage and not on the local temporal ordering of pitches (but see Krumhansl, 2000b, and Krumhansl & Toiviainen, 2001, for an innovation using temporal ordering). This algorithm operates by matching the major and minor hierarchy values with tone duration and/or frequency of occurrence profiles for the chromatic set, based on any particular musical sequence. The result of this comparison is an array of values representing the fit between the relative duration values of a musical passage and the idealized tonal hierarchy values, with the tonal implications of the passage indicated by the strength of the relations between the passage and the idealized tonal hierarchies.

Initial tests of the Krumhansl–Schmuckler algorithm (see Krumhansl, 1990) explored the robustness of this approach for key determination in three different contexts. In its first application, the key-finding algorithm predicted the tonalities of preludes written by Bach, Shostakovich, and Chopin, based on only the first few notes of each piece. The second application extended this analysis by determining the tonality of the fugue subjects of Bach and Shostakovich on a note-by-note basis. Finally, the third application assessed the key-finding algorithm's ability to trace key modulation through Bach's C minor prelude (*Well-Tempered Clavier*, Book II) and compared these key determinations to analyses of key strengths provided by two expert music theorists. Overall, the algorithm performed quite well (see Krumhansl, 1990, pp. 77–110, for details), proving both effective and efficient in determining the tonality of excerpts varying in length, position in the musical score, and musical style.

In general, the Krumhansl–Schmuckler key-finding algorithm has proved successful in key determination of musical scores and has been used extensively by a number of authors for a variety of purposes (Cuddy & Badertscher, 1987; Frankland & Cohen, 1996; Huron & Parncutt, 1993; Takeuchi, 1994; Temperley, 1999; Wright *et al.*, 2000). Interestingly, however, there have been few explicit explorations of the model's efficacy in predicting listeners' percepts of key,[2] although Krumhansl and Toiviainen (2001), in a formalization of this algorithm

---

[2] Most of the research employing the Krumhansl–Schmuckler algorithm has used the model to quantify the tonal implications of the musical stimuli being used in experimental investigations. Such work, although interesting and informative about the robustness of the model, is not, unfortunately, a rigorous test of the algorithm itself.

using a self-organizing map neural network, have provided at least one direct test of this model.

In an attempt to assess more directly the model's ability to predict listeners' percepts of tonality, Schmuckler and Tomovski (1997, 2002a) conducted a series of experiments patterned after the original applications of the algorithm described earlier. Using the probe-tone procedure and modeling this work after the first application of the algorithm, Schmuckler and Tomovski gathered probe tone ratings for the chromatic set, using as contexts the beginning segments (approximately four notes) of the 24 major and minor preludes of Bach (*Well-Tempered Clavier*, Book I) and Chopin (*opus 28*); Fig. 7 presents some sample contexts from this study. Listeners' ratings for preludes from both composers were correlated with the idealized tonal hierarchy values, with these correlations then compared with the key-finding algorithm's predictions of key strength based on the same segments; these comparisons are shown in Table 2. For the Bach preludes, both the algorithm and the listeners picked out the tonality quite well. The algorithm correlated significantly with the intended key (i.e., the key designated by the composer) for all 24 preludes, producing the highest correlation with the intended key in 23 of 24 cases. The listeners showed similarly good key determination, with significant or marginally significant correlations between probe tone ratings and the tonal hierarchy of the intended key for 23 of 24 preludes and producing the strongest correlation with the intended key for 21 of 24 preludes. Accordingly, both the algorithm and the listeners were quite sensitive to the tonal implications of these passages based on just the initial few notes.

Table 2 also displays the results for the Chopin preludes. In contrast to the Bach, both the algorithm and the listeners had more difficulty in tonal identification. For the algorithm, the correlation with the intended key was significant in only 13 of 24 preludes and was the highest correlation for only 11 of these cases. The listeners performed even worse, producing significant correlations with the intended key for 8 of 24 preludes, with only 6 of the correlations with the intended key being the strongest relation. What is intriguing about these failures, however, is that both the algorithm and the listeners behaved similarly. Figure 8 graphs the correlations shown in the final two columns of Table 2 and reveals that the situations in which the algorithm failed to find the key were also those in which listeners performed poorly and vice versa; accordingly, these two sets of data were positively correlated. Thus, rather than indicating a limitation, the poor performance of the algorithm with reference to the Chopin preludes demonstrates that it is actually picking up on the truly tonally ambiguous implications of these short segments.

A subsequent study looked in more depth at the algorithm's modeling of listeners' developing tonal percepts, using some of the Chopin preludes in which listeners did not identify the correct key. Other research, however, mirrored Krumhansl and Schmuckler's third application by exploring the algorithm's ability to track key modulation, or movement through different tonalities, within a single piece. The ability to track key movement is considered a crucial asset

Bach   Chopin

FIGURE 7 Sample contexts used in the probe tone studies of Schmuckler and Tomovski. For the Bach contexts, both the algorithm and the listeners correctly determined the musical key. For the Chopin segments, the first context shown is one in which both algorithm and context correctly determined the musical key. The second context shown is one in which the algorithm (but not the listeners) determined the musical key, and the third context shown is one in which the listeners (but not the algorithm) determined the musical key. Finally, the fourth context is one in which neither algorithm nor listeners determined the correct key.

for key-finding models and has been identified as a potentially serious weakness for the Krumhansl–Schmuckler algorithm (Shmulevich & Yli-Harja, 2000; Temperley, 1999).

Two studies looked in detail at the perception of key movement in Chopin's E minor prelude (see Fig. 9), using the probe-tone methodology. In the first of these studies, eight different probe positions were identified in this prelude. Listeners heard the piece from the beginning up to these probe positions and then

TABLE 2   Correlations between listeners' probe-tone ratings and the algorithm's key predictions with the intended key for the initial segments of preludes by Bach and Chopin

	Bach		Chopin	
Prelude	Algorithm	Listeners	Algorithm	Listeners
C major	.81*	.91*	.81*	.69*
C minor	.92*	.87*	.88*	.83*
C/D major	.83*	.88*	.82*	.68*
C/D minor	.87*	.72*	.25	−.09
D major	.73*	.82*	.27	.61*
D minor	.81*	.91*	.76*	.32
D/E major	.87*	.78*	.59*	.39
D/E minor	.92*	.90*	.71*	.42
E major	.83*	.85*	.88*	.41
E minor	.92*	.80*	.55	.45
F major	.83*	.75*	.76*	.74*
F minor	.85*	.57*	.00	−.10
F/G major	.67*	.76*	.88*	.56
F/G minor	.93*	.61*	.38	.58*
G major	.83*	.74*	.79*	.67*
G minor	.85*	.84*	.21	−.07
G/A major	.87*	.73*	.76*	.03
G/A minor	.83*	.67*	.85*	−.01
A major	.73*	.74*	.49	.58*
A minor	.82*	.88*	−.08	.41
A/B major	.88*	.52	.53	.55
A/B minor	.91*	.88*	.18	.00
B major	.68*	.71*	.38	.03
B minor	.83*	.60*	.92*	.14

*$p < .05$

rated the various probe tones. By playing the different contexts sequentially (i.e., hearing all context and probe pairings up to probe position 1 before probe position 2, and so on; see Schmuckler, 1989, for a fuller discussion), perceived tonality as it unfolded throughout the entire composition was assessed. The second study in this pair examined whether or not the percept of tonality is a local phenomenon, based on the immediately preceding musical context, or is more global in nature, taking into account the entire history of previous musical events.

Because the data from these studies are complex, space limitations preclude a detailed presentation of the findings from this work. However, the results of these studies did reveal that the key-finding algorithm was generally successful at modeling listeners' tonal percepts across the length of the prelude and thus can be used to track tonal modulation. Moreover, these studies indicated that the tonal implications of the piece are a relatively localized phenomenon, based primarily on the immediately preceding (and subsequent) pitch material; this result has been

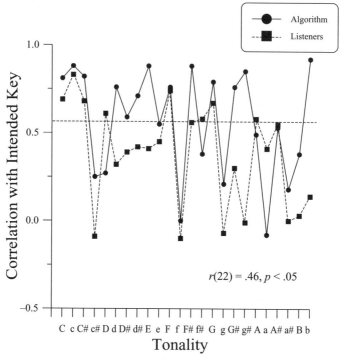

FIGURE 8   The relation between the algorithm and the listeners' abilities to determine the tonality of the Chopin preludes.

both suggested and modeled by others (Shmulevich & Yli-Harja, 2000). Overall, these results provide a nice complement to the third application of the Krumhansl–Schmuckler algorithm (see Krumhansl, 1990) in which the key-finding algorithm successfully modeled expert music theorists' judgments of tonal strength throughout a complete Bach prelude.

Summary of Tonality and Pitch Organization

The findings reviewed in the preceding sections highlight the critical role of tonality as an organizing principle of pitch materials in Western tonal music. Although other approaches to pitch organization, such as serial pattern and linguistic models, underscore important structural relations between pitches, none of them provides as fundamental an organizing basis as that of tonality. And, in fact, the importance of tonality often underlies these other approaches. Serial pattern models (e.g., Deutsch & Feroe, 1981), for example, assume the existence of a special alphabet of pitch materials to which the rules for creating well-formed patterns are applied. This alphabet, however, is often defined in terms of tonal sets (e.g., a diatonic scale), thus implicitly building tonality into the serial patterns. Similarly, many of the bases of the grouping preference rules central to the

FIGURE 9   Chopin's E minor prelude, opus 28. The eight probe positions are indicated by the marking "PP."

operation of the hierarchical reductions that are the goal of linguistic-type analyses (e.g., Lerdahl & Jackendoff, 1983) are based on notions of tonal movement and stability, with less tonally important events resolving, or hierarchically subordinate to, more tonally important events.

Thus, tonality plays a fundamental role in the perception and organization of pitch information. Given its ubiquity in Western music, it might even be reasonable to propose tonality's pattern of hierarchical relations as a form of invariant structure to which listeners are sensitive to varying degrees; this point is returned to in the final discussion. Right now, however, it is instructive to turn to consideration of the organization of pitch in time.

ORGANIZATION OF PITCH IN TIME

Pitch events are not only organized in frequency space, they are organized in time as well. Unlike investigations of frequency, however, relatively little work has examined the organization of pitch in time. Partly this is due to a different emphasis in the temporal domain of music. Traditionally, concern with musical organizations in time has described the metrical structure of musical events (e.g., Benjamin, 1984; Cooper & Meyer, 1960; Large & Palmer, 2002; Lerdahl & Jackendoff, 1983; Lewin, 1984); accordingly, little attention has focused explicitly on how pitch events are organized temporally.

Work that has looked at this issue has tended to examine relations between pairs of tones, investigating questions such as what tone is likely to follow another given a particular event and so on. Examples of this approach can be found in early work on information theory (Cohen, 1962; Coons & Kraehenbuehl, 1958; Knopoff & Hutchinson, 1981, 1983; Kraehenbuehl & Coons, 1959; Youngblood, 1958) and persist to this day in work on musical expectancy (Carlsen, 1981, 1982; Carlsen, Divenyi, & Taylor, 1970; Krumhansl, 1995; Schellenberg, 1996, 1997; Unyk & Carlsen, 1987). The examinations of Narmour's implication-realization model (Cuddy & Lunney, 1995; Krumhansl, 1995; Narmour, 1989, 1990, 1992; Schellenberg, 1996, 1997; Schmuckler, 1989, 1990), for example, have been most successful in explaining expectancy relations for single, subsequent events.

One perspective that has tackled the organization of pitch in time for more extended pitch sequences has focused on the role of melodic contour in musical perception and memory. Contour refers to the relative pattern of ups and downs in pitch through the course of a melodic event. Contour is considered to be one of the most fundamental components of musical pitch information (e.g., Deutsch, 1969; Dowling, 1978) and is the aspect of pitch structure most easily accessible to subjects without formal musical training.

Given its importance, it is surprising that few quantitative theories of contour structure have been offered. Such models would be invaluable, both as aids in music-theoretic analyses of melodic materials and for modeling listeners' perceptions of and memory for musical passages. Fortunately, the past few years have witnessed a change in this state of affairs. Two different approaches to musical contour, deriving from music-theoretic and psychological frameworks, have been advanced to explain contour structure and its perception. These two approaches will be considered in turn.

Music-Theoretic Contour Models

Music-theoretic work has attempted to derive structural descriptions of melodic contour based on the relative patterning of pitch differences between notes in melodic passages (Friedmann, 1985, 1987; Marvin & Laprade, 1987; Quinn, 1999). Early work on this topic (Friedmann, 1985, 1987; Marvin & Laprade, 1987) proposed a set of tools to be used in quantifying the contour of short melodic patterns. These tools summarized the direction, and in some cases the size, of relative pitch differences between all pairs of adjacent and nonadjacent tones (called an *interval* in musical terms) within a pattern (see Schmuckler, 1999, for an in-depth description of these tools). These summarized interval descriptions could then be used to identify similarity relations between contours, with these relations presumably underlying perceived contour similarity. Although these authors do not provide direct psychological tests of their approaches, this work does convincingly demonstrate the efficacy of these models in music-theoretic analyses of short, 20th century atonal melodies.

This approach has culminated in a model by Quinn (1999) based again on the pitch relations between adjacent and nonadjacent tones in a melody. Extending the previous work, though, Quinn uses these tools to derive predicted similarity relations for a set of seven-note melodies and then explicitly tests these predictions by looking at listeners' contour similarity ratings. In this work Quinn (1999) finds general support for the proposed contour model, with similarity driven primarily by contour relations between adjacent (i.e., temporally successive) tones and to a lesser extent by contour relations between nonadjacent tones.

Psychological Contour Models

Although the previous models clearly capture a sense of contour and can predict perceived similarity, they are limited in that they neglect an intuitively critical aspect of melodic contour—namely, the contour's overall shape. In an attempt to characterize this aspect of contour, Schmuckler (1999) proposed a contour description based on time series, and specifically Fourier analyses, of contour. Such analyses provide a powerful tool for describing contour in their quantification of different cyclical patterns within a signal. By considering the relative strengths of some or all of these cycles, such analyses thus describe the repetitive, up-and-down nature of the melody, simultaneously taking into account slow-moving, low-frequency pitch changes as well as high-frequency, point-to-point pitch fluctuation.

Schmuckler (1999) initially tested the applicability of time series analyses as a descriptor of melodic contour, looking at the prediction of perceived contour similarity. In two experiments listeners heard 12-note melodies, with these stimuli drawn either from the prime form of well-known 20th century pieces (Experiment 1) or from simple, tonal patterns (Experiment 2); samples of these melodies appear in Fig. 10. In both experiments listeners rated the complexity of each contour, and from these complexity ratings derived similarity measures were calculated. Although an indirect index, such measures do provide a reliable quantification of similarity (Kruskal & Wish, 1978; Wish & Carroll, 1974).

The derived similarity ratings were then compared with different models of contour similarity based on the time series and music-theoretic approaches. For the music-theoretic models, contour similarity was based on the degree of overlap between contours in their interval content and the overlap of short contour subsegments (e.g., sequences of 3, 4, 5, and so on notes). For the time series model, all contours were Fourier analyzed, with similarity determined by correspondences between melodies in the strength of each cyclical component (the amplitude spectra) and by the starting position in the cycle of each component (the

Experiment 1 Melodies   Experiment 2 Melodies

FIGURE 10   Sample 12-note stimuli from Schmuckler (1999). Experiment 1 employed the prime form of different well-known, 20th century 12-tone compositions. Experiment 2 employed simplistic tonal melodies composed explicitly to contain different cyclical patterns.

phase spectra); Schmuckler (1999) describes both quantifications and predictions in greater detail.

The success of the predictions of similarity ratings from both sets of models was consistent across the experiments. The music-theoretic models, based on both interval content and contour subsegments, failed to predict derived complexity similarity ratings. In contrast, the Fourier analysis model did predict similarity, with amplitude spectra correlating significantly in the first study and both amplitude and phase spectra correlating significantly in the second study.[3] Interestingly,

---

[3] The lack of consistency for phase spectra is intriguing, in that one of the differences between the two studies was that the stimuli of Experiment 2 were constructed specifically to contain different phase spectra similarities between melodies. Hence, this study suggests that phase information can be used by listeners when melodies explicitly highlight such phase relations. Whether listeners are sensitive to such information when it is not highlighted, however, is questionable.

and as an aside, neither experiment found any influence of the tonality of the melody on similarity. Although a lack of tonal effects seemingly belies the spirit of the previous section, this result is understandable in that both studies actively worked to ameliorate influences of tonality by randomly transposing melodies to different keys on every trial.

Although supporting the Fourier analysis model, this work has some important limitations. First, and most significantly, the stimuli used in this work were highly specialized, schematized melodies of equal length that contained no rhythmic variation. To be useful as a model of melodic perception, however, this approach must be applicable to melodies of differing lengths and note durations. Second, there is the issue of the use of the derived similarity measure. Although such a measure is psychometrically viable, it would be reassuring if such results could be obtained with a more direct measure of perceived similarity. Moreover, it is possible that even stronger predictive power might be seen if a direct measure were employed.

Research has addressed these questions, employing naturalistic folk melodies as stimuli and using a direct similarity rating procedure. Using melodies such as shown in Fig. 11, listeners rated the perceived similarity of pairs of melodies, with these ratings then compared with predicted similarity based on the Fourier analysis model. These melodies were coded for the Fourier analysis in two formats. The first, or *nondurational* coding, coded the relative pitch events in 0–n format (with 0 given to the lowest pitch event in the sequence and n equal to the number of distinct pitches), ignoring the different durations of the notes. This coding essentially makes the sequence equitemporal for the purpose of contour analysis. The second format, or *durational* coding, weights each element by its duration. Thus, if the first and highest pitch event were 3 beats, followed by the lowest pitch event for 1 beat, followed by the middle pitch event for 2 beats, the code for this contour would be $\langle 2\ 2\ 2\ 0\ 1\ 1 \rangle$; these two types of codings also appear in Fig. 11. These contour codes were Fourier analyzed, with correspondences in the resulting amplitude and phase spectra used to predict similarity.[4] Figure 12 shows the results of a Fourier analysis of the nondurational coding of two of these contexts.

Generally, the findings of this study confirmed those of Schmuckler (1999), with contour similarity based on corresponding amplitude (but not phase) spectra predicting listeners' perceived similarity. Interestingly, this study failed to find differences in predictive power between the two forms of contour coding. Such a finding suggests that it is not the correspondence of cyclical patterns in absolute time that is critical (as would be captured in the durational but not the nondurational code), but rather it is the cyclical patterns over the course of the melody

[4] Actually, it is an interesting problem how to compare melodies of different lengths. Melodies of different lengths produce amplitude and phase spectra with differing numbers of cyclical components. Unfortunately, a discussion of the issues involved here is beyond the scope of this chapter, but it should be recognized that, although difficult, such comparisons are possible.

Non-durational   1 2 3   3 2   1   2 2   3 2 1 2 3   3 2 2 1 2   3 2 1 0 1

Durational   11223333333322221111222222223322112233333333222211223322211001111

Non-durational   2 3 4 3 2 1 0   0 2 3 4 5 5 4 2 3 3 2   3 4 3 2   1 0 0 2 3   4 5 5 4 2   3

Durational   2223444322210000222344455422333322234443222100002224444554223333

Non-durational   1 2 3 3 1 1   0 0   1 2 3 3   3   1 2 1 2 3 3   1 1 0 0   1 3 3 3 2 2 1

Durational   1112333311110000111233333331222211123333111100001112333322221111

Non-durational   0   1 2 2 2   0 3 3 3   2 2 2 2   0 1 0 1 2 2 2   2 3 4 5 5   4 3 2 2 1 0

Durational   0001222222203333333222222220111100012222220333455554443221100000

FIGURE 11   A sample set of folk melodies used in the direct contour similarity study. Also shown are the nondurational and duration contour codings. For both codings, contours are coded for analysis in 0–n format, with n equal to the number of distinct pitches in the contour.

itself (which is captured equally well by both coding systems) regardless of the absolute length of the melody that is important. One implication here is that a very short and a very long melody having comparable contours will be heard as similar despite the differences in their lengths. Such a finding has not been explicitly tested to date but, if true, implies that the melodies could be represented in a somewhat abstract fashion in which only relative timing between events is retained. This idea, in fact, fits well with the intuition that a melody retains its essential properties irrespective of its time scale, with some obvious limits at the extremes.

Non-durational   1 2 3   3 2 1   2 2 3 2 1 2 3   3 2 2 1 2 3 2 1 0 1

		A_m	B_m	R_m	M_m
Harmonic	1	0.1872	-0.0690	0.1995	0.3531
Harmonic	2	-0.0914	0.1794	0.2013	1.0996
Harmonic	3	0.1674	-0.1210	0.2066	0.6259
Harmonic	4	-0.2329	0.2987	0.3788	0.9085
Harmonic	5	-0.1061	0.1401	0.1757	0.9224
Harmonic	6	0.0855	-0.0122	0.0863	0.1423
Harmonic	7	-0.0173	0.1222	0.1234	1.4301
Harmonic	8	0.0082	0.0688	0.0693	-1.4517
Harmonic	9	-0.0064	0.0028	0.0070	0.4149
Harmonic	10	0.0601	-0.1242	0.1380	1.1202
Harmonic	11	-0.0108	0.0009	0.0108	0.0833

Non-durational   2 3 4 3 2 1 0 0 2 3 4 5 5 4 2 3 3 2 3 4 3 2 1 0 0 2 3 4 5 5 4 2 3

		A_m	B_m	R_m	M_m
Harmonic	1	0.0148	-0.0168	0.0224	0.8491
Harmonic	2	0.3822	-0.5432	0.6641	0.9576
Harmonic	3	-0.0758	0.0797	0.1100	0.8106
Harmonic	4	-0.5664	0.4493	0.7230	0.6706
Harmonic	5	0.0818	-0.0632	0.1033	0.6577
Harmonic	6	-0.0254	-0.0381	0.0458	-0.9830
Harmonic	7	0.0698	-0.0276	0.0750	0.3769
Harmonic	8	0.0896	-0.0012	0.0896	0.0131
Harmonic	9	0.0387	-0.0708	0.0807	1.0701
Harmonic	10	0.0921	-0.1769	0.1994	1.0906
Harmonic	11	0.0152	0.0262	0.0303	-1.0472
Harmonic	12	0.0877	-0.0477	0.0999	0.4980
Harmonic	13	-0.0264	-0.0057	0.0270	-0.2146
Harmonic	14	0.0325	-0.0907	0.0964	1.2264
Harmonic	15	-0.0404	0.0509	0.0650	0.8995
Harmonic	16	-0.0184	-0.0282	0.0337	-0.9911

FIGURE 12   Fourier analysis results for two of the sample contours. This table lists the real (A_m), imaginary (B_m), amplitude (R_m), and phase (M_m) values for each cyclical component of the contour. Similarity between contours can be assessed by correlating amplitude and phase values, calculating absolute difference scores, and so on; see Schmuckler (1999) for a fuller description.

Summary of Contour Models

The previous sections described two alternative proposals for the organization of pitch material in time. Although one might assume these two approaches to be mutually exclusive, there is actually no reason why both models could not be simultaneously operative in contour perception. Of course, one problem for any rapprochement between these views is that they do not necessarily make the same predictions for perceived contour similarity; Schmuckler (1999), for example, found little correspondence between the various music-theoretical and time series predictions.

There are two answers to this concern. First, neither of these models explains all of the variance in perceived contour similarity. Thus, it is possible that contour perception is a weighted combination of multiple approaches, one not fully explainable by a single model. Second, it might be that the approaches of Quinn (1999) and Schmuckler (1999) are most applicable to contexts of different lengths. Quinn's (1999) approach, which quantifies the interval content of melodies, is quite powerful when applied to short contours in which interval content may be especially noticeable. However, because interval content increases exponentially with each note added to a contour, longer contours would place increasingly heavy demands on processing and memory of interval information. Moreover, contour descriptions would become correspondingly homogenized with increasing length, resulting in less differentiated descriptions. Accordingly, this model probably loses its power to discriminate contours as length increases.

In contrast, Schmuckler's (1999) time series model has the opposite problem. When applied to longer contours this model produces multiple cyclic components that are quite useful in characterizing the contour. Although it is unclear how many components are necessary for an adequate description, there nevertheless remains a wealth of information available. However, because the number of cyclical components produced by Fourier analysis equals the length of the sequence divided by two, short contours will contain only a few cycles and will thus be poorly described. Accordingly, this model loses discriminative power as contour length decreases.

These two approaches, then, might be complementary, with Quinn's (1999) model predicting perception of short contours and Schmuckler's (1999) model applicable to longer contours. It remains to be seen whether this prediction is borne out and, if it is, at what length the predictive powers of the two models reverse. Moreover, this hypothesis raises the intriguing possibility of a region in which the two models are both operative; such a region has a number of interesting implications for the processing and memory of musical passages.

ORGANIZATION OF PITCH IN SPACE AND TIME

One concern raised initially was that, although pitch organization in space and time could be discussed independently, this division is nevertheless forced. Obviously, there is an important interplay between these two aspects of auditory events, with factors promoting organization in one dimension clearly influencing organization in the other dimension. A classic example of this interrelation is provided in research on auditory stream segregation (e.g., Bregman, 1990; Bregman & Campbell, 1973; Bregman & Dannenbring, 1973; Miller & Heise, 1950; Van Noorden, 1975). Although this topic is explored in depth elsewhere in this book (Chap. 2), and so will not be focused on here, one important finding from this research involves the complex interchange between the rate at which pitch elements are presented and the frequency difference between these elements, with both factors simultaneously influencing perceptual organization.

Thus, the preceding discussions of pitch organization in space and time would be incomplete without some consideration of the integration of pitch organization in space and time. It is worth noting that, although not a great deal of attention has been paid to this topic, there are some notable precedents for a focus on organizing pitch in space and time. Jones and colleagues, for example, have been concerned with this topic for a number of years (see Chap. 3 for a review). In this work Jones has proposed a dynamic model of attending (Barnes & Jones, 2000; Boltz, 1989, 1993; Jones, 1993; Jones & Boltz, 1989; Jones, Boltz, & Klein, 1982, 1993; Large & Jones, 2000) in which one's expectancies for, and attention to, future events in space–time are driven by explicit space–time parameters of the context pattern. Thus, listeners use a pattern's temporal layout, along with the range of the pitch events, to track and anticipate when future events will occur as well as what these future events might be (Barnes & Jones, 2000; Jones, 1976). In general, this model has successfully predicted attention to and memory for auditory sequences, and although there remain some open questions here (e.g., the weighting of space and time parameters, or how variations in one component, say pitch range, influence variations in temporal expectancies, and vice versa), this work nevertheless represents an innovative approach to integrating space–time organizations in auditory processing.

An alternative, or at least complementary, approach to integrating space and time pitch organizations might involve coordinating the model of tonal relations (the Krumhansl–Schmuckler key-finding algorithm) with the model of contour information (Schmuckler, 1999). In fact, the recognition of the fundamental roles played by tonality and contour in music cognition is not new; Dowling (1978), in a seminal paper, identified these two factors as the basic building blocks of melodic perception. Thus, the real innovation in the current work is not the identification of these components but rather the formal quantification of these factors afforded by these models that allows the measurement of their independent and interactive influences on musical perception and memory. For example, with these models it is possible to determine the relative influences of tonality and contour on simple, undirected percepts of music. In the same vein, it is possible to examine selective attention to one or the other dimension by looking at listeners' abilities to use that dimension solely as a basis for judgments about a passage. Such work provides parallels to research on the primacy of auditory dimensions in perceiving single tones (e.g., Melara & Marks, 1990); in this case, however, the question involves the primacy, or integrality versus separability, of large-scale musical dimensions.

Finally, it is possible to determine how these dimensions function in different musical contexts. What are the relative roles of tonality and contour in the perceptual organization of passages, or in auditory object formation, versus, say, the perceived similarity of musical passages? What are their roles in driving expectancies or in structuring memory for passages? Clearly, integrating these two sources of pitch structure provides a new, and potentially powerful, means for understanding auditory and musical events.

SUMMARY AND FINAL THOUGHTS

Although many of the ideas *vis-à-vis* pitch in this chapter have been worked out and presented relative to musical structure, it should be realized that the concepts developed here are applicable to auditory events more generally. Nonmusical environmental sounds, for example, can be characterized by their contour. And contour certainly plays a crucial role in one's understanding of speech, although work on the prosody of speech (e.g., Hirschberg, 2002; Ladd, 1996; Selkirk, 1984) has focused not on large-scale contour but instead on local effects such as the use of prosodic cues for signaling questions (Nagel, Shapiro, & Nawy, 1994; Straub, Wilson, McCollum, & Badecker, 2001). Moreover, many environmental sounds, including speech and language, have tonal properties, although none contain the type of structure found in musical contexts. Nevertheless, it is an interesting idea to attempt to delineate the nature and/or form of any tonal structure, if present, in such environmental contexts.

Pulling back for a minute, it is clear that although this chapter has accomplished one of its initial goals—providing an overview to pitch and pitch perception—its second goal—the delineation of an ecological perspective on pitch and pitch perception—has, as originally feared, remained elusive. Fortunately, there have been a few themes running throughout this chapter that are relevant to this issue, and it is worth highlighting these ideas. First, there is the importance of considering the environmental context for understanding pitch perception. In music cognition, the importance of context has resulted in a trend toward the use of realistic musical passages as stimuli (as opposed to the short, artificial sequences that had previously dominated the field) and the adoption of real-time responses and dynamical models (e.g., Krumhansl & Toiviainen, 2000; Toiviainen & Krumhansl, 2003). In terms of its relevance to ecological theory, even though this focus on perception "in the environment" is not a particularly deep or illuminating perspective on ecological acoustics, it is nevertheless important in that one of the ecological approach's most important lessons involved its situating perception within more general, goal-directed behavior in the complex environment. Such an approach has implications for how one characterizes the perceptual apparatus itself (Gibson, 1966) as well as how one describes the environment with reference to the capabilities of the animal.

Along with the contextual nature of pitch perception, there has also been an emphasis on the perceptual structures formed as a result of the operation of perceptual constraints (e.g., Balzano, 1986). Such constraints may, in fact, be operating to create different invariant structures critical for auditory and musical processing, with the question then centered around listeners' sensitivity to such invariant information. This review has identified at least two different constraints in the perception of pitch—that of tonality[5] and that of contour. Whether or not these two aspects are truly ecological invariants, in the same way that the cardiodal strain transformation is for the perception of aging (e.g., Pittenger, Shaw, & Mark, 1979; Shaw, McIntyre, & Mace, 1974; Shaw & Pittenger, 1977) or the cross ratio is for perceiving rigidity (e.g., Cutting, 1986; Gibson, 1950; Johansson, von Hofsten, & Jansson, 1980), is an open, and ultimately metatheoretical question. For the moment it is sufficient to recognize the potential role of such abstractions as general organizing principles for the apprehension of musical structure.

A final implication of much of the material discussed here, and clearly the ideas presented in the sections on pitch structures, is that much of this work actually provides support for some of Gibson's more radical ideas, namely the argument for direct perception and for naïve realism (Cutting, 1986; Gibson, 1967, 1972, 1973; Lombardo, 1987). Although these notions have a variety of meanings (see Cutting, 1986, or Lombardo, 1987, for discussions), some underlying themes that arise from these ideas are that perception is not mediated by inference or other cognitive processes and that perception is essentially veridical. Although it might, at first blush, appear somewhat odd and contradictory, both the key-finding and contour models fit well with these ideas as they place the critical information for the detection of these structures within the stimulus patterns themselves (e.g., patterns of relative durations of notes and cyclical patterns of rises and falls in pitch), without the need for cognitively mediating mechanisms to apprehend these structures.

Music cognition research in general has been quite concerned with specifying the information that is available in the stimulus itself, often employing sophisticated analytic procedures in an attempt to quantify this structure (e.g., Huron, 1995, 1997, 1999). Moreover, music cognition work has benefited greatly from a close association with its allied disciplines of musicology and music theory, which have provided a continuing source of sophisticated, well-developed ideas about the structure that is actually present in the musical stimulus itself. Intriguingly,

---

[5] One concern with the idea of tonality as an invariant is that the details of tonal hierarchies vary from culture to culture. In this regard, it is reassuring to see the results of cross-cultural investigations of tonality (e.g., Castellano et al., 1984; Kessler et al., 1984, reviewed earlier) reaffirm the general importance of hierarchical organization in perceptual processing of musical passages, irrespective of the specific details of the composition of the hierarchy.

despite the fact that music research spends an inordinate amount of time and energy analyzing and specifying its stimulus structure, work in this vein has not, as with the ecological approach, seen fit to deny either the existence or importance of internal representation. One implication of such a situation, and in a deviation away from traditional orthodoxy in the ecological approach, is that it is at least conceivable to suggest that simply because the perceptual apprehension of complex stimulus structure might not require the use of internal representation does not mean that such representations either do not exist or have no place in perceptual and cognitive processing. Determining the form of such representations, and the situations in which the information contained within such structures may come into play, is a worthwhile goal.

Of course, the preceding discussions really only scratch the surface of an attempt to delineate an ecological approach to pitch perception. Audition is typically the weaker sibling in discussions of perception, and hence theoretical innovations that have been worked out for other areas (i.e., vision) are often not easily or obviously transplantable to new contexts. One possible avenue for future thought in this regard is to turn one's attention to how ecological theory might be expanded to incorporate the experience of hearing music, as opposed to the reinterpretation (and sometimes deformation) of musical experience and research to fit into the existing tenets of the ecological approach. How, then, might ecological psychology be modified, extended, or even reformulated to be more relevant to the very cognitive (and ecologically valid) behavior of music listening? The hope, of course, is that extending the scope of both contexts will ultimately provide greater insights into the theoretical framework of interest (the ecological perspective) as well as the particular content area at hand (auditory perception).

ACKNOWLEDGMENTS

Much of the work described in this chapter and preparation of the manuscript were supported by a grant from the Natural Sciences and Engineering Research Council of Canada to the author. The author would like to thank Katalin Dzinas for many helpful discussions about this chapter and Carol Krumhansl and John Neuhoff for their insightful comments and suggestions on an earlier draft of this work.

REFERENCES

Adolph, K. E., Eppler, M. A., & Gibson, E. J. (1993). Development of perception of affordances. In C. Rovee-Collier and L. P. Lipsett (Eds.), *Advances in infancy research* (Vol. 8, pp. 51–98). Norwood: Ablex.

Balzano, G. J. (1986). Music perception as detection of pitch-time constraints. In V. McCabe and G. J. Balzano (Eds.), *Event cognition: An ecological perspective* (pp. 217–233). Mahweh, NJ: Lawrence Erlbaum Associates.

Barnes, R., & Jones, M. R. (2000). Expectancy, attention, and time. *Cognitive Psychology, 41,* 254–311.

Benjamin, W. E. (1984). A theory of musical meter. *Music Perception, 1*, 355–413.

Boltz, M. (1989). Rhythm and "good endings": Effects of temporal structure on tonality judgments. *Perception and Psychophysics, 46*, 9–17.

Boltz, M. (1993). The generation of temporal and melodic expectancies during musical listening. *Perception and Psychophysics, 53*, 585–600.

Bregman, A. S. (1990). *Auditory scene analysis: The perceptual organization of sound*. Cambridge, MA: MIT Press.

Bregman, A. S., & Campbell, J. (1973). Primary auditory stream segregation and perception of order in rapid sequences of tones. *Journal of Experimental Psychology, 89*, 244–249.

Bregman, A. S., & Dannenbring, G. L. (1973). The effect of continuity on auditory stream segregation. *Perception and Psychophysics, 13*, 308–312.

Brown, H. (1988). The interplay of set content and temporal context in a functional theory of tonality perception. *Music Perception, 5*, 219–249.

Brown, H., & Butler, D. (1981). Diatonic trichords as minimal tonal cue-cells. *In Theory Only, 5*, 37–55.

Brown, H., Butler, D., & Jones, M. R. (1994). Musical and temporal influences on key discovery. *Music Perception, 11*, 371–407.

Browne, R. (1981). Tonal implications of the diatonic set. *In Theory Only, 5*, 3–21.

Bruce, V., & Green, P. (1985). *Visual perception: Physiology, psychology and ecology*. Hillsdale, NJ: Lawrence Erlbaum Associates.

Butler, D. (1989). Describing the perception of tonality in music: A critique of the tonal hierarchy theory and a proposal for a theory of intervallic rivalry. *Music Perception, 6*, 219–241.

Butler, D. (1990). A study of event hierarchies in tonal and post-tonal music. *Music Perception, 18*, 4–17.

Butler, D., & Brown, H. (1984). Tonal structure versus function: Studies of the recognition of harmonic motion. *Music Perception, 2*, 6–24.

Butler, D., & Brown, H. (1994). Describing the mental representation of tonality in music. In R. Aiello and J. A. Sloboda (Eds.), *Musical perceptions* (pp. 191–212). London: Oxford University Press.

Carlsen, J. C. (1981). Some factors which influence melodic expectancy. *Psychomusicology, 1*, 12–29.

Carlsen, J. C. (1982). Musical expectancy: Some perspectives. *Council for Research in Music Education, 71*, 4–14.

Carlsen, J. C., Divenyi, P., & Taylor, J. A. (1970). A preliminary study of perceptual expectancy in melodic configurations. *Council for Research in Music Education, 22*, 4–12.

Castellano, M. A., Bharucha, J. J., & Krumhansl, C. L. (1984). Tonal hierarchies in the music of North India. *Journal of Experimental Psychology, 113*, 394–376.

Cohen, A. J. (2000). Development of tonality induction: Plasticity, exposure, and training. *Music Perception, 17*, 437–460.

Cohen, E. J. (1962). Information theory and music. *Behavioral Science, 7*, 137–163.

Coons, E., & Kraehenbuehl, D. (1958). Information theory as a measure of structure in music. *Journal of Music Theory, 2*, 127–161.

Cooper, G., & Meyer, L. B. (1960). *The rhythmic structure of music*. Chicago: Chicago University Press.

Cuddy, L. L., & Badertscher, B. (1987). Recovery of the tonal hierarchy: Some comparisons across age and levels of musical experience. *Perception and Psychophysics, 41*, 609–620.

Cuddy, L. L., & Lunney, C. A. (1995). Expectancies generated by melodic intervals: Perceptual judgments of melodic continuity. *Perception and Psychophysics, 57*, 451–462.

Cutting, J. E. (1986). *Perception with an eye for motion*. Cambridge, MA: MIT Press.

Cutting, J. E., & Proffitt, D. R. (1981). Gait perception as an example of how we may perceive events. In R. D. Walk and H. L. Pick, Jr. (Eds.), *Intersensory perception and sensory integration* (pp. 249–273). New York: Plenum.

Dai, H. (2000). On the relative influence of individual harmonics on pitch judgement. *Journal of the Acoustical Society of America, 107*, 953–959.

Dawe, L. A., Platt, J. R., & Welsh, E. (1998). Spectral-motion aftereffects and the tritone paradox among Canadian subjects. *Perception and Psychophysics*, *60*, 209–220.

Deliège, I. (1987). Grouping conditions in listening to music: An approach to Lerdahl & Jackendoff's grouping preference rules. *Music Perception*, *4*, 325–360.

Deutsch, D. (1969). Music recognition. *Psychological Review*, *76*, 300–307.

Deutsch, D. (1972a). Effect of repetition of standard and comparison tones on recognition memory for pitch. *Journal of Experimental Psychology*, *93*, 156–162.

Deutsch, D. (1972b). Mapping of pitch interactions in the pitch memory store. *Science*, *175*, 1020–1022.

Deutsch, D. (1972c). Octave generalization and tune recognition. *Perception and Psychophysics*, *11*, 411–412.

Deutsch, D. (1973a). Interference in memory between tones adjacent in the musical scale. *Journal of Experimental Psychology*, *100*, 228–231.

Deutsch, D. (1973b). Octave generalization of specific interference effects in memory for tonal pitch. *Perception and Psychophysics*, *11*, 411–412.

Deutsch, D. (1980). The processing of structured and unstructured tonal sequences. *Perception and Psychophysics*, *28*, 381–389.

Deutsch, D. (1982a). The influence of melodic context on pitch recognition judgment. *Perception and Psychophysics*, *31*(407–410).

Deutsch, D. (1982b). The processing of pitch combinations. In D. Deutsch (Ed.), *Psychology of music* (pp. 271–316). New York: Academic Press.

Deutsch, D. (1986a). A musical paradox. *Music Perception*, *3*, 27–280.

Deutsch, D. (1986b). Recognition of durations embedded in temporal patterns. *Perception and Psychophysics*, *39*, 179–186.

Deutsch, D. (1987). The tritone paradox: Effects of spectral variables. *Perception and Psychophysics*, *41*, 563–575.

Deutsch, D. (1991). The tritone paradox: An influence of language on music perception. *Music Perception*, *8*, 335–347.

Deutsch, D. (1994). The tritone paradox: Some further geographical correlates. *Music Perception*, *12*, 125–136.

Deutsch, D. (1997). The tritone paradox: A link between music and speech. *Current Directions in Psychological Science*, *6*, 174–180.

Deutsch, D. (Ed.). (1999). *The psychology of music* (2nd ed.). San Diego: Academic Press.

Deutsch, D., & Feroe, J. (1981). The internal representation of pitch sequences in tonal music. *Psychological Review*, *88*, 503–522.

Deutsch, D., Kuyper, W. L., & Fisher, Y. (1987). The tritone paradox: Its presence and form of distribution in a general population. *Music Perception*, *5*, 79–92.

Deutsch, D., North, T., & Ray, L. (1990). The tritone paradox: Correlate with the listener's vocal range for speech. *Music Perception*, *7*, 371–384.

Dewar, K. M., Cuddy, L. L., & Mewhort, D. J. (1977). Recognition memory for single tones with and without context. *Journal of Experimental Psychology: Human Learning and Memory*, *3*, 60–67.

Dibben, N. (1994). The cognitive reality of hierarchic structure in tonal and atonal music. *Music Perception*, *12*, 1–26.

Dowling, W. J. (1978). Scale and contour: Two components of a theory of memory for melodies. *Psychological Review*, *85*, 341–354.

Dowling, W. J. (2001). Perception of music. In E. B. Goldstein (Ed.), *Blackwell handbook of perception* (pp. 469–498). Oxford: Blackwell Publishers.

Dowling, W. J., & Harwood, D. (1986). *Music cognition*. Orlando, FL: Academic Press.

Dowling, W. J., & Hollombe, A. W. (1977). The perception of melodies distorted by splitting into octaves: Effects of increasing proximity and melodic contour. *Perception and Psychophysics*, *21*, 60–64.

Fletcher, H., & Munson, W. A. (1933). Loudness, its definition, measurement and calculation. *Journal of the Acoustical Society of America, 5*, 82–108.

Fowler, C. A., & Dekle, D. J. (1991). Listening with eye and hand: Cross-modal contributions to speech perception. *Journal of Experimental Psychology: Human Perception and Performance, 17*, 816–828.

Fowler, C. A., & Rosenblum, L. D. (1991). Perception of the phonetic gesture. In I. G. Mattingly and M. Studdert-Kennedy (Eds.), *Modularity and the motor theory* (pp. 33–50). Hillsdale, NJ: Lawrence Erlbaum Associates.

Frankland, B. W., & Cohen, A. J. (1996). Using the Krumhansl and Schmuckler key-finding algorithm to quantify the effects of tonality in the interpolated-tone pitch-comparison task. *Music Perception, 14*, 57–83.

Friedmann, M. L. (1985). A methodology for the discussion of contour: Its application to Schoenberg's music. *Journal of Music Theory, 29*, 223–248.

Friedmann, M. L. (1987). My contour, their contour. *Journal of Music Theory, 31*, 268–274.

Giangrande, J. (1998). The tritone paradox: Effects of pitch class and position in the spectral envelope. *Music Perception, 15*, 23–264.

Gibson, E. J. (1969). *Principles of perceptual learning and development.* New York: Appleton Century Crofts.

Gibson, E. J. (1982). The concept of affordances in development: The renascence of functionalism. In W. A. Collins (Ed.), *The concept of development: The Minnesota symposia on child psychology* (Vol. 15, pp. 55–81). Hillsdale, NJ: Lawrence Erlbaum Associates.

Gibson, E. J. (1984). Perceptual development from the ecological approach. In M. E. Lamb, A. L. Brown, and B. Rogoff (Eds.), *Advances in developmental psychology* (vol. 3, pp. 243–286). Hillsdale, NJ: Lawrence Erlbaum Associates.

Gibson, E. J., & Pick, A. D. (2000). *An ecological approach to perceptual learning and development.* New York: Oxford University Press.

Gibson, E. J., & Spelke, E. S. (1983). The development of perception. In J. H. Flavell and E. M. Markman (Eds.), *Handbook of child psychology: Vol. III, Cognitive development* (pp. 1–76). New York: John Wiley & Sons.

Gibson, J. J. (1950). *The perception of the visual world.* Boston: Houghton Mifflin.

Gibson, J. J. (1960). The concept of the stimulus in psychology. *American Psychologist, 15*, 694–703.

Gibson, J. J. (1961). Ecological optics. *Vision Research, 1*, 253–262.

Gibson, J. J. (1966). *The senses considered as perceptual systems.* Boston: Houghton Mifflin.

Gibson, J. J. (1967). New reasons for realism. *Synthese, 17*, 162–172.

Gibson, J. J. (1972). A theory of direct visual perception. In J. R. Royce and W. W. Rozeboom (Eds.), *The psychology of knowing* (pp. 215–240). New York: Gordon & Breach.

Gibson, J. J. (1973). Direct visual perception: A rely to Gyr. *Psychological Bulletin, 79*, 396–397.

Gibson, J. J. (1975). Events are perceivable but time is not. In J. T. Fraser and N. Lawrence (Eds.), *The study of time, II* (pp. 295–301). New York: Springer-Verlag.

Gibson, J. J. (1979). *The ecological approach to visual perception.* Boston: Houghton Mifflin.

Grau, W. J., & Kemler Nelson, D. G. (1988). The distinction between integral and separable dimensions: Evidence for the integrality of pitch and loudness. *Journal of Experimental Psychology: Human Perception and Performance, 117*, 347–370.

Handel, S. (1989). *Listening: An introduction to the perception of auditory events.* Cambridge, MA: MIT Press.

Hartmann, W. M. (1996). Pitch, periodicity, and auditory organization. *Journal of the Acoustical Society of America, 100*, 3491–3502.

Helmholtz, H. L. F. (1885/1954). *On the sensations of tone.* New York: Dover Publications.

Hirschberg, J. (2002). Communication and prosody: Functional aspects of prosody. *Speech Communication, 36*, 31–43.

House, W. J. (1977). Octave generalization and the identification of distorted melodies. *Perception and Psychophysics, 21*, 586–589.

Huron, D. (1995). *The Humdrum toolkit: Reference manual*. Stanford, CA: Center for Computer Assisted Research in the Humanities.

Huron, D. (1997). Humdrum and Kern: Selective feature encoding. In E. Selfridge-Field (Ed.), *Beyond MIDI: The handbook of musical codes* (pp. 375–401). Cambridge, MA: MIT Press.

Huron, D. (1999). *Music research using Humdrum: A user's guide*. Stanford, CA: Center for Computer Assisted Research in the Humanities.

Huron, D., & Parncutt, R. (1993). An improved model of tonality perception incorporating pitch salience and echoic memory. *Psychomusicology, 12*, 154–171.

Idson, W. L., & Massaro, D. W. (1978). A bidimensional model of pitch in the recognition of melodies. *Perception and Psychophysics, 24*, 551–565.

Irwin, R. J., & Terman, M. (1970). Detection of brief tones in noise by rats. *Journal of the Experimental Analysis of Behavior, 13*, 135–143.

Johansson, G. (1973). Visual perception of biological motion and a model for its analysis. *Perception and Psychophysics, 14*, 201–211.

Johansson, G. (1975). Visual motion perception. *Scientific American, 232*, 76–89.

Johansson, G., von Hofsten, C., & Jansson, G. (1980). Event perception. *Annual Review of Psychology, 31*, 27–66.

Jones, M. R. (1976). Time, our lost dimension: Toward a new theory of perception, attention, and memory. *Psychological Review, 83*, 323–345.

Jones, M. R. (1981). A tutorial on some issues and methods in serial pattern research. *Perception and Psychophysics, 30*, 492–504.

Jones, M. R. (1993). Dynamics of musical patterns: How do melody and rhythm fit together •• In T. J. Tighe and W. J. Dowling (Eds.), *Psychology and music: The understanding of melody and rhythm* (pp. 67–92). Hillsdale, NJ: Lawrence Erlbaum Associates.

Jones, M. R., & Boltz, M. (1989). Dynamic attending and responses to time. *Psychological Review, 96*, 459–491.

Jones, M. R., Boltz, M., & Kidd, G. (1982). Controlled attending as a function of melodic and temporal context. *Perception and Psychophysics, 32*, 211–218.

Jones, M. R., Boltz, M., & Klein, J. M. (1993). Expected endings and judged durations. *Memory and Cognition, 21*, 646–665.

Jones, M. R., & Hahn, J. (1986). Invariants in sound. In V. McCabe, and G. J. Balzano (Eds.), *Event cognition: An ecological perspective* (pp. 197–215). Mahweh, NJ: Lawrence Erlbaum Associates.

Jones, M. R., Maser, D. J., & Kidd, G. R. (1978). Rate and structure in memory for auditory patterns. *Memory and Cognition, 6*, 246–258.

Justus, T. C., & Bharucha, J. J. (2002). Music perception and cognition. In S. Yantis (Ed.), *Stevens handbook of experimental psychology* (3rd ed., vol. 1: *Sensation and perception*, pp. 453–492). New York: John Wiley & Sons.

Kallman, H. J. (1982). Octave equivalence as measured by similarity ratings. *Perception and Psychophysics, 32*, 37–49.

Kallman, H. J., & Massaro, D. W. (1979). Tone chroma is functional in melody recognition. *Perception and Psychophysics, 26*, 32–36.

Kessler, E. J., Hansen, C., & Shepard, R. N. (1984). Tonal schemata in the perception of music in Bali and in the West. *Music Perception, 2*, 131–165.

Knopoff, L., & Hutchinson, W. (1981). Information theory for musical continua. *Journal of Music Theory, 25*, 17–44.

Knopoff, L., & Hutchinson, W. (1983). Entropy as a measure of style: The influence of sample length. *Journal of Music Theory, 27*, 75–97.

Kraehenbuehl, D., & Coons, E. (1959). Information as a measure of the experience of music. *Journal of Aesthetics and Art Criticism, 17*, 510–522.

Krumbholz, K., Patterson, R. D., & Pressnitzer, D. (2000). The lower limit of pitch as determined by rate discrimination. *Journal of the Acoustical Society of America, 108*, 1170–1180.

Krumhansl, C. L. (1979). The psychological representation of musical pitch in a tonal context. *Cognitive Psychology, 11*, 346–374.

Krumhansl, C. L. (1990). *Cognitive foundation of musical pitch.* London: Oxford University Press.

Krumhansl, C. L. (1991). Music psychology: Tonal structures in perception and memory. *Annual Review of Psychology, 42*, 277–303.

Krumhansl, C. L. (1995). Music psychology and music theory: Problems and prospects. *Music Theory Spectrum, 17*, 53–80.

Krumhansl, C. L. (2000a). Rhythm and pitch in music cognition. *Psychological Bulletin, 126*, 159–179.

Krumhansl, C. L. (2000b). Tonality induction: A statistical approach applied cross-culturally. *Music Perception, 17*, 461–480.

Krumhansl, C. L., & Iverson, P. (1992). Perceptual interactions between musical pitch and timbre. *Journal of Experimental Psychology: Human Perception and Performance, 18*, 739–751.

Krumhansl, C. L., & Kessler, E. J. (1982). Tracing the dynamic changes in perceived tonal organization in a spatial representation of musical keys. *Psychological Review, 89*, 334–368.

Krumhansl, C. L., Sandell, G. J., & Sargeant, D. C. (1987). The perception of tone hierarchies and mirror forms in twelve-tone serial music. *Music Perception, 5*, 31–78.

Krumhansl, C. L., & Schmuckler, M. A. (1986a). *Key-finding in music: An algorithm based on pattern matching to tonal hierarchies.* Paper presented at the 19th annual Mathematical Psychology Meeting, Cambridge, MA.

Krumhansl, C. L., & Schmuckler, M. A. (1986b). The *Petroushka* chord: A perceptual investigation. *Music Perception, 4*, 153–184.

Krumhansl, C. L., & Shepard R. N. (1979). Quantification of the hierarchy of tonal functions within a diatonic context. Journal of Experimental Psychology Human Perception & Performance, *5*(4), Nov 579–594.

Krumhansl, C. L., & Toiviainen, P. (2000). Dynamics of tonality induction: A new method and a new model. In C. Woods, B. B. Luck, R. Rochard, S. A. O'Neil, and J. A. Sloboda (Eds.), *Proceedings of the Sixth International Conference on Music Perception.* Keele, Staffordshire, UK.

Krumhansl, C. L., & Toiviainen, P. (2001). Tonal cognition. *Annals of the New York Academy of Sciences, 930*, 77–91.

Kruskal, J. B., & Wish, M. (1978). *Multidimensional scaling.* Beverley Hills, CA: Sage Publications.

Ladd, D. R. (1996). *Intonational phonology.* Cambridge, England: Cambridge University Press.

Lantz, M. E. (2002). *The role of duration and frequency of occurrence in perceived pitch structure.* Queen's University, Kingston, ON, Canada.

Lantz, M. E., & Cuddy, L. L. (1998). Total and relative duration as cues to surface structure in music. *Canadian Acoustics, 26*, 56–57.

Large, E. W., & Jones, M. R. (2000). The dynamics of attending: How we track time varying events. *Psychological Review, 106*, 119–159.

Large, E. W., & Palmer, C. (2002). Perceiving temporal regularity in music. *Cognitive Science, 26*, 1–37.

Lerdahl, F., & Jackendoff, R. (1983). *A generative theory of tonal music.* Cambridge, MA: MIT Press.

Lewin, D. (1984). On formal intervals between time-spans. *Music Perception, 1*, 414–423.

Lombardo, T. J. (1987). *The reciprocity of perceiver and environment: The evolution of James J. Gibson's ecological psychology.* Hillsdale, NJ: Lawrence Erlbaum Associates.

Marvin, E. W., & Laprade, P. A. (1987). Relating musical contours: Extensions of a theory for contour. *Journal of Music Theory, 31*, 225–267.

McAdams, S., & Bigand, E. (Eds.). (1993). *Thinking in sound: The cognitive psychology of human audition.* Oxford, UK: Oxford University Press.

McAdams, S., & Drake, C. (2002). Auditory perception and cognition. In S. Yantis (Ed.), *Stevens' handbook of experimental psychology* (vol. 1: *Sensation and perception*, pp. 397–452). New York: John Wiley & Sons.

McCabe, V. (1986). Memory for meaning: The ecological use of language. In V. McCabe, and G. J. Balzano (Eds.), *Event cognition: An ecological perspective* (pp. 175–191). Mahweh, NJ: Lawrence Erlbaum Associates.

Melara, R. D., & Marks, L. E. (1990). Perceptual primacy of dimensions: Support for a model of dimensional interaction. *Journal of Experimental Psychology: Human Perception and Performance, 16*, 398–414.

Michaels, C. F., & Carello, C. (1981). *Direct perception.* Englewood Cliffs, NJ: Prentice-Hall.

Miller, G. A., & Heise, G. A. (1950). The trill threshold. *Journal of the Acoustical Society of America, 22*, 167–173.

Moore, B. C. J. (1993). Frequency analysis and pitch perception. In W. A. Yost, A. N. Popper, and R. R. Fay (Eds.), *Human psychophysics* (pp. 56–115). New York: Springer-Verlag.

Moore, B. C. J. (2001a). Basic auditory processes. In E. B. Goldstein (Ed.), *Blackwell handbook of perception* (pp. 379–407). Oxford, UK: Blackwell Publishers.

Moore, B. C. J. (2001b). Loudness, pitch and timbre. In E. B. Goldstein (Ed.), *Blackwell handbook of perception* (pp. 408–436). Oxford, UK: Blackwell Publishing.

Nagel, H. N., Shapiro, L., & Nawy, R. (1994). Prosody and the processing of filler-gap dependencies. *Journal of Psycholinguistic Research, 23*, 473–485.

Narmour, E. (1989). The "genetic code" of melody: Cognitive structures generated by the implication-realization model. *Contemporary Music Review, 4*, 45–63.

Narmour, E. (1990). *The analysis and cognition of basic melodic structures.* Chicago: University of Chicago Press.

Narmour, E. (1992). *The analysis and cognition of melodic complexity.* Chicago: University of Chicago Press.

Olsho, L. W., Schoon, C., Sakai, R., Turpin, R., & Sperduto, V. (1982). Preliminary data on auditory frequency discrimination. *Journal of the Acoustical Society of America, 71*, 509–511.

Oram, N., & Cuddy, L. L. (1995). Responsiveness of Western adults to pitch-distributional information in melodic sequences. *Psychological Research, 57*, 103–118.

Palmer, C., & Krumhansl, C. L. (1987a). Independent temporal and pitch structures in determination of musical phrases. *Journal of Experimental Psychology: Human Perception and Performance, 13*, 116–126.

Palmer, C., & Krumhansl, C. L. (1987b). Pitch and temporal contributions to musical phrases: Effects of harmony, performance timing, and familiarity. *Perception and Psychophysics, 51*, 505–518.

Patterson, R. D., Peters, R. W., & Milroy, R. (1983). Threshold duration for melodic pitch. In W. Klinke, and W. M. Hartmann (Eds.), *Hearing: Physiological bases and psychophysics* (pp. 321–325). Berlin: Springer-Verlag.

Pierce, J. R. (1983). *The science of musical sound.* New York: Scientific American Books.

Pitt, M. A. (1994). Perception of pitch and timbre by musically trained and untrained listeners. *Journal of Experimental Psychology: Human Perception and Performance, 20*, 976–986.

Pittenger, J. B., Shaw, R. E., & Mark, L. S. (1979). Perceptual information for the age level of faces as a higher-order invariant of growth. *Journal of Experimental Psychology: Human Perception and Performance, 5*, 478–493.

Platt, J. R., & Racine, R. J. (1985). Effect of frequency, timbre, experience, and feedback on musical tuning skills. *Perception and Psychophysics, 38*, 345–353.

Plomp, R. (1967). Pitch of complex tones. *Journal of the Acoustical Society of America, 41*, 1526–1533.

Preisler, A. (1993). The influence of spectral composition of complex tones and of musical experience on the perceptibility of virtual pitch. *Perception and Psychophysics, 54*, 589–603.

Pressnitzer, D., Patterson, R. D., & Krumbholz, K. (2001). The lower limit of melodic pitch. *Journal of the Acoustical Society of America, 109*, 2074–2084.

Quinn, I. (1999). The combinatorial model of pitch contour. *Music Perception, 16*, 439–456.

Ralston, J. V., & Herman, L. M. (1995). Perception and generalization of frequency contours by a bottlenose dolphin (*Tursiops truncatus*). *Journal of Comparative Psychology, 109*, 268–277.

Ranvaud, R., Thompson, W. F., Silveira-Moriyama, L., & Balkwill, L.-L. (2001). The speed of pitch resolution in a musical context. *Journal of the Acoustical Society of America, 109*, 3021–3030.

Rasch, R., & Plomp, R. (1999). The perception of musical tones. In D. Deutsch (Ed.), *The psychology of music* (2nd ed., pp. 89–112). San Diego, CA: Academic Press.

Ritsma, R. J. (1967). Frequencies dominant in the perception of the pitch of complex sounds. *Journal of the Acoustical Society of America, 42*, 191–198.

Robinson, K., & Patterson, R. D. (1995). The duration required to identify the instrument, the octave, or the pitch chroma of a musical note. *Music Perception, 13*, 1–15.

Rosch, E. (1975). Cognitive reference points. *Cognitive Psychology, 7*, 532–547.

Rossing, T. D. (1982). *The science of sound*. Reading, MA: Addison-Wesley.

Schellenberg, E. G. (1996). Expectancy in melody: Tests of the implication-realization model. *Cognition, 58*, 75–125.

Schellenberg, E. G. (1997). Simplifying the implication-realization model of musical expectancy. *Music Perception, 14*, 2945–2318.

Schmuckler, M. A. (1989). Expectation in music: Investigation of melodic and harmonic processes. *Music Perception, 7*, 109–150.

Schmuckler, M. A. (1990). The performance of global expectations. *Psychomusicology, 9*, 122–147.

Schmuckler, M. A. (1999). Testing models of melodic contour similarity. *Music Perception, 16*, 295–326.

Schmuckler, M. A. (2001). What is ecological validity? A dimensional analysis. *Infancy, 2*, 419–436.

Schmuckler, M. A., & Tomovski, R. (1997, November). *Perceptual tests of musical key-finding*. Paper presented at the 38th annual meeting of the Psychonomic Society, Philadelphia.

Schmuckler, M. A., & Tomovski, R. (2002a). Perceptual tests of an algorithm for musical key-finding. Unpublished manuscript.

Schmuckler, M. A., & Tomovski, R. (2002b). Tonal hierarchies and rare intervals in musical key-finding. Unpublished manuscript.

Seebeck, A. (1843). Über die Sirene. *Annals of Physical Chemistry, 60*, 449–481.

Selkirk, E. O. (1984). *Phonology and syntax: The relation between sound and structure*. Cambridge, MA: MIT Press.

Semal, C., & Demany, L. (1991). Dissociation of pitch from timbre in auditory short-term memory. *Journal of the Acoustical Society of America, 89*, 2404–2410.

Semal, C., & Demany, L. (1993). Further evidence for an autonomous processing of pitch in auditory short-term memory. *Journal of the Acoustical Society of America, 94*, 1315–1322.

Sergeant, D. (1982). Octave generalization in young children. *Early Child Development and Care, 9*, 1–17.

Sergeant, D. (1983). The octave: Percept or concept. *Psychology of Music, 11*, 3–18.

Shaw, R. E., McIntyre, M., & Mace, W. (1974). The role of symmetry in event perception. In R. B. MacLeod, and H. L. Pick, Jr. (Eds.), *Perception: Essays in honor of James J. Gibson* (pp. 279–310). Ithaca, NY: Cornell University Press.

Shaw, R. E., & Pittenger, J. B. (1977). Perceiving the face of change in changing faces: Implications for a theory of object recognition. In R. E. Shaw, and J. Bransford (Eds.), *Perceiving, acting and knowing: Toward an ecological psychology* (pp. 103–132). Hillsdale, NJ: Lawrence Erlbaum Associates.

Shepard, R. N. (1964). Circularity in judgments of relative pitch. *Journal of the Acoustical Society of America, 36*, 2346–2353.

Shepard, R. N. (1982a). Geometrical approximations to the structure of musical pitch. *Psychological Review, 89*, 305–333.

Shepard, R. N. (1982b). Structural representations of musical pitch. In D. Deutsch (Ed.), *The psychology of music* (pp. 343–390). San Diego: Academic Press.

Shepard, R. N. (1999a). Cognitive psychology and music. In P. R. Cook (Ed.), *Music, cognition, and computerized sound: An introduction to psychoacoustics* (pp. 21–35). Cambridge, MA: MIT Press.

Shepard, R. N. (1999b). Pitch perception and measurement. In P. R. Cook (Ed.), *Music, cognition, and computerized sound* (pp. 149–165). Cambridge, MA: MIT Press.

Shepard, R. N. (1999c). Tonal structure and scales. In P. R. Cook (Ed.), *Music, cognition, and computerized sound: An introduction to psychoacoustics* (pp. 187–194). Cambridge, MA: MIT Press.

Shmulevich, I., & Yli-Harja, O. (2000). Localized key finding: Algorithms and applications. *Music Perception, 17,* 531–544.

Siegel, R. J. (1965). A replication of the mel scale of pitch. *American Journal of Psychology, 78,* 615–620.

Simon, H. A. (1972). Complexity and the representation of patterned sequences of symbols. *Psychological Review, 79,* 369–382.

Simon, H. A., & Kotovsky, H. (1963). Human acquisition of concepts for sequential patterns. *Psychological Review, 70,* 534–546.

Simon, H. A., & Sumner, R. K. (1968). Pattern in music. In K. B. (Ed.), *Formal representation of human judgment* (pp. 219–250). New York: John Wiley & Sons.

Singh, P. G., & Hirsch, J. J. (1992). Influence of spectral locus and F0 changes on the pitch and timbre of complex tones. *Journal of the Acoustical Society of America, 92,* 2650–2661.

Smith, N. A., & Schmuckler, M. A. (2000). Pitch-distributional effects on the perception of tonality. In C. Woods, B. B. Luch, R. Rochard, S. A. O'Nei, and J. A. Sloboda (Eds.), *Proceedings of the Sixth International Conference on Music Perception and Cognition.* Keele, Staffordshire, UK.

Smith, N. A., & Schmuckler, M. A. (2004). The perception of tonal structure through the differentiation and organization of pitches. *Journal of Experimental Psychology: Human Perception & Performance, 30,* 268–286.

Stevens, S. S., & Volkmann, J. (1940). The relation of pitch to frequency: A revised scale. *American Journal of Psychology, 53,* 329–353.

Stevens, S. S., Volkmann, J., & Newman, E. B. (1937). A scale for the measurement of the psychological magnitude of pitch. *Journal of the Acoustical Society of America, 8,* 185–190.

Straub, K., Wilson, C., McCollum, C., & Badecker, W. (2001). Prosodic structure and wh-questions. *Journal of Psycholinguistic Research, 30,* 379–394.

Suen, C. Y., & Beddoes, M. P. (1972). Discrimination of vowel sounds of very short duration. *Perception and Psychophysics, 11,* 417–419.

Takeuchi, A. (1994). Maximum key-profile correlation (MKC) as a measure of tonal structure in music. *Perception and Psychophysics, 56,* 335–346.

Temperley, D. (1999). What's key for key? The Krumhansl-Schmuckler key-finding algorithm reconsidered. *Music Perception, 17,* 65–100.

Toiviainen, P., & Krumhansl, C. L. (2003). Measuring and modeling real-time response to music: Tonality induction. *Perception, 32*(6), 741–766.

Turvey, M. T. (1977). Preliminaries to a theory of action with reference to vision. In R. E. Shaw & J. Bransford (Eds.), *Perceiving, acting, and knowing* (pp. 211–265). Hillsdale, NJ: Lawrence Erlbaum Associates.

Turvey, M. T. (1990). The challenge of a physical account of action: A personal view. In H. T. A. Whiting, O. G. Meijer, and P. C. Wieringen (Eds.), *The natural-physical approach to movement control* (pp. 57–93). Amsterdam: Free University Press.

Turvey, M. T., & Carello, C. (1986). The ecological approach to perceiving and acting: A pictorial essay. *Acta Psychologica, 63,* 133–155.

Turvey, M. T., & Shaw, R. E. (1979). The primacy of perceiving: An ecologic reformulation of perception for understanding memory. In L. G. Nilsson (Ed.) *Perspectives on memory research* (pp. 167–189). Hillsdale, JN: Erlbaum.

Turvey, M. T., Carello, C., & Kim, N.-G. (1990). Links between active perception and the control of action. In H. Haken & M. Stadler (Eds.), *Synergetics of cognition* (pp. 269–295). New York: Springer-Verlag.

Unyk, A. M., & Carlsen, J. C. (1987). The influence of expectancy on melodic perception. *Psychomusicology, 7,* 3–23.

Van den Toorn, P. C. (1983). *The music of Igor Stravinsky*. New Haven, CT: Yale University Press.

Van Egmond, R., & Butler, R. (1997). Diatonic connotations of pitch-class sets. *Music Perception, 15*, 1–31.

Van Noorden, L. P. A. S. (1975). *Temporal coherence in the perception of tone sequences*. Eindhoven University of Technology, Eindhoven, The Netherlands.

Vos, P. G. (2000). Tonality induction: Theoretical problems and dilemmas. *Music Perception, 17*, 403–416.

Vos, P. G., & Leman, M. (2000). Guest editorial: Tonality induction. *Music Perception, 17*, 401–402.

Wagman, J. B., & Miller, D. B. (2003). Nested reciprocities: The organism-environment system in perception-action development. *Developmental Psychobiology, 42*(4), 362–367.

Wapnick, J., & Freeman, P. (1980). Effects of dark-bright timbral variation on the perception of flatness and sharpness. *Journal of Research in Music Education, 28*, 176–184.

Warren, W. H. J., & Verbrugge, R. R. (1984). Auditory perception of breaking and bouncing events: A case study in ecological acoustics. *Journal of Experimental Psychology: Human Perception and Performance, 10*, 704–712.

Warrier, C. M., & Zatorre, R. J. (2002). Influence of tonal context and timbral variation on perception of pitch. *Perception and Psychophysics, 62*, 198–207.

Whitfield, I. C. (1979). Periodicity, pulse interval and pitch. *Audiology, 18*, 507–517.

Wier, C. C., Jesteadt, W., & Green, D. M. (1977). Frequency discrimination as a function of frequency and sensation level. *Journal of the Acoustical Society of America, 61*, 178–184.

Wish, M., & Carroll, J. D. (1974). Applications of individual differences scaling to studies of human perception and judgment. In E. C. Carterette, and M. P. Friedman (Eds.), *Handbook of perception* (vol. 2, pp. 449–491). New York: Academic Press.

Wright, A. A., Rivera, J. J., Hulse, S. H., Shyan, M., & Neiworth, J. J. (2000). Music perception and octave generalization in rhesus monkeys. *Journal of Experimental Psychology: General, 129*, 291–307.

Youngblood, J. E. (1958). Style as information. *Journal of Music Theory, 2*, 24–35.

12

LOUDNESS

ROBERT S. SCHLAUCH

Loudness is the subjective magnitude of a sound. It is a concept that has implicit meaning for nearly everyone, but a formal definition is the purview of psychoacoustics, the field concerned with relating acoustics and perception. Loudness has been a topic of considerable scientific inquiry since 1920, when a renaissance in psychoacoustics followed the invention of the vacuum tube, a device that enabled the accurate quantification of sound levels (Boring, 1942). One goal of these early studies was to define the functional dependences among loudness, intensity, duration, bandwidth, and frequency. Another goal of these classic studies of loudness was to relate loudness to the underlying physiological processes responsible for perception. The classic approach continues today as we discover more about the function of the cochlea and the central auditory pathways.

Throughout its long history, loudness has almost exclusively been explored using simple stimuli—specifically, stimuli that are simple in their temporal envelope. But listen to the sounds in your environment; virtually nothing we hear outside the laboratory has the temporal characteristics of those laboratory stimuli. What characterizes environmental sounds? It is their spectral and temporal complexity and their nearly constant mélange of auditory stimulation. Of course, prior to the programmable laboratory computer and the capabilities of accurate analog-to-digital and digital-to-analog converters, it was virtually impossible to explore these issues rigorously, but now we can, and in the past 25 plus years we have made only a modest amount of progress.

The goal of this chapter is to review studies of ecological loudness—the relation between loudness and the naturally occurring events that they represent—and to contrast them with the more traditional studies. The topics addressing issues in ecological loudness in this chapter are diverse, but so is the auditory world. The areas of inquiry include loudness constancy, dynamically changing sounds, source segregation, selective attention, the middle ear and the acoustic reflex, and uncomfortably loud sounds. Before delving into these topics, I review some methodological issues related to loudness measurement and the results of some studies that attempt to relate loudness to the physiological mechanisms responsible for its percept.

METHODS FOR MEASURING LOUDNESS

Loudness is a subjective impression of stimulus magnitude and, as such, the validity of listeners' judgments can be assessed only by comparisons with loudness judgments obtained with procedures assumed to be influenced by different nonsensory factors or biases (i.e., convergent validity). This is in contrast to objective paradigms such as a discrimination task, where the experimenter knows which interval contains the more intense sound and can measure the percentage of occasions that a listener was able to discriminate correctly between sounds that differ in their physical levels. By comparison, the experimenter can only infer loudness from objective measures.

Several methods are employed to measure loudness. These methods are common to the classic studies of loudness and more recent studies of ecological loudness. The data obtained from a particular method can be used to derive a scale, a method of assigning numbers to events or objects (Stevens, 1951).

Scales provide a means to summarize and compare data. In sensory psychology, scales provide a quantitative specification of perception for a range of values representing a physical dimension. Common types of scales that are relevant for loudness are ordinal scales and ratio scales. With ordinal scales, any mathematical function that preserves the order of the ranks leaves the scale invariant (Stevens, 1951). It is meaningful to state that one scale value is greater than or less than another scale value for an ordinal scale, but the differences or intervals between scale values are not quantifiable. Ratio scales have an absolute zero point and equal intervals between units of measure (Stevens, 1951). For ratio scales, computation of the ratio of scale values is permissible. Weight (kilograms) is an example of a ratio scale. It is meaningful to say that 50 kg is double the weight of 25 kg. This two-to-one ratio is preserved even when the units are changed from kilograms to pounds. By contrast, the Fahrenheit and centigrade temperature scales, with their arbitrary zero points, are not ratio scales, nor is it meaningful to say that 50°F (or C) is double the temperature of 25°F (or C).

PAIRED COMPARISONS

In this method, listeners are presented with two sounds in succession and are asked to select the one that is louder. Multiple judgments using this method yield useful but limited quantitative information about the relative loudness of sounds (i.e., the percentage of time that one is judged louder than the other). The experimenter can order sounds according to their relative loudness (an ordinal scale), but based on this type of measure one cannot conclude that one sound is twice as loud or four times as loud as another sound. For such comparisons, one needs to derive a scale of loudness using a method such as magnitude scaling.[1]

MAGNITUDE SCALING

Magnitude scaling (Hellman & Zwislocki, 1963, 1964; Stevens, 1975), which includes magnitude estimation and magnitude production, is the most widely accepted method for measurement of loudness in psychoacoustical experiments. In magnitude estimation, listeners assign numbers to match the perceived stimulus magnitude. In magnitude production, a listener adjusts a stimulus level to produce a sensation equal in perceived magnitude to a stimulus number. Both of these methods are sometimes combined to yield an estimate of a loudness function.[2] The product of magnitude scaling, under optimal circumstances, is a ratio scale of sensation.

Figure 1 illustrates loudness functions obtained using magnitude scaling for long-duration tones at three frequencies. For tones in the most sensitive range of hearing (0.5 to 10.0 kHz), loudness doubles for every 10-dB increase in the stimulus level once the level exceeds about 30 dB SPL. This region of the loudness function, between 30 and 90 dB SPL in the most sensitive region of hearing, is well described as a compressive function of intensity, a power function with an exponent of 0.3 (Hellman, 1991; Hellman, Takeshima, Suzwki, Ozawa, & Sone, 2001). Hellman (1991) summarized 78 studies of magnitude estimation (ME) for 1.0-kHz tones and found that the average exponent was 0.3 with a standard deviation of 0.045.

---

[1] Paired comparisons obtained with sounds that differ only in their level are used to obtain an estimate of the just-noticeable difference in intensity (JNDI). Fechner (1860) theorized that loudness could be inferred by summing JNDI, the unit of sensation for his scale. A number of assumptions were required to derive a loudness function from JNDI, and subsequent studies have proved that Fechner's theory for relating these measures was incorrect (e.g., Hellman, Scharf, Teghtsoonian, & Teghtsoonian, 1987; Newman, 1933). Nonetheless, the appeal of an objective discrimination measure has motivated researchers to pursue this approach to generating a loudness function for more than 140 years (e.g., Allen & Neely, 1997; Hellman & Hellman, 1990; Schlauch, Harvey, & Lanthier, 1995). Modern efforts to relate loudness and intensity discrimination still require assumptions (e.g., the variance of neural population response as a function of stimulus level), and the results are still compared with loudness functions obtained using subjective methods, typically magnitude scaling (Hellman & Hellman, 1990), a method that relates numbers to perceived magnitude to derive a scale of sensation.

[2] The combined methods of magnitude estimation and magnitude production are believed to reduce potential judgment bias in the slope of the loudness function due to subjects shortening the metric that they adjust (Stevens, 1972). This bias labeled the regression effect is well known, but many experimenters base their loudness measures on only magnitude estimation.

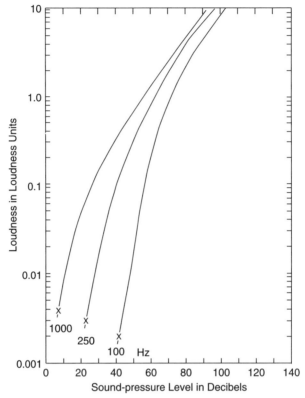

FIGURE 1   Loudness functions for 100-, 250-, and 1000-Hz tones obtained with magnitude scaling. Detection thresholds for the tones are denoted by crosses. (From Hellman & Zwislocki, 1968.)

The loudness functions for sustained broadband noise and for speech are similar to the ones for tones from sensitive regions of hearing. However, a direct comparison shows that at low sound levels the loudness of a wideband stimulus, such as white noise, grows more rapidly than the loudness for a tone in the most sensitive region of hearing (Scharf, 1978).

CATEGORY RATING

Category rating is another method employed to measure loudness (Stevens & Galanter, 1957). Listeners are provided with a range of numbers (e.g., 1–7 or 1–100) or a series of adjectives (e.g., very very soft, very soft, soft, medium, loud, very loud, very very loud), and values from within these ranges are assigned to individual stimuli to derive a loudness function. These descriptors have their origin in music. Verbal descriptions such as very loud, loud, and very soft correspond to the musical notations ff, f, and pp. According to Fletcher (1995), these verbal descriptors are not precise. Examples of loudness functions obtained with category rating are shown in Fig. 2. These functions are much different from the ones obtained with magnitude scaling procedures shown in Fig. 1. Category rating is believed to yield an ordinal scale of sensation.

LOUDNESS MATCHING AND
CROSS-MODALITY MATCHING

Loudness matching and cross-modality matching are methods for assessing relative loudness growth that do not require the use of numbers. In loudness-matching tasks, listeners compare the loudness of two sounds presented sequentially, separated by a short delay. A fixed-level sound is presented to the same ear or opposite ear relative to a comparison sound. During the task, pairs of sounds, the fixed-level sound and the comparison sound, are presented and following each pair, the observer selects the louder stimulus. The level of the comparison sound is adjusted by the listener or by computer control based on the listener's responses until a point of equal sensation magnitude is achieved. Cross-modality matching

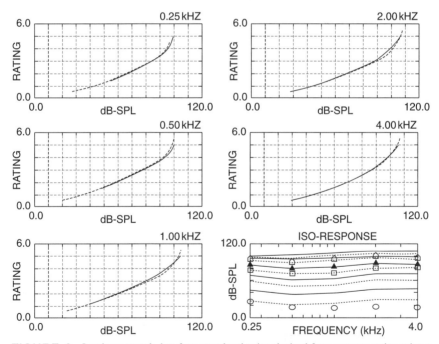

FIGURE 2 Loudness growth data for narrowband noise obtained from category rating using a seven-point scale: 0 (inaudible) to 6 (too loud). Average data are shown for 11 listeners with normal hearing. The center frequency of the noise is shown in the top right corner of each panel. The lower right panel shows equal-loudness contours derived from the rating data in the other panels. (From Allen *et al.*, 1990.)

works on the basis of the same principle, but for this task, the perceived magnitude of a sound is compared with the perceived magnitude of a stimulus from a modality other than hearing, such as the brightness of a light or the length of a line (Stevens, 1975). Line length judgments and the matching function between a sound and line length are used to derive a loudness function (Hellman & Meiselman, 1988).

Loudness-matching and cross-modality matching procedures are often cited as methods for validating data obtained using category rating and magnitude scaling.[3] Magnitude scaling procedures and loudness functions derived from cross-modality matching between a sound and line length and line length judgments yield the same result. Loudness matching also shows good agreement with data from scaling procedures. Loudness matches are published for a variety of conditions. Loudness matches are often made between tones of different frequencies or between tones presented to an ear with normal hearing and one with a cochlear threshold shift. When such results are compared with matching functions derived from category rating and magnitude scaling procedures for the same sounds used in the matching task, they usually yield the same results (e.g., Hellmen & Zwislocki, 1964; McCleary, 1993) or, as in the case of Allen, Hall, and Jeng (1990), results that have the general shape for equal-loudness contours obtained using a matching procedure (see the lower right panel of Fig. 2). However, Hellman (1999) cautions that loudness functions derived from category rating procedures sometimes yield a reduced rate of loudness growth relative to the actual state of a cochlear-impaired person's auditory system. Given that auditory nerve disorders often result in shallower loudness functions for tones than cochlear disorders, this bias observed in loudness functions measured using category rating possibly could lead to an incorrect labeling of the type of hearing loss.

BIAS IN LOUDNESS MEASUREMENT

There is considerable evidence that loudness measurement methods, including category rating and magnitude scaling, are affected by response biases, and some critics believe that this limits their value as scaling techniques (Mellers & Birnbaum, 1982; Stevens & Galanter, 1957). In any event, these methods should not be thought of as producing a scale that is a direct map to underlying

---

[3] A loudness summation procedure has also been used to validate loudness functions obtained using magnitude scaling (Buus, Musch, & Florentine, 1998). In this procedure, loudness matches between multiple narrowband sounds processed in separate auditory channels and a single narrowband sound are made. The decibel difference at equal loudness represents the loudness ratio corresponding to the number of stimuli in the complex sound. This is based on the assumption that loudness grows in proportion to the number of sounds in the stimulus (Scharf, 1978). Loudness functions derived using this method show excellent agreement with ones obtained with magnitude scaling for low stimulus levels (below about 40 dB), but for higher levels the assumption of independence of the channels is violated by the well-known physiological spread of excitation in the cochlea (Buus et al., 1999).

physiological mechanisms without considering the role of cognitive factors. Magnitude estimation and category rating are affected by the way in which participants use numbers or labels (Hellman, 1976; Hellman & Zwislocki, 1961, 1963; Zwislocki & Goodman, 1980). Studies of the subjective number scale, independent of loudness, show evidence of nonlinearity for many observers (Schneider, Parker, Ostrosky, Stein, & Kanow, 1974). If participants use numbers nonlinearly, this cognitive factor would be reflected in the derived loudness scale. Scaling judgments are also affected by the range of stimuli (e.g., Parducci, 1965; Lawless, Horne, & Spiers, 2000; Teghtsoonian & Teghtsoonian, 1978) and the order in which stimuli are presented (sequential dependencies; Jesteadt, Luce, & Green, 1977).

For magnitude estimation, loudness functions become distorted when participants are forced to use numbers outside their natural scales, as they would be when reference tones are paired with a number at the beginning of an experiment. For this reason, the current trend is to present no implicit or explicit reference or standard under the assumption that subjects are able to make absolute judgments using their own internal scale (Zwislocki, 1983; Zwislocki & Goodman, 1980).

Category rating is subject to additional criticisms. In category rating tasks many participants are reluctant to use the entire range of labels from the set and this behavior can distort the shape of the function (Stevens & Galanter, 1957). Another limitation of this method is related to the finite range of labels. For instance, if a listener assigns an extreme value (one end of the range of labels) to a stimulus and a subsequent stimulus is judged to be beyond that extreme value, the response to that latter stimulus will not reflect the listener's perception. By contrast, the range of numbers available in a magnitude estimation task is unconstrained.

PHYSIOLOGICAL CORRELATES OF LOUDNESS

An early and continuing goal of psychoacoustics is to relate perception to the underlying physiological processes responsible for producing the sensation. This bottom-up approach is valuable for understanding the functional mechanisms of the auditory system and has practical application in the design of hearing prostheses and systems designed to reproduce sounds for listeners (e.g., home entertainment equipment, public address systems).

At the time when early loudness experiments were conducted, researchers assumed correctly that the cochlea played an important role in the filtering of sounds presented to an ear. Helmholtz (1954/1862) had proposed an important role for the basilar membrane, a tuned strip within the cochlea hypothesized to be responsible for frequency-selective hearing. However, it was von Bekesy (1960/1928) who first described a rough approximation to the displacement pattern for this membrane as a function of stimulus level and frequency. Fletcher and his colleagues at Bell Laboratories knew of anatomical and physiological studies of the cochlea, such as von Bekesy's, and attempted to relate behavioral masking-detection data for different frequencies to different places along the basilar membrane (Fletcher & Munson, 1933). This frequency-to-place mapping along with knowledge about threshold elevation caused by a masking noise became the basis for a loudness model that was able to predict loudness growth based on a listener's hearing thresholds and, if present, type of hearing loss. The pattern of masking produced by a stimulus was assumed to represent closely its excitation pattern or its internal representation in the cochlea, and the summed area under this pattern was used as an estimate of loudness.

Steinberg and Gardner (1937), Fletcher's colleagues at Bell Laboratories, compared the predictions of their model of loudness with loudness-matching data for tones obtained from persons with different causes of hearing loss. Fletcher's model made excellent predictions. The accuracy of these predictions is noteworthy because loudness functions vary with frequency and the degree and type of hearing loss in a nonlinear manner. Persons with cochlear threshold shifts, due to hearing loss or the presence of a noise masker, display an increased rate of loudness growth over a region of their dynamic range between 4 and 30 dB sensation level, a phenomenon known as recruitment (Buus & Florentine, 2002; Fowler, 1928, 1937; Hellman & Meiselman, 1990; Hellman & Zwislocki, 1964; Stevens and Guirao, 1967). By contrast, persons with elevated thresholds due to a middle-ear disorder, which results in a simple attenuation of sound entering the cochlea, do not show recruitment. Instead, the loudness function is simply displaced along the abscissa by the amount of the loss. Representative loudness functions for normal hearing and cochlear hearing loss are shown in Fig. 3.

Early physiological evidence that the peripheral auditory system plays an important role in loudness encoding came from measurements of the cochlear microphonic (CM) (Wever & Bray, 1930).[4] The CM is a voltage that can be measured by placing electrodes within the cochlea or by recording from an electrode placed in close proximity to the cochlea. The CM faithfully reproduces the input stimulus for stimulus levels as high as 80 dB SPL; for higher levels, saturation is observed (Moller, 2000). We know now that the CM is produced when the cochlea converts mechanical to electrical energy. The motile outer hair cells are the source of this voltage (Moller, 2000).

Stevens and Davis (1936) measured the CM as a function of level in guinea pig and found good agreement between the magnitude of the CM with level for a 1000-Hz tone below levels that produced saturated responses and loudness functions obtained from humans for the same stimulus conditions. They also reported good agreement between an equal-loudness contour across frequency (a 1000 Hz, 45 dB SPL tone was the standard) and the levels required to produce equal-magnitude CM responses.

---

[4] Wever and Brey, at the time of their measurements, thought the auditory nerve was the source of what we now call the cochlear microphonic.

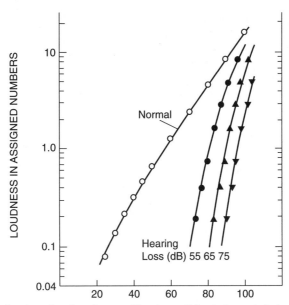

FIGURE 3   Loudness functions for normal hearing participants (open circles) and groups of listeners with different amounts of cochlear hearing loss (filled symbols). The amount of the hearing loss is shown beneath each group's loudness function. These functions were fitted using an equation suggested by Zwislocki (1965). Note that the functions for cochlear hearing impairment are steeper than the ones for normal hearing, a phenomenon known as loudness recruitment. (From Hellman & Meiselman, 1990.)

Physiological evidence reinforces the notion that cochlear output shapes loudness responses. Direct and inferred measures of the basilar membrane (BM) input–output (I/O) function (Ruggero, Rich, Recio, Narayan, & Robles, 1997; Yates, Winter, & Robertson, 1990) for tones in the most sensitive region of hearing have a compressive shape, as do loudness functions. The striking similarity in these shapes, for the loudness function and for the BM I/O function, is shown in Fig. 4. This compressive shape is linked to the motility or movement of outer hair cells (OHCs), the source of the CM. The motility of OHCs is associated with an active process that provides a significant amount of amplification or gain for low-level sounds that becomes progressively smaller as level is increased. This nonlinear "cochlear amplifier" improves the ability to discern sounds that are similar in frequency. When OHCs are damaged, as in cochlear hearing loss caused by disease or ototoxic drugs, the BM I/O function shows an elevated threshold and the response becomes linear (and steeper) (Ruggero *et al.*, 1997). Changes in the loudness function due to cochlear hearing loss are also consistent with what is known about the vibration pattern of the basilar membrane (Moore, Glasberg, & Baer, 1997; Schlauch, DiGiovanni, & Ries, 1998). All of this evidence is consistent with the notion that loudness growth is a compressive function of intensity in normal hearing and that the compressive aspects

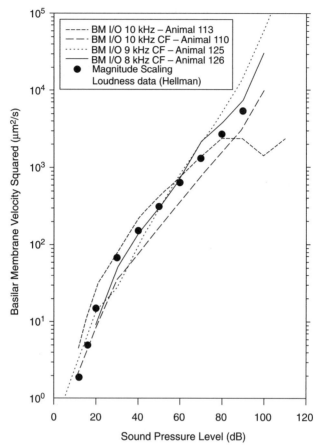

FIGURE 4   A comparison of basilar membrane I/O functions (lines) from four chinchillas and a human loudness function for a 3.0-kHz tone (filled circles). The basilar membrane I/O functions are from Ruggero *et al.* (1997). The loudness functions, which were obtained using magnitude scaling, are from Hellman (1976). Basilar membrane velocity was squared to mimic a process more central than the basilar membrane. (From Schlauch *et al.*, 1998.)

are determined by the nonlinear response of the BM (see also, Buus, Musch, & Florentine, 1998; Buus & Florentine, 2002).

The loudness function measured using magnitude scaling procedures is a compressive function of intensity with an exponent of 0.3 for frequencies between roughly 500 and 10,000 Hz (Hellman *et al.*, 2001). For frequencies below 350 Hz, where thresholds become higher, the loudness function becomes steeper (Hellman & Zwislocki, 1968). One explanation for this threshold elevation and the corresponding steepening of the loudness function is that cochlear gain is reduced in these lower frequency regions relative to higher frequencies. Estimates of cochlear characteristics, both physiological (Cooper & Rhode, 1996) and behavioral (Hicks & Bacon, 1999), suggest that the cochlea is more linear in low frequencies compared with high frequencies, but the frequency at which the reduction in nonlinearity occurs and the amount of the reduction and its relation to cochlear gain/amplification are unknown. Unfortunately, direct physiological measures of basilar membrane compression, which would resolve this issue, are difficult to obtain from regions of the cochlea responsible for coding low frequencies, and, even if they were available, the animals used to obtain these measures might code sounds at these frequencies differently than humans.

Attempts to model loudness based on physiological responses more central than the cochlea have been made as well. One popular approach relates stimulus power to peripheral spike counts in the auditory nerve, but this method fails even for pure tones according to an analysis of neural data by Relkin and Doucet (1997). Other researchers report a relation between loudness and brainstem evoked potentials (Serpanos, O'Mally, & Gravel, 1997) and cortical evoked potentials (Stevens, 1970) obtained by placing electrodes on a person's scalp.

A model for predicting loudness from physical spectra of long-duration sounds was proposed by Moore *et al.* (1997). This model represents an extension to the masking-excitation models proposed earlier (Steinberg & Gardner, 1937; Zwicker, 1970). In the current model, the stimulus is shaped initially by the transfer functions for the external and middle ears. Then, in the next two stages, physiological response is altered by the gain and frequency selectivity of the cochlea. The transformation of cochlear excitation to "loudness" is accomplished using the compressive function of intensity, as observed in BM I/O functions. The integral of the "loudness" excitation pattern predicts the overall loudness for a given stimulus. This physiologically weighted, spectral-based model accounts well for many loudness phenomena, including monaural and binaural threshold and loudness effects, the loudness of complex sounds as a function of bandwidth, and equal-loudness measures across frequency (equal-loudness contours).

ECOLOGICAL LOUDNESS: SOME AREAS OF INQUIRY

LOUDNESS CONSTANCY

Perceptual constancy is the ability to perceive a physical property of a stimulus as the same even as the proximal stimulus varies (Goldstein, 2002). For instance, retinal images of objects vary depending on the lighting, angle, and distance of the object from the retina of the observer. Despite this instability of the proximal stimulus under everyday conditions, some perceived properties of the distal stimulus remain stable. In vision, size constancy is frequently cited as an example of perceptual constancy. For example, observers are able to infer or estimate the actual size of an object by taking into account the distance of an object from the retina. If this did not occur, persons would appear to become smaller as their distance from an observer increased (Goldstein, 2002). Although most of the prior work on perceptual constancy has been in vision, loudness constancy is an area of study in hearing that has received some attention.

Warren proposed the "physical correlate theory" of perception, a method of relating sensory magnitude to environmental correlates applicable to a number of senses (Warren, 1981). As part of this theory, Warren hypothesized that the compressive nature of the loudness function is related to our experience in hearing sounds at different distances. Warren argued that loudness constancy is important for survival, so it is only natural that a relation exists between loudness and distance. In contrast to the more traditional psychoacoustic approach, Warren argued that the expectation for a neurophysiological correlate of the loudness function is unnecessary. He stated that the central nervous system is able to evaluate complex events and that these representations need not bear a resemblance to external events any more than the letters forming a word bear a resemblance to the object it symbolizes (Warren, 1999).

Warren's predicted link between loudness and distance is based on the physical properties of sound. In an anechoic environment, the level of a sound decreases by 6 dB for every doubling of the distance from the sound source, a phenomenon known as the inverse square law. This relation predicts a loudness function that is a power function of intensity with an exponent of 0.5 rather than the average value of 0.3 found in magnitude scaling experiments. He argues that the deviation of the loudness function from the prediction of his relation is within the error of measurement considering biases inherent in loudness scaling. To test his hypothesis, he asked more than 1000 persons in a number of experiments to make one judgment of loudness each in order to avoid a judgment bias resulting from sequential, contextual effects. The task for each subject was to attenuate a comparison sound until it was perceived to be half as loud as a standard level stimulus. These studies (e.g., Warren, 1970) yielded a half-loudness point corresponding to −6 dB for moderate level 1000-Hz tones and broadband noise, a result consistent with the predictions of the inverse square law and his hypothesis.

Some authors have raised concerns about Warren's theory relating the loudness function and experience with hearing sounds at different distances (see Warren, 1981, and commentary). For instance, Marks (1981) points out that loudness growth changes with frequency; low-frequency tones have a much steeper loudness function than midfrequency tones. This difference, which is illustrated in Fig. 1, is not predicted by the physical correlate theory, but it is consistent with known physiological properties of the cochlea, including the reduction in cochlear gain for low-frequency tones (Cooper & Rhode, 1996). The physical correlate theory also does not account for the steeper loudness function in cochlear hearing loss (Fig. 3), binaural loudness additivity, or the steeper growth of the loudness function near threshold in normal hearing persons (Fig. 1) (Scharf & Hellman, 1981), but these results are consistent with known characteristics of the basilar membrane's response to sound.

Another possible criticism of Warren's notion that loudness constancy is based on a listener's experience with the inverse square law is that extreme deviations from this law are observed in reverberant environments, such as rooms. Human listeners gain most of their experience with sound in reverberant environments. Reverberation has a profound effect on distance judgments, but regardless of the environment, studies have shown that listeners are poor judges of the distance of sound sources (see Zahorik, 2002, for a review). The trend is for listeners to overestimate the distance of close sound sources and to underestimate more distant sound sources.

Zahorik and Wightman (2001) published data that suggest that loudness constancy is determined by reverberant sound energy rather than perceived distance. They performed two experiments to examine the relation between loudness and perceived distance in a virtual sound-field environment. This virtual environment took into account the manner in which each person's head and external ear modify sound as it enters the ear canal along with the characteristics of the room. The transfer functions corresponding to these characteristics, known as binaural room impulse responses (BRIRs), are produced by making recordings of sound using miniature microphones placed at the entrance of each experimental participant's ear canal while the person is seated in the room. The listeners were blindfolded to limit their experience with the room's characteristics. Afterward, BRIRs for individual listeners were used to shape sounds presented over earphones to produce the virtual sound-field environment. The advantages of using this method of sound presentation are many, including a reduction in ambient background noise and level control for repeated presentations of stimuli. The sounds for these experiments were all recorded in an auditorium with a seating capacity of 264 persons. In this environment, overall stimulus intensity dropped at 4.25 dB for every doubling of the distance from the source (from 0.3 to 13.8 m). Note that this differs from the 6 dB per doubling decrease that Warren's hypothesis predicts in an anechoic environment. The direct-to-reverberant energy ratio decreased linearly by 3.63 dB for every doubling of the distance from the source.

In Zahorik and Wightman's (2001) first experiment, listeners assigned numbers to perceived source loudness (a magnitude estimation task) as a function of distance of the source from the participant for different presentation levels of a noise burst. For all of the conditions but the lowest level, perceived source loudness remained constant, regardless of distance, even though the level at the ears changed by more than 20 dB for the distances sampled in this study. Zahorik and Wightman (2001) argue that this finding supports the idea that loudness constancy is based on a judgment of reverberant energy. For the low-level condition where the level of the noise was just above the listeners' thresholds, reverberant energy, which was several dB less than the direct energy in the stimulus, was probably inaudible. For this condition, source loudness was perceived to change by a factor of about 4.

In Zahorik and Wightman's (2001) second experiment, listeners judged the apparent distance of the virtual sound source. As in prior studies of source distance, participants were inaccurate in their judgments. This result demonstrates that loudness constancy can occur without veridical knowledge of source distance. This study also presents a problem for traditional psychoacoustic approaches of modeling loudness based on peripheral neural spike counts (Zahorik & Wightman, 2001). The auditory nerve spike count would vary roughly proportionately with stimulus power at the ear rather than remain constant as found in the loudness judgments in Zahorik and Wightman's (2001) experiment. This result is also inconsistent with models based on masking-excitation patterns (e.g., Moore *et al.*, 1997; Zwicker, 1970).

THE LOUDNESS OF DYNAMICALLY CHANGING SOUNDS

Most prior studies of loudness have used steady-state stimuli that were turned on and off abruptly. That is, they reach their maximum amplitude immediately after being turned on (rise time) and their minimum amplitude immediately after being terminated (decay time). In some instances, experimenters employed more gradual onsets and offsets of a few milliseconds to limit spectral splatter. This technique enabled accurate quantification of loudness as functions of stimulus duration and frequency, the goal of the traditional psychoacoustical approach.

Many natural sounds change dynamically in frequency and intensity. For instance, an approaching sound source produces a rising intensity and the sensation of a rising pitch even though frequency is falling, a phenomenon known as the Doppler illusion (Neuhoff & McBeath, 1996). In this case, loudness influences pitch. A study by Neuhoff, McBeath, and Wanzie (1999) demonstrated that dynamic frequency change also influences loudness and that this change occurs centrally in the auditory system. In one of their experiments, changes in the loudness of a noise presented to one ear were influenced by a harmonic tonal complex presented to the other ear. Given that equal loudness and equal pitch contours are determined by the peripheral auditory system (Stevens & Davis, 1936), the interaction of pitch and loudness of dynamically varying sounds is not accounted for using traditional approaches.

Marks (1988, 1992, 1994, 1996) and Marks and Warner (1991) have reported other examples in which loudness judgments of a tone are influenced by stimulus context in a sequence of tones of different frequencies. When a relatively loud sound at one frequency precedes a soft sound at a different frequency, the soft sound is judged louder than it is in isolation. The loudness change induced by this contextual effect is equivalent to a level change of 24 dB for some stimulus combinations. Marks (1996) showed that ipsilateral contextual effects are larger than contralateral ones. Further, the effect occurs only for stimuli outside the analysis bandwidth of the cochlea (i.e., in separate channels) (Marks, 1994; Marks & Warner, 1991). These results are argued to be consistent with a perceptual phenomenon as opposed to a response bias (Marks, 1996). Parker and Schneider (1994) believe that this effect has potential ecological significance. For instance, if the loudness of soft sounds presented in a sequence was boosted, it would improve their likelihood of being processed.

Although the dynamic interaction of frequency and loudness raises questions for traditional models, more limitations of the traditional models are revealed in studies of the temporal envelope of sounds. Many natural sounds have rise and decay times that are asymmetrical and often much longer than the times employed in traditional experiments, especially for the decays. Stecker and Hafter (2000) point out that the rise time of many sounds is the result of a striking force (e.g., striking a drum or a cymbal) whereas the decay time is determined by the filtering properties of an object. The filtering characteristics could include several coupled filters. Speech sounds produced in a reverberant environment provide an example of coupled filters that include the vocal tract of the talker and the characteristics of the room in which the utterance was spoken followed by the listener's body, head, and outer, middle, and inner ear's cumulative response characteristics.

The waveforms of two natural sounds, a drum strike and the word "time" spoken in a near-anechoic environment and a simulated reverberant environment, are shown in Fig. 5. Sounds such as these, with a rapid rise time and a gradual decay time, can be described as damped. When the same sounds are reversed in time, they are described as "ramped sounds." That is, they are characterized by gradual onset times and rapid decay times. A ramped stimulus generated by reversing a damped sound shares the same duration and long-term spectrum with the damped stimulus from which it was derived (Patterson, 1994a, 1994b). Some ramped stimuli occur naturally, such as the bowed string of a violin or the note of an organ, but in most experiments with ramped and damped sounds, ramped sounds are created by reversing damped sounds to maintain experimental control. There is converging evidence from several types of experiments that ramped sounds are perceptually more prominent than damped sounds (Neuhoff, 1998, 2001).

Stecker and Hafter (2000) measured the loudness of ramped and damped sounds with envelopes similar to the ones in Fig. 5. The 250-ms carrier stimuli in their study were broadband noise, high-frequency tones, and low-frequency tones. The ramped and damped envelopes were superimposed on these carriers during the digital stimulus generation process. Loudness was measured using two methods: magnitude estimation and paired comparisons. For both methods, ramped sounds were judged louder than damped sounds. In physical terms, the loudness difference was equal to about 1 to 3 dB difference in level.

Stecker and Hafter (2000) found traditional approaches to modeling loudness differences for their ramped and damped sounds unsuccessful. For instance, spectral models that infer loudness from excitation across frequency regions do not predict loudness differences for these sounds that have identical long-term spectra. Likewise, a peripheral model of the auditory system that takes into account basilar membrane responses and neural adaptation is also unable to predict their results. However, the peripheral model did show an asymmetry

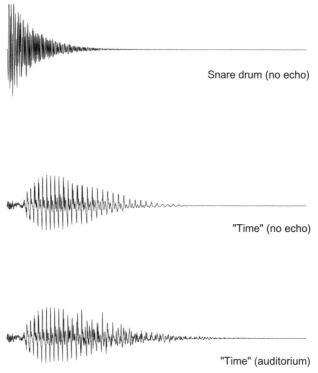

Snare drum (no echo)

"Time" (no echo)

"Time" (auditorium)

FIGURE 5   Examples of waveforms for naturally occurring damped sounds. The top waveform is for a single strike of a snare drum. The middle and lower waveforms are for the word "time" spoken in a near-anechoic environment and in a simulated, highly reverberant environment, respectively. The amount of reverberation corresponds to that of an auditorium.

in the response consistent with their results for low-frequency tones. The model predicted no difference for high-frequency tones even though one was observed.

Stecker and Hafter (2000) proposed a cognitive explanation for loudness and other perceptual differences between ramped and damped sounds. According to their explanation, the auditory system parses damped sounds into segments representing direct sound, which provides information about the source, and reverberant sound, which provides information about the listening environment. This would provide the listener with more precise detail about the distal stimulus, a form of perceptual constancy. The framework for this approach was developed by Rock (1997), who proposed two modes for interpreting features of stimuli. In the literal mode, participants judge a stimulus according to the proximal stimulus. In constancy mode, the stimulus is reinterpreted to recover information about the distal stimulus. Applied to the current situation, listeners judge ramped sounds in the literal mode because with an abrupt decay there is no information about reverberation in the stimulus. By contrast, damped sounds are judged in the constancy mode to maintain accurate information about the sound source. This implies that listeners ignore a portion of the decay of a damped sound, a finding consistent with studies of the subjective duration that show that damped sounds are judged to be about half as long as ramped sounds and sounds that begin and end abruptly (rectangular gated sounds) (Grassi & Darwin, 2001; Schlauch, Ries, & DuGiovanni, 2001). These findings from studies of subjective duration are also consistent with the loudness studies; that is, damped sounds that are perceived to have a shorter duration are perceived as less loud.

Schlauch, DiGiovanni, & Donlin (submitted) presented evidence that supports Stecker and Hafter's (2000) idea that listeners may use two modes for judging the perceptual attributes of ramped and damped sounds. Two groups of subjects participated in a subjective duration experiment and each group was instructed differently when asked to match the duration of ramped and damped sounds to rectangular gated sound (abrupt onset and offset). The key aspects of the two instruction sets were (1) simply match the duration and (2) include all aspects of the sounds. Judgments of damped sounds were affected significantly by these instruction sets. Asking listeners to include all aspects of the sounds in their judgments increased significantly the perceived duration of damped sounds, consistent with the idea that listeners are able to switch between literal mode and constancy mode, as predicted by the explanation offered by Stecker and Hafter (2000) for the ramped–damped perceptual differences.

Neuhoff (1998) has taken a different approach to the study of perceptual differences between ramped and damped sounds. In one study, Neuhoff (1998) asked listeners to estimate the change in loudness of ramped and damped sounds rather than to estimate their overall loudness. The stimuli were tones, a harmonic complex, and broadband noise. The level of these sounds changed by 15 dB from their onset to their offset. Listeners reported that ramped sounds changed in loudness more than damped sounds for the sounds with tonal components. The broadband noise did not show an asymmetry in the loudness. In a second study, rhesus monkeys oriented longer to a rising intensity harmonic complex than a falling intensity harmonic complex (Ghazanfar, Neuhoff, & Logothetis, 2002). An orienting preference was not shown for rising and falling intensity white noise. These findings represent a perceptual bias for rising level tones, a bias that Neuhoff argues has ecological import. For instance, an increase in intensity is one cue that indicates an approaching sound source, and overestimation of this intensity change could provide the listener with a selective advantage for earlier preparation for the arrival of the source. It was argued that the effect was not seen with noise because noise is often associated with background stimuli, such as the rustling of leaves in the wind. This line of work is discussed in more detail in Chap. 4, localization and motion.

Whether ramped–damped differences in perception are under complete cognitive control or mediated by a more automatic, subcortical mechanism is a topic requiring further study. The work of Schlauch *et al.* (submitted) with different instruction sets is consistent with the idea that listeners can perceive damped sounds in their entirety or ignore the decay portion, which is the natural bias subjects have when neutral instructions are given. This explanation is also consistent with Neuhoff's finding that listeners judging the loudness change of ramped and damped sounds perceive damped sounds to change less in loudness than ramped sounds. That is, if listeners ignore a portion of the decay of a damped sound, it would not change as much in loudness as a ramped sound that was judged over its entire duration or a damped sound that adapted over time to a subaudible level. On the other hand, neural responses from subcortical and cortical regions of the auditory pathway respond differently to ramped and damped sounds. For instance, two studies in the auditory brainstem of guinea pigs (Neurt, Pressnitzer, Patterson, & Winter, 2001; Pressnitzer, Winter, & Patterson, 2000) and the auditory cortex of monkeys (Lu, Liang, & Wang, 2001) found asymmetries in the response of neurons to ramped and damped sounds. In work relevant to Neuhoff's hypothesis about a bias for looming auditory motion with its accompanying increase in level as a sound approaches, the brainstem of the echolocating moustache bat shows a greater response for sounds approaching its receptive field than for those leaving it (Wilson & O'Neill, 1998). A neural imaging study (functional magnetic resonance imaging) of ramped and damped sounds in humans also showed an asymmetry in response to sounds with ramped and damped envelopes; cortical regions of the brain responsible for space recognition, auditory motion perception, and attention were more active for ramped sounds than for damped sounds (Seifritz et al., 2002). Although physiological measurements in the auditory pathways show asymmetries in the response for ramped and damped sounds, the relation to psychophysical measures is not straightforward (Neurt et al., 2001). Additional work, combining physiological and psychophysical approaches, needs to be done in this area.

SOUND SOURCE SEGREGATION AND SELECTIVE ATTENTION

A fundamental operation of the auditory system is to segregate sound sources perceptually so that we may attend to a single sound source in the presence of other sounds. This ability, which is important for tasks ranging from people conversing with friends at a cocktail party (Broadbent, 1958) to animals listening for a predator or prey among other background sounds, is known as sound source segregation or auditory stream segregation. The normal auditory system accomplishes this task transparently, but the difficulty of this task is appreciated when one views a sound spectrographic representation (a display of frequency as a function of time with intensity shown by the darkness of the trace) of the speech of multiple talkers. The speech of individual talkers is not clearly represented in this analysis. Another example of the difficulty of this problem is the lack of success in developing a system for automatic speech recognition that is able to function in a noisy environment.

A number of stimulus factors have been identified experimentally as playing an important role in sound source segregation by human listeners (Bregman, 1990). There is a tendency for sequences of acoustical stimulus elements to be grouped perceptually when they (1) originate from a single spatial location, (2) share a common fundamental frequency, (3) make up a sequence of sounds that are close together in frequency, (4) have synchronous onsets and offsets, or (5) share modulation characteristics, in either frequency or intensity. The common link among these stimulus factors is that naturally produced sounds typically consist of stimulus components with mixtures of these characteristics.

Changes in physical intensity, and its psychological correlate loudness, play a role in sound source segregation when source loudness changes over time. Rogers and Bregman (1998) reported the results of a study that examined stream segregation using 100-ms tones. Two sequences of alternating high-frequency tones (H) and low-frequency tones (L) were played consecutively. The first sequence, called an "induction sequence," lasted for 4.8 seconds and contained several iterations of the pattern HLH-, where the "-" represents a 100-ms delay. The test sequence was composed of the same pattern, but its duration was only 1.2 seconds and was presented without delay following the first sequence. When the two sequences were identical in overall level, the second sequence was perceived as containing two distinct streams: a low-frequency stream and a high-frequency stream. This result follows the grouping principle that tones similar in frequency are judged to originate from a common source. The same result was obtained when the first sequence either increased or decreased gradually in level over time or decreased abruptly in level prior to the presentation of the second sequence. On the other hand, an abrupt increase in level of the 4.2-second induction sequence resulted in the perception of the alternating low-frequency tones and high-frequency tones in the second sequence as a single auditory stream. This restoration of single stream perception occurred only for an increase in intensity. Rogers and Bregman (1998) suggest that a differential response to rising intensity would be evolutionarily advantageous because rising intensity represents the presence of a new acoustic event. This asymmetry in the effect for rising and falling level is consistent with findings from other studies (see Neuhoff, 1998) that show a perceptual bias for rising intensity.

There is some evidence that 6-month-old infants have difficulty listening selectively in the presence of moderately loud distracter sounds. Werner and Bargones (1991) studied the behavior of 6-month-old infants and adults in a tonal detection task. Participants were conditioned to turn their head in the direction of a speaker that produced a 1.0-kHz tone. Correct responses were reinforced with the activation of a mechanical toy bear. Thresholds for the 1.0-kHz tone were measured in a quiet background and in the presence of a high-pass noise called a "distraction masker" that was presented either simultaneously with the tone or continuously. The cut off frequency of the distraction masker was selected based on knowledge of the frequency-selective properties of the cochlea to enable the tone and noise to be processed in separate channels or bands. Based on the frequency separation, there is no peripheral physiological explanation for threshold elevation for the tone due to the presence of the noise. However, in all conditions with noise, children's thresholds for the tone were elevated compared with the quiet condition. Adult's thresholds were unaffected by the noise. This finding is evidence that sound-source segregation and selective listening is an ability that develops with age and perhaps experience.

Leibold and Werner (2002a, 2002b) have presented evidence that infants listen less selectively than adults and that this behavior affects loudness growth. Loudness growth rates for infants were inferred from reaction time measures. Reaction time measures in adults show an inverse relation with level, and the infant loudness functions inferred from reaction time measures show a steeper rate of growth than the functions from adult listeners. To demonstrate that nonselective listening is consistent with a steeper loudness function, they had adult listeners perform a competing attention task while measuring loudness growth using magnitude estimation (Leibold & Werner, 2001). They found that the adults, when forced by task demands to monitor frequency regions other than the one of the target tone that was scaled in loudness, yielded steeper loudness functions. In other words, when the competing task diverted their attention from the target tone's frequency, the loudness function grew at a faster rate. This result is consistent with the steeper functions measured in infants and the idea that infants listen nonselectively under normal listening conditions.

THE ECOLOGICAL SIGNIFICANCE OF
THE ACOUSTIC REFLEX

The middle ear of mammals, an air-filled cavity in the temporal bone that contains the eardrum and ossicles, also contains a tiny muscle that contracts in the presence of loud sounds. In humans this occurs for the stapedius muscle; in some other mammals it is the tensor tympani muscle. Numerous studies have demonstrated a close correspondence between stimulus conditions, loudness behavior, and middle-ear muscle contractions (Hellman & Scharf, 1984). Ecological considerations for this relation have been proposed, but some are more convincing than others.

The primary role of the middle ear of mammals is to convert acoustic energy into mechanical energy with a minimal loss in gain as the ossicles provide an efficient transmission path for vibrations of the eardrum caused by sound to enter the cochlea. Although the middle-ear muscles may play a secondary role in this efficient transmission system by keeping the ossicles in proper alignment for precise functioning of the middle ear, other theories have been proposed that suggest a function independent of this role (Borg, Counter, & Rosler, 1984).

To gain an appreciation of the theories proposed to account for the presence of middle-ear muscles, it is important to understand the conditions under which they contract. The middle-ear muscles contract (1) prior to and during vocalization, (2) randomly and intermittently, (3) in the presence of loud sounds,

(4) during mastication, and (5) in some cases, volitionally (Moller, 2000; Simmons, 1964). The primary effect of this contraction is the attenuation of low-frequency sounds entering the cochlea (Moller, 2000).

A number of theories for the existence of the acoustic reflex have been proposed, but the theory receiving the most attention is "protection from loud sounds" (Borg *et al.*, 1984). According to this theory, the delicate sensory cells in the inner ear are protected from overstimulation when the middle-ear muscles contract and attenuate the level of sound entering the cochlea. There are several criticisms of this theory that call into question its viability (Borg *et al.*, 1984). For instance, it is only within the last 100 years or so that industrialization has produced levels of sound that make noise-induced hearing loss a major concern, so it is difficult to identify evolutionary forces that might have produced such a mechanism. Also, prior to industrialization, intense sounds that could result in inner ear damage occurred infrequently and were probably impulsive in nature, such as thunder. Given that the middle-ear muscles are slow to contract, contraction of the muscles would offer little or no protection from impulsive sounds. Furthermore, the attenuation afforded by these muscle contractions affects the amplitude of low-frequency vibrations entering the cochlea, whereas it is the regions of the cochlea responsive to high frequencies that are most susceptible to damage from intense sounds.

Simmons (1964) proposed a "perceptual theory" of middle-ear muscle function that focuses on its ecological importance. He noted that there are a number of conditions that result in a contraction of the middle-ear muscles that are not a result of stimulation by intense, external sounds and that these situations may be the ones that provide insight into the role of these muscles. For instance, he noted that these muscles contract during mastication and prior to and during vocalization. This would render chewing and self-vocalizations less loud. In the case of an animal grazing, the reduction of low-frequency noise could increase the likelihood of detecting an approaching predator. In some specialized mammals, such as the bat, the attenuation of self-vocalizations used for echolocation would help the bat distinguish among self-produced sound and echoes that may represent its next meal (Simmons, 1964).

Simmons (1964) presented evidence for another facet of his perceptual theory from measurements made in cats. In his study, he presented high-frequency sounds to cats while monitoring their middle-ear muscle activity along with the cochlear microphonic, a voltage produced in the cochlea that provides an estimate of the level of sound entering the cochlea. He found that presentation of a novel stimulus resulted in contractions of the middle-ear muscles, which in turn modulated the level of high-frequency sound entering the cochlea. Middle-ear muscle contraction normally results in the attenuation of low-frequency sounds, but cats have a middle ear composed of two cavities, and these two cavities result in an antiresonance that causes a significant dip in the transfer function of the cat middle ear at around 5.0 kHz. The contraction of middle-ear muscles changes the frequency of this antiresonance, which Simmons suggests a cat might use to assess whether a sound is external or internal (e.g., tinnitus, a "ringing" in the ear). The system works as follows. A cat hears a sound and contracts its middle-ear muscles. If the sound is external, it waxes and wanes in loudness when spectral components in the sound pass through the antiresonance of the middle ear. On the other hand, if the sound does not change in loudness during contractions of the middle-ear muscles, the cat can ignore the sound as one produced internally.

UNCOMFORTABLY LOUD SOUNDS

Knowledge of the level of sound at which sound becomes excessively loud has practical applications in situations such as the setting of volume[5] levels in auditoria and movie theaters and the upper limit of sound levels for hearing aids. The level of sound that is judged uncomfortably loud, a level known as a loudness discomfort threshold, depends on psychophysical factors (measurement technique), psychosocial factors, and, to some degree, on stimulus factors such as intensity, frequency, and bandwidth.

The threshold of pain describes an upper limit on the range of audible sounds and, as such, an upper limit for the loudness discomfort threshold. Silverman (1947) conducted an experiment to quantify the threshold of pain along with thresholds for discomfort and tickle. This experiment was completed prior to human subject review boards and the knowledge that intense sounds presented for just a short period may be harmful to hearing. In his experiment, thresholds rose substantially over sessions indicating increased tolerance. For a normal hearing group, the mean "threshold of discomfort" initially was 112 dB SPL, but by the end of the sixth session it increased to nearly 120 dB SPL. The same pattern was seen for the "threshold of pain," which increased over sessions from 135 to 141 dB SPL, the upper output limit of the equipment used in the experiment. The threshold of tickle was just a few dB below the threshold for pain for each session. Bekesy (1960/1936) stated that the source for the "threshold for tickle" is the middle ear and that this measure is independent of loudness. Silverman's (1947) measurements with hearing-impaired listeners showed higher tolerance levels than those of normally hearing listeners, but by only a small amount. Similar thresholds for all three measures were obtained for speech and for tones, and all thresholds increased over sessions.

Nowadays, only loudness discomfort thresholds are measured, mainly for purposes of hearing aid fitting. A category rating task is often used, with categories corresponding to labels such as very soft; soft; comfortable, but slightly soft; comfortable; comfortable, but slightly loud; loud, but o.k.; uncomfortably loud; extremely uncomfortable; and, painfully loud (Hawkins, Walden, Montgomery,

---

[5] Volume is a colloquial term signifying the strength or loudness of a sound (e.g., the volume control on a radio), but in the psychophysical literature loudness and volume are not synonyms (Stevens, Guirao, & Slawson, 1965).

& Prosek, 1987). Although this method seems straightforward, the result is highly dependent on the instructions presented to the participants in studies as well as on the psychophysical procedures (Hawkins *et al.*, 1987). Loudness discomfort levels across studies range from 88 to nearly 120 dB SPL, the level reported by Silverman (1947) after multiple sessions. Most studies find average levels nearer to the lower end of this range. Silverman's results are anomalous, perhaps due to his instructions (Skinner, 1980). He asked listeners to indicate when they would remove their headphones rather than when the level reached a value to which the listener would not want to listen for a long time, a common instruction in the more recent studies.

The physical properties of sounds influence their loudness and also the levels of sounds that are judged uncomfortably loud. Scharf (1978) reports that an increase in stimulus bandwidth results in increased loudness when overall stimulus power is held constant, and there is some empirical evidence that this summation of loudness affects discomfort levels as well (Bentler & Pavlovic, 1989). There is also evidence that peaks in the stimulus waveform influence loudness. For instance, a series of harmonically related tones added in cosine phase, which has a high crest factor (the ratio of peak to root-mean-square [rms] value), is judged louder than noise bands or harmonically related tones added in random phase when these stimuli have equal rms levels (Gockel, Moore, & Patterson, 2002).

Filion and Margolis (1992) attempted to test the validity of laboratory measurements of loudness discomfort levels. They recruited one study group from a nightclub and compared their laboratory judgments of loudness discomfort levels with their responses on a questionnaire regarding the comfort or loudness levels in the nightclub. Actual levels recorded in the nightclub at the listeners' ears were judged to be comfortably loud even though they exceeded the levels found uncomfortably loud in the laboratory setting more than 90% of the time. This finding shows the possible influence of cognitive–social factors in judgments of loudness discomfort.

The role of cognitive–social factors has been documented extensively in studies of sound "annoyance" (e.g., Berglund & Lindvall, 1995), which is correlated with loudness judgments (Hellman, 1982, 1985). Annoyance, which might play a role in loudness discomfort measures, is influenced by culture, expectation, and risk or fear. For instance, some cultures are more tolerant of loud sounds than others (Jonsson, Kajland, Paccagnella, & Sorensen, 1969; Namba, Kuwano, & Schick, 1986). Also, listeners often report that sound levels that are annoyingly loud indoors are acceptably loud outdoors. Outdoors there is more flexibility on the part of the listener to move away from the annoying sound environment. Finally, the perceived risk or fear associated with a particular sound influences its annoyance (Borsky, 1979). For example, aircraft noise levels would be more annoying following a recent crash than just prior to the crash.

Although there is a large cognitive component that influences measures of uncomfortable loudness levels, there are physiological limitations on the levels of exposure that our ears can process without harm. Listening to speech at levels judged uncomfortably loud often corresponds to a reduction in speech recognition ability compared with conditions in which speech is presented at levels judged comfortably loud (Skinner, 1980; Studebaker, Sherbecoe, McDaniel, & Gwaltney, 1999). Also, prolonged exposure to levels exceeding 90 SPL can result in permanent damage to the delicate sensory cells in the inner ear. The Occupational Safety and Health Administration (OSHA, 1983) mandates that the average level for an 8-hour workday not exceed 90 dBa and that no single exposure be greater than 115 dBa, except for impulsive sounds. The risk increases for shorter exposures as the level increases. There is evidence that sound levels of 125 dB SPL presented for only 10 seconds can result in permanent hearing loss (Hunter, Ries, Schlauch, Levine, & Ward, 1999). Although these high levels of exposure are sometimes accompanied by dizziness, a symptom reported by some of Silverman's (1947) participants in his study of the "threshold of pain," the hearing loss caused by long periods of exposure to less intense sounds is often insidious. There are no pain receptors in the inner ear, and the hearing loss associated with exposure to intense sounds often happens without discomfort. The loss usually remains undetected by the victim until an extensive amount of damage has occurred. It is well known that rock-and-roll musicians suffer from hearing loss due to exposure to sound produced by the powerful amplifiers used during their concerts (Palin, 1994; Speaks, Nelson, & Ward, 1970), but members of orchestras also suffer from losses due to exposure to the playing of their own instruments (Royster, Royster, & Killion, 1991), which one might expect would unlikely to be judged "uncomfortably loud." Evidently, persons can adapt to, or in some extreme cases even become addicted to, listening in environments with intense sound levels that are potentially harmful to hearing (Florentine, Hunter, Robinson, Ballou, & Buus, 1998). The role of cultural or generational factors in this process is captured in the spirit of the statement promoted by some rock-and-roll musicians in the 1970s by the statement "if it's too loud, you're too old." What this statement does not convey is that intense sounds, even enjoyable ones that are judged comfortably loud, can result in a permanent hearing loss.

CONCLUSIONS

Traditional models of loudness based on excitation in the auditory periphery make accurate predictions for many laboratory sounds. The limitations of these models become apparent when the loudness of natural sounds is examined. For instance, the traditional models fail in cases in which loudness is judged in a reverberant environment, in the context of varying pitch, and when the loudness of sounds being judged has asymmetrical temporal envelopes. Future studies should explore the relation between the loudness of natural sounds and their representation in the central auditory pathways as well as the relation between the loudness of natural sounds and reverberation in sound-field or virtual sound-field environments. Such studies will help to resolve some of the shortcomings of the current body of loudness theory to deal with the realities of listeners' ecological listening experiences.

REFERENCES

Allen, J. B., Hall, J. L., & Jeng, P. S. (1990). Loudness growth in $\frac{1}{2}$-octave bands (LGOB)—a procedure for the assessment of loudness. *Journal of the Acoustical Society of America, 88,* 745–753.

Allen, J. B., & Neely, S. T. (1997). Modeling the relation between the intensity just noticeable difference and loudness for pure tones and wide-band noise. *Journal of the Acoustical Society of America, 102,* 3628–3646.

von Bekesy, G. (1960). *Experiments in hearing* (pp. 404–429). New York: McGraw-Hill. Original German version appeared in 1928.

von Bekesy, G. (1960). *Experiments in hearing* (pp. 257–267). New York: McGraw-Hill. Original German version appeared in 1936.

Bentler, R. A., & Pavlovic, C. V. (1989). Comparison of discomfort levels obtained with pure tones and multitone complexes. *Journal of the Acoustical Society of America, 86,* 126–132.

Berglund, B., & Lindvall, T. (1995). *Community noise.* Stockholm: Center for Sensory Research.

Borg, E., Counter, S. A., & Rosler, G. (1984). Theories of middle-ear function. In S. Silman (Ed.), *The acoustic reflex: Basic principles and clinical applications* (pp. 63–99). New York: Academic Press.

Boring, E. G. (1942). *Sensation and perception in the history of experimental psychology.* New York: Appleton-Century Crofts.

Borsky, P. N. (1979). Sociopsychological factors affecting the human response to noise exposure. *Otolaryngologic Clinics of North America, 12,* 521–535.

Bregman, A. (1990). *Auditory scene analysis: The perceptual organization of sound.* Cambridge, MA: MIT Press.

Broadbent, D. E. (1958). *Perception and communication.* Oxford: Pergamon Press.

Buus, S., & Florentine, M. (2002). Growth of loudness in listeners with cochlear hearing loss: Recruitment reconsidered. *Journal of the Association for Research in Otolaryngology, 3,* 120–139.

Buus, S., Musch, H., & Florentine, M. (1998). On loudness at threshold. *Journal of the Acoustical Society of America, 104,* 399–410.

Cooper, N. P., & Rhode, W. S. (1996). Fast travelling waves, slow travelling waves and their interactions in experimental studies of apical cochlear mechanics. *Auditory Neuroscience, 2,* 289–299.

Fechner, G. (1966). Elements of psychophysics. Translation edited by D. H. Howes, and E. C. Boring (Eds.), H. E. Adler. Originally published in 1860. New York: Holt, Reinhart, & Winston.

Filion, P. R., & Margolis, R. H. (1992). Comparison of clinical and real-life judgments of loudness discomfort. *Journal of the American Academy of Audiology, 3,* 193–199.

Fletcher, H. (1995). *The ASA edition of speech and hearing in communication* (J. Allen, Ed.). Woodbury, NY: Acoustical Society of America. Reissue of Fletcher's (1953) *Speech and hearing in communication.*

Fletcher, H., & Munson, W. A. (1933). Loudness, its definition, measurement and calculation. *Journal of the Acoustical Society of America, 5,* 82–108.

Florentine, M., Hunter, W., Robinson, M., Ballou, M., & Buus, S. (1998). On the behavioral characteristics of loud-music listening. *Ear and Hearing, 19,* 420–428.

Fowler, E. P. (1928). Marked deafened areas in normal ears. *Archives of Otolaryngology, 8,* 151–155.

Fowler, E. P. (1937). The diagnosis of diseases of the neural mechanisms of hearing by the aid of sounds well above threshold. *American Otological Society, 27,* 207–219.

Ghazanfar, A. A., Neuhoff, J. G., & Logothetis, N. K. (2002). Auditory looming perception in rhesus monkeys. *Proceedings of the National Academy of Sciences of the United States of America, 99,* 15755–15757.

Gockel, H., Moore, B. C. J., & Patterson, R. D. (2002). Influence of component phase on the loudness of complex tones. *Acta Acustica united with Acustica, 88,* 369–377.

Goldstein, E. B. (2002). *Sensation and perception* (6th ed.). Belmont, CA.: Wadsworth.

Grassi, M., & Darwin, C. J. (2001). Perception of the duration of ramped and damped sounds with raised cosine amplitude. In E. Summerfield, R. Kompass, and T. Lachmann (Eds.). *Proceedings of the Seventeenth Annual Meeting of the International Society of Psychophysics* (pp. 385–390).

Hawkins, D. B., Walden, B. E., Montgomery, A., & Prosek, R. A. (1987). Description and validation of an LDL procedure designed to select SSPL90. *Ear and Hearing, 8,* 162–169.

Hellman, R. P. (1976). Growth of loudness at 1000 Hz and 3000 Hz. *Journal of the Acoustical Society of America, 60,* 672–679.

Hellman, R. P. (1982). Loudness, annoyance, and noisiness produced by single-tone-noise complexes. *Journal of the Acoustical Society of America, 72,* 62–73.

Hellman, R. P. (1985). Perceived magnitude of two-tone-noise complexes: Loudness, annoyance, and noisiness. *Journal of the Acoustical Society of America, 77,* 1497–1504.

Hellman, R. P. (1991). Loudness measurement by magnitude scaling: Implications for intensity coding. In S. J. Bolanski, Jr., and G. A. Gescheider (Eds.), *Ratio scaling of psychological magnitude* (pp. 215–227). Hillsdale, NJ: Lawrence: Erlbaum.

Hellman, R. P. (1999). Cross-modality matching: A tool for measuring loudness in sensorineural impairment. *Ear and Hearing, 20,* 193–213.

Hellman, W. S., & Hellman, R. P. (1990). Intensity discrimination as the driving force for loudness: Application to pure tones in quiet. *Journal of the Acoustical Society of America, 87,* 1255–1265.

Hellman, R. P., & Meiselman, C. H. (1988). Prediction of individual loudness exponents from cross-modality matching. *Journal of Speech and Hearing Research, 31,* 605–615.

Hellman, R. P., & Meiselman, C. H. (1990). Loudness relations for individuals and groups in normal and impaired hearing. *Journal of the Acoustical Society of America, 88,* 2596–2606.

Hellman, R. P., & Scharf, B. (1984). Acoustic reflex and loudness. In S. Silman (Ed.), *The acoustic reflex: Basic principles and clinical applications* (pp. 469–510). New York: Academic Press.

Hellman, R. P., Scharf, B., Teghtsoonian, M., & Teghtsoonian, R. (1987). On the relation between the growth of loudness and the discrimination of intensity for pure tones. *Journal of the Acoustical Society of America, 82,* 448–453.

Hellman, R. P., Takeshima, H., Suzuki, Y., Ozawa, K., & Sone, T. (2001). Equal-loudness contours at high frequencies reconsidered. *Journal of the Acoustical Society of America, 109,* 2349.

Hellman, R. P., & Zwislocki, J. (1961). Some factors affecting the estimation of loudness. *Journal of the Acoustical Society of America, 33,* 687–694.

Hellman, R. P., & Zwislocki, J. (1963). Monaural loudness function at 1000 cps and interaural summation. *Journal of the Acoustical Society of America, 35,* 856–865.

Hellman, R. P., & Zwislocki, J. (1964). Loudness function of 1000-cps tone in the presence of masking noise. *Journal of the Acoustical Society of America, 36,* 1618–1627.

Hellman, R. P., & Zwislocki, J. (1968). Loudness determination at low sound frequencies. *Journal of the Acoustical Society of America, 43,* 60–63.

Helmholtz, H. L. F. (1954). *On the sensations of tone.* New York: Dover. Original German edition appeared in 1862.

Hicks, M. L., & Bacon, S. P. (1999). Psychophysical measures of auditory nonlinearities as a function of frequency in individuals with normal hearing. *Journal of the Acoustical Society of America, 105,* 326–338.

Hunter, L. L., Ries, D. T., Schlauch, R. S., Levine, S. C., & Ward, W. D. (1999). Safety and clinical performance of acoustic reflex tests. *Ear and Hearing, 20,* 506–514.

Jesteadt, W., Luce, R. D., & Green, D. M. (1977). Sequential effects in judgments of loudness. *Journal of Experimental Psychology: Human Perception and Performance, 3,* 92–104.

Jonsson, E., Kajland A., Paccagnella, B., & Sorensen, S. (1969). Annoyance reactions to traffic noise in Italy and Sweden. *Archives of Environmental Health, 19,* 692–699.

Lawless, H. T., Horne, J., & Spiers, W. (2000). Contrast and range effects for category, magnitude and labeled magnitude scales in judgments of sweetness intensity. *Chemical Senses, 25,* 85–92.

Leibold, L. J., & Werner, L. A. (2001). *The effect of listening strategy on loudness growth in normal-hearing adults.* Paper presented at the annual meeting of the Association for Research in Otolaryngology, St. Petersburg Beach, FL.

Leibold, L. J., & Werner, L. A. (2002a). The relationship between intensity and reaction time in normal-hearing infants and adults. *Ear and Hearing, 23,* 92–97.

Leibold, L. J., & Werner, L. A. (2002b). *Examining reaction time (RT)-intensity functions in normal-hearing infants and adults.* Paper presented at the annual meeting of the Association for Research in Otolaryngology, St. Petersburg Beach, FL.

Lu, T., Liang, L., & Wang, X. (2001). Neural representation of temporally asymmetric stimuli in the auditory cortex of awake primates. *Journal of Neurophysiology, 85,* 2364–2380.

Marks, L. E. (1981). What (good) are scales of sensation? *Behavioral and Brain Sciences, 4,* 199–200.

Marks L. E. (1988). Magnitude estimation and sensory matching. *Perception and Psychophysics, 43,* 511–525.

Marks, L. E. (1992). The contingency of perceptual processing: Context modifies equal-loudness relations. *Psychological Science, 3,* 285–291.

Marks, L. E. (1994). "Recalibrating" the auditory system: The perception of loudness. *Journal of Experimental Psychology: Human Perception and Performance, 20,* 382–396.

Marks L. E. (1996). Recalibrating the perception of loudness: Interaural transfer. *Journal of the Acoustical Society of America, 100,* 473–480.

Marks, L. E., & Warner, E. (1991). Slippery context effect and critical bands. *Journal of Experimental Psychology: Human Perception and Performance, 17,* 986–996.

McCleary, E. A. (1993). *The ability of category rating and magnitude estimation to predict loudness growth in ears with noise simulated hearing loss.* Unpublished master's thesis, University of Minnesota, Minneapolis.

Mellers, B. A., & Birnbaum, M. H. (1982). Loci of contextual effects in judgment. *Journal of Experimental Psychology: Human Perception and Performance, 8,* 582–601.

Moller, A. R. (2000). *Hearing: Its physiology and pathophysiology.* Boston: Academic Press.

Moore, B. C. J., Glasberg, B. R., & Baer, T. (1997). A model for the prediction of thresholds, loudness, and partial loudness. *Journal of Audio Engineering Society, 45,* 224–240.

Namba, S., Kuwano, S., & Schick, A. (1986). A cross-cultural study on noise problems. *Journal of the Acoustical Society of Japan, 7,* 279–289.

Neuert, V., Pressnitzer, D., Patterson, R. D., & Winter, I. M. (2001). The responses of single units in the inferior colliculus of the guinea pig to damped and ramped sinusoids. *Hearing Research, 159,* 36–52.

Neuhoff, J. G. (1998). Perceptual bias for rising tones. *Nature, 395,* 123–124.

Neuhoff, J. G. (2001). An adaptive bias in the perception of looming auditory motion. *Ecological Psychology, 13,* 87–110.

Neuhoff, J. G., & McBeath, M. K. (1996). The Doppler illusion: The influence of dynamic intensity change on perceived pitch. *Journal of Experimental Psychology: Human Perception and Performance, 22,* 970–985.

Neuhoff, J. G., McBeath, M. K., & Wanzie, W. C. (1999). Dynamic frequency change influences loudness perception: A central, analytic process. *Journal of Experimental Psychology: Human Perception and Performance, 25,* 1050–1059.

Newman, E. B. (1933). The validity of the just-noticeable difference as a unit of psychological magnitude. *Transactions of the Kansas Academy of Sciences, 36,* 172–175.

Occupational Safety and Health Administration (OSHA). (1983). 1910.95 Occupational noise exposure. 29 CFR 1910.95 (May 29, 1971). *Federal Register, 36,* 10466. Amended March 8, 1983. *Federal Register, 48,* 9776–9785.

Palin, S. L. (1994). Does classical music damage the hearing of musicians? A review of the literature. *Occupational Medicine, 44*, 130–136.

Parducci, A. (1965). Category judgment: A range frequency model. *Psychological Review, 72*, 407–418.

Parker, S., & Schneider, B. (1994). The stimulus range effect: Evidence for top-down control of sensory intensity in audition. *Perception and Psychophysics, 56*, 1–11.

Patterson, R. D. (1994a). The sound of a sinusoid: Spectral models. *Journal of the Acoustical Society of America, 96*, 1409–1418.

Patterson, R. D. (1994b). The sound of a sinusoid: Time-interval models. *Journal of the Acoustical Society of America, 96*, 1419–1428.

Pressnitzer, D., Winter, I. M., & Patterson, R. D. (2000). The responses of single units in the ventral cochlear nucleus of the guinea pig to damped and ramped sinusoids. *Hearing Research, 149*, 155–166.

Relkin, E. M., & Doucet, J. R. (1997). Is loudness simply proportional to the auditory nerve spike count? *Journal of the Acoustical Society of America, 101*, 2735–2740.

Rock, I. (1997). *Indirect perception.* Cambridge, MA: MIT Press.

Rogers, W. L., & Bregman, A. S. (1998). Cumulation of the tendency to segregate auditory streams: Resetting by changes in location and loudness. *Perception and Psychophysics, 60*, 1216–1227.

Royster, J. D., Royster, L. H., & Killion, M. C. (1991). Sound exposures and hearing thresholds of symphony orchestra musicians. *Journal of the Acoustical Society of America, 89*, 2793–2803.

Ruggero, M. A., Rich, N. C., Recio, A., Narayan, S. S., & Robles, L. (1997). Basilar-membrane responses to tones at the base of the chinchilla cochlea. *Journal of the Acoustical Society of America, 101*, 2151–2163.

Scharf, B. (1978). Loudness. In E. C. Carterette, & M. P. Friedman (Eds.), *Handbook of perception*, Vol. 4. *Hearing* (pp. 187–242). New York: Academic Press.

Scharf, B., & Hellman, R. P. (1981). Objections to physical correlate theory, with emphasis on loudness. *Behavioral and Brain Sciences, 4*, 203–204.

Schlauch, R. S., DiGiovanni, J. J., & Ries, D. T. (1998). Basilar membrane nonlinearity and loudness. *Journal of the Acoustical Society of America, 103*, 2010–2020.

Schlauch, R. S., Harvey, S., & Lanthier, N. (1995). Intensity resolution and loudness in broadband noise. *Journal of the Acoustical Society of America, 98*, 1895–1902.

Schlauch, R. S., Ries, D. T., & DiGiovanni, J. J. (2001). Duration discrimination and subjective duration for ramped and damped sounds. *Journal of the Acoustical Society of America, 109*, 2880–2887.

Schlauch, R. S., DiGiovanni, J. J., & Donlin, E. E. (Submitted). Examining explanations for differences in perceived duration for ramped and damped sounds. *Journal of the Acoustical Society of America.*

Schneider, B., Parker, S., Ostrosky, D., Stein, D., & Kanow, G. (1974). A scale for psychological magnitude of number. *Perception and Psychophysics, 16*, 43–46.

Seifritz, E., Neuhoff, J. G., Bilecen, D., Scheffler, K., Mustovic, H., Schachinger, H., Elefante, R., & Di Salle, F. (2002). Neural processing of auditory "looming" in the human brain. *Current Biology, 12*, 2147–2151.

Serpanos, Y. C., O'Mally, H., & Gravel, J. S. (1997). The relationship between loudness intensity functions and click-ABR wave V latency. *Ear and Hearing, 18*, 409–419.

Silverman, S. R. (1947). Tolerance for pure tones and speech in normal and defective hearing. *Annals of Otology, Rhinology and Laryngology, 56*, 658–677.

Simmons, F. B. (1964). Perceptual theories of middle ear muscle function. *Annals of Otology, Rhinology and Laryngology, 73*, 724–739.

Skinner, M. W. (1980). Speech intelligibility in noise-induced hearing loss: Effects of high-frequency compensation. *Journal of the Acoustical Society of America, 67*, 306–317.

Speaks, C., Nelson, D., & Ward, W. D. (1970). Hearing loss in rock-and-roll musicians. *Journal of Occupational Medicine, 12*, 216–219.

Stecker, G. C., & Hafter, E. R. (2000). An effect of temporal asymmetry on loudness. *Journal of the Acoustical Society of America, 107*, 3358–3368.

Steinberg, J. C., & Gardner, M. B. (1937). Dependence of hearing impairment on sound intensity. *Journal of the Acoustical Society of America, 9*, 11–23.

Stevens, S. S. (1951). Mathematics, measurement and psychophysics. In S. S. Stevens (Ed.), *Handbook of experimental psychology* (pp. 1–49). New York: John Wiley & Sons.

Stevens, S. S. (1970). Neural events and the psychophysical law. *Science, 170*, 1043–1050.

Stevens, S. S. (1972). *Psychophysics and social scaling*. Morristown, NJ: General Learning.

Stevens, S. S. (1975). *Psychophysics*. New York: John Wiley & Sons.

Stevens, S. S., & Davis, H. (1936). Psychophysiological acoustics: pitch and loudness. *Journal of the Acoustical Society of America, 8*, 1–13.

Stevens, S. S., & Galanter, E. H. (1957). Ratio scales and category scales for a dozen perceptual continua. *Journal of Experimental Psychology, 54*, 376–411.

Stevens, S. S., & Guirao, M. (1967). Loudness functions under inhibition. *Perception and Psychophysics, 2*, 460–465.

Stevens, S. S., Guirao, M., & Slawson, W. (1965). Loudness, a product of volume times density. *Journal of Experimental Psychology, 69*, 503–510.

Studebaker, G. A., Sherbecoe, R. L., McDaniel, D. M., & Gwaltney, C. A. (1999). Monosyllabic word recognition at higher-than-normal speech and noise levels. *Journal of the Acoustical Society of America, 105*, 2431–2444.

Teghtsoonian, R., & Teghsoonian, M. (1978). Range and regression effects in magnitude scaling. *Perception and Psychophysics, 24*, 305–314.

Warren, R. M. (1970). Elimination of biases in loudness judgments for tones. *Journal of the Acoustical Society of America, 48*, 1397–1403.

Warren, R. M. (1981). Measurement of sensory intensity. *Behavioral and Brain Sciences, 4*, 175–188.

Warren, R. M. (1999). *Auditory perception: A new analysis and synthesis*. Cambridge, UK: Cambridge University Press.

Werner, L. A., & Bargones, J. Y. (1991). Sources of auditory masking in infants: Distraction effects. *Perception and Psychophysics, 50*, 405–412.

Wever, E. G., & Bray, C. W. (1930). Action currents in the auditory nerve in response to acoustical stimuluation. *Proceedings of the National Academy of Science of the United States of America, 16*, 344–350.

Wilson, W. W., & O'Neill, W. E. (1998). Auditory motion induces directionally-dependent receptive field shifts in inferior colliculus neurons. *Journal of Neurophysiology, 79*, 2040–2063.

Yates, G. K., Winter, I. M., & Robertson, D. (1990). Basilar membrane nonlinearity determines auditory nerve rate-intensity functions and cochlear dynamic range. *Hearing Research, 45*, 203–219.

Zahorik, P. (2002). Assessing auditory distance perception using virtual acoustics. *Journal of the Acoustical Society of America, 111*, 1832–1846.

Zahorik, P., & Wightman, F. L. (2001). Loudness constancy with varying sound source distance. *Nature Neuroscience, 4*, 78–83.

Zwicker, E. (1970). Masking and psychological excitation as consequences of the ear's frequency analysis. In R. Plomp, and G. F. Smoorenberg (Eds.). *Frequency analysis and periodicity detection in hearing* (pp. 376–394). Leiden: Sijthoff.

Zwislocki, J. J. (1965). Analysis of some auditory characteristics. In R. D. Luce, R. R. Bush, & E. Galanter (Eds.), *Handbook of mathematical psychology* (vol. III). New York: John Wiley & Sons.

Zwislocki, J. J. (1983). Absolute and other scales: Question of validity. *Perception and Psychophysics, 33*, 593–594.

Zwislocki, J. J., & Goodman D. A. (1980). Absolute scaling of sensory magnitudes: a validation. *Perception and Psychophysics, 28*, 28–38.

INDEX